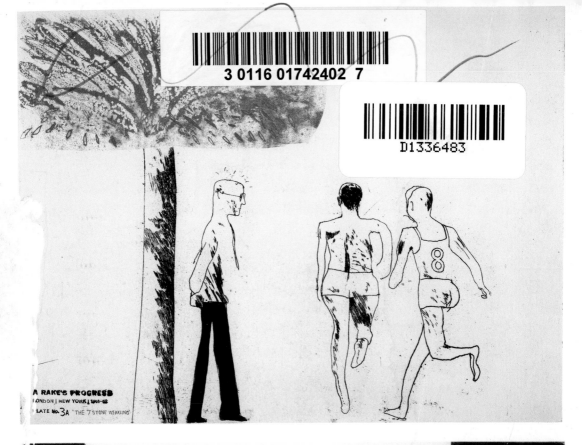

A RAKE'S PROGRESS
LONDON | NEW YORK | 1961-62
PLATE No. 3A 'THE 7 STONE WEAKLING'

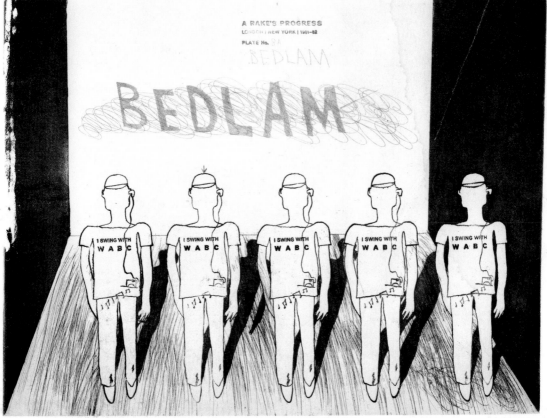

HOCKNEY: THE BIOGRAPHY

Also by Christopher Simon Sykes

AS AUTHOR

The Visitor's Book
Private Palaces
Black Sheep
Country House Camera
The National Trust Country House Album
The Big House
Eric Clapton (with Eric Clapton)

AS AUTHOR AND PHOTOGRAPHER

Ancient English Houses

AS PHOTOGRAPHER

The Front Garden
The Rolling Stones on Tour
The Perfect English House
English Country
Private Landscapes
Scottish Country
Corfu: The Garden Isle
At Home With Books
At Home With Art
Great Houses of England and Wales
Great Houses of Scotland
Great Houses of Ireland
The English Room
English Manor Houses
The Gardens of Buckingham Palace

HOCKNEY:
THE BIOGRAPHY

VOLUME I

1937-1975

Christopher Simon Sykes

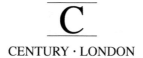

CENTURY · LONDON

Published by Century 2011

2 4 6 8 10 9 7 5 3 1

First published in Great Britain in 2011 by Century
Random House, 20 Vauxhall Bridge Road,
London SW1V 2SA

www.randomhouse.co.uk

Addresses for companies within The Random House Group Limited can be found at:
www.randomhouse.co.uk

The Random House Group Limited Reg. No. 954009

A CIP catalogue record for this book
is available from the British Library

ISBN 9781846057083

The Random House Group Limited supports The Forest Stewardship Council (FSC®), the
leading international forest certification organisation. Our books carrying the FSC label are
printed on FSC® certified paper. FSC is the only forest certification scheme endorsed by
the leading environmental organisations, including Greenpeace. Our paper procurement
policy can be found at www.randomhouse.co.uk/environment

Printed and bound in Great Britain by
MPG Books Ltd, Bodmin

For my family – Isabella, Lily, Ditta and Joby.
And in memory of Christopher IV.

CONTENTS

LIST OF ILLUSTRATIONS ix

ACKNOWLEDGEMENTS xv

INTRODUCTION xvii

1: MY PARENTS 1

2: SELF-PORTRAIT 26

3: DOLL BOY 55

4: 'WE TWO BOYS TOGETHER CLINGING' 85

5: MAN IN A MUSEUM 113

6: A HOLLYWOOD COLLECTION 140

7: IN THE DULL VILLAGE 169

8: A BIGGER SPLASH 185

9: PETER 1969 211

10: MR AND MRS CLARK AND PERCY 235

11: PORTRAIT OF AN ARTIST 259

12: CONTRE-JOUR IN THE FRENCH STYLE 283

13: THE RAKE'S PROGRESS 307

NOTES 329

BIBLIOGRAPHY 345

INDEX 347

ILLUSTRATIONS IN THE TEXT

Page

Man, 1964. Lithograph (Photolithograph from a drawing on paper).
Edition: 60, 18 x 22¼″ © David Hockney   xvii

Kenneth and Laura Hockney's wedding, 1929, photograph © David
Hockney   1

Bradford Town Hall © Mary Evans Picture Library/Francis Frith   3

Kenneth Hockney, *circa* 1928, photograph © David Hockney   9

'Untitled' (date unknown), drawing © David Hockney   19

Sunday lunch Hutton Terrace. Picture supplied by Derek Stafford   27

'Untitled' (date unknown), drawing © David Hockney   28

'Untitled' (date unknown), drawing © David Hockney   29

Hockney at about ten, in his Cub cap, photograph © David
Hockney   31

Self Portrait, 1954, pencil on paper 15 x 11″ © David Hockney/Photo
Credit: Richard Schmidt   43

David Hockney and John Loker. Hockney family photograph   54

Breakdown en Route to Aldermaston (Left to Right: John Loker,
David Hockney, Unknown), photograph © Rod Taylor, fellow
student and author   60

Skeleton, 1959, charcoal and gouache, 15⅝ x 22″ © David Hockney
Photo Credit: Richard Schmidt   63

David Hockney in Painting School. Photograph © Geoffrey Reeve   70

David Hockney and Derek Boshier in Painting School.
Photograph © Geoffrey Reeve   78

Portrait of John Kasmin   84

Peter Crutch with Peter C. Photograph © Geoffrey Reeve   92

The Diploma, 1962, etching and aquatint in two colours © David
Hockney   109

Bradford, 1962, photograph © David Hockney/Photo Credit:
Richard Schmidt   111

Left to Right: Andy Warhol, Henry Geldzahler, David Hockey and
Jeff Goodman, 1963. Gelatin silver print, 16 x 24″ © The Dennis
Hopper Trust. Courtesy of The Dennis Hopper Trust.   113
John Kasmin and Lord Dufferin in the Kasmin Gallery
© Photograph by Snowdon, Camera Press London   132
Christopher Isherwood, photograph © Peter Schlesinger   148
Patrick Procktor, photograph by Peter Rand for Vogue
© Peter Rand   160
In the Dull Village from Illustrations for Fourteen Poems from C.P.
Cavafy, 1966-67. Etching, 22½ x 15½″ © David Hockney   168
Polish Army from Ubu Roi, 1966, crayon © David Hockney/Collection
of the Museum of Modern Art (MOMA), New York   177
Peter Schlesinger and David Hockney, colour photograph © David
Hockney/Photo Credit: Richard Schmidt   181
Peter in Carennac, 1967, ink on paper, 14 x 17″ © David Hockney   184
Peter, 1969, etching in black © David Hockney   210
Paris, December 1967, © David Hockney/Photo Credit: Richard
Schmidt   215
Mr. and Mrs. Clark and Percy, Linden Gardens, London, 1970 ©
David Hockney/Tate, London 2011   236
David Hockney with Pentax, photograph © Camilla McGrath   258
Gregory Evans and Nicholas Wilder, Appian Way, Hollywood,
1973, photo collage © David Hockney/Photo Credit: Richard
Schmidt   281
Artist and Model, 1973–1974, etching © David Hockney   284
Henry Geldzahler and David Hockney, photograph © Camilla
McGrath   291
David Hockney and Mo McDermott, photograph © David
Hockney/Photo Credit: Richard Schmidt   294
Yves Marie, New York, 1974, crayon on paper © David Hockney/
Photo Credit: Richard Schmidt   303
Gregory. Palatine, Roma. Dec. 1974, 1974, ink on paper © David
Hockney/Photo Credit: Richard Wedemeyer   306
The Glyndebourne Picnic, painting by Bob Marchant   311

PLATES

Section 1

Self Portrait, 1954. Oil on board, 14 x 14″ © David Hockney

Self Portrait, 1954. Edition 5 (approximately). Lithograph in five colours, 11½ x 10¼″ © David Hockney

Portrait of my father, 1955. Oil on canvas, 20 x 16″ © David Hockney. Photo Credit: Richard Schmidt

Doll Boy, 1960 – 61. Oil on canvas, 48 x 39″ © David Hockney/ Collection of Hamburger Kunsthalle. Photo credit: Paul Oszvald

We Two Boys Together Clinging, 1961. Oil on board, 48 x 60″ © David Hockney/Collection of Arts Council, Southbank Centre, London. Photo credit: Prudence Cuming Associates

The most beautiful boy in the world, 1961. Oil on canvas, 70 x 39½″ © David Hockney

Flight Into Italy - Swiss Landscape, 1962. Oil on canvas, 72 x 72″ © David Hockney/Collection of The Museum of Modern Art (Kunstmuseum), Dusseldorf

Life Painting for a Diploma, 1962. Oil on canvas with charcoal on paper collage, 70⅞ x 70⅞″ © David Hockney. Photo credit: Sotheby's, London

Man in a Museum (Or You're in The Wrong Movie), 1962. Oil on canvas, 60 x 60″ © David Hockney/Collection of The British Council

Section 2

David Hockney. Photograph by Snowdon/Vogue, Camera Press London

Picture emphasizing Stillness, 1962. Oil and letraset on canvas, 62 x 72″ © David Hockney

The Second Marriage, 1963. Oil, gouache and collage on canvas, 77¾ x 90″ © David Hockney/Collection of National Gallery of Victoria, Melbourne

Play Within A Play, 1963. Oil on canvas and plexiglass, 72 x 78″ © David Hockney

Domestic Scene, Los Angeles, 1963. Oil on canvas, 60 x 60″ © David Hockney

Domestic Scene, Notting Hill, 1963. Oil on canvas, 72 x 72″ © David Hockney

Shell Garage, Luxor, 1963. Colored crayon, 12¼ x 19¼″ © David Hockney

Great Pyramid at Giza with Broken Head From Thebes, 1963. Oil on canvas, 72 x 72″ © David Hockney

California Art Collector, 1964. Acrylic on canvas, 60 x 72″ © David Hockney

Boy About to Take A Shower, 1964-69. Acrylic on canvas, 36 x 36″ © David Hockney

Section 3

Picture of a Hollywood Swimming Pool, 1964. Acrylic on canvas, 36 x 48″ © David Hockney

Rocky Mountains and Tired Indians, 1965. Acrylic on canvas, 67 x 99½″ © David Hockney/Collection of National Galleries of Scotland, Edinburgh

From *A Hollywood Collection*, 1965 © David Hockney
Top Row, Left to Right:
Picture of a Still Life That Has an Elaborate Silver Frame. Lithograph in seven colours. Edition: 85. 30¼ x 22¼″
Picture of a Landscape in an Elaborate Gold Frame. Lithograph in six colours. Edition: 85. 30¼ x 22¼″
Picture of a Portrait in a Silver Frame. Lithograph in five colours. Edition: 85. 30¼ x 22¼″

Bottom Row, Left to Right:

Picture of Melrose Avenue in an Ornate Gold Frame. Lithograph in six colours. Edition: 85. 30¼ x 22¼″

Picture of a Simple Framed Traditional Nude. Lithograph in four colours. Edition: 85. 30¼ x 22¼″

Picture of a Pointless Abstraction Framed Under Glass. Lithograph in six colours. Edition: 85. 30¼ x 22¼″

Beverly Hills Housewife, 1966-67. Acrylic on canvas, 72 x 144″ © David Hockney. Photo Credit: Richard Schmidt

A Bigger Splash, 1967. Acrylic on canvas, 96 x 96″ © David Hockney Collection of The Tate Gallery, London

The Room, Tarzana, 1967. Acrylic on canvas, 96 x 96″ © David Hockney

The Room, Manchester Street, 1967. Acrylic on canvas, 96 x 96″ © David Hockney

Christopher Isherwood and Don Bachardy, 1968. Acrylic on canvas, 83½ x 119½″ © David Hockney

Section 4

Henry Geldzahler and Christopher Scott, 1969. Acrylic on canvas, 84 x 120″ © David Hockney

Le Parc des Sources, Vichy, 1970. Acrylic on canvas, 84 x 120″ © David Hockney. Photo credit: Chatsworth House Trust

Mr. and Mrs. Clark and Percy, 1970-71. Acrylic on canvas, 84 x 120″ © David Hockney/Collection of The Tate Gallery, London

Sur La Terrasse, 1971. Acrylic on canvas, 180 x 84″ © David Hockney

Portrait of an Artist (Pool with Two Figures), 1972. Acrylic on canvas, 84 x 120″ © David Hockney. Photo credit: Steven Sloman

Contrejour In The French Style, 1974. Etching, 39 x 36″ © David Hockney

Celia in a Black Dress with Red Stockings, 1973. Crayon on paper, 25½ x 19½″ © David Hockney/Collection of National Gallery of Australia, Canberra

Celia Half Nude, 1975. Crayon on paper, 30 x 22″ © David Hockney

Drop Curtain for The Rake's Progress. From The Rake's Progress, 1975-79. Ink and collage on cardboard, 14 x 20½″ © David Hockney. Photo Credit: Richard Schmidt

Bedlam. From The Rake's Progress, 1975. Ink on cardboard, 16 x 21 x 12 (Model) © David Hockney

Endpapers

Top Row, Left to Right:

The Gospel Singing (Good People) Madison Square Garden, From A Rake's Progress (Portfolio of Sixteen Prints), 1961-63. Etching, aquatint. Edition: 50. 15 ½ x 22 ½″ © David Hockney

The Seven Stone Weakling, From A Rake's Progress (Portfolio of Sixteen Prints), 1961-63. Etching, aquatint. Edition: 50. 16 ¾ x 20 ½″ © David Hockney

Bottom Row, Left to Right:

Cast Aside, From A Rake's Progress (Portfolio of Sixteen Prints), 1961-63. Etching, aquatint. Edition: 50. 19 ½ x 24 ½″ © David Hockney

Bedlam, From A Rake's Progress (Portfolio of Sixteen Prints), 1961-63. Etching, aquatint. Edition: 50. 17 ¾ x 11 ½″ © David Hockney

ACKNOWLEDGEMENTS

It was not easy to persuade Hockney to consent to be the subject of a new biography. 'I'm not in the mood for reflection,' he told me. 'I've got too much to look forward to.' But the prospect of a major new show at the Royal Academy in January 2012 – not a retrospective, but an exhibition of new work, bringing with it many requests for such a book – eventually persuaded him that this was a subject that was not going to go away, and he agreed to let me do it. The rules were simple. He would talk to me in his time, not mine, and would authorise the book, but not endorse it.

My aim in writing this book has not been to add to the hundreds of thousands of words already written about Hockney's work, but to conjure up the man that he is and in doing so to put his paintings and drawings in the context of his extraordinary life. Though it was not originally intended to be in two volumes, the richness of the available material eventually necessitated it. Since I could not have started out on this project without his agreement, my first thank you is to David Hockney himself for giving me such a wonderful opportunity. I pray that I will not let him down.

Next I have the Hockney siblings to thank for their cooperation, for allowing me to read and use extracts from their mother's diaries, and for all the memories they have shared with me. So thank you to Paul Hockney, Philip Hockney, Margaret Hockney and John Hockney.

In all my visits to Bridlington, I have received help and sustenance from all the Hockney household, in particular delicious lunches and dinners cooked by John Fitzherbert, advice and beautiful accordion playing from Jean-Pierre Goncalves de Lima, technical help and a superb Wagner soundtrack from Jonathan Wilkinson, and many cups of tea perfectly made by Dominic Elliott. Thank you all. A special thanks must also go to those who were such a great help to me in California, where Hockney has lived for so many years and where his archives are kept, in particular, Gregory Evans, Richard Schmidt and George Snyder.

My agent, Ed Victor, had faith in my idea from the start, and was ably supported by Maggie Phillips. Thank you to Oliver Johnson at Century for buying it, to Jack Fogg and Caroline Gascoigne for editing it and to Briony Gowlett for working tirelessly gathering material for it. And without the cooperation of the following, who all helped in one way or another, either with reminiscences or with illustrations or with moral support, there would be no book. So thank you:

Don Bachardy * Mark Bell * Adrian Berg * Mark Berger * Murray Biggs * Benedict Birnberg * Celia Birtwell * Simon Blow * David Bolger * Eric Boman * Derek Boshier * Melvyn Bragg * Katherine Bucknell * David Cammell * Melissa Chassay * Tchaik Chassay * George Christie * Mary Christie * Paul Cornwall-Jones * John Cox * Richard Davenport-Hines * Johnny Dewe Matthews * Lindy Dufferin * Mike Duggleby * Aurora Dunluce * Mary Fedden * Chris Fletcher * Bella Freud * Cherry Glazebrook * Grey Gowrie * Ann Graves * David Graves * Allen Jones * Jane Kasmin * John Kasmin * Lem Kitaj * Arthur Lambert * Mark Lancaster * Jack Larson * George Lawson * Wendy Lindbergh * John Loker * Ian Massey * Roddy Maude-Roxby * David and Susan Neave * Neil Parkinson * Maurice Payne * David Pilling * David Oxtoby * John Naylor * Philip Naylor * Philip Powell * Geoff Reeve * John Richardson * Jacob Rothschild * Charlie Scheips * Peter Schlesinger * Graham Sherriff * Lizzie Spender * Derek Stafford * Nona Summers * Hugo Vickers * Jacqui Wald * Marinka Watts * Norma Williamson * Richard Wentworth * Bruno Wollheim

Christopher Sykes
London
July 2011

INTRODUCTION

I first met David Hockney when I was seventeen, up in London for a day from school and hanging out at the Kasmin Gallery, whose owners, John Kasmin and Sheridan Dufferin, were friends of my mother. As a rather innocent and conventional Etonian, I was intrigued by Hockney's bleached-blond hair, his brightly coloured clothes and the fact that he was so obviously homosexual. His Yorkshire accent reminded me of home, for I had been brought up on the East Yorkshire Wolds, though my southern schooling meant there was not a trace of dialect in my own voice. I was immediately fascinated by his paintings, with their childish figures, and the words and numbers scrawled on them. I tried to persuade my mother to buy one for me, but she had no intention of spending over £200 on what she considered a foolish whim, though she did fork out a fiver for a small etching of a man's head perched

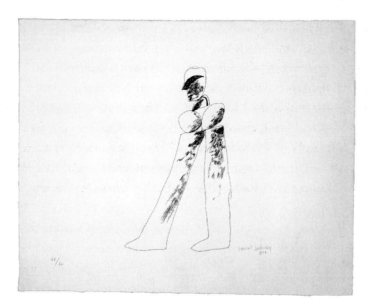

Man, 1964

precariously on two enormous legs. It was the first work of art I ever owned.

Over the next few years, though I did not get to know Hockney himself any better than as an occasional acquaintance, encountered at parties and openings, I did get to know and love his work, and was thrilled when three friends, Bobby Corbett, Rory McEwen and Henry Herbert, all bought paintings by him, respectively *Two Men in a Shower*, *The Room, Tarzana* and *Great Pyramid at Giza with Broken Head*, which from time to time I could look at enviously. Then Hockney disappeared to California, and I followed his career through exhibitions and TV programmes, the likelihood of my ever owning another of his pictures receding into the distance as the prices of his work soared. I remained a fan and loved the fact that though the extraordinary images he continued to produce, of swimming pools and Hollywood and the Grand Canyon, seemed to redefine him as a Californian, he remained first and foremost a Yorkshireman. 'I've got Bradford,' he told his old friend R. B. Kitaj; 'they'll never take that from me.'

Then one August afternoon in 2005, I was at home in Yorkshire when the telephone rang and it was my friend, the artist Lindy Dufferin, saying that she was at the bottom of the drive with David Hockney and could she bring him up for tea. It turned out that he had moved back to England and was living and painting in Bridlington, only half an hour's drive away. He had quite fallen in love with the landscape of the Wolds, where he used to take summer holiday jobs as a farmhand when he was a pupil at Bradford Grammar School. For my wife and me, this was the beginning of a new friendship, and we have since spent many happy hours in his company, always marvelling at his ability to refresh one with his enthusiasm. I have never known anyone so engaged in his work and in the exploration of all the possibilities it throws out. Recently his childlike excitement at discovering what he can achieve firstly on his iPhone and latterly on his iPad has been a wonder to behold. 'Turner would definitely have used one of these if they'd been around then,' he says breathlessly. When I asked him how come it took a 73-year-old to be the first artist to have a major show using this device, he said, 'That's because none of the young ones can draw any more.'

HOCKNEY: THE BIOGRAPHY

CHAPTER ONE

MY PARENTS

The life of David Hockney almost ended when it had barely begun. Sometime in the small hours of 31 August 1940, a German bomber on a raid over Bradford in West Yorkshire released a stick of bombs, one of which fell on Steadman Terrace, a steeply inclined street on its northern outskirts. In number 61, the second house from the top, the seven members of the Hockney family and their neighbour, Miss Dobson, were huddled in a tiny space beneath the stairs, barely seven foot long. As the bomb came down, filling their ears with its

Kenneth and Laura Hockney's wedding, 1929

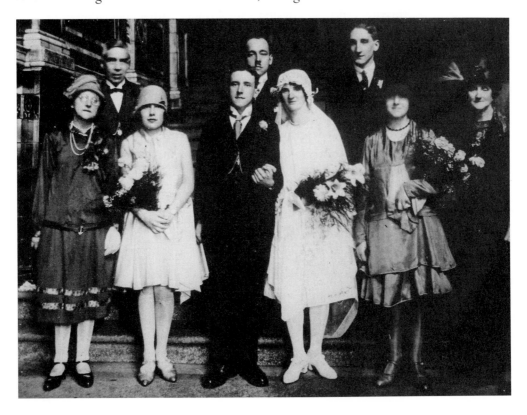

high-pitched whistle and electrifying them with fear, three-year-old David's older brother Philip clambered over his siblings, threw his arms round their mother and cried out, 'Mum, say a prayer for us.' Laura Hockney clutched at a small 'promise box' containing verses from the Bible before being hurled forward by the force of the bomb as it exploded, letting out a piercing scream that her children were never to forget. A timber merchant at the bottom of the street had taken a direct hit which all but destroyed it and left the road littered with wood. Every house in the street had its windows broken or the roof damaged. Yet miraculously number 61 was untouched. Forever after Laura was convinced it was the promise box that had protected them.

The city in which the family huddled that night, and in which David Hockney had been born three years earlier, on 9 July 1937, was the thriving centre of England's wool trade, with a population of close to 300,000. Commonly thought of as a Pennine town, like its neighbours Halifax, Wakefield, Dewsbury, Shipley and Huddersfield, Bradford can in fact be considered as part of the Yorkshire Dales, lying as it does in the valley of the Bradford Beck, known locally as Bradforddale. Before the advent of steam, it was a market town with a population who raised sheep, sold home-grown fleeces and made cloth on handlooms. Then came the Industrial Revolution and, benefiting from the water power provided by the many streams rushing down the steep surrounding hillsides, the small town began to grow. As the hills became covered with woollen mills rather than sheep, there was a shortage of local wool, and Bradford looked to the empire for its raw material, importing from South America, India, South Africa, New Zealand and Australia. It was not long before it became one of the world's central markets for wool and wool products.

The city was immortalised in the popular imagination of the day as 'Bruddersford' in J. B. Priestley's best-selling novels *The Good Companions* and *Bright Day*. 'Lost in its smoky valley among the Pennine hills, bristling with tall mill chimneys, with its face of blackened stone,' wrote Priestley, 'Bruddersford is generally held to be an ugly city; and

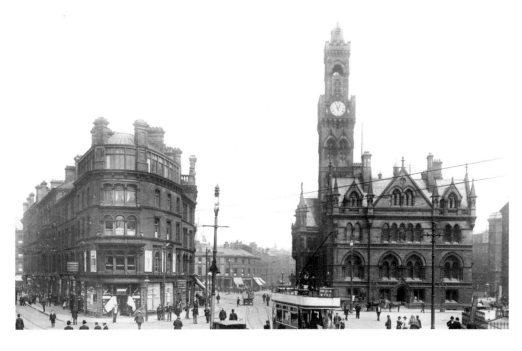

Bradford Town Hall

so I suppose it is; but it always seemed to me to have the kind of ugliness that could not only be tolerated but often enjoyed.'[1] Travellers on the London Midland railway, perhaps following in Priestley's footsteps, would have spilled out of the Exchange Station to find themselves in the heart of the city, in an area dominated by public buildings such as St George's Hall, where Dickens gave his first reading of *Bleak House*, the Wool Exchange, a great Gothic-revival building with a tall clock tower which was the centre of all the wool-trading, and, most striking of all, the Venetian Gothic town hall, with its 200-foot-high tower inspired by the campanile of the Palazzo Vecchio in Florence. Whether they would have seen the top of the tower is a moot point, however, for the two hundred or so chimneys of the woollen mills were belching out fumes all day, which sank slowly into the basin in which the city lies, and made Bradford then one of the smokiest cities on earth. 'When you come down into the centre of Bradford,' wrote a local author, Lettice Cooper, in 1950, 'dipping into that cauldron of smoke, your first impression is that everything is black, everything is solid, every doorway bears some legend connected with wool – "Wool Merchants",

"Wool Staplers", "Tops and Noils", "Textile Machinery", "Dyers and Spinners Association".[2]

Though there was some wool in the blood of David Hockney's parents, their forebears were engaged in a variety of different professions, beginning with that of agricultural labourer. Robert Hockney, his paternal great-grandfather, was born in Lincolnshire in 1841, one of the twelve children of a farm worker, and his first job was as a carter on an isolated farm at Ottringham in East Yorkshire. By 1881, the agricultural depression had driven him, his wife, Harriet, and their two sons to Hull, where he got himself a job as a 'rullyman', driving a horse and wagon delivering goods to and from the docks. It was a profession he remained in until his death in 1914.

Seeking to better himself, his younger son, James William, David's grandfather, worked as an insurance agent in Hull, which suggests that he must have been clever as well as ambitious. He also appears to have had little regard for the conventions of the time, since he lived out of wedlock with Louisa Kate Jesney, the daughter of a Lincolnshire farm labourer, for eleven years, during which time she bore him three children. They were finally married in Leeds in November 1903, Louisa being pregnant yet again, and soon after moved to Bradford where their fourth child, David's father, Kenneth, was born on 9 May 1904.

Everyone who knew Kenneth Hockney had the same thing to say about him, which was that had he had the benefit of further education there was no knowing how far he might have gone. As it was, he was born at a time when the ethos of his class demanded he should get through school and out to work as quickly as possible, and in this the Hockneys were no different from the other families in the neighbouring terraced houses of St Margaret's Road. Like his sisters, he left school at fourteen, taking up a job as a telegram boy; it was 1918, and he had already suffered the trauma of seeing his beloved older brother come back from the war a broken man, having been gassed in the trenches.

Kenneth had too much of an enquiring mind to want to spend his life delivering telegrams, and as soon as he was old enough he became a clerk for a local firm, Stephenson Brothers, a company of dry-salters, trading from a large Victorian warehouse, who sold chemical products, and goods such as flax, hemp, glue and dye. His wage was three pounds a week, out of which he paid twenty-five shillings to his mother. One of his first jobs was to sit in a small cubicle at one end of the store and open the container with the money that was catapulted along a wire from one end of the store to the other. It was a mindless activity from which he was able to escape in his spare time when, rather than go drinking down the pub with his father and his brother, who had managed to get a job working in a pawnbroker's, he pursued artistic hobbies. He took evening classes in art and developed a serious interest in photography, moving on from a box Brownie he had had since childhood to buying a serious quarter-plate camera, complete with tripod and hood, which he took everywhere. He often practised on his colleagues, taking a series of portraits of them at work at Stephenson Bros. The family had moved up in the world, to a more spacious house in St Andrew's Villas, Princeville, once a street for the smarter citizens of Bradford; the servants' bells in the hallway indicated the social standing of its former owners.

Kenneth was carrying his camera when he met Laura Thompson properly for the first time, on a Methodist ramble on the moors. Methodism played an important part in Kenneth's early life, following his conversion by Rodney 'Gipsy' Smith, a celebrated evangelist, at the vast mission, Eastbrook Hall, which was at the centre of the social and religious life of hundreds of local working-class young men. After the Sunday-afternoon meetings, the 'Brotherhood', as they were known, would walk home, crowds of them in their best suits, 'their faces radiant with joy, some of them humming over the strains of the last hymn they had been singing, others discussing the address they had heard',[3] a scene that was being repeated outside all of Bradford's seventy-four Methodist halls and chapels. The Methodist hope was that the experience would have uplifted them so much that it would keep them out of the pubs and clubs that proliferated all over the city, and were the ruin of many poor families, for whom drink obliterated the reality of the appalling conditions in which they worked and lived. Kenneth, a teetotaller, was so inspired by the Brotherhood that he eventually became both a lay preacher and a Sunday school teacher.

Since one of the Brotherhood's aims was the fostering of a spirit of community, they would organise various social events for this purpose, among the most popular of which were rambles up onto the moors above Bradford. 'No Bruddersford man,' wrote Priestley, 'could be exiled from the uplands and blue air; he always had one foot on the heather; he had only to pay his tuppence on the tram and then climb for half an hour, to hear the larks and curlews, to feel the old rocks warming in the sun, to see the harebells trembling in the shade.'[4] One Saturday afternoon in 1928, Kenneth loaded his camera onto a tram to the Exchange Station, to catch a train up to Ilkley, his intention being to walk to Bolton Abbey, a local beauty spot, to take some photographs. It was pouring with rain when he reached his destination, and as he stood on the platform he noticed a group of four girls laughing and staring at him, two of whom, Laura Thompson and her friend Doris, he recognised from chapel. Realising that they must be on a Brotherhood ramble, he decided to follow them. 'He soon caught up with us,' Laura later remembered, 'and we all went together. He had this great big box camera which he carried about with him everywhere, and I can remember him putting it down in the wet and taking our photograph, right in front of Bolton Abbey. So he took our photograph and after that he just stayed with us.'[5]

Laura came from a similar background to Kenneth. Her grandfather, Robert Thompson, was an agricultural labourer at Scarning in Norfolk who fathered eight children and ended up living on poor relief from the parish. His son Charles, Laura's father, escaped this life of poverty by joining the Salvation Army, and when he was in his early thirties set up as a coal merchant in Bradford. In 1894, he married a fellow Salvationist, Mary Sugden, the daughter of a family of weavers. Laura was the youngest of their four daughters, and by the time she was born, on 10 December 1900, her father was working as a 'manufacturer's carter'. He soon had his own cart and set up as a second-hand furniture dealer. Her earliest memories of home were of a house in Ripon Street. 'The house had a central door,' she remembered, 'and on one side of it my dad had a second-hand shop, while the other side my mother used as a sweet shop. She made her own jam and sweets and her own bread and she sold them at all hours. There were no opening and closing times, and she did all her baking and cooking in the evenings. Dad was out a lot on his horse and cart, often going to sales out in the country where he would buy furniture. Sometimes he would take me to school on his horse and cart.'[6]

Naturally clever, Laura won a scholarship to secondary school. She left at sixteen, however, to take up a job as a pattern-maker at Tolson's, a firm owned by a friend of her father's. Her sharp mind soon got her promoted to being in charge of the pattern books, earning seven shillings and sixpence a week for an eleven-hour day, from eight thirty in the morning to seven at night. She loved the work, which gave her a wide knowledge about different kinds of cloth, but her happiness was short-lived when a bullying colleague had her pushed out of her job, and put back on to more menial tasks. This deeply undermined her confidence, and the girl's continuing unkindness became so bad that Laura fell ill with what were then referred to as 'nerves', and she had to leave work. In effect, she had a nervous breakdown and it was a long time before she was able to think about looking for work again.

At the time she and Kenneth met, about eight years later, Laura had returned to work in a draper's shop in Manchester Road, earning twelve shillings a week. She was happy in the job and it had given her back her confidence. Religion played as important a role in Laura's life as it did in Kenneth's. She read the Bible every day, as she had done since she had learned to read, was an active member of the local Methodist chapel and taught beginners' class at Sunday school. Inspired by seeing her Salvationist parents going out among the slum-dwellers, particularly on Friday and Saturday nights when drunkenness was rife, she harboured a genuine, if secret, ambition to become a missionary. This was forgotten, however, when she met Kenneth and discovered that they had so much in common. Like her, he was an ardent Methodist, and she was impressed at how proud he was to have been converted by 'Gipsy' Smith. He too taught at Sunday school, and was a lay preacher to boot. They held the same unswerving views on the perils of drinking and smoking. She decided there and then that she was going to marry him and have a family.

There were, however, one or two problems. To begin with Kenneth's parents, James and Louisa Hockney, were not religious and were quite unconcerned as to whether or not their children attended chapel on Sundays, a trait she found worrying. Then there was the fact that, while her parents were quite fastidious and kept their house spotlessly clean, the Hockneys were the very opposite. 'When I first went to his home,' she later told her youngest son, John, 'it was awful. His family lived in St Andrew's Villas and we'd been walking out for a while before he took me there. It was a lovely big house, but his mother didn't see very well and she didn't hear very well either. I'd never seen anything as grubby and untidy. It was horrible.'[7] What she did notice, which confirmed her belief that she had chosen the right man, was how much smarter Kenneth was than the rest of his family, and how much his sisters, Harriet, Lillian and Audrey, admired him. A small man, about five foot four, he was both handsome and dashing, with brown hair and greenish eyes.

Kenneth Hockney was a bit of a dandy, whose strong character was reflected in his clothes. This was the era when Montague Burton stores used to offer a 'five-guinea suit for 55 shillings' and every working man had one. The fashion was for three-piece suits, usually worn on a Sunday, but Ken wore his every day. His waistcoats were made with lots of pockets, which were always full of bits and pieces, and he had the knack of brightening up his outfits with his own unique touches, using great ingenuity to look smart on his tiny weekly wage. He bought paper collars from Woolworths, specially manufactured for shirts with detachable collars, and covered them with an adhesive material on which he could paint checks and different patterns, and then easily wipe clean (his white collars, invariably black by the end of the day because of the smog, he used to clean with toothpaste). He would buy plain bow ties, and stick coloured paper dots onto them to add colour to his outfits. His shoes were always beautifully polished, and he never went out without a trilby hat, or a cane, of which he had a large collection, a fashion statement inspired by his great love of Charlie Chaplin.

Laura was soon faced with a dilemma: Ken was somewhat slow in

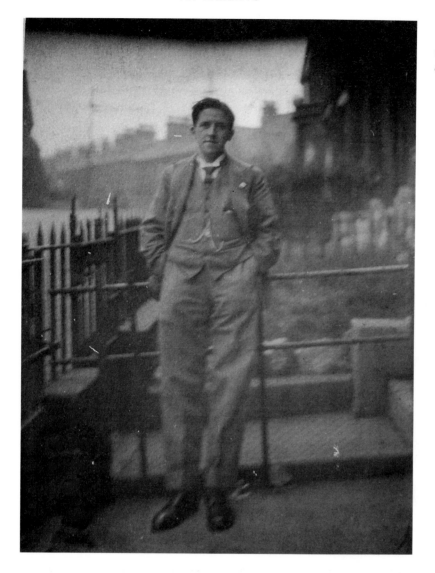

Kenneth Hockney,
circa 1928

coming forward, a fact that drove her to distraction, and after twelve
months of walking out and no sign of a proposal, she was unsure
of what to do. 'There was nothing wrong,' she said, 'but there was
nothing happening. So one day I went to my mother and said, "Is it
possible for a girl to say something to a boy rather than for the boy to
say something to the girl?"'[8] Her mother's advice was that she should
write to Kenneth to find out if he felt the same way about her as she

did about him. After the letter, things began to move faster, and in June 1929 they became engaged. He bought her a bar of chocolate every week, took her to London to visit the zoo, gave her a leather overnight case and a leather sewing box, and, on 4 August, put down £100 of his savings on a tiny house in Steadman Terrace. They were married on 4 September 1929, at the Eastbrook Methodist Mission, walking down the aisle to the strains of the march from Wagner's *Lohengrin*.

The marriage did not receive the enthusiastic support of Kenneth's mother, who believed that her elder son, Willie, should have been the first to marry. She was also reluctant to lose the twenty-five shillings she received weekly for Kenneth's board and lodging. 'So because Ken wanted to get married very quickly,' Laura remembered, 'she put it around that he'd had to get married because I was pregnant, and there were a lot of people who talked about it.'[9] This did little to endear Laura to her new mother-in-law.

Number 61 Steadman Terrace was a typical West Riding working man's terraced house, in one of row upon row of such houses, built of grey-yellow stone or soot-blackened brick. At the top of a very steep street off Leeds Road, with panoramic views across the city to the Pennines beyond, it was mercifully free from the smog that hung about the lower ground. There was no garden at the front, just steps up to the entrance, while at the back there was a tiny yard, just big enough to hang a washing line and to house a small shed for coal and one for the outside toilet. Laura paid her father a shilling a week to furnish their new home with second-hand furniture from his shop, starting with four dining chairs, two armchairs and a sofa. It was to be their home for the next fourteen years.

David Hockney was Laura's fourth child, following Paul, born in 1931, when she was thirty (then considered quite old to have a first baby), Philip in 1933 and Margaret in 1935. Four children under seven meant that space was at a premium in the tiny house, a 'two-up two-down'. The front room was furnished with the dining chairs, armchairs and sofa, as well as a marble-topped mahogany sideboard and a large glass-fronted bookcase. It also housed a 'Yorkist' coal-fired range, upon which water was heated both for washing-up and the weekly bath. There was no bathroom; instead, the kitchen or the back room was dominated by a large wooden board used in the week for storage space and for preparing food, then lifted up on Friday nights to reveal an enamel bath. Friday night was bath night, and wartime restrictions dictated that everyone shared the same water. After Kenneth and Laura, the boys all got in the bath together, while Margaret, being a girl, had the luxury of having it to herself. The waste water was used to flush the outside toilet, known as a 'Tippler'. On the upper floor, there were two rooms, one shared by the parents, the other by the children.

Money was as tight as space, the only income in the family now coming from Kenneth's three pounds a week job at Stephenson Bros where he had graduated to the accounts department. Every weekday morning he would leave home, walk down the hill to Leeds Road and catch a tram to Listerhills, where the business was based. Laura stayed at home looking after the children, cleaning, cooking and sewing. She made all the children's clothes. If she took them out to the country at the weekends, she had them all foraging for wild berries and salad leaves, and in the spring she would bring back bundles of young nettles to make non-alcoholic nettle beer. When David once sprained his ankle and had to be off school for a couple of days, a friend came to the house to visit and found him sitting with his foot in a bath of foul-smelling liquid. 'If this was in medieval times,' he told him, 'your mother would be burned as a witch!'[10]

In the evening, Kenneth would return home and the family would sit down together for tea. On Saturdays there were trips into town to look at the shops in the Swan Arcade, an elegant Victorian shopping arcade, with stone and ironwork swans incorporated in its Market Street entrance, or a visit to St John's Market to watch the salesmen give their various spiels, and eat a plate of peas with mint sauce. For a special treat, they might go to Robert's Pie Shop on Godwin Street, celebrated for its meat-and-potato pies, and for the giant pie, nicknamed 'Bertha', which was always in the window, and which was, as Priestley wrote, 'a giant, almost superhuman meat pie, with a magnificent brown, crisp, artfully wrinkled, succulent-looking crust . . . giving off a fine, rich, appetising steam to make your mouth water

. . . a perpetual volcano of meat and potato'.[11] In the summer, they sometimes took a tram ride to Roundhay Park in Leeds, or went for a picnic at a local beauty spot like Shipley Glen, which had a little funfair with swings. Sundays were reserved exclusively for chapel. With the baby David in a pram, the whole family, in their best clothes, would walk down the hill to Leeds Road, to Eastbrook Hall Methodist Chapel for the Sunday service, and back home for lunch. In the afternoon, Kenneth would attend the Brotherhood.

In spite of their relative poverty, there was never any feeling among the children that they went without. On Sunday afternoons, for example, Laura instituted a tradition whereby, as soon as they went off to junior school, each of them could invite four or five friends for tea. 'My mother did all the baking,' remembers Hockney, 'and Sunday teas were big, with cakes and buns and jelly all laid out on the table. We thought they were terrific.'[12] His brother Paul remembers 'this one friend of mine, Duncan. When we used to go to his house, all his mother used to give us was two sardines on a plate on a piece of lettuce, and when he came to our house for tea he thought it was wonderful – it was a real feast. It might have been plain stuff, but there was always plenty of it and she always made it herself.'[13] Being a girl, Margaret benefited less from these teas than the boys, as she was always required to help.

What mattered to Kenneth and Laura more than anything, however, was education. The children started their school life aged three in the babies' class at Hanson Junior School, a ten-minute walk from Steadman Terrace, and were encouraged as they grew up to work hard in order to better themselves, under the close and united eye of their parents. Kenneth and Laura, too, continued to learn from everything they saw around them. They both had a healthy respect for culture. Laura was a keen reader, and there were always books in the house. Kenneth had never stopped educating himself, visiting museums, the theatre and opera, reading anything he could get his hands on and taking advantage of any experience that came his way; in 1927 he travelled to Giggleswick, for example, when the Astronomer Royal, Sir Frank Dyson, set up camp in the school grounds to observe the total eclipse of the sun. He was a member of the Bradford Mechanics Institute in Bridge Street, which had a library with a large selection of daily newspapers. Kenneth paid them five shillings a year to let him take away all their papers after two days, and he read these voraciously. The world was in a state of upheaval and being a very religious man with a natural inclination to take up extreme causes – he became a member of the Independent Order of Rechabites, a strict anti-alcohol society – he found himself deeply affected by accounts of the Spanish Civil War, and fearful that the unfolding events in Hitler's Germany might lead to another world war; his brother Willie was a constant reminder of the horrors that that might unleash. Though he never actually joined the Communist Party, he was fired by its ideals. He stopped attending chapel, and became vehemently anti-war, announcing in September 1939, when war on Germany was finally declared, that he was a conscientious objector and would not fight. He adopted a position of moral absolutism, and refused to engage in any work for the war effort, even working as a fire warden.

This was an impossibly difficult time for Laura, seven months pregnant with her fifth child. As a 'conchie', Kenneth was an outcast in a world that was convinced of the rightness of going to war. He was physically attacked at work, and found himself ostracised wherever he went. People spat at him in the street and scarcely a morning went by without Laura having to scrub away the words YELLOW HOCKNEY painted during the night on the front steps by one of their neighbours, a policeman. Philip began to suffer from recurring nightmares. 'I used to dream,' he remembers, 'that the Germans had landed and had herded all the children onto a piece of land, and were asking, "Who is going to protect the children and who is not," and my father would always say, "I can't fight," and I thought, "We're not going to be protected," and would wake up night after night terrified.'[14]

It was especially hard for Laura because Kenneth's refusal to fight meant that she received no war pay, while his rejection of any kind of work connected to the war meant that there was no other money coming in, when they needed it more than ever. A yawning gulf opened up between them. 'He refused to do any fire-watching,' she later commented, 'which he could have done really even if he was against the war. My way of looking at it then was that he could have been protecting his children, and he would have got five shillings a night, which was a lot of money and would have helped us a lot. He wouldn't talk about it at home . . . He didn't share his troubles, and I think if he had done it would have been much nicer for us. Perhaps I would have understood things better.'[15]

To begin with, the children were spared the knowledge of what was going on, because, since the authorities were convinced that Bradford was sure to be bombed, it was thought safer to evacuate the family until the new baby was born. While Kenneth remained in Bradford, the heavily pregnant Laura and their four children were sent to Nelson in Lancashire. A bus took them from the train station to a local school, where they waited with hundreds of other evacuees to be allocated to local families. Paul and Philip, dressed in little red blazers, with white shirts and socks, and navy-blue trousers, all made by Laura, went first. 'We were sitting on this kind of grass verge,' Paul remembers, 'waiting to be allocated somewhere and this lady came by in a car and she said she'd take two little boys. So they gave her Philip and me. She just took us off and that was it. We'd never been in a car before.'[16] Nobody wanted a pregnant woman with two small children, so Laura was the very last person to be chosen, and then only reluctantly, by a woman who was mainly interested in the food she had brought with her – a carrier bag given to each family by the authorities and filled with corned beef, cocoa, dried milk and tea. Her name was Mrs Lund, and she lived across the road from the school with her husband and daughter, both of whom worked in the local woollen mill. 'She was a very strict person,' said Laura, 'but very kind.'[17] The Hockneys were given a room with a double bed for Laura and Margaret, and a cot for David. They sat at the same table as the Lund family, but cooked their own meals, and Kenneth was allowed to visit once a week. It was not mentioned that he was a conscientious objector.

Two weeks after the birth of the new baby, a boy they named John, Laura and the children returned to Bradford and David was enrolled in the babies' class at Hanson. Because of the blackout, wartime school started late and finished early and it was drummed into the children that if the air-raid sirens started while they were on their way to school or home, then they should run as fast as possible back to whichever was nearest. The school day was also punctuated with routines like the daily gas-mask practice. All the children, of whatever age, had to have a gas mask and know how to put it on, and they were given little cardboard boxes to carry them in. To Laura Hockney, these did not seem quite good enough, so she made her children special leatherette cases to provide adequate protection in the rain. They never actually had to wear one.

With no job and no prospect of any other kind of employment, Kenneth was thrown back on his wits. He had always been good with his hands so he decided to start a little business reconditioning prams, both dolls' prams and babies' prams, which he found through the advertisements in local papers, like the *Bradford Telegraph and Argus*, or the *Dewsbury Gazette*. Laura put her dressmaking skills to use repairing or remaking the hoods and aprons, while Kenneth put new springs on them and painted the bodies to make them look new. Though this work brought in relatively little money, with careful use of her ration books, Laura was able to make ends meet. A family of seven was allowed one book for each member of the family. She had three books for meat, and since she was a strict vegetarian, all her ration went to the children. With the other four books, she could get plenty of cheese, milk and butter or margarine. 'She was very good at feeding us,' Margaret remembers, 'and she certainly didn't expect us to be vegetarians, though she did make very nice vegetarian food.'[18]

The family had scarcely been back a few months when the bomb struck that nearly annihilated them. It was one of 116 bombs dropped on Bradford that night, doing considerable damage to the city centre and surrounding areas. Lingards, the great department store, took a direct hit and was gutted, as was the adjoining Kirkgate Chapel. Rawson Market was badly damaged, and in Manchester Road a bomb crashed through the roof of the Odeon Cinema, then the largest in Britain, landing in the front stalls and bringing the ceiling and heavy metal chandeliers down onto the seats. Miraculously, the audience for

It's a Date, starring Deanna Durbin and Walter Pidgeon, had left ten minutes earlier. Robert's Pie Shop had its front blown off, but when Priestley visited the city a month later, at the end of September, just after the Battle of Britain had been won, the giant pie was back in the window, still steaming, 'every puff defying Hitler, Goering and the whole gang of them'.[19]

Then, quite suddenly, in 1943, Kenneth announced that they were moving house, a decision which angered Laura, who had not been consulted. Kenneth's reasoning was that, with five children, they needed more space, and that it would be good for the whole family to get away, since the cruel taunts of their neighbours in Steadman Terrace were not going to cease. The new house, 18 Hutton Terrace, was in Eccleshill, a suburb high up on the northern outskirts of the city. It had a proper cellar, a kitchen with an open range for cooking, and a separate front room. Upstairs there were two bedrooms on the first floor and two attic rooms, and it had a bathroom and an inside toilet. There was a decent garden at the back, the air was fresh, and the front looked out over green fields, with extensive views across the Aire Valley. It was certainly a good environment and in time, Kenneth believed, Laura would come round to it, but night after night Margaret, who had the room next to them, would hear them arguing into the small hours.

Kenneth set up his pram business in the cellar of the new house, and with the extra space it afforded, he also began to buy and restore bicycles. When work was completed and they were ready to be sold, he would advertise them in the local papers, giving the number of the nearest telephone box and telling prospective buyers to call it between a certain time. Then he would take his favourite chair and set it up outside the box and sit down and wait till somebody called. For the young David, this seemed logical. 'People considered him eccentric for doing this,' Hockney says now, 'but it just made me think . . . "What a sensible man. That's just what I'd do."'[20]

It was in his father's pram workshop, watching him at work, that the seeds of Hockney's ambition to become an artist were sown. 'The fascination of the brush dipping in the paint, putting it on,' he later wrote, 'I loved it . . . it is a marvellous thing to dip a brush into paint and make marks on anything, even on a bicycle, the feel of a thick brush full of paint coating something.'[21] And on another occasion he recalled how 'he'd put silver paint on the wheels, but the one thing I remember was he'd paint a straight line down the bar. He had a special brush and he would hold his finger along the brush so he could paint a perfect line. I thought: incredible that you can make a straight line like that with just your eye. It's like watching Michelangelo draw a circle.'[22]

The young Hockney drew from the moment he was old enough to hold a pencil. 'My earliest memory of David drawing,' recalls John, 'was when we used to get up in the morning and I used to come down to get my comics or the newspaper. The edge all the way around, where there was no writing, was usually covered in little drawings and cartoons. That was the only paper he could get, and this was before school every day and he'd already be drawing. I used to get annoyed because I was looking forward to getting my own comic and he had already drawn all over it.'[23] If he couldn't get hold of a scrap of paper, he would draw with chalk on the linoleum floor of the kitchen, and when his mother got fed up with the mess she put up a blackboard. The golden rule was 'No drawing on the wallpaper!'

On Saturday mornings Hockney would enter the painting and drawing competitions for children that used to appear regularly in the *Daily Express*, and when the family went on Sundays to their local Methodist church in Victoria Road, he would doodle away on the fly leaves of the hymn books. After chapel, there would be Sunday school, at the end of which the children were broken up into small classes and asked to do illustrations of what they had learned. Hockney used to draw cartoons of subjects such as 'Jesus Walking on the Water', much to the amusement of the rest of the class. At one point his mother arranged for him and Margaret to have piano lessons. 'After the third lesson,' he remembers, 'I thought to myself, "I'm going to have to put an awful lot of time into this," [24] so I said to my mam, "I'd rather put my time into drawing." So I gave up. My parents always encouraged me with my drawing.' They also put it to good use. When Laura

'Untitled'
(date unknown)

drew up a washing-up rota, David illustrated it with caricatures of himself and his siblings in various moods, of which he was the eternally cheerful one.

The children's new school was Wellington Road Primary, and on 8 May 1945, a two-day holiday was announced to the children there — the war was officially over. Hockney rushed home to tell his mother who already knew from listening to the radio, which was kept on permanently. It struck his eight-year-old self, as he looked at the large console and the coloured map of Europe above it, on which they had followed the progress of the war, that from now onwards there would be no more boring news coming endlessly out of the radio, but just music and songs. 'When the blackout was over,' he remembers, 'and the lights came on again, Bradford Corporation Buses organised a bus route that took you along the hills round the edge so you could see the city lit up. Well, it was probably a pretty miserable sight, but to a small kid this was like Las Vegas.'[25]

Many of Hockney's early influences developed during this period. 'He always seemed to be worldly-wise at a very young age,' Margaret remembers. 'From the age of five or six, he seemed to know what to do in the world. He really enjoyed life.'[26] With Eccleshill Library nearby, the house was always full of books and he read a lot, everything from Biggles to the Brontës, the local classics, to Dickens. His father took them all to museums, and to look at the collection of Victorian and Edwardian paintings in Cartwright Hall, the civic art gallery in Lister Park. On Saturday nights they would often go to the Alhambra Theatre in Morley Street, taking fish and chips up to the balcony, where they'd have cheap standing tickets at the back. Though pantomime and music hall were the usual acts, there were the occasional more upmarket evenings, on one of which Hockney saw his first performance of Puccini's *La Bohème*, performed by the Carl Rosa Opera Company. 'It stuck in my mind,' he recalls, 'because it was about artists in Paris, and the music was better than usual and the orchestra was bigger. My father didn't really care for it. He just said, "Well, some nights it's like that . . ."'[27]

First and foremost, however, Hockney loved the movies, his

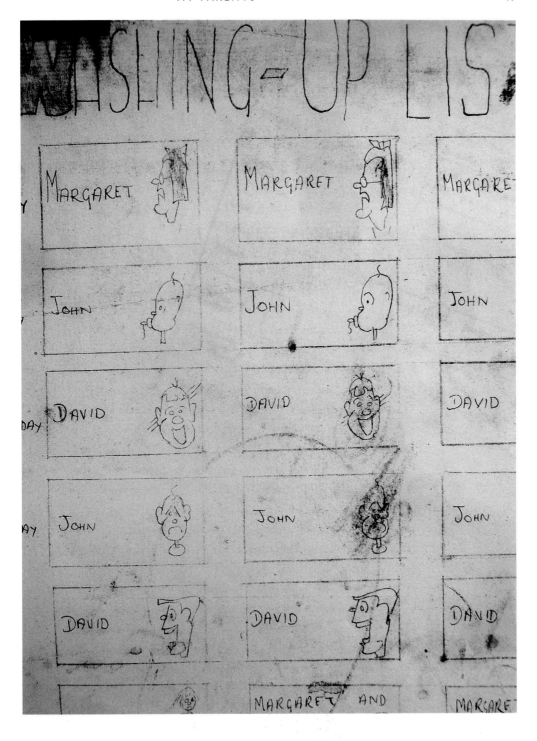

early experiences of them being during the war when, because of
the blackout, to get to the cinema they had to feel their way down
the street by running their hands along the wall. It was a passion he
inherited from his father. 'I used to say, "Can we go to the pictures?"'
he remembers, 'and my dad used to say, "You'll have to ask your
mother." And we knew that was fatal, because she ran everything
and she didn't like the pictures. She was very much in charge, and
if she said no that meant no. I suppose she was worried about the
expense.'[28] For that reason, on the occasions when Laura relented,
they never went in the main entrance of the cinema, but in the side
entrance for the cheap seats at the front. And there were ways to
get in free. Kids would often manage to push open the exit doors
to let in their friends waiting outside, while Hockney remembers
learning 'that if you walk in backwards, people think you're coming
out.'[29]

In the 1940s Bradford had more than forty cinemas, or 'picture
houses'. The Arcadian and the Empress, the Odeon and the Coliseum,
and the New Victoria, which stood next to the Alhambra and had
the third largest auditorium in the country, showed first-run films.
Then there were the 'fleapits' like the Oxford, the Elysian and the
Idle, which had a sheet for a screen, and films that were likely to be
very scratched and have poor sound. Because by the mid-1940s he was
beginning to go deaf, Kenneth sought out cinemas with the state-of-
the-art Western Electric Sound System, which gave a sharper sound.
The films they showed were invariably American. 'I was brought up,'
says David, 'in Bradford and Hollywood, because Hollywood was the
cinema. American films were technically superior, because they had
good lighting and good sound.'[30]

Saturday mornings meant Kids' Club at the Greengates Cinema
on New Line, where David and John watched serials such as *Superman*,
Flash Gordon and *Hopalong Cassidy*. 'There was excitement on that
screen,' Hockney later wrote. 'The screen, as if by magic, was opening
up the wall to you. It showed you another world, even in the dingiest
little cinema in suburban Bradford.'[31] He also shared his father's love of
what Kenneth referred to as 'comical' films, starring Charlie Chaplin

or Laurel and Hardy. 'He used to laugh so hard,' Hockney remembers, 'that it loosened his false teeth.'[32]

Though Bradford is an industrial city, it is small, and to the north and the west there is beautiful countryside that can be reached very quickly. From an early age, the young David was an avid hiker and cyclist. A tuppenny bus ride would take him to Saltaire where the great mill built by Sir Titus Salt belched out smoke, and from there it was a short walk to Shipley Glen, with its funfair, or a three- to four-hour hike to Ilkley, fifteen miles away and advertised for its 'bracing air'. With Kenneth's help, David and John built themselves a tandem from second-hand parts and they would cycle all over. York was a favourite destination because, once they'd got through the hilly country around Leeds, the journey was all on the flat. They'd set off at eight in the morning and it would take them four hours. Once there, they would climb the tower of the Minster, walk the city walls or visit the railway museum before returning home. Sometimes they went to Leeds where there was a much bigger art gallery that had French paintings, and there were stores such as Woolworths which had modern cafeterias. 'Some of the trams in Leeds,' Hockney remembers, 'had New York Road written on the front, meaning the new road to York, but I used to think, "New York! You'd never see that written in Bradford."'[33]

Very occasionally Kenneth took the whole family on a summer holiday, but while most people went to Morecambe or Blackpool, for which the Hockney children yearned, they went to Withernsea. There were two reasons for this. First of all it was close to Hull, where they could stay with their Great-Aunt Nell, their father's aunt, an eccentric woman who adopted an exaggerated 'posh' accent. Second, it was cheap, a short bus ride from Hull and there was nothing to spend their money on when they got there. 'All Dad had to do was give us a few pennies, because there was just one tiny little arcade. I mean, compared to Withernsea, Bridlington was like Monte Carlo, which is why we weren't allowed to go there.'[34]

When he was at home, he was encouraged to study at all times. So far as his parents were concerned, it was Bradford Grammar or nothing, and his school reports show what achievements he made. In February

1946, when he was fourth in his class of thirty-six, his headmaster, Irvine R. Bakes, wrote: 'David has shown great interest in his work. He tries at all times.'[35] The next term he had reached top place with an overall score for all his subjects of 274 out of a possible 280. 'David has done excellent work this year,' wrote Mr Bakes. 'I could do with more like him.'[36] This was in spite of the fact that he had had to scold David in front of the whole class for sketching the teacher during the problem exam, something he had been caught doing on several other occasions when he was bored in class. Drawing in class did not stop him soaring ahead, however, and the following year, at the end of the summer term, his work was judged 'Excellent throughout the term. All subjects reach a high standard. Outstanding in art.'[37] Parents of children at Wellington Road were encouraged to sign off the reports, with a view to encouraging their children in their work at school. 'I am very pleased with his progress,'[38] wrote Laura Hockney.

This was a time when the education system in Britain was being revolutionised. Hockney and his generation were the first beneficiaries of the 1944 Butler Act, a landmark in English education which greatly expanded access to secondary education by making it free for all pupils. 'The throwing open of secondary education to all,' wrote Harold Dent, the editor of the *Times Educational Supplement*, '[would] result in a prodigious freeing of creative ability, and ensure to an extent yet incalculable that every child shall be prepared for the life he is best fitted to lead and the service he is best fitted to give.'[39] Pupils were assessed in a new exam, the eleven-plus, intended to allocate them to schools best suited to their abilities and aptitudes.

All Hockney's hard work paid off when, in the spring of 1947, like his brother Paul before him, he won a scholarship to Bradford Grammar School, one of the oldest academic institutions in the country, founded in 1548 and granted its charter by Charles II in 1662. For parents like his, with their great ambition for their children, this was manna from heaven. Such schools were known for their high academic standards, emulating the curriculum, ethos and ambitions of the major public schools, and retaining a classical core of Latin and Greek alongside modern subjects. Discipline was rigorous, however, and the naturally rebellious Hockney was not particularly keen on going there. 'David very difficult,' Laura wrote in her diary on 7 September 1948. 'Does not want to go to Grammar School.'[40] He had no choice.

While David's first term at Bradford Grammar was spent in the old premises near the parish church on Stott Hill, the following term the whole school was moved to a brand-new building in Keighley Road, Frizinghall, opened on 12 January by the Duke of Edinburgh. Hockney's class were asked to write an essay on the subject of the opening but, because he had been seated far to the right of the stage, and had to crane his neck to see what was going on, instead of handing in an essay on how splendid the whole occasion was, he wrote about his cricked neck. This was typical of the subversiveness that increasingly epitomised his character, along with a quick wit and an ability to answer back. There were times when he just couldn't resist going too far. 'There was a place in the school called the Long Corridor,' he remembers, 'and one afternoon I was walking along the corridor and there was this prefect coming towards me. When he passed me, he didn't say anything, so I turned round to him and said, "Less of your cheek!" He came straight back to me and I got detention, but I thought, "It's worth it."' [41]

As a scholarship boy, Hockney was expected to work hard and to do well, which would not have been a problem had he been able to study art. But he soon discovered that in the top form, art was only on the syllabus during the first year, and only for one double period of one and a half hours a week. After that there was no more art until the sixth form, when art appreciation was taught. On the other hand, boys who found themselves in the bottom form doing a general course were allowed to study art. 'They thought art was not a serious study,' he recalls, 'and I just thought, "Well, they're wrong."'[42] Taking a conscious decision to do less work, he spent mathematics classes drawing the cacti on the classroom windowsill, doodled endlessly on all his notebooks, and, during a science exam, left the paper blank save for a line of writing which read 'am no good at science, but I can draw', under which was a sketch of the invigilator.[43] In his class, Form 3D, which had thirty pupils, he came thirtieth. This infuriated the headmaster, Mr Graham, who demanded to know why a scholarship boy like him was so lazy, while his form mistress, Margaret Baker, wrote in her report: 'He should realise that ability in and enthusiasm for art alone is not enough to make a career for him.'[44]

As a result of his tactical idleness Hockney achieved his wish to be relegated to the non-academic level of the bottom division, where he was able to continue in the art class. Here he thrived under the genial art teacher, Reggie Maddox, who encouraged him to get involved in creating posters for the various school societies – particularly enjoyable was dreaming up pictures according to the themes of the Debating Society's debate. These ended up on the school noticeboard, where everybody saw them, and which Hockney began to regard as his own personal exhibition space. It was, he later wrote, 'the first time I had the opportunity to carry out my fantasy about being an artist'.[45] That people liked them so much was borne out by the fact that they were invariably stolen.

Hockney was also greatly inspired by his English teacher, Kenneth Grose, who recognised that, in spite of his inability to work hard at anything except drawing, he was full of curiosity. He encouraged him to pursue his love of reading, and made no attempt to stifle his artistic ability. 'I remember once when I was supposed to have done some essay for my homework,' Hockney recalls, 'and I hadn't done the essay – instead I'd spent all my time doing a collage self-portrait for the art class – and he said to me in front of the whole class, "Hockney, can you read your essay?" So I said to him, "Well, I didn't do the essay, but I did this," and showed him the collage. He said, "That's very good," and I was quite knocked over. He was a stimulant and he encouraged me in my ambitions to be an artist.'[46]

Grose also edited the school magazine, the *Bradfordian*, and often got Hockney to illustrate articles, usually with drawings done on scraperboard, since they required a high degree of contrast and the school block-makers weren't very sophisticated. A typical cartoon ridiculed compulsory sports, one of the features of school life that Hockney most hated, showing first a caricature of him standing with a crutch, one foot bandaged up, holding a notice reading 'Complaint about compulsory running', and second one of him being pushed in a wheelchair by an able-bodied runner.

It was becoming clear that art really was the only subject at which Hockney excelled. When he discovered that Bradford School of Art had a junior school attached to it, which took students from the age of fourteen, he pleaded and pleaded with the headmaster to let him go there, until Mr Graham, seeing that he was never going to give up, finally caved in and wrote to his father: 'David's Form Master and those who teach him have been considering his future, and they think it worth while my writing to you to suggest that as his ability and keenness appear to be on the artistic side he might suitably transfer, before long, to a School of Art, and there prepare himself for a career in some branch of drawing or painting.'[47] Kenneth and Laura gave him their full support. But they were reckoning without the forces of traditional education in Bradford.

CHAPTER TWO

SELF-PORTRAIT

On 25 March 1950, at Eccleshill Methodist Chapel's anniversary concert, the young David Hockney gave a public demonstration of his skills, sitting on the stage and doing lightning sketches of the performers and of various members of the congregation. Hockney was happy, confident both in the knowledge of his headmaster's recommendation that he should be allowed to transfer to Bradford School of Art, and in his parents' support. But his wish to leave grammar school early would turn out to be a pipe dream. 'May I suggest that in "Reasons for Application",' Mr Graham had written to Kenneth four days earlier, 'that you wish the boy to be withdrawn from the school *only* if he is admitted to the School of Art.'[1] On 5 April after Kenneth had submitted the application, and both he and Laura had gone before the Education Committee at the town hall, the Director of Education himself, Mr Spalding, wrote back: 'After careful consideration the Committee believed that your son's best interests would be served by completion of his course of general education before specialising in Art. They, therefore, were not prepared to grant your request.'[2]

The twelve-year-old Hockney's disappointment at this blow was deep and bitter. It is something he has never forgotten. He would have liked to go even earlier. 'I would have gone to art school at the age of eight,' he says. 'You learn a lot when you're eight. I mean, how old were Rembrandt and Michelangelo when they started art? I don't think they were much older than twelve.'[3] His anger sent his schoolwork into a downward spiral, and he lingered at the bottom of the class. He did virtually no homework, spending most of his time drawing posters for the school societies. 'Doing the posters at home,' he later wrote, 'did save me from trouble . . . my mother would say to me, "What about

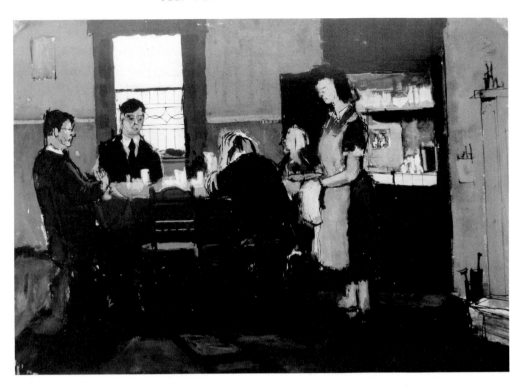

your homework? Are you doing it?" and I'd say, "Yes," when really I'd be doing a poster. I'd say, "This is for the school."[4]

Sunday Lunch
Hutton Terrace

His form master, Mr Ashton, was frustrated by his lazy habits and the knowledge that he had real ability. It was as if he couldn't be bothered. 'He still does not really believe,' wrote his loyal supporter, Ken Grose, in his December 1950 English report, 'that an artist needs occasionally to use words', while his report at the end of the Lent term in 1951 was abysmal. His geography was 'very lethargic', 'he makes little or no effort with any of his mathematical work', and even Mr Grose couldn't find a good word to say for him, simply writing: 'There is no point in his coming to English lessons.' Though he continued to be first in art, even in that subject his teacher reported 'little progress', and the headmaster demanded periodic reports on Hockney during the next term, a sure sign that his future at the school was in doubt. 'Is he really silly?' Mr Graham wrote at the bottom of the December report. 'He can't afford even to pretend to be.'[5]

The decline in Hockney's schoolwork did not escape his parents' notice as he became more and more untidy, his school notebooks increasingly desecrated by doodles. Linking these facts, Laura had the idea of sending him to a neighbour, Mr Whitehead, a teacher at the Bradford School of Art who gave calligraphy lessons in his spare time. 'He obviously thought I was talented,' Hockney recalls, 'and people like that, if they find some talented person, will give their lessons for free so my parents didn't have to pay. I remember he used to chew hard little sticks of Italian liquorice, which made his teeth all black. He was old-fashioned and smoked a pipe, and I used to go to him once a week and be given some exercises to do. He taught me how to use a pen and to make the serif so that the curve was perfect. I liked it because it was teaching me about form, so at least I thought I was learning some skill. He was eager to have a young pupil who was obviously keen and it made the whole business of not being allowed to go to the art school easier to deal with.'[6] It was an inspired idea of Laura's, and Hockney's schoolwork began to show immediate improvement. 'I have been very pleased with his work and his general attitude,' wrote his form master at the end of July, while the headmaster wrote simply: 'Most encouraging. His best term so far.'[7]

'Untitled'
(date unknown)

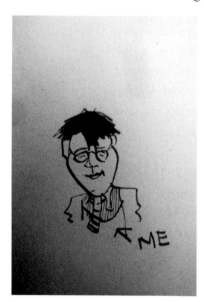

Over the next two years, Hockney managed to keep his head above water, in spite of the fact that his natural desire to clown around often overcame the need to pay attention. He developed a reputation for being funny, and made every effort to live up to it. If this meant tripping over when he came into the classroom, then he would do exactly that. He was an excellent mimic. Nineteen fifty-two was the year of a new radio show that was, the *Radio Times* announced, 'based upon a crazy type of fun evolved by four of our younger laughter-makers'. Their names were Peter Sellers, Harry Secombe, Michael Bentine and Spike Milligan, and the show was called *The Goon Show.* At a time when almost every family in the country gathered round the radio in the

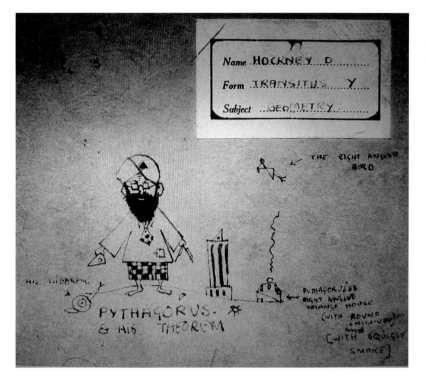

'Untitled'
(date unknown)

evenings to listen to such programmes, Hockney's impersonation of Henry Crun, a character played by Peter Sellers, was certain to raise a laugh. A natural anarchist, he would arrive at school without wearing his cap and blazer if he could, which gave him semi-heroic status. 'He won the art prize every year,' Laura was to remember, 'but at speech days we couldn't understand the reaction of the other boys when David went up for his award. They stamped their feet, booed, clapped and shouted and made a terrific noise. We spoke to the head about it and he said it was because David was so amusing.'[8]

At the same time as playing the clown, Hockney was also growing up. When he accompanied Laura every Sunday to Methodist chapel, she may have looked upon him as the perfect son, but there was a lot going on in his life that she didn't know about, not least his burgeoning sexuality. 'There were loads of things I never told my mother,' he remembers. 'Actually, I didn't tell my parents anything that was going on.' One night, for example, he went off on his own to see a film in one of the local fleapits. 'I was sitting near the front enjoying the picture when a man sitting next to me suddenly reached over and took my hand and placed it on his erect cock. I remember thinking, "I can't tell my mother about this." I enjoyed it and it gave me a lifelong love of cinemas.'[9]

Sex was simply not discussed in families in the 1950s, and most children found out about it by trial and error, or from dirty jokes and graffiti in public urinals. They learned precious little in school. The novelist Derek Robinson recalled that, at the institution he attended in Bristol, 'the two periods of biology scheduled to cover human reproduction left many of us more confused than before. That tangle of plumbing created in chalk on the blackboard; did it really have something to do with our bodies? There was a rumour that sex was supposed to be fun. It didn't look like fun. The way the biology master described it, it sounded slightly less fun than unclogging a drain with a bent plunger.'[10] For Hockney, it was Scout camp that provided the stamping ground for sexual exploration.

He had joined the Cubs at primary school; by the time he went to grammar school he was a member of the Fourth Bradford East Scouts from Eccleshill Church, and celebrated for his very particular participation in the annual gang shows (variety shows at which all the Scouts would sing songs and perform sketches to raise money for local charities) in which, standing onstage with a large easel and a drawing pad, he would do lightning sketches of the Scoutmaster, the vicar and other local people, to great applause. When the group went on camping trips, he would keep the logbook, filling it with drawings and cartoons that depicted their various activities. 'David would always make us laugh,' remembers Philip Naylor, a friend of his brother John. 'Once at camp he climbed right up into the high branches of a tree and announced that he was the King of the Twigs. Then the branch gave way and he plunged earthwards, and for quite a while after that he was known as "Twiggy".'[11]

'David is off at last with a pack almost as big as himself,' wrote Laura in her diary on 30 December 1952. '. . . an old Scoutmaster . . . is allowing the boys to camp in a stable where there is a stove and plenty of coke. They do have good times these days.'[12] 'When I was in the Boy Scouts,' says Hockney, 'I used to be quite naughty, but you'd never talk about it. I mean, you'd put your hand on someone's cock, but you'd never mention it later. I liked the camping because it was sexy. It was an opportunity to get into someone else's sleeping bag. We were just kids, teenage boys messing around.'[13]

Hockney had a bit of a crush on one of the boys on this trip, David Johnson, who was the captain of the school rugby team. '. . . they are big pals,' wrote fellow Scout, Mike Powell. '. . . the two Davids found a flooded air-raid shelter and Johnson decided he would dive in and investigate, but he had no swimming kit. It had been raining all week at camp and

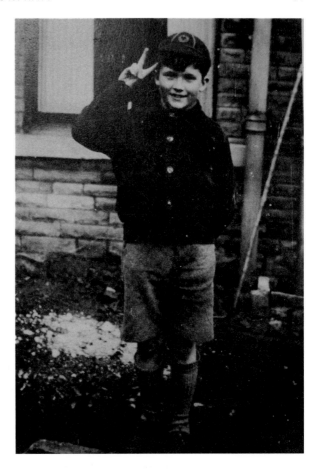

Hockney at about ten, in his Cub cap

to minimise the number of soakings we were having, my patrol leader had the idea of making some of us wear swimming trunks. Hockney looked at me and said, "Take off your trunks and give them to Johnson." I sheepishly did so, quickly slipping into some shorts. David J., school rugby captain, squeezed into my tiny costume and promptly jumped in. The water looked horrible in there and he was soon out, handing back my trunks now stretched to twice the size. The Scoutmaster was so annoyed with the two Davids for being somewhat irresponsible that he ordered them both to take a P B [public bath] in a stream by the camp. They both stripped completely, lay in the stream and the Scouts had to scrub them both with soil-filled turf we had recently dug up during the building of the latrines.'[14] On her son's return from this trip, a week later, on 8 January, Laura noted, 'David came home from camp. He has had a fine time and is looking forward to going again. He certainly does get much out of life.'[15]

The early part of 1953 was clouded for Laura by the sudden death in her sleep of her mother, Mary, on 19 February. 'Today seemed strange and empty outwardly,' she wrote the following morning, '– but a strange feeling of calm and quiet within, something I have never experienced before.' The funeral took place on 24 February. 'The service at Eastbrook was beautiful – not mournful, but more like an Easter service, as fitted her beautiful life – just called to a Higher service, and quite ready,' and afterwards Laura took Hockney to visit Bradford Regional College of Art. She was armed with a good reference from his headmaster, Mr Graham, and some of his drawings, and the following Friday she wrote: 'I took some of David's work to the College of Art – and Mr Rhodes, the Principal, and Mrs Peters, the head of the Commercial Art department, were very much impressed and assured me that definitely commercial art should be David's career. We want to give him a chance – but shall have to apply for a grant from the Education department.'[16]

Hockney sat the all-important GCE exams in July. The papers that have survived give an extraordinary glimpse of a boy sitting in an examination hall, daydreaming and doodling. In his French paper, for example, which required translation of a scene set in a Paris hotel and featuring Madame Noublard, her daughter Jacqueline and the manager, le Gérant, he made no attempt at the work, merely writing, 'I'm afraid I know no French but will draw some pictures instead.'[17] Caricatures of 'Madame Noublard et sa fillette et le Gérant' are drawn at the top of the page; the word 'Bluebeard' is mysteriously written at the bottom. Not surprisingly he failed the exam. He did rather better in English literature, which required the design of a stage set for *Twelfth Night*, and he naturally scored the highest mark for art. He scraped through in most of the other subjects, covering all the exam papers with little sketches.

On his last speech day, when he went to pick up the customary art prize, the whole school gave him a huge cheer. 'He has undoubted ability in art,' wrote his form master on his final report, 'especially in cartoon and sign-writing work ... we have enjoyed his company.' The headmaster bade him best wishes on his new start. 'He will be glad to get rid of the figure of fun,' he concluded, 'and to establish himself as a sincere and serious person by steady work and merit.'[18]

Hockney left with a skip in his step only to meet another hurdle – in the previous few months his parents had modified their enthusiasm for his going to art school. This was partly for financial reasons, and partly to be fair to his older siblings, all of whom had left school and gone straight to work. Paul in particular had wanted to be an artist, having got credits in art in his School Certificate, but had failed to find a job in commercial art and had ended up as a clerk in a firm of accountants. Philip had gone to night school to study engineering, and Margaret was training to be a nurse. Encouraged by the views of Mr Rhodes, the principal of the art college, that their son's work had commercial potential, Kenneth and Laura now encouraged him to go out and find a job as a commercial artist.

Mr Graham helped out, arranging an interview with Percy Lund Humphries & Co., a Bradford firm of printers, binders and publishers, and to please his parents Hockney went along with their wishes, putting together a portfolio of lettering and other things he thought commercial artists might do. This included a series of drawings of the various textile processes he had seen – Sorting, Washing, Drying and Carding – on a school visit to the local Airedale Combing Co. He also arranged to take the portfolio round other studios and advertising agencies in Leeds. Lund Humphries turned him down saying that he was not suitable for their class of work, while most of the other firms suggested that he returned after attending art school. With his heart still set on going there, 'I told my parents then,' Hockney remembers, 'that it was essential for me to go to art school to get a job. I was determined. I would have cheated and lied and used every trick in the book to get there.'[19]

Finally convinced, Kenneth and Laura applied for a grant from the Education Committee, and the sum of £35 was awarded, the first instalment of £11 to be paid in November 1953. In the meantime, his

rucksack on his back, Hockney set off for a six-week holiday job to earn
some money, helping with the harvest on a farm in the East Riding.
This was a summer job he had been doing since he was fourteen, a
gruelling cycle ride of fifty-four miles to Foxcovert Farm in Huggate,
high up on the Yorkshire Wolds. A continuation of the chalk hills of
Lincolnshire, the Wolds undulate gently from the River Humber to
the coast of the East Riding, occupying an area of about 200,000 acres.
Up until the nineteenth century, when they were first cultivated to
meet the agricultural needs of the Industrial Revolution, they were
little more than a barren wasteland, devoid of trees and vegetation,
unvisited by Victorian tourists and largely ignored by artists such as
J. M. W. Turner, James Ward and Alexander Cozens, who painted
the more romantic grandeur of the West Riding. Yet the summers that
Hockney spent working on the land here remain etched in his memory.

'When I first came to the Wolds,' he remembers, 'I cycled everywhere and I quickly noticed the very beautiful cultivated landscape,
so different from West Yorkshire and amazingly unspoiled.'[20] There
was no farmhouse attached to Foxcovert Farm; the farmer, Mr Hardy,
lived in a house in Huggate. The seasonal workers, all young boys,
lodged in outbuildings, the accommodation consisting of a dormitory
on the first floor, with three big shared double beds, and a room below
for eating and cooking. Across the foal yard was a room known as the
'Slum', which was for recreation and contained a large coke stove, a
settle and a dartboard. Each day the boys were out in the fields by
seven, helping to bind and stook the corn, and they worked there till
seven in the evening, when, exhausted, they would wander down to
the local pub, the Huggate Arms. Here the young Hockney, free from
parental restraints, tasted his first pint of beer. His mind was never
far from home, however. 'He once sent us a parcel containing a dead
rabbit,' Laura remembered. 'The poor postman couldn't wait to get
rid of it. He said, "I don't know what's in this parcel, but it stinks to
high heaven." David thought he was sending us a lovely meal!'[21]

The full-time workers consisted of the foreman, the stockman,
a man to look after the horses, and the shepherd, an old man called
Tommy Jackson, who never washed and used to chew and spit tobacco.

'The thing that struck me,' says Hockney, 'was how feudal it all was. The farm labourers all referred to Mr Hardy as "The Master". Nobody in Bradford would have called their employer that, not in the mills anyway. It was a terrific experience. The job was boring, but I took home eight pounds at the end and it instilled in me a love of the landscape which I never forgot.'[22] After six weeks on the farm he returned to Bradford to prepare for his first term at Bradford College of Art.

Hockney arrived late, his grant having been delayed for two weeks, but his reputation preceded him: his calligraphy tutor, Mr Whitehead, had told his class that a boy who would soon be joining them could knock spots off the lot of them. Not only that, he cut an intriguingly theatrical figure. After six weeks working in the fields, he was very tanned, in stark contrast to the pale complexions of the other students. He was also eccentrically dressed. Clothes rationing had just come to an end, and he and his father had taken to going to their favourite shop, Sykes Wardrobes, a high-quality second-hand clothes dealer that specialised in acquiring deceased estate wardrobes, including shoes. 'You don't need money for style,' Hockney says. 'It's about an attitude. People dressed pretty conventionally then, but I'd pick up things to make me look a bit different and which I wore out of a sense of mockery.'[23] Dave Oxtoby, a painting student who was to become his close friend, remembers sitting with a fellow painter, Norman Stevens, in the life class at the moment when David first came in. 'He was wearing a shirt with a high-starched wing collar and a black pinstriped suit with trousers that were far too short. He had on a bowler hat, an incredibly long red scarf, and he was carrying an umbrella. I turned to Norman and I said, "Look at this guy, he looks like a Russian peasant. He looks a right Boris."'[24] This caused some embarrassment for Hockney, who was already struggling to keep his composure in the face of being confronted with his first ever nude female model. The name stuck, and throughout his time at the college he was always to be known as 'Boris'.

Climbing the wide stone steps and entering the pillared portico of the grand old Victorian building that was Bradford College of Art was

the achievement of a dream for Hockney. It was all he had thought of
for the last three years: to be in an environment where he was going to
be learning about nothing except art. 'I was interested in everything at
first,' he wrote. 'I was an innocent little boy of sixteen and I believed
everything they told me, everything. If they said "You have to study
perspective", I'd study perspective; if they told me to study anatomy,
I'd study anatomy. It was thrilling after being at the Grammar School
to be at a school where I knew I would enjoy everything they asked me
to do.'[25] Mr Whitehead had told him that quite a lot of students who
went to the art school wasted their time there by not doing much work.
'I was careful to tell my parents,' he remembers, 'that I would not be
one of those people, and I did work very hard and quickly noticed all
the students who didn't.'[26]

The principal of the college in the autumn of 1953 was Fred
Coleclough, a bureaucrat who liked every department to be run as
though it was the army. So far as he was concerned the business of the
college was to turn out commercial artists who would have successful
careers in the advertising and printing trades. He had little time for
painters, as Hockney was quick to discover. 'When I was asked what
I wanted to do,' he recalls, 'I said that I wanted to be an artist. They
didn't appear to understand what I meant by this, and asked me if I had
a private income. They knew I'd been to grammar school and probably
thought that I was a bit superior. I said I didn't know, because the truth
is I had absolutely no idea what a private income was. They then told
me that if I wanted to do something practical, I would be better off
going into the graphics department.'[27] Happy at this stage to agree to
anything, Hockney lasted just two months in this department, studying
commercial art under John Fleming, who supported Coleclough's
views on student training. All the while, however, he had one eye
firmly fixed on the painting department.

Once again he approached the principal and asked to be transferred.
'They told me that I would have to train to be a teacher, as that was
the only living to be got out of painting. I thought to myself that if the
only way to get into the painting department was to trick them, then
that's exactly what I would do. So I said, "Fine, yes, I really would like

to be a teacher.'" Agreeing to this meant that so long as he had the required number of GCEs, he could now study painting in order to get a certificate to become a teacher of art. 'I sorted this out very quickly,' he says, 'because I was a very determined person. I was determined to have a proper art school education, to learn drawing and painting, and I got it, even though it had meant lying to get there.'[28]

Thus it was that at the beginning of 1954, the sixteen-year-old Hockney joined the painting department of Bradford College of Art. It was tiny, with a core group of five other students: Dave Oxtoby, Norman Stevens, David Fawcett, Rod Taylor and Bernard Woodward. 'Dave Oxtoby was a Teddy boy,' Hockney remembers, 'who wore a bottle-green suit, so I took one look at him and thought that he was probably one of the ones who didn't do much work.'[29] Because the class was so small, he soon got to know them all well, and his first real friend among them was Norman Stevens. 'He came up to me and said, "I've heard of you. I know you come from the Bradford Grammar School."[30] Stevens's disability – he had been badly crippled by polio as a child – had given him a determination to succeed at all costs, and this, combined with a wry sense of humour, endeared him to Hockney. They soon became inseparable.

They joked about everything, even Stevens's limp. One evening, they were out at night in the company of two friends who, along with Hockney, were imitating Norman's awkward way of walking. Suddenly they saw another genuinely disabled man limping towards them. When they were close enough to him, Hockney said loudly, 'All right, Norman, pack it in!' The two friends immediately started walking normally, but of course Norman couldn't, and as the man passed them he shouted at him, 'Cheeky bastard!' This cracked Hockney up.[31] The close friendship with Stevens caused a rift at home, in the relationship between Hockney and his younger brother. 'I became angry,' John says, 'not with David but with Norman, because for the first time ever, David was not mine any more. It was a petty jealousy but I do remember it having a great effect on me. I idolised David. We were buddies, I admired his confidence and openness and we had shared school holidays. We had done so much together. Of course I was the youngest, very immature, and losing him at that time was very difficult.'[32] But Hockney was moving ahead, throwing himself into student life, and from now on home and family life were to come second.

Provincial art colleges in the 1950s were for the most part pretty poverty-stricken: drawing from classical casts was still one of the primary modes of instruction, and heraldry was still on the curriculum in many of them. Prime influences were the Euston Road School, formed by William Coldstream, Victor Pasmore and Graham Bell in 1937 to promote naturalism and realism, and Walter Sickert, who had brought the French influence into English art schools. Bradford was little different and the teachers there were struggling to drag it into the modern world. Yet the four-year course that Hockney signed up to, the National Diploma in Design, which was a completely academic training, is now viewed by him as vital to all his later work.

For two years he was to study painting, together with a subsidiary subject, lithography. Then for the last two years, he would concentrate solely on painting and drawing. Two days a week were devoted to life painting, two days to figure composition, again mostly from life, and one day a week to drawing; and during the first two years, one day a week was devoted to either perspective or anatomy. 'It meant that for four years,' he later wrote, 'all you did was draw and paint, mostly from life.'[33]

There were two tutors in the painting department whom David found particularly stimulating. Fred Lyle, the senior tutor, was bald, with one eye and a beard, which gave him the appearance of Sinbad the Sailor, but it was the younger of the two who turned out to be the real inspiration. Derek Stafford was twenty-six and a fellow Yorkshireman from Doncaster, though there was no trace of his origins in his accent, as a result of his having attended Stowe School, from where he had been awarded a scholarship to the Royal College of Art. His studies had been interrupted by the war, and in November 1944, with a reasonable knowledge of anatomy from his drawing classes, he was placed in the Royal Army Medical Corps. After eight weeks' training he ended up in Belgium, just after the Battle of the Bulge, and from there travelled with the medics wherever they went. This included being among the first people into the concentration camp at Belsen, a horrific experience for the eighteen-year-old boy. 'For years I never spoke about it to anybody,' he says, 'and I still sometimes wake up at night with the smell of it in my nose.'[34]

Stafford took up his place at the Royal College in 1948, one of a generation of artists cut off from the mainstream of modern art by the experience of war at the crucial stage of their developing careers. The government actively encouraged them to take a patriotic approach to their art, and engage with the English landscape and its monuments, the result being the rebirth of a British Romantic movement. Leading lights among these self-styled neo-Romantics included John Minton, Robert MacBryde and Robert Colquhoun, Keith Vaughan, Eric Ravilious and John Craxton, who were simultaneously forward-thinking, and aware of their debt to nineteenth-century artists such as Samuel Palmer and William Blake. Some found a further outlet for their work in another patriotic project, 'Recording Britain', the brainchild of Sir Kenneth Clark, which commissioned artists to paint watercolours that would celebrate the country's natural beauty and architectural heritage. The nostalgic feel to much British painting in the 1940s was exemplified in the work of artists such as John Piper, Edward Bawden, Kenneth Rowntree and Stanley Spencer.

By the early 1950s, this veneration of the Englishness of English life was being eroded by a new movement celebrating, in the words of one of its leading exponents, the young painter John Bratby, 'the colour and mood of ration books, the general feeling of sackcloth and ashes'. 'The painting of my decade,' he commented, 'was an expression of its *Zeitgeist* – introvert, grim, khaki in colour, opposed to prettiness, and dedicated to portraying a stark, raw, ugly reality. The word angst prevailed in art talk.'[35] In December 1954, in the journal *Encounter*, the art critic David Sylvester gave the name to this movement which, he wrote, 'takes us back from the studio to the kitchen' and featured paintings which included 'Everything but the kitchen sink? The kitchen sink too.'[36] The Kitchen-Sink movement, which reached its zenith in 1956 when its main practitioners John Bratby, Derrick

Greaves, Edward Middleditch and Jack Smith – represented Britain at the Venice Biennale, echoed the strength of social realism in art at the time, and this was reflected in the work Hockney saw from his tutors, mostly gritty Bradford street scenes in muted colours.

Derek Stafford had joined the staff of Bradford College of Art in 1953, the year before Hockney arrived, fighting off eighty other applicants after a 'soul-destroying' year working in a furniture store in Doncaster. He had very quickly found a house and studio only four minutes away from the college. 'When I started the job,' he remembers, 'I was determined to teach the students my way and not anybody else's way, and my way was to teach them to think. Drawing is a cerebral process. It is not just imitating what you see, it is understanding what you see. That is what I wanted to put over.'[37]

From the beginning he fell out constantly with the bureaucratic Fred Coleclough. 'I was trying to encourage thinking,' says Stafford, 'and getting the students to do things their way, to come into a life class full of energy, to sit down, to examine, to walk up to the model to look, to walk round the model, to see what was taking place outside of their vision, to make them realise that the edge is only the last part you see before it moves out of your vision. This excited them.'[38] In his life class, the students would start drawing as soon as they came in, for about half an hour. Then the model would take a rest and Stafford would look at the work individually, sometimes making a comment, sometimes just sitting with them and making them watch him draw. 'What I was quick to notice,' Hockney recalls, 'was that the teachers were seeing more than I was seeing. I hadn't looked hard enough, and I quickly saw that, and so I began to look harder myself. And if you are strict with yourself, after a few weeks you begin to get better and better.'[39]

To begin with, Hockney didn't show himself as any more or less talented than the other students. What he was good at was drawing Desperate Dan from the *Dandy*, playing the fool, joking and disrupting the class. 'He'd be throwing rubbers about in life drawing,' Stafford remembers, 'and then before you got to him he'd turn his life drawing upside down so you'd have to strain your neck to look at it. I had to

take him aside and tell him, "David, you've got to take this seriously."
He soon showed himself to be the most industrious of students. He was
tenacious in his approach and would always stay late, and if we weren't
talking during the lunch hour, then he'd be drawing.'[40]

Because most of the group's understanding of art was limited to
what they'd seen in newspapers or comic books, Stafford encouraged
them to scrimp and save up to travel occasionally to London. David
made his first trip on 26 February 1954. 'We went to the National
Gallery, the Victoria and Albert Museum, the British Museum and
the Tate Gallery, all the obvious places, simply because I'd never been
to London before.'[41] John Loker, a student who arrived at the college
in 1955, recalls how they used to leave school on a Friday night, get
themselves down to the Great North Road, the A1, and then hitchhike.
When they arrived, in the early hours of the morning, they would buy
a ticket on the Circle Line and then sleep on the train until the time
the galleries began to open, at which point they would trudge round as
many exhibitions as they could fit in.

'The amazing thing is,' says John, 'that we would do these trips
with virtually no money – we might have half a crown to last us the
whole trip. We used to go to the Lyons Corner House café just off
Trafalgar Square where they used to have a salad counter at which you
could eat as much as you could fit on the plate. We used to get a plate
and pile it up so high you had to hold both the top and the bottom of
the plate to keep the salad from falling off. We'd stuff all this down us
and very little else.' Hitchhiking back on Saturday nights, there were
very few cars on the road, mostly just lorries, and they often ended
up sleeping in a barn in the middle of nowhere, finally getting home
on the Sunday evening. 'It was a great thing to do and we always used
to have a lot of fun doing silly studenty things. I remember one time
in the Tate Gallery Norman Stevens fell asleep on one of the benches,
and David took out a page from one of his notebooks, wrote "DO NOT
DISTURB" on it in block capitals and propped it up on him, and we just
left him there.'[42]

Derek Stafford considered these trips a vital part of the students'
education. 'I encouraged them to go to the National Gallery and look

first at the old masters, and then go and look at the new masters, and they would see there was an evolution from one to the other, each demonstrating in their own way something of their own period. That is what they were going to be doing whether they liked it or not. I told them that they could not live outside their own period. I told them that the influences upon them were going to be the influences that were there just before them, and that they should not ignore them. If they rejected what was new, then they were going to become bad artists. They had to look, they had to absorb, and then evolution would take place which is a natural process of life.'[43]

It was on one of these trips to London that David first saw the work of Picasso, an artist about whom a high degree of philistinism prevailed. This ranged from Sir Alfred Munnings' comment at a Royal Academy dinner that Picasso deserved to be kicked down the steps of Burlington House to the student at Bradford College nicknamed 'Picasso', because he couldn't draw. 'I was horrified,' says David, 'because I knew that Picasso drew beautifully and I just thought to myself, "They haven't been looking at Picasso properly." Well, I had, and I thought that whatever you didn't know about abstraction, you should know that Picasso had done some marvellous paintings. I remember being very struck by Picasso's painting of the Massacre in Korea which he painted in 1951 and which I saw when I was still at Bradford Grammar School. It was reproduced in all the newspapers and I remember at the time how it was dismissed as being nothing but communist propaganda. I thought to myself that whatever they said, Picasso was better than that.'[44]

That Hockney absorbed Stafford's advice is clearly shown in some of his best early work, a series of self-portraits he painted at home. He did a fair amount of work at Hutton Terrace, which was far too small for a studio. 'Our front bedroom is in a terrible state,' wrote Laura on 5 April. 'What it is to have an artist son!! David thought he should be allowed to use the little bedroom for a studio (just decorated and all) but I positively refused. I need the room, and if David had it he would ruin it. We all appreciate his work, but he is getting to expect all and give nothing in return – his own room was dreadfully untidy.

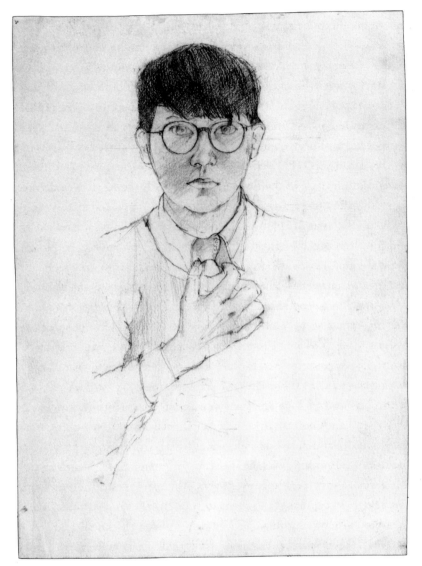

Self Portrait, 1954

We compromised and as our front bedroom has to be decorated, I said David could finish his portrait in there. He is doing a full-length portrait of himself and has the wardrobe mirror dismantled and propped up where he can see it — a table littered with paints — brushes — etc — but he dropped paint on the carpet just where he hadn't covered it with newspapers. Kenneth thinks I should let David use the little room, but I still think he should respect other people's work as well as his own.

He is a happy go lucky fellow, a real anarchist – but it just won't do.'[45]

The portrait Laura was referring to is one of three self-portraits Hockney painted in 1954, the earliest of which shows him three-quarters on, staring intensely into a mirror with a look of both concentration and hesitancy on his face, his hair flopping against his forehead, and a background of the rooftops of Hutton Terrace. It is a remarkably assured portrait of a young man on the threshold of life, a little shy and a little uncertain. While this painting owes much to the traditional academic approach of the Euston Road School, the next self-portrait, painted against a backdrop of newspaper clippings and boldly using blocks of colour to depict his distinctive clothes – a bright yellow tie and long red scarf – takes a much more modern approach. Finally, the third picture – a striking lithograph in five colours, in which he is seated in a chair before a background of yellow wallpaper, the black and white lines in his pudding-basin haircut echoing the stripes of his tie and trousers – is, to quote Mark Glazebrook, 'positively prophetic in its fluent line, its bright colour, its technical experimentation and in its direct, confident, quirky self-presentation'.[46] Here was the evolution at work that Derek Stafford felt was so important.

By the end of 1954 Hockney was living and breathing the life of an art student, and showing the determination and devotion to work that would characterise his life. 'He had this overriding passion for his work and nothing else,' Dave Oxtoby remembers, 'and that was a tremendous influence on everybody.'[47] Through him they suddenly saw that painting was the centre of their world, and it bound them together closely as a group. 'I loved it all,' wrote Hockney, 'and I used to spend twelve hours a day in the art school. There were classes from nine-thirty to twelve-thirty, from two to four-thirty; and from five to seven. Then there were night classes from seven to nine, for older people coming in from the outside. If you were a full-time student, you could stay for those as well; they always had a model, so I just stayed and drew all the time right through to nine o'clock.'[48]

But Hockney also threw himself into the extracurricular activities of the painting department, though he was never without a sketch pad. There were card games in the common room during the lunch hour, where he was likely to be discussing with Stafford subjects varying from vegetarianism and the perils of smoking to the theory of art. In the evenings they would go down to one of several pubs to play darts, sessions that would invariably end up with Hockney singing his favourite song, 'Bye Bye Blackbird', at the piano, or bringing the house down by pulling his face so that he looked exactly like Orson Welles. The games of darts eventually led to them forming a darts team to take on Leeds School of Art at a pub near Leeds Town Hall. During one of these visits, Hockney was introduced to an elderly artist, Jacob Kramer, a former Vorticist and associate of Wyndham Lewis and William Roberts, who had enjoyed a measure of fame in the 1920s but had since fallen on hard times. Often mistaken for a tramp by those who didn't know of his distinguished past, he was reduced to propping up the bar and telling stories in return for drinks. Nevertheless, he made a powerful impression on the young Hockney. 'I had seen some of his work because he had two or three paintings in Leeds City Art Gallery. He had lived and worked in Paris and was living proof to me that it was possible to make a living as an artist. And I thought to myself, "This is a real artist, not just a teacher. He may have met Picasso or Braque or any of those people. He's a real link with bohemian Paris." I was a bold little kid and I thought this was really exciting.'[49]

While Dave Oxtoby, Norman Stevens and John Loker had a skiffle group and played at the occasional college dance – Oxtoby on tea-chest bass, Loker on washboard and Stevens on vocals, alongside three guitarists and a banjo player – skiffle was of little interest to Hockney. He only loved classical music, which he used to play very loudly at home. 'When we used to go to the Hockneys' house,' Philip Naylor remembers, 'the lounge was really tiny and David used to like to tuck himself away in there and listen to his music. One day he decided that we were uncultured little oiks, and made us sit in there and he played us his Mozart records on the Deutsche Grammophon label and conducted for us using a pencil as a baton.'[50] At weekends, Hockney would go down to St George's Hall where he had secured himself and his fellow students jobs selling programmes in return for free seats to hear the world-renowned resident orchestra, the Hallé, conducted by Sir John

Barbirolli. 'I had my free seat all the way through my time at college,'
he recalls, 'and I would just sit and listen and draw. It was lovely.' Pages
of drawings in his sketchbooks reflect this, annotated with titles such
as 'Second Bassoon, Hallé, Saturday 29th', 'Beethoven's Symphoney
[sic] No. 1' and 'Listening to Sibelius'. He also designed the occasional
poster to advertise a concert.

Even in the hallowed atmosphere of St George's Hall, Hockney still
developed a reputation for being a 'character'. Philip Naylor remembers
that 'David would somehow always contrive to be late, arriving after
the orchestra and sometimes even after the conductor. The audience
used to cheer and applaud him because, even if they didn't know him,
he was a feature of the town.'[51]

The friends also used to regularly convene for parties at Derek
Stafford's new studio in Manningham Lane, just off the main road to
Saltaire. Stafford was only ten years older than his students, but they
were in awe of his sophistication. 'It was like a bolt from the blue,
somebody like that turning up at Bradford College,' Dave Oxtoby
recalls. 'His whole attitude was refined.'[52] They discussed the theory
of art, and the latest exhibitions, and he introduced them to cheap
French wine, which was much harder to come by in those days, and
which none of them had ever tasted. 'They used to go down and vomit
in my bath,' Stafford remembers, 'and I would have to clear up the
mess the next day, but they were great evenings and we all got on like
a house on fire.'[53]

Occasionally they discussed politics, more likely than not prompted
by Hockney's father sounding off on one of his favourite rants. The
figure of Kenneth Hockney preaching anti-war and anti-nuclear
sermons from his soapbox was a familiar one in Bradford, particularly
in Foster Square, and he got his son and his friends involved in helping
with propaganda. Rod Taylor, a textile student, had a cellar with a
screen-printing machine which he lent them to print posters. 'I once
saw David and Kenneth,' Mike Powell, a boyhood friend, remembers,
'standing in Bradford's Town Hall Square during a rag-day parade

carrying large placards. David's read 'CHARITY IS HUMBUG IN A WELFARE STATE', while Kenneth's read 'STOP THE WAR – CHRISTIANS SHOULD NOT BOMB CHILDREN'. Such were David's leanings at that time. I saw him occasionally sporting a full khaki "Castro-style" combat outfit complete with forage cap and red star, incongruously sitting on the top deck of the Eccleshill trolley bus. He quickly got the nickname "Boris" in the village, Ken being referred to as Commissar Ken after placing the *Daily Worker* for sale at the local newsagent's at his own cost.'[54] But though Hockney supported his father's anti-war views and those on nuclear disarmament, he couldn't go along with his communist sympathies. 'I was much more of an anarchist,' he says. 'My father had a very rosy view of communism, but of course he'd never been to Russia. He was rather like Mr Kite in the film *I'm All Right Jack* who, when Mr Windrush asks him if he's ever been to Russia, says, "Ah, Russia, all them cornfields and ballet in the evenings." That's what my father thought.'[55]

With the exception of Hockney, most of the boys had girlfriends, or were looking for girlfriends, and the group tried to set him up with a very pretty girl called Terri MacBride who was a regular at Derek Stafford's parties. He showed little interest beyond taking her out on the occasional trip to the cinema, which his friends interpreted as being because his passion for his work overrode any interest he might have in sexual activity. It never occurred to any of them that he might be gay. 'I probably always knew I was gay,' says Hockney. 'I certainly wasn't interested in girls, and I didn't really have to pretend to be because there wasn't much social pressure. I remember that when Paul got engaged, I thought, "That's not for me," and I must have known then that I would never marry. If anyone had asked me if I was gay, I would just have got out of it. I didn't really feel that normal anyway, because I'd begun to realise that my talent made me different.'[56]

On Christmas Eve 1954, Laura wrote in her diary: 'Dad posed for David most of the afternoon.' This was the start of Hockney's first serious portrait in oils, a painting of his father, which took just under a month to complete. It was painted on an old canvas Kenneth had bought at a jumble sale, so Hockney had to paint over whatever was on it. His father was not an easy subject as he was incapable of sitting still, his insatiable curiosity always getting the better of him and causing him to question and comment on everything that was going on. Since he'd paid for the canvas and bought the easel, he felt he had the right to do this. 'My father,' wrote Hockney, '. . . set the chair up for himself, and he set mirrors around so he could watch the progress of the painting and give a commentary. And he would say "Ooh, that's too muddy, is that for my cheek? No, no, no, it's not that colour". . . and I'd say "Oh no, you're wrong, this is how you have to do it, this is how they paint at the art school, and I carried on."'[57] *Portrait of My Father* is a touching and sensitive work, over which the ghost of Walter Sickert lingers, beautifully executed, painted in muted tones, his father seated in a chair, hands clasped and looking almost sheepishly at the floor.

Hockney worked on the painting at home, mostly on Saturday afternoons when Kenneth had finished work, creating further chaos in the house and upsetting the orderly life of his brother John, who had just started working for Montague Burton, the tailors. 'The sharing became difficult when David began painting in the attic,' wrote John. 'He was very untidy. Clothes dropped where he got out of them, sometimes hiding a tube of paint which, when accidentally stood on, squelched over whatever had been lying there. This became the topic of typical brotherly arguments, David's total lack of any consideration except for his painting and my own growing ego about having to look smart. The two opposed. It was never bitter, frustrating perhaps, but Mum and Dad were great moderators. It must have been very difficult for David whose world then was purely focused on painting and drawing, and mine thinking looking good was important.'[58]

Portrait of My Father was finished towards the end of January 1955, and submitted, along with a small landscape of Hutton Terrace, to Leeds Art Gallery for their biannual Yorkshire Artists Exhibition. This was a prestigious event to which all the staff of the art college sent work, along with teachers from other local art schools. Much to David's surprise, both pictures were accepted, though he didn't bother to put a price tag on them as he thought no one would buy them. The exhibition opened on Saturday, 29 January. 'Kitchen upset all morning,' Laura wrote that day, '– David sketching in it. He went off soon after lunch for the opening of the Exhibition at Leeds . . . Ken and I went. We were proud of David's pictures; they looked quite at home amongst the others.'[59] After his parents had gone home, David was approached by a man called Bernard Gillinson, a friend of Fred Lyle's, who offered him £10 for the portrait, a considerable sum then. After checking with Kenneth that he was happy for the painting to be sold, Hockney accepted the offer and called Laura to tell her. 'He rang me up and said, "Hello, Mum. I've sold my Dad." It was so funny the way he said it. He got £10, which was a fortune to him at the time. He was so proud.'[60] It was his first sale and to celebrate he took all his friends to the pub. 'That probably cost a pound,' he later wrote. 'The idea of spending a whole pound in a pub seemed absurd, but with the rest of the ten pounds I got some more canvases and painted some more pictures.'[61]

After passing the Ministry of Education intermediate exam at the end of 1955, Hockney decided to apply for a place at the Royal College of Art in London, a decision in which he was greatly influenced by Derek Stafford, who believed him to be the most talented student he had ever taught. But he had his own reasons too. 'I knew that it would take me out of Bradford, and I wanted to leave Bradford because I scarcely knew of an artist who lived in Bradford.'[62] So he devoted his last two summers there, 1956 and 1957, to preparing himself for this important step. He converted one of his father's prams into a mobile art studio – an idea borrowed from Stanley Spencer, of whom he was a great admirer, aping his appearance, right down to the National Health glasses, fringed haircut and ubiquitous umbrella – and loaded into it all his oils and watercolours, brushes and pencils, his sketchbooks and canvases and his easel, to transport them around Bradford to paint. 'I had become quite interested in Stanley Spencer,' he wrote. '. . . I knew he was regarded as a rather eccentric artist out of the main class of art both by the academics who favoured Sickert and Degas, and by the abstractionists who dismissed him.'[63] When Hockney's brother

Paul was doing his national service in 1956, stationed quite close to Spencer's home in Cookham, Hockney asked him if he would go and ask for the painter's autograph. So one evening in the early summer Paul set off on the bus from Maidenhead to Cookham, where he was directed by a passer-by to Spencer's house.

'I knocked on the door,' Paul recalls, 'and it was soon answered by this little man wearing round rimless spectacles. He identified himself as Mr Spencer and I told him that my brother was an admirer of his. He asked me to come in. The house wasn't scruffy exactly, but there was junk all over the place, piles of papers and books and all sorts of things. I remember there were loads of mugs everywhere with the remains of tea in them, and plates with bits of bun and biscuit on them. He was wearing a little pullover with holes in it and paint all over it. He said, "You don't mind if I carry on with my painting?" On the wall he had this massive canvas. It was *Christ Preaching at Cookham Regatta* and I remember thinking what a peculiar hat Christ was wearing. It was half finished, and he had these two stepladders and would go up one and put on a little paint and then come down and take a look, and then put some more on. He didn't say much. Eventually he signed the book I'd brought and I left.'[64]

Hockney soon became a familiar sight in Bradford, pushing the pram around the city looking for suitable subjects. He painted, among other subjects, street scenes, the interiors of shops, people sitting about in a launderette, a fish and chip shop, and his family sitting down to Sunday lunch in their best suits. 'He was the first person I ever saw,' says Derek Stafford, 'who painted semi-detached houses. But he took them on and he did remarkably interesting things with them. His subjects were carefully observed. He looked at his own environment and said, "This big city I live in may be grey and black, a dirty city, but there is a magic in it if I look at it closely,"'[65] while Dave Oxtoby recalls, 'There was a solidity, a weight, to David's work at that time. Even his little drawings were very heavy, in particular some pictures of pubs on corners and things like that which were really solid. I remember also he did a painting once of the tram wires and the trees, and the break-up of the trees. He actually painted in between the branches with different colours, slightly different blues so that the branches would disappear and the difference in the blues carried the line of the branch as it went through. I thought the way he handled his paint then was really amazing. He was constantly trying new things.'[66]

He experimented with colour and developed his own technique for doing his outdoor paintings. He found an unusual colour which he called 'Indian yellow', a synthetic dye that he would wash all over his board and work on while it was still wet, so that the underlying Indian yellow influenced every colour he painted into it. 'It created a kind of homogeneous sensation over the landscape he was painting,' says Stafford. 'It did work for him and he created some very interesting landscapes.'[67]

The only restriction was the cost of paint, which was prohibitively high for all the students. When Hockney went to an exhibition of van Gogh at the Manchester City Art Gallery in 1956, what struck him most was how rich the artist must have been, to use a whole tube of blue to paint the sky, something that not even one of Hockney's teachers could afford. He found novel ways of raising funds to buy paint, which also enhanced his reputation for being an eccentric. These included taking money in return for dares. 'We'd go painting round the canal,' Dave Oxtoby remembers, 'and come the end of the day David would say, "Give me sixpence and I'll jump in the canal," and he'd jump in just to get some money.'[68]

Depending on how many people were involved, the dares could prove quite lucrative. 'David was painting with other students near the canal at Apperley Bridge,' Laura wrote in her diary one day. 'During lunch hour they dared him to walk the edge of the Spring Bridge – he did it, but fell in at the end and came home dripping wet – but just in time for the last lot in the washer. He earned 10 shillings with his daring.'[69]

At the beginning of 1957, Hockney took the Royal College of Art entrance exam and passed with flying colours. 'Mr Coleclough wishes me to convey to you his congratulations,' wrote his deputy. 'He is delighted with your success.'[70] Then, at the end of the summer term, he sat for the National Diploma in Design. For this he spent a week making a painting of a nude model, and he showed some of the pictures he had made of Eccleshill and its surroundings. The examiners were impressed enough to award him a first-class diploma with honours, and his painting, *Nude*, was picked for a travelling exhibition of art students' work. He now waited anxiously for further word from the Royal College, which had required successful applicants to submit a portfolio of drawings, watercolours, lithographs, etc., along with a number of actual paintings. Hockney had sent life drawings, life paintings and figure compositions, and paintings he'd done at the art school and at home during the holidays. Just in case he failed the interview, he had also sent similar work to the Slade School. He was told there were three hundred people applying for the Royal College and thirty places available. He successfully passed the first hurdle, and was selected for interview.

The interview process took two days, so students from the provinces had to stay at least one night in London. Applicants would spend the first day in the Life Room drawing a nude model, and on the second day would show these drawings, along with all the other work they had submitted, to the college professors. 'I naturally thought I wouldn't have much of a chance,' Hockney recalls, 'because all the London people would be much better than me. You had to do a life drawing as part of the interview and I remember going round looking at the other people's drawings and thinking to myself, "Well, I can do just as well as that. Maybe I will be OK."'[71]

At the end of the first day Hockney and Norman Stevens, who had also been selected, returned to the bed and breakfast off the Earls Court Road the college had recommended. In the hall they ran into Derek Boshier, a graduate student from Yeovil College of Art in Somerset and a fellow applicant. 'I recognised David straight away from having seen him in the Life Room,' Boshier remembers, 'because of his straight jet-black hair and the tweed suit he was wearing. He told me he had his interview the next day, and asked me rather sheepishly in his broad Yorkshire accent, "Do you think we'll get in?"'[72] Boshier had planned to cruise the streets of Earls Court looking for nightlife, but ended up going up to Hockney and Stevens's room to discuss the interview and help them drink their way through the crate of Guinness they had bought. The following morning, a little woolly-headed, they walked back to the college buildings in Queen's Gate to face the selection panel. 'You had to lay out all your work on a table,' Hockney recalls, 'which consisted of about six paintings, lots of drawings, including the life drawings of a nude, in front of a panel of old people. Actually it was very exciting.'[73] The 'old people' were the college professors: Carel Weight, the head of the painting department, who took centre stage, with Ruskin Spear, Roger de Grey, Colin Hayes, Ceri Richards and Rodney Burn, all distinguished artists, on either side of him. What Hockney did not know, and which was very much in his favour, was that Carel Weight was becoming increasingly disillusioned by the number of his students, such as Dick Smith and Robin Denny, who were turning to the abstract. He was deliberately looking for young artists who showed the figurative in their work. On the strength of what he saw, Weight decided to offer Hockney a place on the postgraduate course in painting.

Hockney was also offered a place at the Slade, but his heart was set on the Royal College, whose offer he happily accepted.

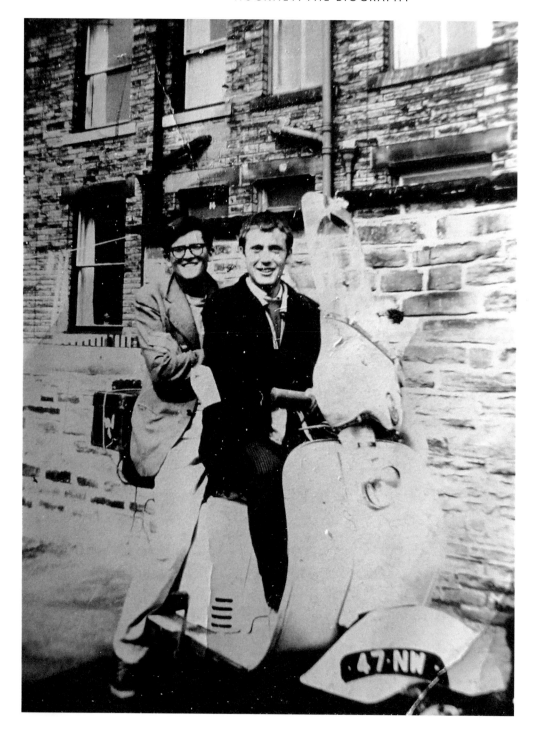

CHAPTER THREE

DOLL BOY

'Before university . . . there was national service to be got through,' says Alan Bennett in his memoir, *Writing Home*, 'regarded at best as a bore, but for me, as a late developer, a long-dreaded ordeal.'[1] Just as this compulsory military service, reintroduced in 1947, delayed Bennett's going up to Oxford for two years, so it delayed David Hockney's arrival at the Royal College of Art till September 1959. Like his father, Hockney registered as a conscientious objector, at a point when the authorities were taking a more relaxed view of ethical objectors. Hockney was told he would be called for interview in September 1957, and assigned suitable work in the community. But first there was a long summer of painting to enjoy.

David Hockney
and John Loker

In Hockney's last year at Bradford, he and John Loker decided to enter an annual competition, the David Murray Landscape Scholarship, named after the famous Scottish landscape painter. The prize was £48, and they made a deal that if one of them won it, they would share the prize money and go off painting together for the whole summer. Loker also agreed to put into the pot any winnings from his lunch-hour card games. Luck was with both of them: Hockney won the scholarship and Loker won at cards. With their mutual love of Constable, they settled on Suffolk as the best place to paint, and placed advertisements for accommodation in the local papers. Being young and impatient, however, they decided that they couldn't waste time sitting around waiting for the replies to come in, but would head straight off for St Ives in Cornwall, the centre of the thriving colony of artists headed by Ben Nicholson and Barbara Hepworth.

They packed their paints for the journey in a large trunk. 'What we used to do,' John Loker remembers, 'was buy a half-hundredweight tin of white lead paint. Then we used to buy small tins or big tubes of titanium white and mix the two together for our white paint. We also bought lots and lots of tubes of different-coloured oil paints. We needed an easel, so we smuggled one out of Bradford College and took it with us.'[2] When they set off for the south-west from Paddington station, the trunk, which they struggled to carry, went on the scales and weighed in at two hundredweight. Eventually they managed to get all their stuff on the train and set off for Cornwall.

Penniless as they were, the best accommodation they could come up with on arrival was some way out of St Ives, up a steep hill on the road to Zennor, where a farmer gave them the use of a derelict barn in return for their cleaning it out. 'It was chicken droppings on chicken droppings on chicken droppings,'[3] says Loker. They spent hours scrubbing it and putting disinfectant down, and finally laid their sleeping bags on the stone floor with every intention of staying there for some time. The following morning, they borrowed a wheelbarrow from the farmer and went down to the station in St Ives to fetch the trunk, which they then had to push up the hill. While Loker organised setting up the barn into some kind of studio, Hockney went off to the post office in St Austell, to which they had arranged for their mail to be sent. Events had moved quickly: he returned with a cheque for £24, the first half-payment of the landscape prize, and a letter offering them a cottage in the Suffolk village of Kirton for £3 a week.

'The upshot was that we decided to go to Suffolk there and then,' Loker recalls. 'The only problem was we were unable to cash the cheque anywhere because we didn't have a bank account, so we decided that the best course to take was to go and see Barbara Hepworth, who we knew was rich and who lived nearby. Arrogant as we were, we just turned up on her doorstep, knocked on the door and asked if she could cash a cheque for us. She was very friendly, and organised to have it cashed by the Newlyn Art Society. As it turned out, we didn't do any painting in Cornwall. All we did was clean out someone's barn for them. We took the trunk to the station, returned the barrow to the farmer and set off on the train that night.'[4]

The journey to Suffolk was long and tortuous, involving going through London and changing trains, but when they finally arrived they were delighted with their accommodation: an old horseman's cottage in the grounds of a much larger house, with an outside lavatory and no bathroom. Their landlords, John and Margaret Burton, lent them bicycles and they became familiar figures cycling around the local countryside looking for suitable views to paint or draw. They worked happily like this for a few weeks, Hockney painting small landscapes, few of which have survived, and Loker slightly larger ones, until they ran out of money, before the second half of the prize money was due. After three days without food, Loker, driven by desperation, went scavenging in the fields and came back with what he thought were some turnips. He scrounged some Oxo cubes from the Burtons' maid, and boiled up what turned out to be not turnips but sugar beet, which made an inedibly sweet mush.

'It was then that I got a clear notion about life,' says Hockney. 'We were on the point of starving, so I rang up my parents, reversing the charges as you could in those days, and I explained to them that we had absolutely nothing, and by that I mean not even threepence. I told them that the second cheque for £24 would be arriving in a few days and could they possibly send something for us. The next day I received a postal order for two and sixpence. When I opened it I spent two shillings of it on a packet of cigarettes, but at that moment I thought to myself, "From now on, you're on your own, David." What I didn't realise at the time was that, aged twenty, that was a very, very useful thing to know. I suddenly felt freer, that I'd finally escaped the family.'[5]

By this time Hockney and Loker had fallen somewhat out of favour with their landlords who, their novelty value having worn off, now saw them not as tame young artists, but rather as scruffy students who kept an untidy house and cleaned their paintbrushes on their trousers. But in the long hours of painting and cycling around the county, they had made other friends, two of whom, Ken Cuthbert, a local artist, and his friend Denis Taplin, a future gallery owner, invited them to exhibit at the Felixstowe Amateur Arts Show.

'We were a bit arrogant at first,' Loker recalls, 'thinking we didn't really want to show our work in that kind of environment, but we were short of money and he said they would put some screens up and we could have our own exclusive corner, so we decided to do it.'[6] The evening of the private view got off to a bad start when Hockney's cycle light fell off into the front wheel, catapulting him straight over the handlebars and writing off the bike, an incident unlikely to further endear them to their landlords. But when they eventually limped into the show, they were overwhelmed with people rushing up to greet them and demanding to know the prices of their work. 'We were selling drawings for two and sixpence, next to nothing really,' Loker remembers. 'I even sold a five-foot painting for six or seven pounds. But it was a fortune in those days and we were suddenly rich. We'd made about equivalent to half the value of the scholarship and that meant that we didn't have to go home. The paintings were mostly landscapes but they were landscapes in which we were trying to do something slightly different. The workings of the paintings were all there to see. They were serious pictures for us. The way we painted was the way Derek Stafford had taught us, which was that unless we were totally committed to our work there was no point in painting at all. And we were willing committers.'[7]

At the end of this idyllic summer, Loker returned to Bradford College of Art and Hockney reported to the Ministry of Labour and National Service in Leeds to be assigned employment. His first job was as a medical orderly in the skin diseases ward of St Luke's Hospital, Bradford. He lived at home and worked long hours at the hospital, a salutary experience. His jobs included putting ointment on the patients, one of whom, a pot-bellied old man whom he particularly loathed, had to be regularly dabbed with calamine lotion. The old man took pleasure in standing stark naked in front of the shy young orderly and reminding him, 'Don't forget the testicles, David.'[8] 'I swept the floors, put the ointment on, and was the caller in the afternoon bingo games. If the TV broke down, or if you didn't give them anything to do, they just sat and scratched. I was also the runner. I used to collect all their bets, mostly sixpences and shillings, and take them to a porter who took them to a bookie. I soon knew which patients won

regularly, so I backed the same horses and won too.'⁹ There was no
time for painting and Hockney used to scrub the floors singing, 'Roll
on September 1959!' The one pastime he did indulge in was reading.
Even though he'd never been abroad, he decided to take the time to
read Proust, because he'd been told that *À la recherche du temps perdu* was
one of the greatest works of art of the twentieth century. He struggled
through it, feeling that he wasn't sure he was getting that much out
of it. 'I remember that asparagus was mentioned in it,' he says, 'but I
didn't even know what an asparagus was.'¹⁰

Living at home, Hockney was at close proximity to his father's
increasingly vociferous political views, which had made him a celebrated
figure in Bradford. Kenneth left copies of *Peace News* on Bradford's
buses or on benches in the city parks, and he hired public hoardings
and painted slogans on them in bright colours – BAN THE BOMB or
BAN SMOKING or END HANGING NOW – adding fairy-lights during
the Christmas period. He worked so hard for Sidney Silverman's anti-
hanging bill that when it was finally passed in June 1956, he was invited
down to the House of Commons for the final vote.

None of this carried much weight with Laura, who felt her husband's
role should be supporting the family, not squandering money on such
causes. Audrey Raistrick, a fellow Bradfordian and a founder member
of CND (the Campaign for Nuclear Disarmament), remembered going
round to the house in Eccleshill one winter morning to collect some
goods promised by Kenneth for the *Daily Worker* Bazaar. It was a cold
and snowy day and Laura was busy shovelling snow off the front steps.
'I greeted her warmly,' she recalled, 'and asked if Mr Hockney was in.
"No," she replied. "He's out doing good!"'¹¹

Kenneth's political campaigning also took the form of enthusiastic
letter writing, usually several a day and often using pseudonyms,
such as K. Aitch, K. Kenlaw, and the Russian-sounding K. Yenkcoh,
which was simply Hockney reversed. He wrote not only to newspaper
editors and publishers, but to politicians and world leaders such as
Nasser, Stalin and Mao Tse-tung. He encouraged his children and their
friends to question everything. 'He taught us a lesson,' John Hockney
remembers. 'He purchased the *Soviet Weekly*, *China News*, *The Times*,

Breakdown
en route to
Aldermaston (*left
to right:* John Loker,
David Hockney,
unknown)

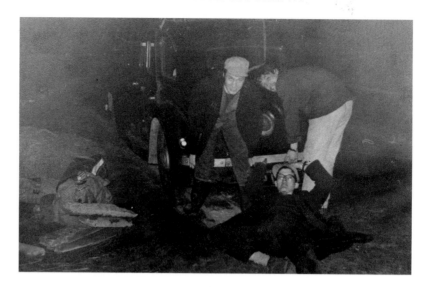

Manchester Guardian, Daily Express and *Daily Mail, Peace News* and the
Daily Worker. He then asked Margaret, David and me to read about
a particular incident that was reported by all the papers, and asked
what we thought. All of us were confused as the reporting varied so
much, depending on the persuasion of editorial licence. He told us,
"That is why you must always find out the truth yourself; you cannot
always believe what you read."'[12] Into Hockney he drummed the adage,
'Never mind what the neighbours think.'

Over the Easter weekend of 1958, CND held the first of its Aldermaston marches, a four-day anti-nuclear protest march from Trafalgar
Square in London to the atomic weapons establishment at Aldermaston
in Berkshire. Hutton Terrace became a hive of activity, with Kenneth
busy painting posters in the attic in his best suit, much to the annoyance
of Laura, while Hockney and John Loker sorted out their own posters
printed by Rod Taylor. 'They were the kind of thing I was doing in graphic
design,' Loker recalls, 'with big bold letters. I remember one that I
particularly liked which just had huge letters filling the whole page
saying BAN THE BLOODY BOMB. Bloody was painted in red.'[13] Taylor
bought a clapped-out old car for a few pounds, and he, Hockney and
Loker all piled in and drove down to London for the march, a saga of
punctures, changing tyres, bumpers falling off, and cold nights spent

in sleeping bags in church halls that was to be repeated over the next few years.

The autumn of 1958 was a happy time for Hockney. John Loker had left Bradford College and, as a fellow conscientious objector, had decided to fulfil his military service in Hastings, doing agricultural work. With Peter Kaye and Dave Oxtoby, he rented a cottage where Hockney joined them at the end of September, and for a while he, Kaye and Loker worked as apple-pickers at an orchard along the coast in Rye, following the itinerant harvesters, and collecting anything they might have missed, such as the fruit from the tops of the trees. Because their names were Hockney, Kaye and Loker, they called themselves Hockeylok Apples Inc.

When the work started to get monotonous, Hockney decided to apply for another hospital job. 'We are beginning to get things ship-shape down here,' he wrote to his parents on 10 October '(That doesn't mean we've moved into the sea).' On 21 October he told them, 'I commenced work at St Helen's Hospital Hastings yesterday. It is alright. The ward is rather similar to the one at St Luke's . . . Dad, don't worry about my appearance at the hospital, we are keeping house very well, and in fact I think we can congratulate ourselves. We even washed some sheets the other day and I ironed them all – and they were "Persil White".'[14] As an orderly in the heart patients' ward his jobs included bathing the patients, and occasionally those who had died. Hockney struck up a friendship with the mortuary attendant and on more than one occasion found himself eating his picnic lunch surrounded by the bodies of the dead.

With one year left before starting at the Royal College, Hockney began to think about painting again, and he and his friends enrolled for Monday-evening life-drawing classes at Hastings College of Art. He also wrote to his father on 21 October instructing him to dispose of his surplus pictures. 'Dad, if Mr Ashton is interested in buying pictures cheap, all those stacked in the attic can be sold, apart from the Road Menders. This painting is on a canvas worth at least £5, so that would be "cheap" at anything around say £10.' He was sending paintings to the Yorkshire Artists' Exhibition, to next year's Royal Academy Summer

Exhibition and had already started three new pictures and done quite a bit of drawing. He finished the letter by telling him that they had had a visit from David Fawcett, their fellow student at Bradford. '. . . he was saying that this new school he is teaching at wants some original paintings, and they are interested in young painters, so he's put our names forward – not bad eh.'[15]

While Hockney worked out his time in the hospital, John Loker and Peter Kaye were employed on a farm, initially pulling mangles, a really horrible job. On the whole, however, it was a good year. 'At weekends,' Loker recalls, 'Norman Stevens, who was already at the Royal College, used to come down and bring various students with him. Dave Oxtoby used to visit from the Royal Academy Schools with friends, and we used to go round the countryside seeing things like the Lewes bonfire, where they burn an effigy of the Pope. They were some great times, and it gave us the opportunity to meet some students of the Royal College, and occasionally we used to go up to London and hang out with them, so when we actually got there it wasn't so strange.'[16]

When Hockney finally arrived in London in September 1959, he was entering one of the best art schools in the world at a time when it was on the threshold of one of its most productive periods. The Royal College of Art was spread about South Kensington in what the principal, Robin Darwin, described as a series of 'shacks and mansions',[17] with some sites a quarter of a mile from each other. While the main premises on Exhibition Road, behind the V&A, housed the School of Painting and Graphic Design, the School of Sculpture was in a shed in Queen's Gate, the School of Fashion in a large house in Ennismore Gardens, and the Junior and Senior Common Rooms were in the Cromwell Road. However unsatisfactory the set-up, the college's results spoke for themselves: recent graduates included Peter Blake, Frank Auerbach, Robin Denny, Bridget Riley and Richard Smith.

Robin Darwin had already wrought miraculous changes at the college since arriving, on 1 January 1948, to discover 'Morrison Shelters doing duty for printing tables in the Textile Department . . .

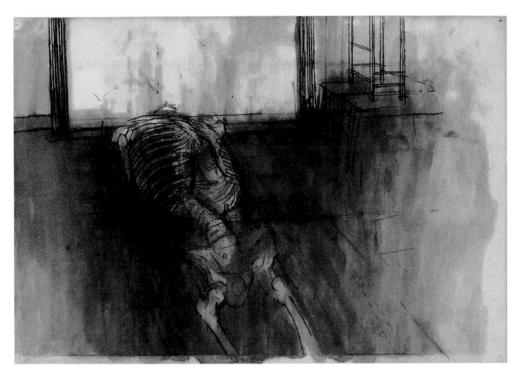

Skeleton, 1959

no drawing offices anywhere in the College, and only two studios for the whole School of Design; nor was there a lecture theatre. There were virtually no records of any sort, no paintings or other works by former students . . . A single secretary served the whole of the College . . .'[18] An unconventional figure, Darwin had been secretary to the British Camouflage Committee during the war, where he had brought in artists to work alongside architects, engineers and scientists. Striking in appearance – 'brooding with thick dark hair, heavy spectacles underlined by an equally heavy moustache, a piercing eye that stared one down, a merciless tongue, an old Etonian tie and a dark double-breasted business suit, a perpetual cigarette'[19] – he had become a brilliant administrator as a result of his wartime experience, and by appointing lively professors and letting them manage their own departments in the way they wanted he soon had the place up and running. The senior tutor was Roger de Grey, a distinguished landscape and still-life painter, who was not afraid to speak his mind, and alongside him were Professors Carel Weight, Ruskin Spear, Ceri Richards, Robert Buhler, Colin Hayes and Mary Fedden, the first woman ever to be employed at the college. By the time Hockney arrived the college was thriving, and there was a real buzz about it. He arranged to lodge with Norman Stevens in one tiny room of an Earls Court boarding house, 47 Kempsford Gardens, owned by an actor, John Bennett. Hockney wrote home on 3 October, 'Dear all, I have settled down and am working hard. The digs (one room with two beds, gas ring and wash basin, and kitchen, toilet and bath downstairs) are about 10 minutes walk from the college or a 3d ride on the tube . . .'[20]

On his first day at college, Hockney felt like 'a little provincial. I thought that, coming from a place like Bradford, everyone else would be much more sophisticated than me.' Though he soon found out that this was not the case, he did suffer from the occasional teasing about his then quite thick Yorkshire accent. 'There was quite a lot of "trooble at mill" stuff to begin with, which I'd never really come across before. It didn't worry me. In fact, it quite amused me, though I did sometimes bite back. I remember saying to someone who was taking the mickey, "Well, if I drew as badly as you, I'd keep my mouth shut." I wasn't intimidated at all.'[21] It had also occurred to him that going to the Royal College when he was that little bit older was probably a good thing, as he would get more out of it, and he had Norman Stevens to keep an eye on him. 'My first impression of David and Norman,' remembers Roddy Maude-Roxby, the editor of the college magazine, *Ark*, 'was of these two northern lads who were like a comic double act, and they both spoke as if each other's mother had told him to look after the other lad. People used to imitate their accents as well, but I think they were quite at ease with it. They both had a great sense of humour and a lot of rapport with people.'[22]

The students Hockney met in those first days were an unusual mishmash, most of them stepping out into the world for the first time. Of those his own age perhaps the most sophisticated was Allen Jones, a Londoner, who had not only attended another leading art college, Hornsey School of Art, but had already travelled abroad, in particular to Paris, where he had fallen under the influence of Delaunay and had come back to paint large, colourful, abstract canvases. A jazz lover with a penchant for wearing three-button suits, at first Jones felt a little out of place among his fellow students. 'When I arrived at the RCA,' he recalls, 'I seemed to be the only person not from the provinces. The only time I had heard north country accents was when I heard comedians, so I was always expecting punchlines every time anyone spoke with a northern accent even though it wasn't funny.'[23]

With one exception, the rest of the new intake were pretty green. There was Peter Phillips who came from Birmingham, where he had studied at Birmingham College of Art; Derek Boshier, whom Hockney had befriended at his interview, and who came from Yeovil Art College in Somerset; and Norman Stevens, Hockney's fellow Bradfordian. In addition, there was also an American ex-serviceman, Ron Kitaj, who was a few years older than the rest of them and correspondingly more worldly.

This was an interesting collection of young men, thrown together at a time when there were stirrings beneath the surface of austerity Britain. 'Growing up in the 1950s, we dreamed the American dream,' wrote the film-maker Derek Jarman thirty years later. 'England was grey and sober. The war had retrenched all the virtues – Sobriety and Thrift came with the Beveridge plan, utility furniture and rationing, which lasted about a decade after the end of hostilities. Over the Atlantic lay the land of Cockaigne; they had fridges and cars, TV and supermarkets. All bigger and better than ours . . . Then as the decade wore on, we were sent Presley and Buddy Holly, and long-playing records of *West Side Story*, and our own *Pygmalion* transformed. The whole daydream was wrapped up in celluloid . . . How we yearned for America! And longed to go west.'[24]

Having spent two years doing relatively little painting, Hockney was determined to make up for lost time. His problem was how to begin. 'The first thing I thought,' he says, 'was that I had to unlearn everything I'd learned at Bradford, because they didn't really deal with modern art, and that was something I had become aware of.' A powerful new influence was American painting, which he'd been exposed to for the first time in December 1958, when he went to the

Jackson Pollock show put on by Bryan Robertson at the Whitechapel Gallery in London, and realised that here was a modern artist who was part of an utterly different tradition. 'I'd become aware of how many artists came out of Picasso – Henry Moore, Francis Bacon and so many others – and suddenly there was this very free-looking art which when you looked closely at it you could see how organised it was. It was not just random splashes of paint. There was order to it. It was because it was so unlike Picasso and so American that young art students found it so lively and fresh.'[25] Seeing the Pollock show made Hockney realise that his teaching had never addressed the problems of the modern movement, partly, he suspected, because his teachers didn't really understand it.

Temporarily at a loss, Hockney threw himself back into drawing. 'I hadn't done any drawing to speak of for a couple of years, so I thought I'd get back into it by drawing something a little bit difficult and complicated. There was a skeleton hanging up in the studio so I decided to draw that. I realised that if I was going to do it properly, drawing in detail the ribcage and the pelvis, etc., then it would take some time and get me back into the routine of work.'[26] Establishing a routine was important, and as his living conditions were hardly conducive to work, each morning he would get up at the last possible moment and walk the half-mile to the college from Kempsford Gardens, to be there to start at eight. Invariably he would put his name down on the list to work after hours and stay at the college studios till ten at night, only returning home when he was ready for bed. On Sundays, when the college was closed, he would methodically tour London's museums and galleries.

Hockney spent six weeks on his two skeleton drawings, executing the first, a vertical study of the skeleton hanging from a rail, in pencil, and the second, a more dramatic study looking down upon it and foreshortening the perspective, in turpentine washes. Because the size of the paper he had access to was limited, as the drawing got bigger, he would just roughly paste on a new piece. Janet Deuters, another painting student, noticing how good the drawings were, told him that because he could draw so well, he should take greater care in the way he glued the paper together. She told her friends about him and word soon began to spread about this extraordinary-looking new student. The drawings rapidly drew praise. 'They were a tour de force,' says Allen Jones. 'They exhibited so much panache and so much language, but it was done with such authority that you didn't view it as a trick.'[27] The young American, Ron Kitaj, also came to take a look. 'During our first days at the Royal College,' he later wrote, 'I spotted this boy with short black hair and huge glasses, wearing a boilersuit, making the most beautiful drawing I'd ever seen in an art school. It was of a skeleton. I told him I'd give him five quid for it. He thought I was a rich American. I was – I had $150 a month GI Bill money to support my wife and son. I kept buying drawings from him . . .'[28]

Ronald Brooks Kitaj had arrived in England from the United States in 1958 courtesy of the GI Bill, to study art at Ruskin College in Oxford, from where he had graduated to the Royal College of Art. A former merchant seaman, he was five years older than Hockney, and the younger man immediately looked up to him, both for being American and for his experience of the world; Hockney had never been abroad. They discovered a mutual love of reading and Kitaj was able to pass on his knowledge of his favourite American expatriate writers such as T. S. Eliot, Henry James and Ezra Pound; he had also read one of Hockney's favourite books, George Orwell's *The Road to Wigan Pier*. But more than anything it was Kitaj's attitude to painting that impressed Hockney. He was by far the slowest painter at the college, because he took his time. Painting was something to be studied seriously, he passionately believed, though it was a point of view not held by every student at the college. 'There were these two groups of people at the RCA,' Allen Jones recalls, 'and the difference between them was noticeable. I was aware that some of the people there were behaving like men. While I was drawing away, it was often a source of wonder to me that some of my fellow students had been digging trenches in Korea only six months previously. These students were men and they handled themselves differently. They all blew their grants immediately and bought Lambrettas and hung out at the Serpentine picking up girls, and I remember thinking, "That's all very well, but what will they do for buying paint?"'[29]

Still finding his way, and not a little spurred on by the large abstract-expressionist-style canvases he saw being worked on by his fellow students Derek Boshier and Peter Phillips, Hockney decided to follow up the skeleton drawings with his own attempts at abstraction. In working on these, he was much influenced by a 1958 show at the Wakefield City Art Gallery, a retrospective of the work of the Scottish artist Alan Davie. Davie's use of symbols and graffiti in his quite unique paintings seduced Hockney, as did the gaudy colours he employed. The fact that Davie was also a recipient of the Gregory Fellowship in Painting from Leeds University and was working in Leeds at the same time Hockney was at Bradford made him all the more real, and Davie was very much in Hockney's mind when he started work on a series of large images painted on pieces of four-foot-square hardboard. 'Young students had realised,' he later wrote, 'that American painting was more interesting than French painting . . . American abstract expressionism was the great influence. So I tried my hand at it. I did a few pictures . . . that were based on a kind of mixture of Alan Davie cum Jackson Pollock cum Roger Hilton. And I did them for a while, and then I couldn't. It was too barren for me.'[30]

These experiments with abstraction lasted about three months through the winter of 1959–60, and most of what Hockney produced was either destroyed or painted over by him, or by fellow students needing a fresh supply of hardboard. The few that have survived were given proper titles, suggesting a dislike for the fashion set by Pollock of referring to paintings by numbers, which, Pollock claimed, made 'people look at a picture for what it is – pure painting'.[31] Thus *Erection* suggested the stirrings of an as-yet-subverted desire to address sexual themes, while *Growing Discontent* firmly stated Hockney's ever increasing dissatisfaction with the road he was going along.

Hockney discussed his insecurities in many conversations with Ron Kitaj who, far more than any of the college staff, he came to look upon as his mentor. 'He had an incredible conscience about his work,' said Hockney, 'which brushed off on other people. He wasn't flippant or easily put off work . . . He stood there in front of a canvas from 10.00am till 5.00pm and worked.'[32] Since Kitaj didn't drink or smoke and liked to be in bed soon after ten, their discussions usually took place over a morning cup of tea or coffee in the cafe of the Victoria and Albert Museum. Hockney confessed that he was so frustrated by what he was doing that it sometimes seemed pointless to go on. 'He told me,' Hockney remembers, 'that I should look upon painting as a means of exploring all the things that most interested me, and that I should paint pictures that reflected this. This was the best advice he ever gave me.'[33] Kitaj probed his interests, discovering them to be politics, literature, relationships, vegetarianism, and encouraged him to consider using these as subject matter for paintings. 'I thought it's quite right; that's what I'm complaining about, I'm not doing anything that's from me. So that was the way I broke it. I began to paint those subjects.'[34]

The first paintings were inspired by vegetarianism. 'I was a militant vegetarian at the time, and handed out leaflets about the cruelty involved in making the terrible sausages you got in the common room. At Kitaj's suggestion I started painting vegetarian propaganda pictures and they became absurd and interesting.'[35] Once again painted on hardboard, these were abstract paintings with various vegetables represented by areas of colour – red for tomatoes, orange for carrots, green for lettuce, for example – with the names of the vegetables written on them in paint. The employment of words, an idea that came from the cubists' use of collage, also forced the spectator to confront the interests of the artist, in the same way that the words on Kenneth Hockney's posters confronted people with his ideas. 'You realise,' says Hockney, 'that the moment you put a word on a painting, people do read it. It's also like an eye. If there's an eye in a painting, you can't not look at it, and you can't not read a word.'[36] Using words also helped him solve a problem he had been grappling with for some time, which was his reluctance to use figures in his paintings for fear of being considered 'anti-modern'. 'When you put a word on a painting,' he wrote, 'it has a similar effect in a way to a figure; it's a little bit of a human thing . . . it's not just paint.'[37] That the vegetable paintings have long since disappeared seems irrelevant in the light of what Hockney did next, which was finally to address the one, and most important,

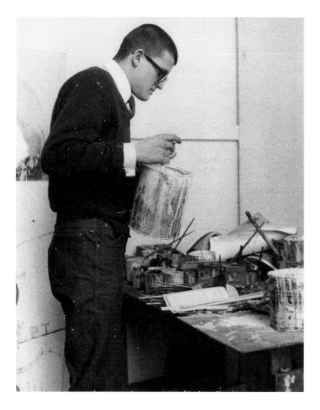

David Hockney in
Painting School

subject that he had been till now studiously avoiding: his sexuality.

Space was at a premium in the Painting School. Once the new students had graduated from working in the Life Room and the Still Life Room, which was compulsory in the first six weeks, it was up to them to stake out a space in the studios, which were part of the old V&A. Hockney used to try and grab the biggest area by getting in before anyone else, but those who were not quite so determined ended up in the corridor, where partitions had been erected to take the overflow. It was here that Kitaj worked, in a space he shared with another, older, painter, Adrian Berg, who had previously studied at Chelsea School of Art and had already been at the college for a year. Berg was openly gay, and when Kitaj introduced the two, they immediately hit it off. Just as at Bradford, Hockney's reputation had preceded him: Norman Stevens had repeatedly warned Berg, 'You wait till Hockney arrives.'

Adrian Berg was the first man that Hockney had met for whom being gay was not a problem. 'I wasn't confused about my sexuality,' he recalls, 'though I was cautious, because you had to be in those days. I was queer and David was queer, and we were of help to one another.'[38] He also appealed to Hockney because he had studied literature at Cambridge and was able to share his great knowledge of books. They discussed poetry, and Berg told him of the work of the homosexual poets Walt Whitman and Constantine Cavafy. 'I suddenly felt part of a bohemian world,' Hockney remembers, 'a world about art, poetry and music. I felt a deep part of it rather than any other kind of life. I finally felt I belonged. I met kindred spirits and the first homosexuals who weren't afraid to admit what they were. Adrian Berg lived in a free world, and fuck the rest of it. I thought, "I like that. That's the way I want to live. Forget Bradford." Once I accepted all this, it gave me a great sense of freedom, and I started to paint homosexual subjects.'[39]

Baring his soul on canvas was not easy for Hockney who, though gradually blossoming, was still quite shy. Contemporaries remember him looking at his feet a lot when speaking. Searching for a way of expressing his deepest emotions in his work while retaining some feeling of anonymity, he looked to Jean Dubuffet, whose spindly figures took their inspiration from children's art. 'I got taken with the deliberate childish thing,' he recalls, 'and felt I could use this to deal with a lot of subjects and ideas.'[40] He also drew on graffiti as an inspiration, and reviewed for the college news-sheet the graffiti in the men's toilet of the students' common room, as if it were art hanging in the Latrine Gallery and he was the critic from *Art Review*. To begin with, he approached the subject of his sexuality in his paintings very tentatively, one of his first paintings about love being simply a picture of a heart with the word LOVE written in small letters along its lower edge. As he developed his technique, however, managing to keep one step away from his subject, he grew gradually bolder and was soon painting the word QUEER on a canvas and using the then explicit word as its title. Graffiti was also the inspiration for a series of 'Fuck' drawings he produced during this period.

By the end of his first year at the RCA, Hockney was beginning to find himself. The painting staff, however, seemed to be at a loss as to know how to deal with the class of '59. To begin with, they didn't like the students doing enormous paintings, and Peter Phillips, Derek Boshier and Kitaj were all painting pictures of motorcyclists, movie stars and cowboys and Indians on a large scale. Add to this the fact that the painting studio had become so cluttered with big canvases that it was like trying to enter a maze, and it is perhaps understandable that this older, wartime generation of professors came to be so antagonistic towards their charges. 'The staff said that the students in that year,' wrote Hockney, 'were the worst that they'd had for many, many years. They didn't like us; they thought we were a little bolshy.'[41] Allen Jones remembers the day a warning light came on. 'One day Ruskin Spear, who was going round looking at the work of each student, came up to my picture and asked, "What's going on here? What's all this bright colour?" Everyone was painting away, secretly listening to me getting a barracking, and I was thinking, "He's just got to be joking." But then I realised he was absolutely serious and he could not understand what I was doing, and would not be able to talk about it. I asked him what was wrong and he said, "This is a grey day, this is grey South Kensington, this is a grey model, she's got grey prospects, so what's all this red and green all over the place?"'[42]

Jones was one of the painters who stayed on regularly to paint after hours, till the doors closed at ten, and one particular evening, when they were all dying for a cup of tea, Hockney said he couldn't be bothered to walk to the nearest cafe, and in typically anarchic style suggested they should raid the staff common room, where there was a plentiful supply of tea and biscuits. As long as they replaced whatever they used, no one would be any the wiser. 'So we started going there to have a quick cup of tea,' Jones recalls, 'and David would read the staff memos to all of us, and I kept thinking we were on dangerous ground. I remember there was a memo from Robin Darwin, the principal, to Carel Weight and company just saying "Who is running the painting school?"'[43]

The result of the memo was that the painting students who were thought to be out of line were all gathered together and were read the riot act by Carel Weight, who told them that in their first year they were there to observe nature and prove themselves to be proficient, and that they should wait till their third year to experiment. But Darwin wanted more than this. *Pour encourager les autres*, he wanted a head on the block, and that head turned out to be Allen Jones. 'For me it was the end of my world,' says Jones. 'I demanded an interview with Robin Darwin and he agreed to see me. He told me he had five minutes because he was going off to a lunch appointment. So I said my piece, and at the end of it he said, "Well, I've known you for five minutes and I've known Prof. Weight for most of my life. So who do you think I should believe?" and that was that.'[44] Most people were baffled by Jones's dismissal, but his friend Peter Phillips always believed that they singled him out because his determination and independence made him potentially the most dangerous student. As for Hockney, of whom the same might be said, it was the skeleton drawings that had saved him.

By the time Allen Jones learned his fate, it was the last day of term and most of the students had gone home. Hockney had returned to Bradford and a summer job as a caretaker at a school in the centre of the city and next to the library, where he went every day. Remembering his talks with Adrian Berg, he made two literary discoveries there which would inspire future work. First were the poems of the American writer Walt Whitman, many of which had explicit homosexual themes. 'In the summer of 1960, I read everything by Walt Whitman. I'd known his poetry before, but I'd never realised he was that good. There are quite a few of my paintings based on his work.'[45] He also explored the work of the Greek poet Constantine Cavafy, whose work was not put out on the open shelves, being considered unsuitable for the general reader, and which had to be asked for specially. Hockney later admitted that he stole the library's copy of Cavafy's poems translated by John Mavrogordato as it was out of print. 'I read it from cover to cover, many times, and I thought it was incredible, marvellous.'[46]

Hockney returned to college that autumn for the start of his second year fired with enthusiasm, and looking forward to the fact that his friends from Bradford Art School, John Loker and Peter Kaye, were taking up places at the Royal College, while Dave Oxtoby was going to the Royal Academy Schools. Since Norman Stevens had now graduated, they all moved into the Kempsford Gardens flat, creating an extra room by erecting a partition across the tiny bedroom. It was horrendously cramped and when the landlord, John Bennett, fresh from playing the part of the Marquess of Queensberry's Friend in *The Trials of Oscar Wilde*, wanted to move in an actor friend of his who had fallen on hard times, he offered Hockney the opportunity of sleeping in the shed at the bottom of the garden at a cheaper rent. 'I liked being on my own, so I jumped at it,' he recalls. 'It was literally a garden shed

with one bed and an electric heater. It had to have electricity because
I needed a light, but it was probably quite illegal. It really wasn't very
comfortable, and there was no water. Every three weeks I would have
a bath in the house. I did everything at the Royal College. I would wash
there in the sink, because it had hot water. In fact, Carel Weight once
caught me having a bath in the sink! I had my mail delivered there,
even my milk.'[47]

Hockney had a clear two hours before anyone else arrived: people
would start coming in and chatting at 10 a.m., and it was then time to
have a cigarette. He knew the times when he couldn't get work done,
and which were the good working hours, and he was always making
sure that he would have the space to work and the time to work. He
also figured out that you could only work for about an hour after lunch.
'I noticed that most people began to end the day about three o'clock
and then they started to put things away and would go round and talk
to the other students. I noticed that they'd come to me at around three
for cigarettes, because I always had plenty of cigarettes. So at three
o'clock in the afternoon I started to go to the cinema. Anyway, it was
the best time to go because the cinemas were empty and I could put my
feet up on the seat in front and be quite carried away, and if I wanted
an ice cream the usherette would come straight to me. Then when I
came out of the cinema at six, I would go back to the college and they
had all gone home. I would then have the place to myself again. So I got
to see the films and missed the times when they were pulling me away
from the easel.'[48]

The autumn term saw the arrival of another American who
was to have a profound influence on Hockney. Mark Berger was a
thirty-year-old mature student on a year-long scholarship break from
teaching painting at Tulane University in New Orleans. His first day
at the college is still etched upon his mind. 'I arrived there before the
semester began,' he reminisces, 'and they gave me a cubicle. I was
totally alone in this building, when suddenly this character walks in
wearing striped clothing and looking like a prisoner. It was David
Hockney and he had been assigned a cubicle right next to me. We
were the only two people there.'[49] Hockney took to Mark immediately

because 'he was openly gay, very American and very amusing'. He also had a collection of American 'beefcake' magazines such as *Physique Pictorial* and *Young Physique* that Hockney picked up on right away. 'We never said to each other "I'm gay" and "You're gay",' Mark remembers, 'but it was just so obvious we were. It was just never discussed.' Mark saw Hockney as a true English eccentric, a man who liked to be regular, but did the irregular. 'One time he went shopping because he needed to buy some socks, and he bought a pair of socks which were in fact women's leggings and they were bright pink, and he said to me, "God forbid I should be in an accident and they find me wearing bright pink stockings!" But he enjoyed the idea.'[50]

Before the summer holidays, Hockney had been developing a series of 'Love' paintings in which he further explored the theme of homosexuality. 'They were inspired,' he recalls, 'by the fact that the sex life of London had opened up to me, rather than by any one particular lover.'[51] These were not yet figurative pictures, but abstract compositions in which words and phrases were used to help make his meaning clear. While the first two of these feature a large red phallic shape rising from the lower edge and the word 'love' prominently displayed, it is the third one, titled *The Third Love Painting*, that is the most extraordinary, for it brings the subject of homosexual desire to the fore and invites anyone looking at it to become a voyeur. Hockney achieved this effect by scattering the canvas with the kind of crude graffiti he had seen in the public toilets of Earls Court Underground station. '. . . you are forced to look at the painting quite closely,' he wrote. '. . . You want to read it . . . When you first look casually at the graffiti on a wall, you don't see all the smaller messages; you see the large ones first and only if you lean over and look more closely do you get the smaller more neurotic ones.'[52] Thus a close look reveals an invitation to 'Ring me anytime at home', a saucily ambiguous propaganda slogan, 'Britain's future is in your hands', and the information that 'My brother is only seventeen', while the artist's inner self calls out, 'Come on David, admit it'. Alongside these base sentiments, written on the same phallic shape as appears in the previous works from the series, are the closing lines of 'When I Heard at the

Close of Day', a poem by Walt Whitman which celebrates the perfect love that can exist between men:

> For the one I love most lay sleeping by me under the same
>   cover in the cool night,
> In the stillness, in the autumn moonbeams, his face was inclined
>   toward me,
> And his arm lay lightly around my breast – and that night I was
>   happy.

The Third Love Painting was completed in the autumn of 1960, a time when Hockney was beginning to show a new self-confidence rooted in the knowledge that he'd finally reached a point at which he could make paintings for himself about the things that excited him. One of his crushes at the time was the young singer Cliff Richard. Though classical music had always been Hockney's first love, his brother John had given him an early Elvis Presley record, and this had started him off listening first to Elvis, then to Tommy Steele and finally to Cliff Richard, who in 1959 had released his number-one album, *Cliff Sings*, and starred in the gritty movie *Expresso Bongo*. With his greased-back hair, leather jackets and skin-tight trousers, Cliff was, Hockney remembers, 'a sexy little thing', a line echoed by a *Daily Sketch* headline that asked: 'IS THIS BOY TOO SEXY FOR TELEVISION?'

Cliff's latest hit single was the Lionel Bart song, 'Living Doll'. In a series of studies and drawings connected to a new painting, *Doll Boy*, Hockney made Cliff himself the object of adulation rather than the girl implied in the song's lyrics. *Doll Boy* is an important picture because it is one of the first of his paintings in which a figure begins to emerge, clothed in a white dress on which is written the word 'QUEEN', leaving one in no doubt as to the meaning of the title. The figure is identifiable as Cliff Richard by the notes emanating from his mouth signifying a singer, and by the figures 3.18, which are written beneath him; these are based on a childish code used by Walt Whitman to disguise the name of his lover, Peter Doyle, in which 1 = A, 2 = B and so on. 3.18 therefore translates as C.R.

This code came into play again in a painting executed at about the

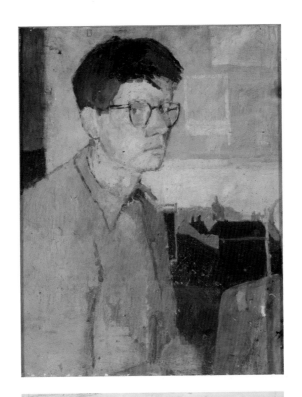

Self Portrait, 1954.
Oil on Board, 18 × 14″

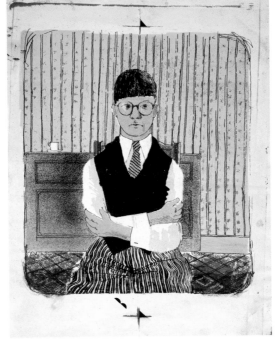

Self Portrait, 1954.
Edition 5
(approximately).
Lithograph
in Five Colours,
11 ½ × 10 ¼″

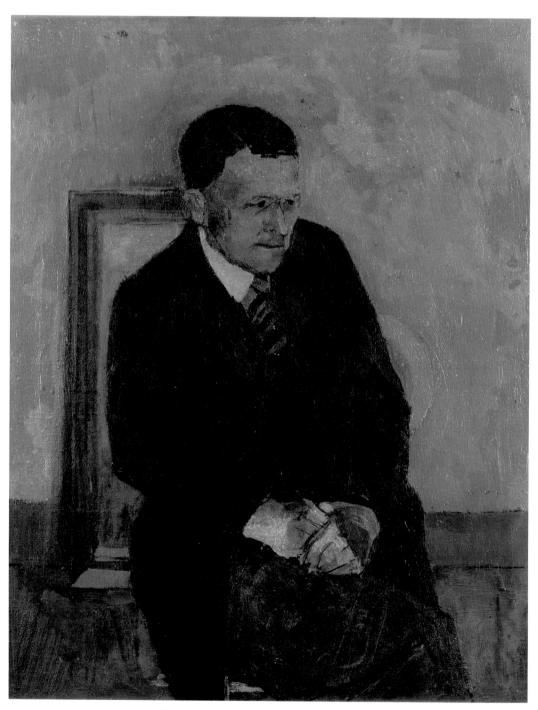

Portrait of my father, **1955.** Oil on Canvas, 20 × 16″

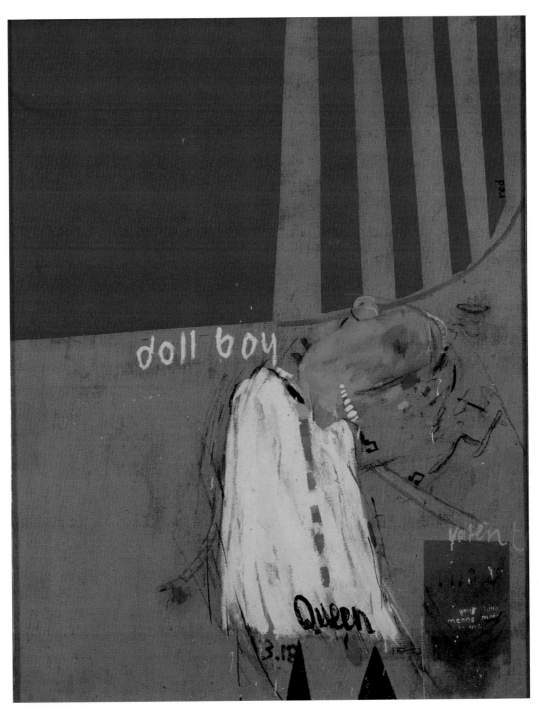

Doll Boy, 1960 – 61. Oil on Canvas, 48 × 39″

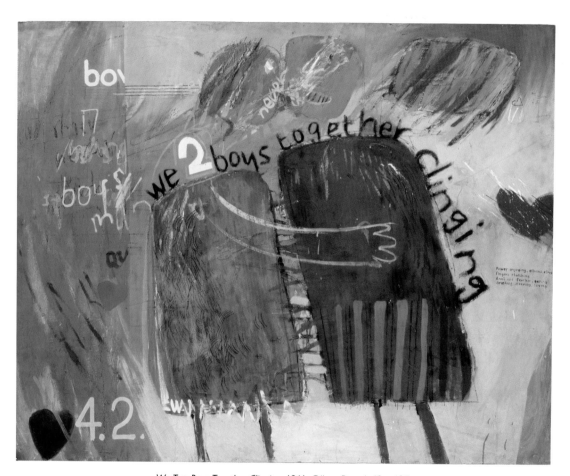

We Two Boys Together Clinging, 1961. Oil on Board, 48 x 60″

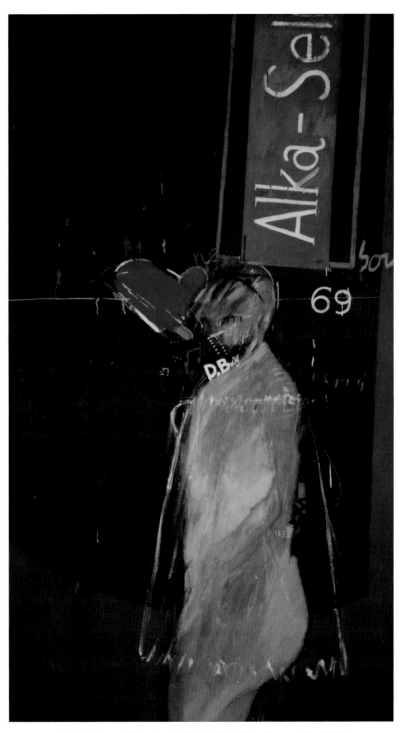

The Most Beautiful Boy in the World, 1961. Oil on Canvas, 70 x 39 ½″

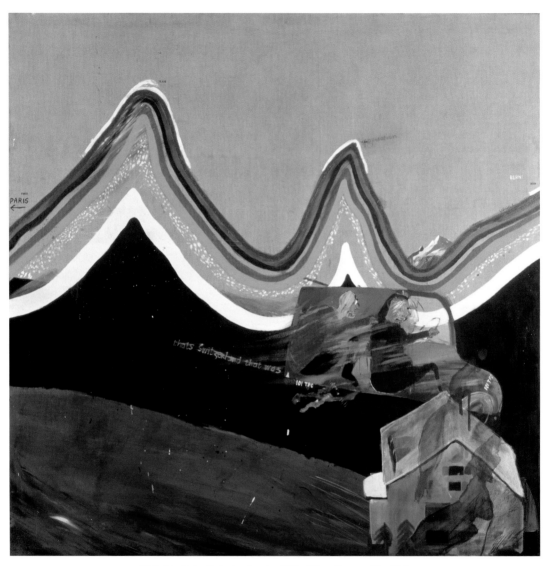

Flight Into Italy - Swiss Landscape, **1962.** Oil on Canvas, 72 × 72″

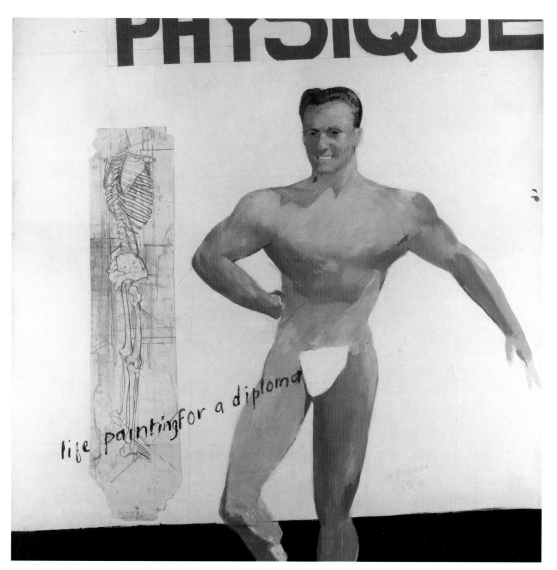

Life Painting for a Diploma, 1962. Oil on Canvas with Charcoal on Paper Collage, 70 ⅞ × 70 ⅞″

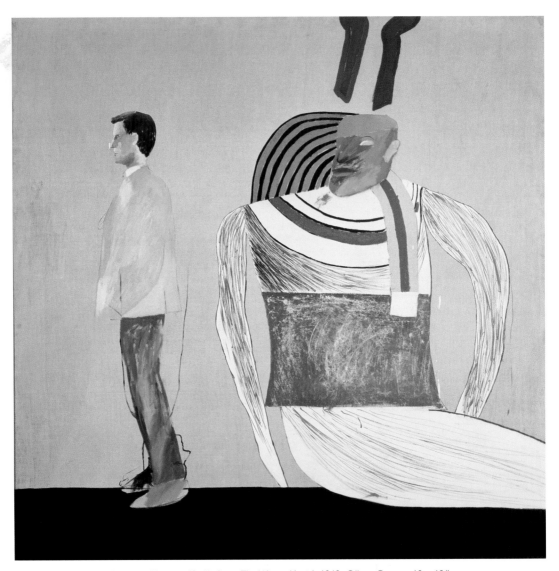

Man in a Museum (Or You're in The Wrong Movie), **1962.** Oil on Canvas, 60 × 60″

same time in which the use of the figure is further explored, and which Hockney referred to as his 'first attempt at a double portrait'.[53] Its title, *Adhesiveness,* is a word used by Walt Whitman to describe friendship; in the poem 'So Long!', he writes:

> I announce adhesiveness – I say it shall be limitless, unloosen'd;
> I say you shall yet find the friend you were looking for.

Adhesiveness is the first picture in which Hockney portrays himself and thus explicitly declares his homosexuality, for it depicts two men engaged in the act of lovemaking, apparently interlocked in the 69 position. One figure is identified by the numbers 4 and 8 for David Hockney, the other by 23 and 23 for his hero, Walt Whitman. 'What one must remember about some of these pictures,' Hockney later wrote, 'is that they were partly propaganda of something I felt hadn't been propagandised, especially among students, as a subject: homosexuality. I felt it should be done.'[54] It was an attitude that was to establish him as something of a hero to campaigners for gay rights over the next few years.

'David was very erudite,' wrote Peter Adam, a young friend of the artist Keith Vaughan, after a visit to Kempsford Gardens, 'and could talk for hours on almost any subject: Walt Whitman, Gandhi, Duccio, Durrell or Cavafy. He struck me as a strange mixture of modesty and self-assurance. He was so intensely alive that ideas just came toppling out, interlacing the most contradictory ideas in a logical pattern.'[55]

Charged with energy, Hockney was quite happy to draw on an enormous variety of influences. At the time, Ron Kitaj, Peter Phillips and Derek Boshier were all drawn towards pop art, depicting the everyday objects of mass culture. 'We weren't interested in wine bottles and fruit,' Boshier recalls. 'We were interested in the world we lived in, in sex and music and culture and advertising. There was a painting by John Bratby which had a cornflakes packet in it, and so I started to paint cornflakes packets and got into pop art.'[56]

Hockney, too, dipped his toes into these waters, in a series of three 'Tea' paintings. Arriving at college before the Lyons Corner House at South Kensington had opened, he always made sure he had a small

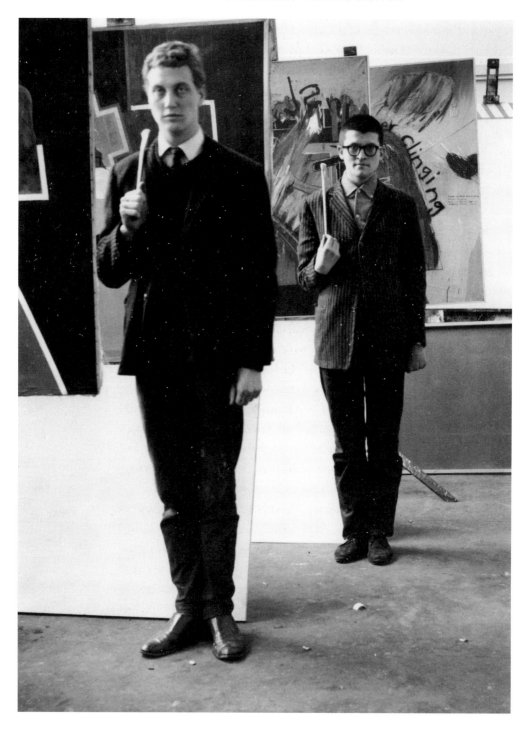

teapot and a cup, a bottle of milk and plenty of tea – his mother's favourite variety, Typhoo, 'The tea,' as the advertisement ran, 'that puts the "T" in Britain'. The distinctive red-and-black packets, piled up on the floor when they were empty along with the tubes and cans of paint, became his inspiration. 'This is as close to Pop Art as I ever came,' admitted Hockney,[57] whose questing nature would never allow him to become too narrowly concerned with solely contemporary images. These paintings were closely followed by a number of pictures based on playing cards, inspired by a book on the history of cards given to him by Mark Berger.

David Hockney and Derek Boshier in Painting School

So prolific was Hockney's output at this time that he ran out of money to buy paint, the consequences of which proved to be extremely important for his subsequent career. Discovering that the printmaking department – headed by the distinguished Edwin La Dell, a fellow Yorkshireman – gave out free materials to the students, and armed with the knowledge of lithography he had gained in his first two years at Bradford, Hockney decided to try his hand at some printing. Under the tutelage of a fellow student, Ron Fuller, he learned the basic techniques and produced three masterful etchings. The first of these, *Myself and My Heroes*, shows the figures of Walt Whitman, Mahatma Gandhi and David himself standing against a background of three panels, as though they are figures in a medieval triptych. Whitman and Gandhi both have halos, while Hockney, wearing an army cap, stands admiring them. Once again, words and phrases play an important part. 'For the dear love of comrades', from his poem 'I Hear It Was Charged Against Me', is written on Whitman. Gandhi has the words 'Mohandas', 'love', and 'vegetarian as well' around him, while Hockney, at a loss to know what to say about himself, has simply written, 'I am 23 years old and wear glasses.' This etching was followed by one based on playing cards, *Three Kings and a Queen*, and by *The Fires of Furious Desire* after William Blake's poem 'The Flames of Furious Desire'. The three completed prints demonstrate a mastery of the craft that was to serve him well in the future, even after so short an apprenticeship.

At the end of the autumn term Mark Berger tried to involve Hockney in the annual Royal College Christmas Revue, the idea being to parallel the satirical comedy that was being pioneered by people such as Jonathan Miller, Peter Cook, Dudley Moore and Alan Bennett in *Beyond the Fringe*, the hit show of the 1960 Edinburgh Festival. The revue was produced by Berger, with the theme of the Hollywood musical, but attempts to persuade Hockney to dress up in drag and sing a number fell on stony ground. This was primarily because only a few weeks previously a young painter called Patrick Procktor, who was studying at the Slade, had talked Hockney into attending their drag ball. 'So I went to Woolworths,' Hockney later told *Gay News*, 'and I got these eyelashes and makeup and I had a T shirt printed with Miss Bayswater on it. I had these rubber tits and I shaved my legs. I thought, "I'll swish into the Slade at 9.30." I arrived and I was the only one in drag. I thought, "Fucking hell, what a terrible dull lot of people. Even Patrick had let me down."'[58]

The Christmas Revue featured an imaginary conversation in Heaven between Beethoven and Errol Flynn, performed by Roddy Maude-Roxby and Derek Boshier; Janet Deuters, in a costume of her own design, doing a striptease to 'You've Gotta Have a Gimmick' from *Gypsy*; and Berger himself, got up in top hat and tails, singing 'I'll Build a Stairway to Heaven' with Pauline Boty, who was studying stained glass, and was known as 'the Wimbledon Bardot' because of her resemblance to the French film star. Berg also wrote a skit making fun of the kind of avant-garde theatre that was going on in New York at the time. 'I had Janet Deuters sitting up on a chair eating a banana, and someone crawling under her speaking nonsense poetry. David didn't like it at all. I remember he was up in the balcony drinking beer shouting "What a crock of shit! What is this lousy stuff?" He was definitely not into avant-garde, though strangely enough he began to do things in his paintings that were extremely advanced.'[59]

The revue also served another purpose in that it brought together students from all the different departments – fashion, graphics and industrial design – creating a great feeling of camaraderie. Favourite out-of-hours haunts included the Hoop and Toy pub round the corner in Thurloe Place, later to feature as a location in Roman Polanski's film *Repulsion*, and, once last orders had been called, the Troubadour on the Old Brompton Road, a popular hangout for artists, poets and musicians, or the Hades coffee bar on Exhibition Road. 'They served spaghetti in bowls for half a crown,' Hockney remembers. 'You had to sit at any table, so if there were six of us and there was a table which already had three people sitting at it, they'd send in me and Norman Stevens to go and sit at it and talk loudly to drive the other people away, so our gang could take it over.'[60]

Cinema was another uniting influence. The Royal College had its own film club, whose unmissable weekly meetings introduced them to the films of Eisenstein, Buñuel and Renoir. 'We used to go to a lot of movies,' Hockney recalls. 'As well as the college film club, there was the International Film Theatre in Westbourne Grove, the Classic in Notting Hill and the Paris Pullman in Drayton Gardens. We saw French films, Russian films and Italian films. Though I could be quite dismissive of French pretension, I was very taken with *L'Année dernière à Marienbad*.'[61]

In February 1961, Hockney exhibited in the annual 'Young Contemporaries' exhibition at the galleries of the Royal Society of British Artists in Suffolk Street. Started in 1949 by Carel Weight as a showcase for student work, it was to give successive generations of young artists their first professional outing. Frank Auerbach, Leon Kossoff, John Bratby, Edward Middleditch, Richard Smith, Robin Denny and Peter Blake had all cut their teeth at it. Peter Phillips was that year's president, and Derek Boshier, Allen Jones – now doing teacher training at Hornsey College of Art – and Patrick Procktor were on the organising committee. Together they appointed as judges Anthony Caro, Frank Auerbach and the influential critic Lawrence Alloway, who was assistant director of the ICA (Institute of Contemporary Arts) and the originator of the term 'pop art'.

'At first we hung the show like a sketch club,' Allen Jones remembers, 'pasting the walls with paintings as best we could. But when it had been hung and everyone had gone home, I was left with Peter Phillips and we looked around and we thought this is not the way to do it. We thought we should put all the pictures that we liked and identified as an idea on one wall, and all the rest on another wall.

So we gave Kitaj a complete wall, and then we had the other Royal College paintings facing the Slade. The Slade at the time was all under the influence of Bomberg, so it was all what I called "struggled mud", while on this other wall there was just this vibrant range of paintings.'[62]

The paintings chosen by the committee included images of toothpaste tubes by Boshier, fruit machines by Peter Phillips and a big red bus by Allen Jones. Hockney's work in the show, Jones believes, was particularly inventive. As well as *Doll Boy*, he showed *The Third Love Painting* and the first two 'Tea' paintings. In the catalogue, Lawrence Alloway drew attention to the group's use of 'the techniques of graffiti and the imagery of mass communication. For these artists the creative act is nourished on the urban environment they have always lived in.' Though he didn't use his term 'pop art' in the introductory essay, this is precisely the label that was given by the press to the work of the Royal College group in this show, and it was one that stuck. Suddenly the attention of the art world was drawn to a collection of young artists who were producing remarkable work while they were still at college, a previously unheard-of phenomenon. 'This year's Young Contemporaries at the RBA,' wrote Keith Sutton in the *Listener*, 'is a particularly good and lively one. The pictures . . . confirm at least one tentative hope, that things have got better since the war; namely that English artists can cope with scale in painting without diminishing content.'[63]

This exhibition was the first really significant moment in Hockney's student career. 'It was probably the first time,' he commented, 'that there'd been a student movement in painting that was uninfluenced by older artists in this country, which made it unusual. The previous generation of students, the Abstract Expressionists, in a sense had been influenced by older artists who had seen American painting. But this generation was not.'[64] People began to beat a path to the Royal College painting studios. 'They used to come in and wander round,' Hockney remembers. 'You would have finished paintings lying around and people would stroll in and look at them, so it was a bit of an exhibition space. You could show off in it, and I'm sure I did.'[65] One person who stopped by was the photographer Cecil Beaton, himself a talented artist. 'When I went to the college to take a few lessons,' he wrote in his diary, 'David and his friends were referred to by the professors as "the naughty boys upstairs". I visited them up there and found David at work on a huge Typhoo Tea fantasy. Everyone seemed to be doing what they wanted and loving it . . . I bought an indecent picture, *Homage to Walt Whitman*,[66] by Hockney who brought it round when Pelham Place [Beaton's home] was in the throes of building alterations. The workmen were startled at his appearance.'[67]

By far the most important thing that happened to Hockney, however, as a result of this show was that he attracted the attention of an extraordinary young dealer, John Kasmin, who was to change his life for ever.

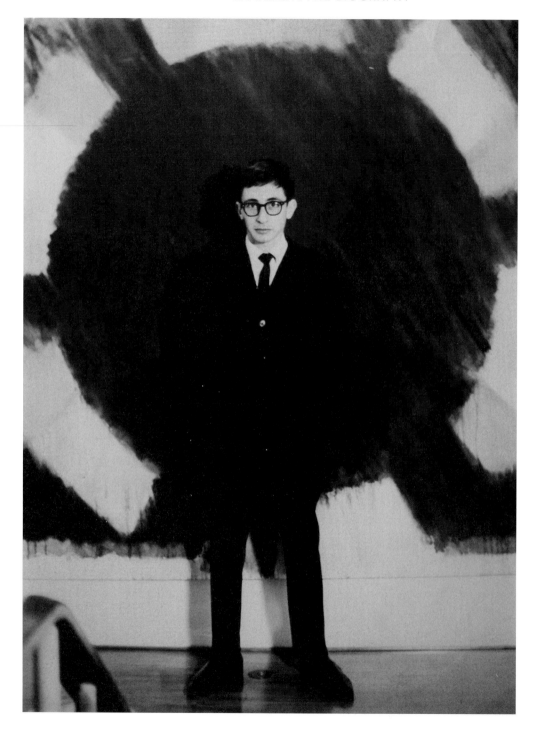

CHAPTER FOUR

'WE TWO BOYS TOGETHER CLINGING'

John Kasmin was the 27-year-old son of a family of Jewish immigrants from Poland. He had grown up in Oxford, where his father ran a garment-manufacturing factory, and had been happily studying classics at Magdalen College School until the business ran into financial difficulties. He was withdrawn from school, put to work in the family business and made to take night classes in accounting, going from a delightful life reading Greek poetry to a miserable one on the factory floor. Determined to escape and get away as far as possible from this dreary existence and a deteriorating relationship with his father, at seventeen he used his bar mitzvah money to travel to New Zealand, where he attended university for a while before dropping out and joining the bohemian fringe of New Zealand life. 'I became a sort of roving character,' he recalls. 'I made many friends and had a very varied and interesting life, rather like being a character in Kerouac's *On the Road*.'[1] In 1956 he returned home, calling himself a poet, and settled in London, soon assimilating himself into the artistic life of Soho, where he would take coffee at Torino's, hang out in David Archer's poetry bookshop in Panton Street, and drink at the French House pub, the Colony Room or the Cave de France. Among his favourite places to visit, particularly in the afternoons, was an art gallery in D'Arblay Street, Gallery One.

In the art scene of the 1950s, money was never the principal consideration, and many galleries were pretty shambolic, often run by slightly rakish gentlemen who spent as much time on the telephone to their bookmakers as they did in the gallery. Victor Musgrave, the owner of Gallery One, was an eccentric bohemian poet married to the

Portrait of
John Kasmin

portrait photographer Ida Karr, who was renowned for her pictures
of artists. Theirs was an open marriage and the whole set-up at 20
D'Arblay Street, where the gallery was on the ground floor and the
basement rented out to a picture framer, reflected the bohemian world
that Soho then was. On the first floor, Colin MacInnes, the author
of *City of Spades* and *Absolute Beginners*, had a room, while Ida had her
studio, sitting room and bedroom on the top floor. She and Victor both
had very active sex lives, he with a variety of prostitutes who inhabited
the neighbourhood, she with lovers of both sexes who would come and
go at all hours. '. . . lovers, lodgers and friends became all mixed up
in the sleeping arrangements as those with not enough money to eat
stayed to eat, and those with nowhere to stay stayed over, lovers came
and went and lodgers brought in their own companions.'[2]

'I was sitting in my gallery,' Victor Musgrave recalled, 'when a
small, eager, enthusiastic figure erupted into it and said in this eager
breathless way, "Hello, hello, are you Victor Musgrave? Where can
I meet painters, writers, artists?"'[3] As a result of this surprising
introduction Kasmin soon found himself working as an unpaid
assistant to Musgrave, as well as being both lover and studio manager
to his wife. He was also paid half a crown a day to do the cooking,
and was allowed to sleep in. One room on the top floor served as
sitting room, dining room, kitchen, bathroom and bedroom, the last
being created by means of a board placed over the bath at night. There
was an outdoor lavatory in the backyard. 'I liked being there,' Kasmin
remembers. 'It was one of the hot spots of Soho, a meeting place for
writers and artists, and after four or five months I managed to prove
my worth in the gallery.'[4]

The show that finally made Gallery One famous internationally
was called *Yves le Monochrome* and was of the work of the French
postmodernist Yves Klein. It took place in 1957, by which time Kasmin
had been promoted and was sleeping in the guest bedroom, often with
a variety of women. 'There was a tremendous amount of sex life that
went on in and around the gallery,' he recalls. 'Victor was very into
prostitutes and had a busy fantasy life, and at that time a lot of the
women who went round galleries were very much open to proposition,

so there was a lot of action. I would take the under twenty-eights. It was a curious and interesting life.'[5]

Having cut his teeth at Gallery One and built up a wide range of contacts and friendships, Kasmin moved on in 1959 to work at the Kaplan Gallery in Duke Street, St James's, under the distinguished Marxist dealer Ewan Phillips, with whom he shared dalliances with the gallery receptionist, who liked to measure their penises during her coffee break. It was a lively scene, and they put on the first London show of Jean Tinguely, featuring his Meta-Matics, robot-like machines which painted their own pictures, as well as early shows by Leonore Fini and Jean Atlan. During this year, Kaplan also recruited a third employee, a young Jewish refugee of great taste called Annely Juda, who would one day become David Hockney's dealer.

By now Kasmin had married into art royalty, his wife Jane being the granddaughter of Sir William Nicholson and the niece of Ben Nicholson, and was living in a cold-water flat off Regent Street. He was also the father of a six-month-old son, Paul. The necessity of supporting his family now pushed him in a new direction.

The most commercially minded gallery in London in 1960 was the Marlborough, founded after the war by two Viennese émigrés, Frank Lloyd and Harry Fischer, who were both feared and disliked on the art scene for their habit of poaching artists from other galleries. Their two greatest coups had been to lure Francis Bacon away from his long-standing dealer, Erica Brausen of the Hanover Gallery, who had nurtured him throughout his career, and Lynn Chadwick, Kenneth Armitage and Ben Nicholson from Peter and Charles Gimpel of Gimpel Fils. Among cash-strapped young art lovers, they were also well known for the excellence of the canapés served at their openings. They planned to open a new gallery, across the road from the Marlborough, in Bond Street, to be called the New London Gallery. Its premises were above Lloyds Bank, which appealed to Frank Lloyd, who had anglicised his name from Levy. Though they failed in their attempts to recruit Ewan Phillips to run it, who considered them ungentlemanly and driven by naked greed and power, he did recommend Kasmin for the job. 'My instincts told me,' Kasmin remembers, 'that it would be dreadful to enter into what was going to be the other side of the art world, the world of money, in which they behaved in a completely contrary fashion to most English art dealers of the time, but I decided to go for the job, and I went along and was interviewed by Mr Lloyd. My brief was to look for artists as well as to run the shows they sent over to me. They gave me an expense account to take out to lunch people whose goodwill would improve the prospects of the Marlborough Gallery, so I immediately set up accounts in Wilton's, Prunier's and a cigar store near Wilton's. I was constantly looking about for new artists whose work I liked and who might be available.'[6]

Kasmin worked at the Marlborough for a year, during which time he attempted, with little luck, to promote the work of artists he liked. The problem was that Fischer did not share his taste. Kasmin's attempt to push John Latham, for example, a conceptual artist who worked in a form of three-dimensional collage called 'Assemblage', was disastrous. Latham's chosen subject at the time was books, which he would torch and paint, producing walls of burned, blackened and coloured books. 'I loved his work and I considered him a visionary,' says Kasmin. 'Fischer, on the other hand, who was a lover of books, absolutely hated him, and on the occasion when I took him into Latham's studio, he was speechless with horror.'[7]

Kasmin also tried to interest Fischer in David Hockney. As part of his brief to search for new talent, Kasmin had gone to the Young Contemporaries show, and out of the extraordinary and exciting crop showing there had identified Hockney as the best of the bunch. 'I liked his touch,' he remembers. 'He seemed to have a really original approach to painting that was between figuration and abstraction. It had cheekiness and bravado and it was lively.'[8] Of the paintings Hockney was exhibiting, Kasmin particularly loved *Doll Boy*, which he bought for £40. 'I liked the writing, the style, the spirit . . . and felt very pleased with myself.'[9]

Keen to get to know the artist better, Kasmin contacted Hockney and invited him to his home in Ifield Road, Fulham, for a cup of tea so that they could talk about the picture. 'I told him I'd like to get to know him a bit and talk about possibly buying some more of his work.'[10] Late home from the gallery that day, he arrived to find his wife Jane sitting alone with Hockney in the kitchen. 'We were both rather shy,' she recalls, 'and didn't know what to say to each other. Our teacups were rattling in their saucers.'[11] Kasmin's first impression was of a rather gauche young man with National Health glasses and crew-cut hair, who was poorly dressed but clean, and spoke with a strong north country accent. Once they got talking and Hockney started to relax, he found him delightful, quickly warming to his open, trusting nature and wry sense of humour. They discussed his lack of money to buy canvas and paint, touched on the subject of what the Marlborough Gallery might be able to do for him, and arranged that Kasmin would look at more of Hockney's work. He was left with a strong sense of a young artist destined to be a success.

Kasmin's attempts to sell Hockney as a potential new star to Fischer, however, were a failure. Like most London galleries, the New London Gallery had a room for showing clients pictures that were not hanging up, complete with floor-to-ceiling grey velvet drapes on runners, an armchair, a sofa and an easel that could be lit from a spotlight. It was a style that might have been suited to showing off a van Gogh portrait or a Cezanne watercolour but for contemporary work it was the most inappropriate setting imaginable. Kasmin, however, persuaded Hockney to bring in some more of his pictures, and stored them behind the curtains. 'Some were particularly scruffy,' he recalls, 'painted on the cheapest canvas with ordinary white household paint, often unfinished, sometimes shaped with bits tacked on. Being so enthusiastic about them, I would have them out quite often, and Mr Fischer would come in and say, "What is all this rubbish? I said you could have it here, but you were to keep it behind the curtains. Get rid of all this stuff!"'[12] Apart from Kasmin, the only person at the Marlborough who liked the pictures was a fellow employee, James Kirkman, who would later buy several for only a few pounds.

*

If the critics were impressed by the work of the RCA students at the Young Contemporaries show, then their tutors were less so. 'The faculty told us, in their own words,' Derek Boshier remembers, 'to "stop all this pop art nonsense". They told us we had to take an old master or classical painting and do a painting based on it. We all thought this was a really boring idea, but in reality we got a lot out of it.'[13] Derek chose a painting by William Blake, *Elohim Creating Adam*, which directly led to him using falling figures in his paintings, while Hockney chose Ford Maddox Brown's *The Last of England*, which depicts the Pre-Raphaelite sculptor Thomas Woolner and his wife emigrating to Australia. Hockney's version cleverly followed the exercise in hand without slavishly copying it, transcribing it into his own work, complete with coded numbers and letters and turning the figures of the man and woman into two men, their faces smudged in the style of Francis Bacon. His justification for this was that, in real life, no onlooker would ever see from a distance the faces in such razor-sharp detail as they appear in the original painting.

The moment that the RCA faculty ceased to dismiss Hockney's work was when Richard Hamilton came to the Painting School and awarded him a prize. Often referred to as the father of pop art, the London-born Hamilton had trained at the Slade before joining the Independent Group and becoming a key figure at the ICA. Here he organised a number of influential exhibitions, such as *The Wonder and the Horror of the Human Head*, curated by Roland Penrose. In 1956 he was a major contributor to *This Is Tomorrow*, a landmark show at the Whitechapel Gallery, which featured a giant cut-out of Marilyn Monroe, Robbie the Robot from the film *The Forbidden Planet* and a jukebox; his poster for the show, a collage of 1950s American consumer culture titled *Just What Is It That Makes Today's Homes So Different, So Appealing?* has become an iconic image. Hamilton was teaching in the interior design department of the Royal College when the painting students asked him to come and judge their sketch club. 'He came and talked about the pictures,' wrote Hockney, 'and gave out little prizes of two or three pounds. He gave a prize to Ron and a prize to me, and from that moment on the staff of the College never said a word to me about my work being awful . . . Richard had come along to the college and seen what people were really doing, and recognized it instantly as something interesting . . . Richard was quite a boost for students; we felt, oh, it is right what I'm doing, it is an interesting thing and I should do it.'[14]

Mark Berger continued to be an important influence on Hockney and encouraged him to further develop his burgeoning skill at etching. Berger had written a gay fairy tale, called *Gretchen and the Snurl*, for his boyfriend in New York. It told the story of an innocent young boy, Gretchen, who goes out into the world fortified only by a cake made by his mother, and meets an alien creature called Snurl. Together they are rescued from a fearsome monster with terrible teeth called the Snatch, which tries to engulf them both. 'I think that in my mind David was Gretchen,' Berger remembers, 'and Snurl was his boyfriend, and I showed it to David and he really liked it, so I asked him if he would do some illustrations. The interesting thing is that one of David's best paintings came directly from the final etching in the story, which is a picture of the two boys hugging each other having been saved from what is really a monstrous vagina.'[15] The painting to which he refers, and which was to become one of Hockney's most iconic images, was called *We Two Boys Together Clinging*.

In his second year at the RCA Hockney was extraordinarily productive, creating a large body of work much of which was of an extremely personal nature. Many of the pictures feature two men embracing, and they manage to be both touching and funny. 'Cheeky' is a word that Hockney often uses about himself and it could be said that it was barefaced cheek which enabled him to tackle such material, together with the use of humour. *We Two Boys Together Clinging* is a perfect example, though when Roger de Grey first saw it, his only comment was: 'Well, I hope they don't get any closer than that!'

The painting was inspired both by a press cutting and by a beautiful poem. On the wall close to where Hockney worked were a number of pin-ups of Cliff Richard, together with a newspaper clipping with the headline 'TWO BOYS CLING TO CLIFF ALL NIGHT', which told the story of a bank holiday mountaineering accident. Hockney's quirky imagination naturally gave the story another interpretation; it also brought to his mind Walt Whitman's poem 'We Two Boys Together Clinging', which has the lines:

We two boys together clinging,
One the other never leaving . . .
Arm'd and fearless – eating, drinking, sleeping, loving . . .

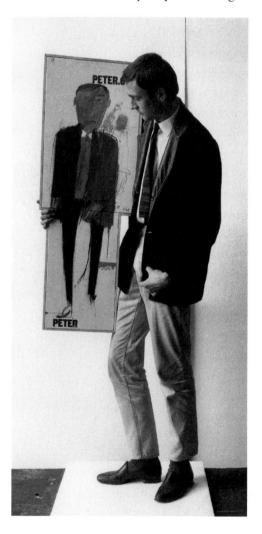

Peter Crutch
with Peter C

His painting, which was preceded by an experimental watercolour study, depicts two figures embracing, their bodies bound together by 'tentacles' of desire emanating from both of them. In the bottom left-hand corner of the canvas, the numerals 4.2 link the painting to *Doll Boy*, while the figures are also identified by codes – the left-hand one, 4.8, being a self-portrait, while his partner on the right has both 3.18, for Cliff, *and* 16.3, for Peter Crutch, a student on whom Hockney had a huge crush. The word NEVER painted across the lips of the Hockney figure, however, hints at the inevitable unrequited passion, in the case of Peter Crutch because he was completely straight.

'David developed this incredible crush on Peter Crutch,' Berger recalls, 'which was perplexing for him because he was still quite shy about his emotions.' Crutch was studying design in the furniture department, and had caught Hockney's eye while in the college bar. 'Oh! He's just so beautiful,'[16] Hockney had said to Berger, immediately besotted. They soon became friends and Hockney began to hang out with Crutch and his fashion-student girlfriend, Mo Ashley, who turned out to

share Hockney's love of Cliff Richard. Though Hockney kept his strong
feelings of sexual desire strictly sublimated, he transferred them into
a number of paintings, notably *We Two Boys Together Clinging* and *The
Most Beautiful Boy in the World*. In the latter painting, which features a
young man naked except for a 'baby doll' nightie, made all the rage in
1956 by Carroll Baker in Elia Kazan's film *Baby Doll*, he expresses his
desire quite openly, using his usual code of numbers and graffiti. 'I
love wrestling,' he scrawls, and 'come home with', the inferred 'me'
hidden by a poster for Alka-Seltzer, which also presumably hides the
word 'love' at the end of 'let's all make', which is written above a large
red heart pushing against the boy's head. The identity of the figure
is made clear by the numbers 16.3 written just above his buttocks.
Crutch, whose friendship with Hockney remained entirely platonic,
was the subject of a number of pictures, including *Cha-Cha-Cha that
was Danced in the Early Hours of 24th March, 1961* and *Peter C*, a portrait
on a shaped canvas which was Hockney's first since *Portrait of My Father*
in 1955.

One rainy April morning, Hockney left the garden shed in which
he was still living to make his usual journey to Exhibition Road
and noticed a taxi dropping off a fare at the Kempsford Gardens
boarding house. 'I had a ten-shilling note in my pocket,' he remembers,
'virtually my last ten shillings, and I thought, "It's pouring with rain.
I'll get a taxi," which would have cost about five shillings to the Royal
College, rather than 6d on the bus. Anyway I took this taxi, which left
me with five shillings to my name, but I knew I could always live on
my wits, and cadge a lunch here, a lift there. But that day I received a
letter containing a cheque for £100 for winning a prize at some print
exhibition, which I hadn't even known about, and I thought, "This is
fantastic. That taxi did it!"'[17]

The prize was for an etching which the head of the printing
department, Alistair Grant, had discovered in the drying racks of the
Print Room and had entered into an exhibition called *The Graven Image*
at the St George's Gallery, Cork Street, where a young Cambridge

graduate, the Hon. Robert Erskine, was spearheading a revival of
English printmaking. He had persuaded the hotel group, Trust Houses
Ltd, to donate prize money for the best five prints of the previous year,
and Hockney had won for his print *Three Kings and a Queen*. For him the
money seemed like a fortune.

More unexpected money came when the Royal College received
a commission from the P&O shipping line, whose chairman, Donald
Anderson, was the brother of the RCA's provost, Sir Colin Anderson.
Their new flagship, the SS *Canberra*, was being built at the Harland
and Wolff shipyard in Belfast, and Hugh Casson, head of the School of
Interior Design, was put in overall charge of this project. He brought in
established artists such as Ruskin Spear, Edward Ardizzone, Humphrey
Spender and Julian Trevelyan, while his senior tutor, John Wright,
offered Hockney the job of decorating a room for teenagers, to be
called 'The Pop Inn'. 'Julian and I decorated the staircase,' remembers
Mary Fedden, wife of Trevelyan and one of Hockney's tutors, 'with
cut-out metal figures of kings and queens. David decorated a room
with an electric poker and most of it was writing, though there were
also little pictures, all burnt onto the walls with this red-hot poker.'[18]

Living in a small hotel in Southampton, Hockney spent five days
on this project, filling every inch of wall space with his characteristic
graffiti, number codes and childish drawings, the cheeky side of his
nature working overtime as he wondered what he might get away with.
'Handsome milkman 21', 'Butch is naughty' and 'Swing it Auntie'
were three typical examples, while he paid homage to the current cool
cigarette advertisement, 'You're never alone with a Strand', with a
drawing showing 'Maisie' arm in arm with 'Jack' and the words 'You're
never alone in the Strand or Piccadilly'. 'I finished the "mural" on this
ship,' he wrote to Berger. 'I had a quite crazy ten days down there – the
crew continually coming up to see me and watch. As I was working, a
cabin boy came up and asked me to write his name up. I agreed and he
told me it was "Jesse" . . . Ten minutes later he came back with all his
mates (all aged about 16), all wanting their names up – "Betty", "Judy",
"Susan" etc. All in a day's work, eh?'[19] Pathé Pictorial made a newsreel
film about the *Canberra*'s maiden voyage in June 1961, which Hockney

caught at the Forum cinema in the Fulham Road. 'This is the Pop Inn,' said the veteran commentator, Bob Danvers-Walker, 'a Rumpus Room for teenagers, where rock 'n' roll has definitely replaced the sailor's hornpipe.'[20] Hockney's idea that the teenagers would add to his graffiti with their own eventually came all too true, the majority of it, unfortunately, being better suited to a gents' toilet, and the result was that the walls were boarded over and the Pop Inn became a camera shop.

Hockney was paid £100 for the *Canberra* mural. 'With the money I'll get,' he wrote to his parents, 'I can have a cheap return air ticket to New York this summer – this is through the college, and I can stay with an ex-student there. I certainly seem to be getting around.'[21] He had been offered a return ticket to New York for £40, and had jumped at it, having been under the impression that a ticket must cost at least a thousand pounds. He arranged to stay with Mark Berger, now back home. 'The address I gave you for New York,' he wrote to his mother shortly before leaving, 'will only be valid for the first fortnight – after that I will be travelling about, most likely down to New Orleans in the South and back through Texas and Oklahoma to New York . . . Tell John if I go to New Orleans, I'll send him some postcards and maybe books from the home of jazz.'[22]

With the sale of pictures, the Erskine fee and the *Canberra* mural, Hockney had amassed about £300 by the time he left. 'I thought I was absolutely in the money,' he remembers. He flew out on 9 July 1961, his twenty-fourth birthday, with Barrie Bates, another Royal College student, carrying with him, on the advice of Robert Erskine, a number of prints to show to the Museum of Modern Art.

Hockney had fantasised about New York ever since boyhood, when 'New York Road' was displayed on the Leeds trams, and more recently, after looking at Mark Berger's *Physique Pictorial* magazines, his fantasies had taken on a more sexual tone. The city did not disappoint him. 'I was taken by the sheer energy of the place,' he recalls. 'It was amazingly sexy, and unbelievably easy. People were much more open, and I felt completely free. The city was a total twenty-four-hour city. Greenwich Village was never closed, the bookshops were open all night so you could browse, the gay life was much more organised, and I thought, "This is the place for me."'[23] Berger was in hospital with hepatitis when Hockney arrived, but had arranged to come home to Long Beach in Nassau County, where he lived with his rather uptight father Benjamin, a pharmacist, and his glitzy stepmother Helen, who had big eyebrows, wore lots of jewellery and had once harboured ambitions to be an actress. 'My father could not figure out David at all,' Berger remembers. 'He enjoyed his company, but he just found him so offbeat in many ways. One of the things my father disliked was things being shifted from where they belonged. One day, for example, Hockney was told off for not putting the blueberries back in the refrigerator exactly where he had found them. Later he did a wonderful drawing based on this scene.'

It was not a match made in heaven, particularly because Hockney was still a radical pacifist vegetarian who was shocked by his host's habit of going round the house killing ants with a spray gun. This oft-repeated scene was the inspiration for both a drawing of the spraying of the insects, and for a painting, *The Cruel Elephant*, which depicts an elephant treading on the words 'crawling insects' and flattening them. Hockney almost fainted one day when Mark's father returned home carrying a live lobster which he intended to cook for dinner. Helen Berger also had her differences with Hockney. 'David didn't care where he worked,' Berger recalls. 'He would work anywhere where he was inspired. My parents had this really nice wall-to-wall white broadloom carpet and David loved to sit on the floor and draw with pen and ink or pencil. One day he was busy drawing when, plop, a big blob of ink dropped on the carpet. My stepmother nearly had a heart attack. "Look what David's done," she wailed, "he's messed up my carpet." I just said, "Look, Mother, cut it out and have him sign it and it'll be worth couple of hundred thousand in a few years." David just laughed, but was so unique in his work and his personality that there was no question to me that one day he was going to be famous.'[24]

This was a view shared by William S. Lieberman, the legendary curator of the print department at the Museum of Modern Art. He was so impressed by the etchings that Hockney showed him, *Kaisarion with All His Beauty* and *Mirror, Mirror on the Wall*, both inspired by Cavafy poems, that he not only bought one of each for the museum, but sold all the rest of the edition on his behalf. Lieberman also sent him to the Pratt Institute in Brooklyn, one of America's leading undergraduate art colleges, where Hockney set to work on a new etching, *My Bonnie Lies Over the Ocean*, an expression of his continuing unrequited pining for Peter Crutch. 'Dear All,' he wrote to his family on 19 July, 'I'm having a fine time here, although the weather is very uncomfortable. (It seems to be always above 90°.) I will be staying in New York for quite a while now, as I am doing some work at the Pratt Institute here . . . New York is a rather confusing city as all the streets are absolutely straight – there are no curved ones – making it difficult to find your way about . . . The museums here (and there are many of them) are quite marvellous, and will take some time to absorb. Still I've plenty of time left.'[25]

This New York trip marked another significant moment: the dramatic transformation of Hockney's appearance. A friend of Berger's called Ferrill Amacker, 'droll, very funny, quite camp and exotic' in Hockney's words, came over to the Long Beach house one evening when Mr and Mrs Berger were out, and the three boys settled down to watch TV. When during one of the commercial breaks there was an advertisement for the hair dye Lady Clairol, with the catchphrase 'Is it true blondes have more fun?', Hockney became very animated. 'This completely captivated David,' Berger recalls, 'because to him the American image was butch football players and blondes, so he decided he was going to become blonde. We were all very excited and in the end all three of us went out and had our hair dyed. My father nearly had a fit when he came home and saw us all sitting there with our bleached hair.'[26]

With the $200 he made from the sale of his etchings Hockney bought himself a real American suit. He also moved in with Amacker, who lived in the Fruit Street area of New York in Brooklyn Heights, which was convenient for the Pratt Institute. 'Ferrill had lived in New York for two or three years,' Hockney remembers. 'He was young and had a bit of money, so he didn't have to work. He had a proper little apartment with a television and a bathroom, things we certainly didn't have in London. He was a bohemian and lived a marvellous bohemian life, and we became occasional lovers. People came and went in his apartment. I didn't quite know who they were. People would get into the bed. It was just like that and I thought it was great. I thought, "This is the life." It's a long way from Bradford, and London is dreary by comparison.'[27]

Hockney drank in everything about the city, staying up all night with Amacker, watching TV, cruising the gay bars, visiting Madison Square Gardens, exploring Harlem and the Bowery, taking part in an anti-nuclear march in Greenwich Village, and visiting all the museums and galleries. He was also thrilled to find plenty of fellow vegetarians, a discovery he enthused about in a letter to Ron Kitaj. 'Ron Old Chap,' he wrote soon after his arrival, 'I like this town – Vegetarian restaurants on every street corner. I haven't been in the Empire State Building yet – but I wouldn't be surprised if the whole of that wasn't one big Veg restaurant. The funny thing is that New Yorkers don't look like animal lovers.'[28] It was 1961, and New York City seemed like the capital of the world.

When Hockney finally returned to London in early September, 'with a yellow crew-cut, smoking cigars and wearing white shoes',[29] he was a different person. Donald Hamilton-Fraser, a landscape artist who taught one day a week at the Royal College, noticed that while previously he had come over as edgy and wanting to plough his own furrow, he was now more relaxed and had definitely found himself. He was also more energised than ever, his head swimming with 'thousands of subjects'. Arriving a week before term started, he decided that his first painting was going to be really big, using a large stretcher, eleven feet by seven feet, which he had bought from a fellow student at the end of the summer term. While in New York, all the paintings he had seen had appeared enormous. Another good reason for painting a large picture was the purely selfish one that it would guarantee him a bigger working area in the studio, where people were already beginning to grab places. Among those who saw the work while it was in progress was Grey, 2nd Earl of Gowrie, a student at Balliol College, Oxford, who was brought along by David Bathurst, a former colleague of Kasmin's at the Marlborough Gallery. 'David took me one day to the Royal College of Art,' Gowrie remembers, 'and there I saw this very interesting young man in wonderful clothes actually painting a practical joke, and the joke was, he told me, that all the other students were enamoured of large paintings, which was the result of the big backwash of Jackson Pollock and Clyfford Still and people like that, so he thought he'd better shape up and do one himself, and I watched him paint *A Grand Procession of Dignitaries in the Semi-Egyptian Manner*. It was a wonderful work, a very remarkable picture, and anyone could see that.'[30]

Once again, a poem by Cavafy, 'Waiting for the Barbarians', was the inspiration for this picture, the first painting of his final year at the RCA. In this, his first ever three-figure composition, he set out to paint a highly theatrical picture, using Egyptian tomb paintings as his stylistic source, depicting three officials – a clergyman, a soldier and an industrialist whose stiff and pompous outward appearance hides the truth that inside they are very small and ordinary. In its use of raw canvas rather than paint to provide background 'colour', it drew on influences ranging from Bacon and Kitaj to American painting. 'This painting,' he wrote, 'and the big works of 1961 . . . are the works where I became aware as an artist. Previous work was simply a student doing things.'[31]

While Hockney was in America, Kasmin had written to tell him that he had left the Marlborough Gallery and was dealing temporarily from home. The Hon. Sarah Drummond, the well-connected debutante who was the receptionist at the New London Gallery, had introduced him to a rich young man who wanted to invest in art, and Kasmin had gone into partnership with him. His name was Sheridan Blackwood, the Marquess of Dufferin and Ava, a shy, diffident and immensely charming young man, with a penchant for fast and expensive cars, and one of the heirs to the Guinness fortune. Still a student at Oxford, where he inhabited a vast suite of rooms hung with good pictures in the

No. Old Library X

Christ Church Quad, he dreamed of becoming a serious art collector. 'He really wanted to be helped to get deeper into modern art,' Kasmin recalls. 'I liked the idea of having someone around who would listen to what I liked and of having someone I could advise, and he liked the idea of being a collector and buying things at a good price.'[32] Within a matter of months, Kasmin had told Dufferin that the time had come for him to strike out on his own. In the autumn of 1961, with the sum of £25,000 put up by Dufferin, they started Kasmin Ltd, and among the first artists they approached was David Hockney.

In spite of his recent successes, Hockney was still extremely short of money, and Kasmin decided to take him out for a business lunch to discuss some kind of contract. His years at the Marlborough had given him plenty of experience of expense-account entertaining, but he hadn't accounted for Hockney being a vegetarian. '"Lunch in the West End?" said David. "Well, there's a vegetarian place I like very much off Leicester Square called the Vega." Well, we went to this restaurant, and when I got the bill at the end it was something like one and ninepence. I couldn't believe it. I was used to having a very good lunch at Wilton's with a bill for two people for five quid. David saw me looking at the bill and said, "Oh, Mr Kasmin, is it too much?" "No," I said, "it's certainly not, but it is very difficult to explain a bill like this to anybody."'[33]

The result of the lunch was a contract forward-dated to when Hockney left college, it being illegal for a student to sign a financial contract. Since Kasmin didn't want him to feel completely signed up, he generously excluded from it the territories of the Gilbert and Ellice Islands in the Western Pacific.

The contract with Kasmin opened up a whole new world. 'If you have someone who is keen on your work,' says Hockney, 'you should follow them. It was exciting for me. He was incredibly energetic and I quickly noticed that he had a good eye, especially for drawings. He was an interesting man, very knowledgeable about pictures, and I was part of his eccentric taste. He used to have a kind of salon every Tuesday night, and this is where I began to meet interesting people. All kinds of people came, and I found myself meeting the art world for the first time.'[34]

Kasmin's gatherings were open-house evenings of food, drink and conversation, and the occasional sale of pictures, which would be on show in the ground-floor rooms. These would be anything from traditional 'bread and butter' works by Klee, Miró, Léger or Ben Nicholson, to newer work by Ellsworth Kelly, Allen Jones and David Hockney. Hockney drawings cost between £10 and £20 each, sold in these early days on a non-profit-making basis to give Hockney an income.

At the Royal College, people passing through could buy prints directly off Hockney for two or three pounds, with no edition number and often in a pretty grubby condition, sometimes with footprints clearly visible on them where they had been trodden on. There was no sense of things being valuable; they were after all just work in progress. Since his time at the Pratt Institute in New York, however, Hockney's interest in printing had intensified as he began to discover its power as a means of expression. He put all of himself into these early prints, creating images of his inner life. He cast himself, for example, in the title role in a version of William Hogarth's celebrated series of paintings and prints, *The Rake's Progress*, in which he reimagined the follies of high and low life in eighteenth-century London as a tale of a young gay man trying to find his place in 1960s New York. Thus *The Seven Stone Weakling*, in America for the first time, visits gay bars and lives the high life until *The Wallet Begins to Empty*.

'One of the things that struck me in New York,' he remembers, 'was that in the Bowery you did see bums on the street, which you didn't see in London at that time, and of course that was perfect for *The Rake's Progress*.' His original plan was to copy Hogarth and produce eight etchings, but when Robin Darwin got wind of this, he approached Hockney with a plan for the Royal College to produce a book of the work for its own imprint, the Lion and Unicorn Press. They would, however, require twenty-four prints. Hockney considered that this would mean padding the story out too much, as well as being far too big a task for a student working without an assistant, and so they compromised on sixteen, some of which would be based on the Hogarth original and some on his own experiences. '*The Gospel Singing*, with the Good People wearing ties with God is Love on them,' he recalls, 'is based on a trip I made to Madison Square Gardens to hear Mahalia Jackson, and there was a choir jumping up and down singing "God is Love". It was amazing, pure Americana. *The Door Opening for a Blonde* was the Lady Clairol advert. *Receiving the Inheritance* was selling etchings to the Museum of Modern Art. *Bedlam*, right at the end, is when they're all plugged into the first transistor radio. I'd seen these people with earplugs, and I thought they were hearing aids, like my father used to wear. In fact they were the first transistor radios, which you wouldn't have got in England then. So it was a combination of things that happened to me.'[35]

That Hockney was making his mark in more ways than one is clear from a letter the RCA registrar, John Moon, sent to his old head at Bradford College of Art, Fred Coleclough. 'I am sorry not to have written to you sooner about David Hockney,' he wrote. 'He has become the College's No. 1 Character, whose influence extends out beyond the Painting School, and his work and doings are watched by all up and coming students. He still spends most of his time painting, but he has done a number of very interesting etchings which have created a great deal of notice.'[36] He went on to list a number of Hockney's achievements: first prize in a student art competition organised by London University Union, a painting being selected for the Arts Council Collection; and three prints being chosen for the Graphic section of the Paris Biennale, suggesting that these 'pretty solid and impressive' details should be passed on to the Lord Mayor of Bradford.

Hockney's growing self-confidence meant that he was less reticent than the previous year about appearing in the 1961 Christmas Revue, and Ferrill Amacker, who was passing through London en route for Italy, persuaded him to do a drag act, in the dress that Janet Deuters had made for her striptease the previous year. 'He managed to get David on stage,' Derek Boshier remembers, 'wearing a frock and a pair of Yorkshire clogs, and he sang a song from *Oklahoma*, "I'm Just a Girl Who Can't Say No", changing the words to "I'm Just a Boy . . .", and it was the first time that a lot of people realised that he was gay.'[37] Amacker was on his way to spend Christmas with Mark Berger, who was living in Florence on a Fulbright scholarship, and when the revue was over he persuaded Hockney to break the habit of a lifetime and accompany him to Italy rather than going home for Christmas. When Michael Kullman, the head of the general studies department, offered them both a lift as far as Switzerland in his little Morris van, they eagerly accepted and set off as soon as term was over.

This was Hockney's first trip to Europe, made possible because his increasing income from painting meant he no longer had to rely on holiday jobs to get by. He was particularly looking forward to seeing the Alps, but because he had felt it only polite to offer Amacker the front seat, he was squashed in the back of the van, without windows, and saw virtually nothing of the landscape all the way to Berne. 'It was Ferrill's first visit to Europe,' he remembers, 'and I was very amused by him referring to the toilets as the "restrooms", especially in France when they were just those holes in the ground. I thought, "I'm not sure you'd call that a restroom." It was a long journey and more than a little uncomfortable.'[38] When they reached Berne, they bid farewell to Kullman, and took the train to Florence.

Hockney had imagined that Italy would be hot and sunny, but the reality was that the temperatures were below freezing. 'It really snowed very heavily,' he wrote, 'and the narrow streets of Florence with the snow on them were like a Dickensian London Christmas Card.'[39]

The trip was primarily an artistic one. Hockney slept on the floor of Mark's studio in a sleeping bag and spent his days plodding round the city with his guidebooks, looking at galleries and ancient sites. He toured the Uffizi, loving the beauty of the medieval paintings while resisting any influences from them, though he did take in, from looking at a large *Crucifixion* by Duccio, that artists had been shaping canvases to suit their subjects for centuries. Evenings were spent with Berg and Amacker in the bars and cafes.

This trip became the basis for another delightful and funny autobiographical painting, *Flight into Italy–Swiss Landscape, 1962*. The fact that Hockney had seen nothing of the Swiss landscape was no barrier, as far as he was concerned, to painting a mountain picture. He would just make it up, incorporating a variety of influences of the time. Thus the main image is taken from a school geography book showing the contours

of the mountains and their height, while peeking in from the back are
some real mountain tops taken from a picture postcard. The unpainted
canvas representing the sky has echoes of Bacon, the multicoloured lines
delineating the mountaintops, of Kenneth Noland and Morris Louis.
From the back of the Morris van charging across the canvas, with its
three blurred and desperate-looking passengers and Hockney himself
represented as a witch, come the words 'That's Switzerland that was', a
reference to a current advertising campaign by Shell.

Hockney painted two versions of this picture, the first of
which, *Swiss Landscape in a Scenic Style*, was entered into the 1962
Young Contemporaries exhibition, one of four paintings he chose
to demonstrate his versatility as an artist. On sending-in day he
consolidated his friendship with Patrick Procktor, who was that year's
treasurer. 'We started talking and we just became friends quickly.
We simply had a lot of interests in common – painting, literature,
and being gay, *then*. Because most people were in the closet at that
time.'[40] Patrick also rescued Hockney's paintings from obscurity in
the back room, insisting that they should all be hung together at the
front. 'Those four pictures I did,' he told the American painter Larry
Rivers, in an interview published in the magazine *Art and Literature*,
'were very concocted pictures. I deliberately set out to prove I could
do four entirely different sorts of picture like Picasso.'[41] The three
other entries were *A Grand Procession of Dignitaries in the Semi-Egyptian
Style*, *Tea Painting in an Illusionistic Style* and *Figure in a Flat Style*, the
last consisting of a canvas shaped like a figure, in which the base of
the easel on which it sat became the legs of the figure. His choice of
long titles for the pictures was by no means random and demonstrates
his shrewdness. 'By titling the pictures in this way,' he wrote, 'in the
catalogues there was more space between the lines, so it stood out. I
knew all those tricks . . .'[42]

The 1962 Young Contemporaries show was an enormous success.
'. . . if this year's brilliant Young Contemporaries exhibition is anything to go by,' wrote the art critic of *The Times*, 'then British Art is in
for a healthy, lively period. The exhibition fairly bubbles with bright
ideas and visual excitement.' He was impressed by the intelligence

of the artists, and singled out 'two markedly influential "art-school movements", the girder-and-iron-plate sculpture at St Martin's, and the raspberry-blowing "new-surrealist school" (for want of a better name) at the Royal College of Art. This last dominates the first room, particularly in the person of its present star turn, David Hockney.'[43] It is no exaggeration to say that this show, which was widely written about and discussed by the press, set Hockney on the road to fame.

The bright star that was the Young Contemporaries cast its light not just across London, but all over the country, thanks to a touring exhibition sent out by the Arts Council. For this a poster was commissioned from Hockney. 'He produced an hilarious image,' said Mark Glazebrook, the Arts Council member who had come up with the idea, 'of a scruffy youth being sick over a reproduction of the Leonardo Cartoon, the famous Da Vinci drawing that belonged to the Royal Academy. The Arts Council, out of the profits of its Picasso exhibition at the Tate, had donated a substantial sum to the Leonardo Appeal to save the cartoon for the nation, the Royal Academy being temporarily broke. My colleagues upstairs at 4 St James's Square, older, wiser and respected heads, were nervous of the effect of this Hockney image on "the provinces"– where David and I had both come from. I didn't put up much of a fight and David didn't kick up a fuss. We were forced to subtract the photo of the Leonardo which sadly left the youth just being sick over the blank piece of paper.'[44]

The exhibition inspired a multitude of ambitious, lively young people to head for the London art world. Among them was a charismatic young textiles student, Mo McDermott, who moved into a flat in Ladbroke Grove, Notting Hill, and found himself a job working for the interior designer Adam Pollock. Mo came from Salford, near Manchester, where he had attended the regional art school and gained a reputation for being both charming and mischievous. His father was away at sea, and he lived most of the time alone with his mother, with whom he had endless rows and who, disapproving both of the art school and his friends, would furiously trawl the local coffee bars looking for him. It was scarcely surprising that he couldn't wait to get out of Manchester.

Mo quickly established himself at the centre of a lively scene revolving around the Elgin pub in Ladbroke Grove, which included his flatmates, two unknown young musicians, Rod Stewart and 'Long' John Baldry, as well as two of his closest friends from Manchester, Ossie Clark and Celia Birtwell, both talented fashion students. At a party given by the Australian artist Brett Whiteley, who was in London on a travelling art scholarship, he was introduced to Hockney, whose work he already loved and he almost immediately asked him for an etching. 'Nobody had asked me for one before,' says Hockney, 'and we quickly became friends. He was a little bit younger than me, very lively, very gay, very cocky, and confident. He was funny and he loved London, and moving in all different kinds of milieus. It was a far cry from Manchester.'[45]

At the time Hockney was desperately looking for a model for the life drawings he was expected to produce for his diploma. His problem was that he found the models provided by the college repulsive. 'They really did have old fat women as models,' he wrote, 'big tits hanging down; they sit on a chair and their ass goes falling over it . . . you couldn't get further away from attractive flesh than this flesh. So I said, "Can't you get some better models?" . . . but the idea of painting an attractive one they thought was rather wicked.'[46] To make his point that all great painters of the nude have always painted models that they liked, he got hold of an *American Physique* magazine and copied the cover, in addition sticking onto the canvas one of his skeleton drawings as a reminder that he could draw something that was absolutely anatomically correct. To this he gave the title *Life Painting for a Diploma*. He then invited his new friend Mo to come in and model for him, and the college eventually agreed to pay him the set rate of £12 a week. Typically Hockney did not do as he was asked, which was to produce a series of three different straight life paintings. Instead, he made one picture featuring Mo in three different poses and wrote 'life painting for myself' across the top. When he left the painting on an easel overnight, somebody added the words 'Don't give up yet' at the bottom. 'We never found out who did it,' Hockney recalled. 'It's still on the painting . . . I remember there was a girl opposite, a very, very quiet girl who'd never said a word, and I just couldn't resist going over to her and saying, "How dare you write that?" And I knew perfectly well that she hadn't done it. But I laughed and so she saw the joke herself. I'm sure it was Ruskin Spear who wrote on it . . .'[47]

His teachers remained distinctly unamused, and the process of completing his diploma turned out to be rather less simple than his extraordinary talent would have suggested. There were other reasons for this, not least of which was the undercurrent of hostility that ran, barely hidden, among certain of the staff. 'One of the sadder places I know,' wrote David Sylvester in the *New Statesman* in March 1962, 'is an art school where the usual mistrust and envy between students and staff is engendered not by the students' resentment of an established order which presents a solid barrier to their fame, but by the staff's resentment that the students have more fame than *they* do.'[48] Ann Martin, a painting student in the year above Hockney, remembers Carel Weight's reaction when she showed him one of her abstract paintings for his opinion. 'If I were you,' he said with barely controlled sarcasm, 'I'd enter it for a competition. It'll probably win a prize.'[49]

More serious was Hockney's running battle with Michael Kullman over the general studies course, which required all students to attend a weekly lecture and produce a 6,000-word thesis in order to gain their diploma. Hockney considered it a complete waste of time. 'I pointed out that there is no such thing as a "dumb artist",' he recalls. 'I was always against it because I thought that if anything was going to be compulsory it should be drawing, not this stuff. I never bothered going to the lectures, not even to sign myself in. I liked Michael Kullman, who was a bit of a mad philosopher, and I got to know him. I just didn't approve of the system.'[50]

The result was that Hockney's hurriedly written thesis on Fauvism was not considered acceptable. 'Dear Hockney,' wrote the registrar on 11 April 1962, 'You will have noticed from the Results Lists which have been posted on the School's notice board that you have failed the Final Examination in General Studies which means that irrespective of the result of your professional work you will not be eligible for the award of the College Diploma at the Convocation Ceremony to be

held on 12th July.'[51] The letter went on to say that if he was prepared
to carry out additional work and be re-examined, then it would be
possible for him to gain the diploma if the new work was considered
satisfactory. Hockney, however, was cocky and confident enough
not to care, especially since he now had a dealer. 'In a way I was set
up professionally even before the diploma show,' he remembers, 'so
when they were going on about diplomas, I thought, "Well, Kasmin
isn't asking to see a diploma." I thought, "Why bother about all this
in painting of all things?" It just seemed ridiculous. I was confident
enough to just simply laugh at it.'[52] With characteristic wit and self-
assurance, his response to the whole episode was to design his own
diploma in the form of a coloured etching depicting, beneath the coat
of arms of the college, a seated Robin Darwin holding up a two-faced
Michael Kullman. The image is contained within a frame which rests
upon the backs of five tiny figures, representing Hockney and four
other failed students, bent double beneath its weight, bowing in shame.

When Hockney went home for a few days at Easter, his mother
confided to her diary, 'He looks well, but I'm not keen on his blond
hair.'[53] He gave her a cheque for £20 to buy a new sewing machine, the
first of his own money that he was able to give her, and the two of them
trailed round the Bradford shops in search of a new machine, to no
avail as she was unable to make up her mind. 'Met Mrs Todd who was
pleased to see David but not keen on the blond hair.'[54] When they got
home, he filled her in on his plans. 'I think he will do very well when
he leaves College in July,' she wrote later, '– already has made quite a
name for himself. He is to make a 3 years contract with "London Art
Dealers" who will pay him a monthly salary – but who also have first
preference to buy his pictures. He hopes to have a one-man exhibition
at Geneva, Switzerland in 6 months' time.'[55] His mother's pride was
not necessarily shared by the neighbours, however. 'I remember . . . I
was walking down the street,' Hockney recalled, 'and I overheard one
of the neighbours saying to another, "Oo, look, 'e's back again, and 'is
brothers did so well, you know." Idle Jack back from London. It's just,
I suppose, what little people are like, who live little, ordered, quiet
lives . . .'[56]

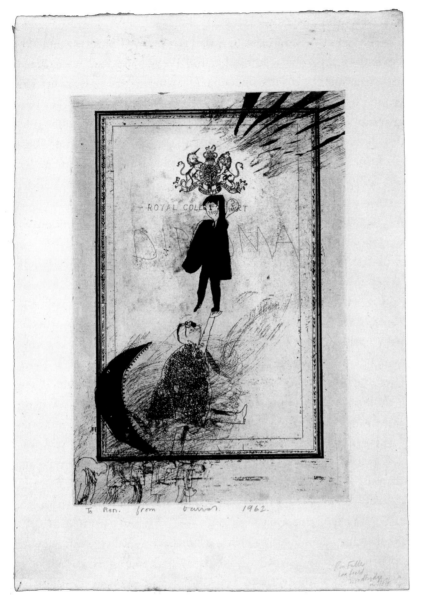

The Diploma, 1962

The diploma fiasco ended in an episode that did not reflect well on the Royal College. It was quite clear to Robin Darwin that, since Hockney was undoubtedly one of the best students they had had for decades, he should be awarded their gold medal, a rare accolade. Much to his horror, he then discovered that this was not possible for a student who had failed the general studies course, so he made it quite clear to the Examinations Board that a sub-committee should be appointed, consisting of himself, Carel Weight and Michael Kullman, to re-examine the results and come up with new ones. This they did, coming to the conclusion that, for some inexplicable reason they must have miscounted the original marks. The committee 'therefore ruled that all the results be set aside and that all the students, including David Hockney, be adjudged to have passed the examination'.[57] No one was convinced by this 'recount' story, which cast a poor light on all the participants, and rankled with Hockney for years after.

The award of the gold medal attracted wider attention for Hockney, and the fashionable men's magazine *Town* dispatched one of its star young reporters, Emma Yorke, to interview him. By now he had moved from the shed into a basement flat in Lancaster Road, Notting Hill Gate, or Rotting Hill Gate as it was then nicknamed by some. It was a tiny premises shared with a fellow painting student, Mike McLeod, that consisted of a bedroom with two beds, a small room off it containing a Baby Belling cooker and an outside toilet. They hung their socks out of the window to eliminate their smell, and at the bottom of the steps, in the well, was a small wall with soil in the top of it, which Hockney had attempted to cheer up by planting it with the plastic flowers that came free in packets of Tide washing powder.

'David Hockney is twenty-five years old,' wrote Emma Yorke, 'and has just been awarded the Gold medal at the RCA for his painting . . . His hair is an improbable buttercup yellow and his heavy spectacles give an air of ridiculous seriousness to his face – he looks in fact distinctly like the characters in his paintings which have a quality reminiscent of Dubuffet. "I have my melancholic days mind you," he said, but looks imperturbable – then a flash of pleasure comes across his face. "I wish I could dye the whole of Bond Street blond, every man, woman and child. I don't really prefer blond people but I love dyeing hair." His hair glints in the sun like a newly thatched cottage . . . This odd Harpo-Marxist swivels his rainbow body in the chair . . . "I've got to go to Cecil Gee's now to buy a gold lamé coat. I'm going to wear it when they present me with the gold medal."'[58]

In the end Hockney was proud to receive the medal, if only for the sake of his parents. 'David rang up on Friday evening,' wrote Laura in her diary on 6 July, 'to tell us he is being given a GOLD MEDAL & has a First CLASS HONOURS. He is so unconcerned – but it is a wonderful honour & he has evidently been persuaded to attend the ceremony, which previously he had no intention of doing. We are very proud of him & would like to go to London to see the ceremony & share the honours. I'm so glad David is still humble – but he has earned the prize. His only love is to paint, so far.'[59]

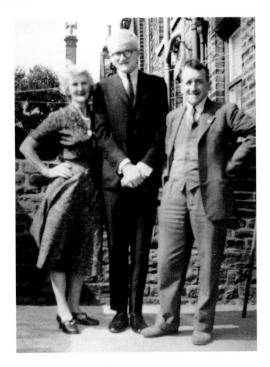

Bradford, 1962

The convocation ceremony, at which various outstanding individuals in the world of the arts had honorary awards and titles conferred upon them, took place annually in the hall of the Royal College of Music, and was attended by all the college students, as well as graduates, family and friends. It was an event that engendered some nervousness among the staff, as it was traditionally the occasion for elaborate practical jokes. 'When I was awarded my diploma,' Roddy Maude-Roxby recalls, 'I organised placards with the words APPLAUSE, LAUGHTER and SILENCE written on them, which the graduates, who were sitting behind the principal and staff on a raked platform, hid under their gowns, only to produce them at the most inappropriate moments possible.'[60] On another occasion, at a signal, the graduates all donned heavy-rimmed glasses and moustaches and imitated in unison the gestures of the principal, while perhaps the most outrageous stunt was when the Duke of Edinburgh was giving a lecture on the importance of 'Artist-engineers', and as he took his place on the rostrum, every single student and graduate released a red plastic toy helicopter which rose in unison to the ceiling.

Hockney, watched by his proud parents, shared his day with the distinguished critic and poet Sir Herbert Read, the architect of Coventry Cathedral, Sir Basil Spence, and the designer of the Mini, Alex Issigonis, all of whom were being awarded fellowships. When it came to his turn to be awarded the gold medal for work of outstanding distinction, he went up to collect it, to deafening applause, resplendent in the gold lamé jacket as well as the traditional and requisite academic gown. 'David looked fine,' wrote Laura in her diary, 'in his gold lamé jacket, and gold-banded black gown and cap – his white (gold) hair to match. The Principal in his speech said that under Hockney's eccentricities his heart was in his work, & that not only was he honoured by the College, but would he thought be one day an honour to his country. I'm glad David is humble enough not to care too much about the presentation, but realizes that his work alone will get him a place in the world.'[61] Laura also recognised that she was witnessing the end of an era and the beginning of a new one: her words were tinged with both pride and regret. 'Oh for the happy days,' she wrote, 'when we all had such fun at home together. We shall never see those days again, but the memory is a tonic.'[62]

CHAPTER FIVE

MAN IN A MUSEUM

'MARILYN MORTA' exclaimed the headlines of the daily papers prominently displayed on the newspaper vendor's stall on the promenade in Viareggio, the Italian seaside town where Hockney was staying in August 1962. He would always remember hearing the news of the blonde goddess's death in the middle of this idyllic Italian holiday. With his final term at the Royal College over, he had decided to celebrate by visiting Mark Berger and Ferrill Amacker in Florence, taking with him a new love interest, a young artist called Jeff Goodman. 'Jeff was a very handsome, attractive Jewish New Yorker,' he remembers. 'He was very American, with crew-cut hair. I didn't really think of him as a lover. We were just sexy friends.'[1] It was a carefree summer. Florence was very different from what it had been like on his last trip there in the winter, and Hockney's spirits were high. 'I had a little motorbike,' Berger recalls, 'and one evening when driving about in

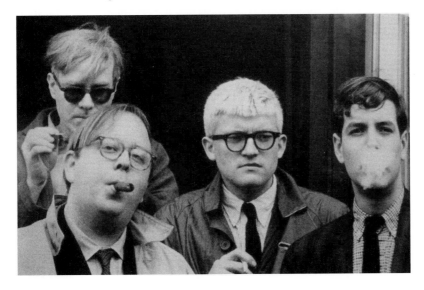

Left to right: Andy Warhol, Henry Geldzahler, David Hockney, Jeff Goodman

central Florence, after David had had a few drinks, he became very exuberant and he was sitting on the back of the motorbike shouting out "Pizza Pie" and "Anna Magnani" and all these kind of Italian phrases, and I kept saying, "Oh my God, David, they're going to beat us to death." It was his spirit and his exuberance. He just wanted to sound a little Italian.'² Amacker had an open-top car and at the end of July they decided to drive to Viareggio. There they enjoyed long tranquil days lying on the beautiful beaches.

From Italy they took a train to Munich, and then to Berlin, drawn there by reading Christopher Isherwood's *Berlin Stories*. Hockney was greatly disappointed to find that the world of the young Weimar Republic invoked by Isherwood, with its eccentric characters and sleazy nightclubs, had been largely swept away; the shadow of the Berlin Wall, erected only one year previously, hung heavily over the city. They did, however, stumble onto one of Isherwood's old haunts, the Kleist Kasino, on Kleiststrasse, a gay nightclub where men could dance together in a room that had blue-and-white-striped awnings hanging from the ceiling, maroon wallpaper, and a bar that was illuminated by two lamps supported by half-size torsos without fig leaves. The other highlights of their tour were eating at numerous *Wurststands*, and a visit to East Berlin to see the Pergamon Museum, so named because it contains the monumental reconstructed Pergamon Altar, built in the first half of the second century BC, as part of the Acropolis of Pergamon in Asia Minor. 'It was quite amazing,' Hockney recalls, 'and looked very splendid in one great big room, but just looking at East Berlin in those days made me realise that communism was a failure. Everybody looked downtrodden and there didn't seem to be a spark about anything or anybody. It was as if a dead hand had come over it.'³

When Hockney returned to London alone, Goodman having flown back to New York, it was to face the reality of his new life. His education was finally over and a career as an artist beckoned. His reputation was beginning to spread, partly because he had won the Royal College gold medal, but mostly because of relentless propaganda by Kasmin. In a letter to Hockney, the American painter Larry Rivers mentioned that 'Kasmin, your gallery dealer, came to see me in Paris and when your name came up he just happened to have 500 photos of your work in his inside pocket.'[4] By the autumn of 1962, Hockney's work had featured in at least ten group shows at many distinguished galleries, including the Walker Art Gallery in Liverpool, the ICA, the Musée d'Art Moderne and the National Museum of Art in Tokyo.

Kasmin had a deft touch when it came to organising Hockney's exhibiting life, and his Tuesday-night gatherings continued to spread the word and sell the odd painting or drawing. An early client was Grey Gowrie, who had wanted to buy a Hockney ever since he had seen *A Grand Procession of Dignitaries*, and now appointed as art buyer for Balliol, his Oxford college, with a brief to find suitable works to hang in the junior common room, was in a position to do so. Unfortunately things did not quite work out as he might have hoped. 'Balliol was then in the vanguard of political correctness,' Gowrie remembers. 'They didn't like you smoking Rothmans, for example, because of their South African connection. Their taste in art at the time was social realism and they had a rather good, though gloomy, Derek Greaves of an industrial landscape. Anyway, I went and bought for £75, which was quite a lot of money for an undergraduate college, *The Most Beautiful Boy in the World*, and it was hung in the JCR where it caused a great deal of uproar and a cup of tea was thrown at it.'[5] Nor did it end there. So much fun was poked at the painting and endless missiles directed at it that Gowrie asked Kasmin to come up and talk to the students about it. 'I had to try and explain what was going on in the picture,' he recalls, 'and put it into some kind of current context with Larry Rivers and Dubuffet, and explain that this wasn't just some kind of one-off madness or childish prank.'[6] At the end of his talk, he asked for a show of hands on whether they liked it or not and the answer was no, so he agreed to buy it back for £80.

The Most Beautiful Boy in the World was one of fifteen pictures sold by Hockney to Kasmin that year. Others included *A Grand Procession of Dignitaries*, sold for £100, *Typhoo Tea No. 4* for £50, *Swiss Landscape* for £60, *Teeth Cleaning* for £55 and *Cha Cha Cha* for £120. The total income Hockney declared to the Inland Revenue was £563 with zero profits. 'I'm sorry I can only find about £30 of bills,' Hockney wrote to his brother Paul, who was now acting as his accountant, 'but if you look at the dates of them you'll notice they only cover about 2 months (average expenditure on materials is about £20 per month). ½ my rent is 35s per week – my visit to Switzerland for inspiration for *Swiss Landscape* was £60 + trips to Bradford £8 per year. If they don't believe how much I spend on materials tell them to inquire about the high cost of canvas and stretchers and Artists quality oil paint.'[7]

As well as selling from his own front room, Kasmin also allowed Hockney's work to be shown by a few galleries who he considered to have an enlightened attitude. One of these was the Grabowski Gallery in Sloane Avenue. Mieczyslaw Grabowski had come to England with the Polish Army in 1940, and after the war opened a pharmacy in Chelsea, and a mail-order business to send medical supplies to Poland. A keen lover of art who liked to promote the work of young and unknown artists of different nationalities, according to the principle of 'art without borders', in 1959 he opened a non-profit-making gallery at 84 Sloane Avenue, next to Grabowski's Pharmacy.

Hockney was showing there in the summer of 1962 as part of a group show also featuring Derek Boshier, Allen Jones and Peter Phillips. What distinguished this particular show was that Grabowski invited each of the participants to write a personal statement for the catalogue on the theme of 'the strange possibilities of inspiration'. Hockney wrote: 'I paint what I like when I like, and where I like, with occasional nostalgic journeys. When asked to write on "the strange possibilities of inspiration" it did occur to me that my own sources of inspiration were wide – but acceptable. In fact, I am sure my own sources are classic, or even epic themes. Landscapes of foreign lands, beautiful people, love, propaganda, and major incidents (of my own life). These seem to me to be reasonably traditional.'[8] It was a philosophy he has adhered to all his working life.

One of the first things Hockney had to do on his return from Berlin was to look for a studio. In the meantime he worked out of a rented lock-up near Lancaster Road. His head was buzzing with ideas from his trip. A small drawing of a leaping leopard, for example, noted in a Berlin museum and quickly sketched from memory on his return to his hotel room, became *Picture Emphasizing Stillness*, which presents the viewer with a conundrum. Two nude men are enjoying a quiet talk close to a small semi-detached house, oblivious of a leopard, which is about to leap upon them. Just as you are getting caught up in the action, you notice a line of type between the leopard and the men which reads 'They are perfectly safe, this is a still'. The inspiration for this picture also came from some battle scenes which had caught his eye in the Tate. 'In spite of one's immediate impression,' he told Guy Brett from the *London Magazine*, 'there is of course no action in these paintings at all. Things don't actually move – the figures are and will always remain exactly where the painter put them. The same thing that struck Keats when he saw the Grecian Urn.'[9]

The Pergamon Museum provided a curious image of duality that lodged in Hockney's mind the germ of an idea that was later to develop in his joint portraits. 'I never seem to be able to go round a museum at the same pace as anybody else,' he later wrote, 'and when I went with Jeff . . . we got separated. Suddenly I caught sight of him standing next to an Egyptian sculpted figure, unconcerned about it because he was studying something on the wall. Both figures were looking the same way, and it amused me that in my first glimpse of them they looked united.'[10] He immediately consigned the image to paper with a couple of drawings, and as soon as he got back to London painted it on to canvas, titling it *Man in a Museum (or You're in the Wrong Movie)*. This was a theme he would return to and concoct into two much more elaborate pictures at the end of the year, the *Marriage* paintings.

Since it was considered de rigueur at the time for a young painter fresh out of art school to do some teaching, as well as beginning to pursue his own career, Hockney also started teaching at Maidstone School of Art. He was offered this work by the flamboyant head of the fine art department, Gerard de Rose, a portrait painter of part Russian descent who had taught at various art colleges and liked to bring fresh young talent into the school (he gave jobs, at one time or another, to Patrick Procktor, Dave Oxtoby, Michael Upton and Norman Stevens). He employed Hockney to teach etching one day a week, for which he was paid £15, and Hockney brought with him not just his talent but his work ethic, painting the word 'WORK' in large letters on the studio wall. 'I taught for one year at Maidstone,' Hockney remembers, 'then I gave it up because I would rather have been working on my own work. I didn't mind teaching once I was there, but in the end I began to resent it.'[11]

The search for a proper studio bore fruit in the autumn when Don Mason, both a fellow student at the Royal College and a resident of Kempsford Gardens, was offered his aunt's flat at 17 Powis Terrace, round the corner from Ladbroke Grove. Since he couldn't afford the five pounds a week rent, he asked Hockney whether he might like to take it on. As soon as he saw it, Hockney jumped at the opportunity. It was on the first floor of a narrow street of four- and five-storey late nineteenth-century houses, and consisted of two large rooms, a kitchen and a bathroom. For the first time in his adult life, he would be able to live and work in the same place.

Notting Hill in 1962 was a far cry from the chic place that it is today. The streets around Powis Terrace consisted mainly of slum properties, with large houses divided into bedsits, mostly for West Indians who had recently arrived in London, or for poor students. Many of these were owned by the notorious slum landlord Peter Rachman, a Pole who had come to England in 1946 and set up a property empire. 'I was amazed at the area,' remembers Kasmin, who had put up the key money for Hockney, 'because opposite where he was living were buildings owned by Peter Rachman. He used to buy properties with sitting tenants at low prices, the sitting tenants being almost always older people who had the right to live there protected by the rent act. He would then move in many large groups of young black people, prostitutes and party people, and encourage them to give parties, which would make life intolerable for the tenants. Opposite 17 Powis Terrace was a whole block of houses that he was gradually emptying out, so there was the constant sound of shrieks of laughter and gorgeous black girls coming in and out of the buildings and walking up the street in a precocious manner. It was like a constant party, with an atmosphere of a Trinidad town at night.'[12]

The street may have been noisy, but it was friendly and neighbourly, and it suited Hockney down to the ground. There were shops, including a chemist's, an off-licence, a motor repair garage, and, on the ground floor of number 17, a grocer's, run by Mrs Evans, where Hockney used to buy his tea, eggs, butter and milk. It was not unusual to see a rag-and-bone man's cart trundling down the road.

Being gregarious by nature, he found himself a lodger, a fellow Yorkshireman called John Pearson, who came from Boroughbridge, and word soon got round that Hockney now had somewhere he could entertain his friends. Charismatic and funny, Hockney made new friends easily, and among the most important of these were a number of strong women. The first great woman friend that he made in London was Anne McKechnie, an extraordinary red-haired Pre-Raphaelite beauty, who wore long corduroy skirts with hooped petticoats and had run away from her convent school at sixteen with the ambition to become an existentialist, even though she was uncertain quite what that meant. After waitressing and a stint at Harrods, she had been employed as a model by John Bratby and then Roger de Grey, through whom she first heard about Hockney.

'I was asked by Roger de Grey to pose for him at the Royal College,' she recalls. 'Nobody seemed to do any work, but the staff obviously found Hockney funny because I used to hear them saying, "Oh, let's call Hockney and see what he's got to say about so-and-so." They didn't do it to tell him off. They just found him amusing.'[13] Her boyfriend, Michael Upton, an ultra-cool and devastatingly handsome painter from the Royal Academy Schools, was sharing a flat with Hockney's friends Derek Boshier and Peter Phillips, which is how Anne met Hockney: she was instantly smitten. 'The reason I liked David was because of his sense of humour,' she says. 'I remember once seeing a mouse and jumping on the bed in my tiny little bed-sitting room, and David, instead of saying "Oh dear, was that a mouse?" just said "Was it Minnie or Mickey? You can tell by the shoes."'[14] They also shared a passion for the movies and Anne became his regular companion on outings to the cinema.

By the time Hockney moved into Powis Terrace, Anne was living with Upton down the road in Colville Square, in a row of derelict houses that had been taken over by students from the Royal Academy Schools, and were heated and lit by paraffin stoves and lamps. Because Hockney had a bit of money and a nice flat, all the friends graduated there for tea parties and evenings of beer and tittle-tattle, and 'going over to Hockney's' soon became the norm. 'As I suddenly had this big apartment,' Hockney recalls, 'it was very attractive to all my friends and the doorbell was always ringing. They knew I was always there, and they would come in and sit down and I would just carry on painting, but I would say to them, "Well, if you'd like a cup of tea, make a cup of tea and I'll have one too." That started almost as soon as I got Powis Terrace, and there was a time when I actually got rather fed up with the amount of people who came to visit.'[15]

Hockney saw order where others saw chaos, and his ability to carry on working surrounded by friends or by untidiness served him in good stead. 'When I moved into Powis Terrace,' he remembers, 'the biggest room was where I painted, and I had my little bed in the corner. At the end of the bed was a chest of drawers on which I painted a message rather carefully that said in large capital letters "GET UP AND WORK IMMEDIATELY". So the first thing I saw every morning when I woke up was the sign, and not only did I read the sign but I remembered that I had wasted two hours painting it, so I jumped out of bed.'[16] In his first few months there, he was amazingly productive. One of the early pictures he worked on, *The First Marriage*, was an elaboration of *Man in a Museum,* his first double portrait. This time he placed the couple together, in an exotic honeymoon-style setting suggested by a simple palm tree, injecting life into the stylised Egyptian figure of the woman by making her look like the man's wife 'who is a bit tired and therefore sitting down'.[17] A Gothic window in the bottom left-hand corner of the canvas was added to make an ecclesiastical connection with the title of the painting. In the more complex follow-up, *The Second Marriage,* painted on a cut-out canvas suggesting the walls of a room, the woman became more realistic, wearing a white dress and high heels, and the couple, the man in a suit and dark glasses, were placed in a stage-like domestic interior complete with curtains and wallpaper. It is a tour de

force that draws in the viewer and forces them into a meditation on the
nature of illusion and art.

A trip to the cinema in January 1963 inspired another painting
using two figures, which was even more theatrical, further developing
the canvas as a stage-like setting, complete with curtains round the
edge. The film was Roger Corman's comedy horror *The Raven*, based
on a story by Edgar Allan Poe, in which two magicians, Dr Erasmus
Craven and Dr Adolphus Bedlo, battle for supremacy, and culminating
in a scene where Dr Craven, played by Vincent Price, uses his hands
like a hypnotist and causes green electric bolts to fly between his
fingertips and Peter Lorre's. The resulting picture, *The Hypnotist*,
shows an evil-looking practitioner casting his spell upon an innocent-
looking boy who, in his long red robe, has the appearance of a young
priest. The model for the hypnotist was Mark Berger. 'I had just arrived
in England,' he recalls, 'and decided to go and visit David. As I walked
in he said, "Quickly Mark, come here and just stand and hold your
hands out in front of you like that." I stood there for hours, and it looks
exactly like me.'[18] An etching made at a later date also taught Hockney
a useful lesson. 'I drew the etching plate,' he wrote, 'with the figures
in the same positions as in the painting, but of course when it was
printed it was reversed. Seeing both pictures together made me realize
that even pictures are read from left to right.'[19]

His inventiveness knew no bounds, though he was quick to
acknowledge his debt to other work. Kasmin had been badgering him to
paint his portrait, but not till he saw *Apollo Killing Cyclops* by the Italian
baroque artist Domenichino in the National Gallery did Hockney
figure out how he could do it. It portrays an elderly man seated on
a chair, his cat at his feet, in front of a tapestry depicting a dramatic
episode from Greek mythology. The floor space between the bottom
of the tapestry and the edge of the canvas is shallow, just enough for the
cat to sit on and to create a *trompe l'oeil* effect whereby you can imagine
the old man getting up and walking out of the picture. No such luck
for Kasmin in *Play Within a Play*, which depicts him standing in front
of a tapestry of Hockney's own invention, yet trapped behind a sheet
of glass. David's thinking was, 'Well, he's been pressing me to do his

portrait. I'll put him in and I'll press him.'[20] The glass was real and to depict the effect of Kasmin's face, hands and clothes pressed against the back of it, David added another level of unreality with painted marks on the front of the glass. 'I must admit,' he wrote later, 'I think of it as one of the more complex and successful pictures of that period.'[21]

Bradford seemed a long way away now to David, and his parents were seeing little of him, something they both took for granted. Laura wrote him weekly letters, though she didn't always get a reply, but he was usually home for Christmas. 'David arrived about 8pm,' she wrote in her diary on 21 December 1962. 'He has made 10 special etchings of Rumplestiltskin [sic] – his version – not to sell, but as gifts, which makes them more valuable. We received the No 1 copy, Paul and Jean no. 2 and so on to others. I have bought a very nice telephone list for David . . .'[22] After Christmas he returned to London, and the unusually harsh winter of 1962–63 in which the temperature often sank to minus sixteen degrees, and in Earls Court there were reports of milkmen doing their rounds on skis. There was no central heating in Powis Terrace, which relied solely on the warmth from two coal fires.

As well as painting, Hockney was all the while still working on *A Rake's Progress*, printing all the proofs himself at the Royal College, since it was now commissioned for their Lion and Unicorn Press, and the colossal workload began to affect his health. 'I got ill because I was anaemic and not eating enough,' he remembers. 'I was living on tins of cold baked beans.'[23] Things came to a head one evening when he failed to turn up to meet Kasmin at a private view at the Rowan Gallery in Lowndes Street, Belgravia. Kasmin then telephoned Powis Terrace and got Hockney's doctor on the line, Patrick Woodcock, a charming homosexual and socialite who relished the arts and numbered John Gielgud and Noël Coward among his patients. Woodcock insisted that Kasmin come round straight away because Hockney was complaining of pains in his right arm, and wanted to make a will in case he was having a heart attack. When Kasmin arrived at Powis Terrace, Dr Woodcock assured him that Hockney was no more than just severely run down. 'He wanted to talk to me,' Kasmin remembers, 'so I went in to see him, and I said, "David, it seems you are feeling quite ill and your right arm hurts. I think it's worth considering that you've probably been masturbating a lot and that it's possible you've got a pain in your arm from overdoing it." "Oh, do you really think that?" he asked. "Well, it's possible," I replied, "and I think it might help if you got dressed and we went out to dinner." So I took him out to a Chinese restaurant and I said I thought it would be a good idea if we got him off the diet of bean curd and that kind of thing, so I suggested that we would eat a lot of vegetables, but that he should try one thing from the animal world. He said, "Well, I don't know about that." I said that it could help cure his anaemia. "I'll tell you what," I said, "we will go gently into it, and we'll just share a small dish of prawns." So I got him to eat the prawns, and he discovered that he quite liked them.'[24] It was the end of Hockney's vegetarianism.

Life in Powis Terrace, though often chaotic, and not helped by Hockney's lack of skills in running a house, was beginning to inspire his work. 'I started painting the domestic scenes,' he recalls, 'because I realised I was having a more domestic life, which is something that I needed.' Since he had also started painting figures again, he felt that doing something from life would fit nicely into this pattern, but there is a touching naivety and disconnection in these paintings, scarcely surprising considering the lack of experience that he so far had in living with anyone.

In *Domestic Scene, Notting Hill*, the first of these pictures, he used as models two regular visitors to Powis Terrace, Mo McDermott, now working part-time as his assistant, and his friend Ossie Clark, who was studying fashion under Professor Janey Ironside at the RCA Fashion Design School. The painting is striking in that the interior is brought to life without walls or a floor, but just through the few objects that happened to catch the artist's eye. The truth, as Hockney explained, is that if you enter a room in which somebody is standing naked, you certainly don't notice the wallpaper. 'When you walk into a room you don't notice everything at once and, depending on your taste, there is a descending order in which you observe things. I assume alcoholics notice the booze first, or claustrophobics the height of the ceiling, and so on. Consequently I deliberately ignored the walls, and I didn't paint the floor or anything I considered wasn't important.'[25] Domestic though the scene is, it is not a cosy domesticity, the figures, one naked, Mo, and one clothed, Ossie, being curiously alien to one another.

He followed this up with another domestic fantasy combining his love of America with his deepest erotic desires. Painted long before he went to California, *Domestic Scene, Los Angeles* was taken from a photograph he had seen in *Physique Pictorial*, which he had been collecting since he was first introduced to it by Mark Berger. Though the magazine, published in Los Angeles by Bob Mizer of the Athletic Model Guild, was aimed at homosexual men, it had to be careful not to openly proclaim its market, so the resulting images, usually of virile young men pretending to be engaged in everyday domestic activities such as vacuuming, showering and washing-up, have a coyness that amused Hockney no end. 'I painted *Domestic Scene, Los Angeles*,' he later wrote, 'from a photograph in *Physique Pictorial* where there's a boy with a little apron tied round his waist scrubbing the back of another boy in a rather dingy American room; I thought, that's what a domestic scene must be like there.'[26] When he finally got to LA, he found much to his delight that his picture was quite close to life.

The shower in *Domestic Scene, Los Angeles* was painted from life. Hockney had longed for a shower of his own ever since his first trip to New York and had one installed as soon as he moved into Powis Terrace. Almost immediately he began to include it in his pictures, and did various experiments using Mo as a model, drawing and painting both through the shower curtain and without it. 'The great thing about showers,' he says, 'is that you can see the body. The body is more visible in a shower, so it's more interesting to watch somebody have a shower rather than take a bath, and that was the appeal, and of course the technical thing of painting water has always interested me, the whole subject of transparency. A lot of the paintings I was doing at that time, like the painting of Kasmin, *Play Within a Play*, were all about making pictures.'[27]

*

Ken and Laura heard nothing from Hockney till April when she recorded, 'At last we have a letter from David who is still busy – says he may be up after Easter for a few days – but is using the College whilst students are on vacation for working on his etchings.' A few days later Hockney telephoned and invited his father to come down to London for the annual Aldermaston march. Laura decided this was the perfect opportunity to see her son and check out his living conditions. 'We discussed my going with Ken on Thursday and staying with David,' she noted. 'He has two beds, but I wrote to ask if it was convenient. He told us Anthony Armstrong-Jones, Princess Margaret's husband, is going to photograph him for the Times on Wednesday.'[28]

In fact, Laura meant the *Sunday Times*, and this photo shoot and subsequent article was to prove one of the turning points in Hockney's career, bringing him to the attention of a huge new audience. On 4 February 1962 the *Sunday Times* had launched its magazine, the first ever colour supplement to accompany an English newspaper and the brainchild of Roy Thomson, the Canadian owner, who had seen such supplements work successfully in North America. It was a colossal gamble, but the paper's editor, Denis Hamilton, knew exactly what was wanted, 'a magazine that would have little interest for anyone over forty. I had watched the build-up of brilliant new graphic design – the outpourings of art schools in the late forties and fifties. No newspaper was storming away in this field and I wanted the magazine to do so.'[29]

To bring reality to his vision, Hamilton appointed as editor a talented thirty-year-old, Mark Boxer, who even as a Cambridge student had developed a reputation 'for being bright and gifted in an undefined way, with a suggestion of . . . naughtiness'[30] and who recently had been editing the ultra-stylish *Queen* magazine. 'I felt he had the necessary kind of iconoclastic attitude,' Hamilton wrote in his memoirs, 'a chap I'd have to restrain rather than ginger up.'[31] Boxer caused controversy almost immediately by appointing Armstrong-Jones as photographic and design adviser. Despite the rows that followed over whether or not it was right for a member of the royal family to work for a newspaper, it turned out to be an inspired choice, for not only was he a brilliant photographer, but he was brimming with ideas.

Thomson was distinctly underwhelmed by the magazine's first issue. He 'came up to Watford', Hamilton recalled, 'specially to see the first copies off the machines, and was appalled . . . "This is a disaster, we'll be a laughing stock." I said, "It doesn't really matter, people will look at it because of its novelty. It's what's coming ahead that matters."'[32] Hamilton was right. The first six months were a disaster, with the magazine having to put up with losses running as high as £20,000 a week, together with the almost total derision of Fleet Street. One commentator, however, absolutely got the point. 'Though most of the people I talked to did not like it much . . .' wrote Francis Williams in the *New Statesman*, 'those under 25 liked it a good deal more. "You're all much too stuffy," exclaimed one young woman. "It's fun and it's new. It's interesting and it makes me want to look inside."'[33] Luckily Thomson was determined to stick with it, having a cast-iron certainty that it would get better and better with each issue. His gamble paid off and after a year, with its profits and circulation finally rising, the *Sunday Times* had the pleasurable experience of watching the rest of Fleet Street falling over themselves to imitate it.

By the time Hockney appeared in it, the magazine was hitting its stride, introducing millions of people each week to a glossy world of youth and style, art and culture, and creating celebrities out of pop singers, hairdressers, photographers, fashion designers, writers and artists. The *Sunday Times* article for which Snowdon photographed him was 'British Painting Now' by the art critic David Sylvester, which appeared in the 2 June edition, and in which he appeared alongside established artists like William Coldstream and Francis Bacon, and the up-and-coming school such as Harold Cohen and Frank Auerbach. While expressing his view that 'David Hockney . . . is usually less effective in his large paintings than in his graphic work, where he is working on the scale of illustration', Sylvester also described him as being 'as bright and stylish a Pop artist as there is',[34] a label Hockney did not take kindly to, having once astonished visitors to a private view of one of his shows by shouting out loud, 'I am not a pop painter!' In the accompanying photographs he was pictured wearing his gold lamé jacket. 'I regret buying that bloody gold coat,' he later wrote. 'For I think people thought I had worn it every day. In actual fact I only ever wore it twice. I wore it for that Gold Medal and my mother thought it was an official coat. And I wore it for some photographs Snowdon took.'[35]

Two days after the photo shoot, his mother got her first look at Powis Terrace, taking a taxi to carry Kenneth's Aldermaston paraphernalia after arriving at St Pancras just after five in the morning. 'Cost 10/3d,' wrote Laura. 'Ken had so much baggage and banners. David had tea and toast in a jiffy & wasn't it welcome! He went back to bed at 6.00am – I washed up and generally cleaned up the kitchen which is very nice and modern. As soon as I thought the world was up, I vacuumed my room – a gorgeous room with such possibilities – but dowdy and in need of much attention – a divan bed <u>but no sheets</u>.'[36] Over the next two days, while Hockney was working on his etchings at the Royal College, and Ken was busy getting everything ready for the march, Laura passed her time shopping for sheets at Pontings and sightseeing – she walked through Hyde Park, explored Portobello Road, and spent a frustrating time failing to find a Methodist chapel. Then on Saturday night 'about 11.15pm door bell rang & there was Kenneth – looking very tired and worried. His rucksack and contents – also large banners – had been stolen – value nearly £20 from behind a tent where he had foolishly left them unattended.'[37]

After this unfortunate event things began to look up. While Hockney and Kenneth went off marching, on Easter Sunday Laura spent her time in the local Salvation Army chapel, and went to a service at Methodist Central Hall in Westminster. On Monday she visited the Houses of Parliament and took a trip up the Thames before making her way to Hyde Park in time to see the CND marchers arrive at Marble Arch. Before they returned home on Tuesday night, Hockney gave each of his parents a special treat. For Laura it was lunch at the Vega ('I enjoyed that very much!!' she noted in her diary), while for Ken this was followed by a trip to the pictures, to see *The Best of Cinerama* at the Casino Cinerama cinema in Soho.

Laura mentions Hockney's work several times: he was almost finished with *A Rake's Progress*. After his parents had left, however, he felt that he had to make one more trip to New York in order to successfully complete the series. In return for one edition of the completed work, Kasmin paid for the voyage, and at the end of April, Hockney set off on the *Queen Elizabeth*, one of the two transatlantic liners of Cunard's White Star Line. On arrival in New York, he went to stay with Jeff Goodman and spent time looking around for ideas. He made two more etchings at the Pratt Institute: number 7, titled *Disintegration*, in which the dissolution of the Rake is presented graphically through his depiction as a limbless bust; and 7A, in which the bust is then *Cast Aside*, to be devoured by a dragon. With these the series was finally complete.

One afternoon, Hockney and Goodman went down to look at a show on East 74th Street at the Stable Gallery, the name of which derived from its original location in a former livery stable on West 58th Street, a place where on damp days the smell of horse urine was said still to linger. It was owned by the New York art dealer Eleanor Ward, who had nurtured the careers of many abstract expressionists and had employed Robert Rauschenberg as a janitor before eventually giving him his own show. In November 1962, she had given Andy Warhol his first New York exhibition of pop art, which included paintings of Marilyn Monroe, Campbell's soup cans, Coke cans and dollar bills. On the day Hockney visited, Warhol happened to be in the gallery and they were introduced. Warhol immediately invited him and Goodman to come that evening to his Upper East Side house on Lexington Avenue.

They arrived at Warhol's brownstone to find three other people there: the actor Dennis Hopper, who had appeared with James Dean in both *Rebel Without a Cause* and *Giant,* his wife, Brooke Hayward, and Henry Geldzahler, the newly appointed assistant curator of twentieth-century art at the Metropolitan Museum of Art, and a good friend of Warhol's. 'Dennis wanted to buy one of Andy's *Mona Lisa* paintings,' Hockney remembers. 'He invited us to come the next day and watch him shooting a television series he was working on.'[38] As soon as Hopper had left, Hockney mentioned to Warhol that he'd just seen a still of Hopper outside a downtown cinema, so they all piled into a cab and went down to 42nd Street to see him in *Night Tide*, directed by Curtis Harrington. Then the following day they took up Hopper's invitation and went up to Harlem to watch him filming an episode of *Naked City*, a popular detective series then playing on TV, which always ended with the line, 'There are eight million stories in the Naked City. This has been one of them.'

This twenty-four-hour episode, immortalised in a famous photograph taken on the set, marked Hockney's first meeting with a man who was to become one of the key figures in his life. Born in Antwerp in 1935, Henry Geldzahler came from a family of European Jews who emigrated to the United States in 1940. He attended Yale University and, on graduation in 1960, joined the staff of the Met. Quick-witted, extremely funny and gay, he was a fountain of knowledge. 'Oh, you know so much,' Andy Warhol once said to him. 'Teach me a fact a day, and then I'll be as smart as you.'[39] Barely able to sit still – he was later to be diagnosed with attention deficit hyperactivity disorder – he hit it off with Hockney right away. 'Henry and I got on instantly,' Hockney remembers. 'First of all he liked the fact that I'd remembered seeing Dennis Hopper in the film still. We then realised we shared a love of music, opera in particular, which I had started to go to a bit, upstairs at Covent Garden, and there was painting of course, and we became friends very quickly. He was very, very funny, very clever, and we had the same kind of taste. I thought we had a similar way of looking at life.'[40]

On his return to London at the end of May 1963, Hockney was introduced to someone who was to further transform his life. Paul Cornwall-Jones was a young architect two years down from Cambridge who with a fellow undergraduate, Michael Deakin, had hit upon a clever way of making money: commissioning topographical prints of their colleges, Emmanuel and Jesus, from the artist Julian Trevelyan and selling them to the staff and students. This venture had been successful enough for them to form a company, Alecto Editions, named after one of the mythical Furies. Cornwall-Jones's big coup was persuading John Piper to do a print for the quattrocentenary of Westminster School; the success suggested the potentially huge audience for an artist with a big name. His lodger, Mark Glazebrook, was a friend of Kasmin's, and told him about David Hockney, and *A Rake's Progress*.

'He thought Hockney was terrific,' Cornwall-Jones remembers, 'and took me round to Powis Terrace to meet him. He was very young and very open and I immediately liked him. As for the work, I thought it was fascinating.'[41] What he saw was the complete set of sixteen images, all stuck up on the wall of the studio. He was intrigued by the fact that the prints were not made from a set of finished drawings that were then copied onto plates – the only drawings that existed were a few studies made on scraps of paper – but were drawn directly on to the plates, Hockney developing the image as he went along. Cornwall-Jones was hugely impressed by the work, and decided to take a gamble: he made an offer for fifty sets of *A Rake's Progress* at £100 each, making the then staggering sum of £5,000.

'. . . they were paying me a hundred pounds each for a set of sixteen prints,' wrote Hockney, 'and they were going to print them. They sold the sets for two hundred and fifty pounds each, and I didn't dare tell people the price because it was so outrageous I was ashamed of it; I thought etchings should cost two or three pounds each; two hundred and fifty pounds – madness!'[42] The typographer Eric Ayers introduced Cornwall-Jones to an elderly jobbing printer who worked in Bushey, on the outskirts of London, and printed the fifty sets over the next few months. It always amused Hockney that when he offered the old man, who had done the job so beautifully, a complimentary edition, he turned it down because he said he didn't like them. 'Every time I went to see him,' he wrote, 'to see how they were going on, he would show me a little etching of a churchyard or something, and he would say, "Can't you do anything like this?" And I would say, "Well one day I'll be able to do something like that."'[43]

Under the terms of Hockney's contract, the money for *A Rake's Progress*, which was to be paid over three years, went through Kasmin, who now had his own gallery in partnership with Sheridan Dufferin. He had operated out of Ifield Road for a year before he began to consider looking for a premises, a step which had become necessary to establish himself and avoid being eclipsed by the other young dealer making his name on the gallery scene, Robert Fraser. Fraser was a 25-year-old ex-army officer and Old Etonian with a remarkable eye for art, who had recently, with the backing of his father, a successful City banker, opened a gallery in Duke Street. His opening exhibition, the first show in England of paintings by Jean Dubuffet, had caused quite a stir, and subsequent shows, which included work by Egon Kalinowski, Richard Lindner, Eduardo Paolozzi, Harold Stevenson and Francis Bacon, had proved to be influential. 'The gallery made an extraordinary impression from the beginning,' commented Bryan Robertson, the director of the Whitechapel Gallery, 'because of its obvious sophistication and style . . . It felt serious. And the kind of work that one saw there, pretty well all the time, was of a very high order.'[44]

Kasmin understood how difficult it would be to find the perfect site, and he was not prepared to accept second best. The British artists he was primarily interested in, like Hockney, Richard Smith, Bernard Cohen, Robin Denny and Anthony Caro, all worked on a scale that was large by London standards, as did the Americans he sought to represent, who included Kenneth Noland, Morris Louis, Frank Stella and Jules Olitski. He needed somewhere bold, where their work would not look out of place and which took them out of the English drawing room. On the site of the old Walker Galleries at 118 New Bond Street, behind a small shopfront, which had already been let, he found what he had been looking for: a series of nineteenth-century galleries with cornices, skylights and a large room, which had infinite possibilities. '. . . the main room was a peach of a space,' he recalled, 'and the gallery was going to be one big room in which you could see everything by turning round.'[45]

The architect Kasmin employed was Richard Burton of ABK, step-son of John Russell, the art critic of the *Sunday Times*, to whom Kasmin wrote: 'I want to show artists no one else wants to here because they are either too difficult, too enormous in picture scale, too expensive (some of the Americans) but are still doing great things; and I want to make new collectors of the young rich and . . . aristocracy who have been neglected too long.'[46]

The finished space was like a temple, with sophisticated fluorescent lighting designed to boost and balance the daylight, which came from

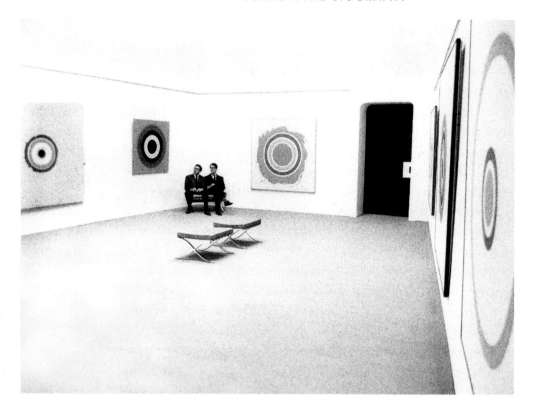

John Kasmin and
Lord Dufferin in the
Kasmin Gallery

a lantern in the roof, electrically operated louvred blinds, and state-of-the-art flooring, a kind of hard-wearing rubbery linoleum, made by Pirelli. (Annoyingly for Kasmin, large numbers of people turned up to look at the floor rather than the pictures.) The Kasmin Gallery opened on 17 April 1963 with a show of concentric circle paintings by Kenneth Noland, Kasmin's favourite artist. It was a glittering evening during which the art world rubbed shoulders with the worlds of society and the aristocracy, and was followed by a party given by Claus von Bülow in Belgrave Square. 'First show over,' Kasmin wrote to the American art critic Clement Greenberg, 'and trying to assess the effect here – great attendance and discussion; generally vapid reviews . . . the world of painters and students very excited and keen; the general public mostly discussed the beauty of the gallery and its lighting – concrete results are a couple of sales and the Tate discussing a possible purchase . . . Nevertheless it was my idea of a success.'[47]

In August, passing through London en route to Paris, a trip that Hockney was taking them on as a treat, Ken and Laura got their first view of both the gallery and Kasmin. 'We went to Bond Street,' wrote Laura on 16 August, 'where J. Kasmin, Hockney's agent, has his gallery. Not very large – but wonderfully modern – with engine-manoeuvred lattice ceiling blinds which commanded light and sunshine in any part of the room . . . White walls and black beams were very striking – also two pictures? in entire black for £500. Mr Kasmin is a small energetic person – full of vitality – he suggested we had an evening playing "Poker" – which David evidently does (I hope not often). One wonders!'

Hockney's gambling habits were not the only thing on Laura's mind that day. A few months earlier, the satirical magazine *Private Eye*, which, launched in 1961 by Peter Cook and Nicholas Luard, had brought back into public life a strain of public insult and personal vilification not seen in England since the eighteenth century, had run a full-page spoof newspaper story titled 'How to Spot a Possible Homo', under the byline Lionel Crane. 'The Admiralty, the Foreign Office and MI5 don't seem to know,' ran the headline, 'so the *Sunday Mirror* offers them some useful advice.' There had then followed a mixture of cartoons and photographs depicting various scenarios, such as . . . 'The man in the bar who drinks alone and is forever looking at other customers over the top of his glass'; 'the middle-aged man unmarried who has an unnaturally strong affection for his mother'; 'the man who is adored by older women' (this one accompanied by a photo of the prime minister, Harold Macmillan); and 'the Obvious those who dye their hair, touch up their lips and walk with a gay little wiggle'.[48]

The scenario titled 'The Toucher – the man who is always putting his hand on another man's shoulder or arm' was accompanied by a photograph of Hockney with his hand resting on the shoulder of the figure modelled by Mo in *Life Painting for a Diploma*. Hockney's brother John saw the piece and mentioned something about it to Laura, before getting cold feet about telling her the content. She was determined to find out, however, so she had asked Paul if he knew what it was about. 'John . . . tantalizingly refused to unfold,' she wrote on 12 August.

'Paul told me — but he did not believe it was true — I can't think so either. So I commend my boy to God and leave it to Him.'[49]

An agreement existed between Hockney and Kasmin that he should have his first one-man exhibition at the new gallery as soon as he had enough paintings completed, and his next trip abroad provided the final picture for the show. One morning Hockney received a call from Mark Boxer at the *Sunday Times*. The previous autumn, Boxer had commissioned some drawings for a piece on colonial governors; his new idea was a series in which well-known artists visited and drew places that had a special meaning for them: would Hockney be interested in going back to Bradford? When Hockney heard that Philip Sutton was being sent to Tahiti and Jan Haworth to California, his response was that he'd only just escaped from Bradford, which was far too J. B. Priestley, and he'd rather go somewhere more exotic. Instead he suggested the furthest place away he could think of and said, 'I'll go to Honolulu; I'll draw the view from the top of the Honolulu Hilton.'[50] Boxer consulted his art critic, David Sylvester, who reminded him of the interest Hockney had shown as a student in Egyptian art; the following day, he called back to suggest it, an idea Hockney accepted eagerly. Travelling alone, Hockney left London on 26 September, wearing a white suit, a white cap and sporting a polka-dot bow tie.

Hockney's initial experience of Egypt was of five-star luxury in Cairo, having been accommodated by the *Sunday Times* in the first Hilton to open in the Middle East. He couldn't wait to draw the view from his window, and the resulting image, *View from the Nile Hilton*, precisely captures the snatched excited glance out of the window that is the first thing any tourist does on being shown their room. It has a lightly sketched palm tree and the outlines of four figures in djellabas crossing the street, but the central image, which dominates the picture and roots the viewer in the country that the artist was so longing to see, is a greatly exaggerated Egyptian flag billowing in the wind, inviting the tourist to leave the international confines of the hotel and come down and explore.

Over the next three weeks Hockney did just that, and the set of beautiful coloured crayon drawings with which he returned to England show him at his skilful and inventive best. This was the first time since his student days at Bradford that he had drawn consistently from life over a long period, and the drawings cover many subjects on his travels from Cairo to Alexandria and finally to Luxor. Among them are an apartment in an eighteenth-century house in Cairo belonging to Mr Milo, a Russian, who gave tours to selected groups, and which was full of 'wonderful spaces and marvellous objects' and where the tranquil sound of a courtyard fountain was omnipresent; two Arab boys walking down a street in Luxor, one wearing a green-striped djellaba, the other sketched in pencil, with his left hand resting on his companion's shoulder; a book of matches with 'These Matches Belong to David Hockney' written on it in Arabic script; a number of objects in the Cairo Museum; and a Shell garage in Luxor, an image made particularly striking by the larger-than-life head of President Nasser painted on the wall next to the Shell sign.

'It was a marvellous three weeks,' Hockney remembers. 'I didn't take a camera, only drawing paper, so I drew everywhere and everything, the Pyramids, modern Egypt, it was terrific. I was very turned on by the place, and on your own you do a lot more work. I carried all my drawings everywhere and a lot of equipment, and I would get up very early in the morning. I loved the cafe life. Egyptians are very easy-going people, very humorous and pleasant, and I liked them very much. It was a great adventure.'[51]

The drawings were due to run in the 24 November edition of the *Sunday Times* magazine, but a world-shattering event intervened. 'President Kennedy has been assassinated,' wrote Laura in her diary on 22 November. 'Died in hospital 25 mins later. Came thro on TV at 7.10 this evening . . . The world feels cold with shock. One can sense the feeling of horror everywhere even to the far ends of the earth.'[52] At the *Sunday Times*, the magazine and twenty-eight pages of the paper had already gone to print, but the editor, Denis Hamilton, was decisive. 'These would all have to be cancelled,' he wrote, 'and the paper torn to pieces and remade if the *Sunday Times* was to give the event the coverage it felt it deserved.'[53] Out went Hockney's drawings of Egypt and in came an album of Kennedy family photographs that Mark Boxer had been saving for a rainy day.

By this time, however, Hockney was too excited to be upset about the story being dropped. He had decided to use the money from Alecto to make a long trip to the land of his dreams: California. He also had two upcoming exhibitions to think about – his first one-man show at the Kasmin Gallery, and a simultaneous showing of *A Rake's Progress* at the Print Centre in Holland Street, Kensington – and he was working hard to finish his last picture, a six-foot-square oil inspired by his visit to the Pyramids at Giza, called *Great Pyramid at Giza with Broken Head*. In it a man in a green striped djellaba stands beside a broken monumental head lying beside a palm tree in front of one of the Great Pyramids. Hockney had decided that all the paintings in his show should have figures in them, thus distinguishing him from the purely abstract painters that made up the rest of Kasmin's stable, and giving him the title of the exhibition, *Paintings with People in*.

Kasmin gave Hockney complete control when it came to organising his show, his only involvement being to put him together with Gordon House, a painter who was also one of the best graphic designers in England, and who had designed all the catalogues for the Marlborough Gallery. Together they designed both the catalogue for the show and the invitation to the private view. Kasmin also made sure that the press got wind of what was going on. 'David is in the news this week,' Laura noted in her diary on 1 December. 'A whole page in this month's *Studio* and his exhibitions are announced in the *Sunday Times*. Also next Sunday "The Critics" on the Home Service discuss his Exhibition. David has not yet let us know if and when we can go.' Two days later she was bemoaning the fact that he was increasingly difficult to get hold of. 'About 7pm we rang his flat, but again there was no reply – Why?!! Well!! When we turned round there he was on "BBC Tonight" programme speaking to Kenneth Allsop who was questioning him about his pictures – some oil paintings and 6 of his Rakes Progress engravings were compared with Hogarth. It was very thrilling to see him there. It makes me choke with a queer mixture of pride & humility that he is our boy. God bless him – may he make good & do good with his success.'[54]

Paintings with People in opened on 6 December. There were ten paintings on show, all the works he had completed since leaving the Royal College, including *The Hypnotist, Domestic Scene, Notting Hill, Two Men in a Shower, Great Pyramid at Giza with Broken Head* and *Play Within a Play,* as well as many drawings. The paintings were priced between £250 and £400, which Kasmin regarded as 'a reasonable price rather than a high-fashion price. We also wanted them to go to the right places, people that we liked and who really liked them and weren't playing games. The fact was that Hockney's work sold briskly from the word go and we could always have asked more.'[55] Anticipating a large crowd at the private view, Kasmin had persuaded the newspaper vendor from whom he regularly bought his *Evening Standard*, who had a stand on the corner of Bond Street and Grosvenor Street, to come and be the commissionaire on the front door. 'The evening was a wonderful mixture of art people, gay people and society people,' Kasmin remembers, 'and the show was a big success. There were people, of course, who thought it was thin and over-praised, Francis Bacon for one. He thought Hockney was overrated, though I think he was also rather peeved at the amount of attention he was getting.'[56]

Among the guests was the director of the Bradford City Art Gallery, Peter Bird, who wrote to Kasmin on 9 December, 'I think there is a possibility of our being able to acquire something for the gallery here, and I mentioned this to David Hockney when I last saw him in Bradford.'[57]

The reviews for the show were mixed. Edwin Mullins, writing in the *Sunday Telegraph*, considered it 'a considerable achievement: to be able to use figurative imagery today in a manner that is neither a painstaking alternative to the photograph nor the excuse for some striking patterns of light and movement. But to use them in fact as dramatic material. Bacon has done it, but very few others besides.'[58] John Russell said the show 'had given foreign visitors something to bite on when they ask what is happening in British art',[59] while Hugh Gordon Porteous, in the *Listener*, wrote that when he had worked all the 'perilous adolescent stuff out of his system, Hockney . . . promises to develop into that kind of artist – and here we may think of the imperfections of Blake as well as of the rare perfections of Hogarth or

Goya – who is indeed a rather special kind of man'.[60] Neville Wallis, writing in the *Spectator*, took a more measured view. 'The importance of being Hockney,' he wrote, 'is not to be ignored at this moment when the reputation of the golden youth from the Royal College is ballooning . . .' but, he continued, 'in his large and lightly brushed paintings at the Kasmin Gallery . . . his natural sense of the bizarre can degenerate into frivolous exhibitionism . . . Oriental tags and shreds of what-nots are all pressed into the service of this self-consciously naive imagery. It exhibits a magpie alertness. But overshadowed by Bacon's dreadful power and the intense subjectivity of Larry Rivers and Kitaj, their attitudinizing junior is cut down to his size.' On the other hand, he continued, 'his darty, needly drawing is another matter',[61] and to a man the critics all raved about *A Rake's Progress*, showing simultaneously at the Print Centre.

Much to the annoyance of his father, who had been looking forward to spending a long weekend in London, Hockney did not invite his parents to the private view, but fixed up instead for them to make a day trip to see the show on 10 December, an arrangement that Ken took 'very badly'.[62] 'David met us at Kings Cross,' wrote Laura, 'where first we had coffee. Then went to the Kasmin Gallery. I was pleasantly surprised with the exhibition and had David to interpret what I did not understand.'[63] After lunch at a vegetarian restaurant in Kensington, he took them to look at the prints. 'My parents didn't really comment on my pictures,' says Hockney. 'As far as my mother was concerned, if they were by me then she liked them. That's what mothers do. I don't think they were that interested in pictures and I don't think they would have known the good ones from the bad ones.'[64]

Among the many members of London's artistic elite who attended the show was Hockney's early patron, Cecil Beaton. '. . . on to crowded David Hockney exhibition,' he wrote in his diary on 11 December. 'He is undoubtedly an original, and his engravings for *Rake's Progress* are beautiful. This Bradford boy with the yellow glasses, yellow dyed hair and exaggerated north-country accent was accosted at vernissage by an irate lady. In a loud voice she challenged him for drawing his nude women in such a distorted manner. "Can you really imagine that is the way the arm comes out of the socket? Look at their bosoms – they're nowhere near where they should be. Have you ever seen a naked woman?" "A dorn't knogh ars ah harve!"[65]

Before leaving for America, he went home for Christmas. 'David had brought gifts for everyone,' wrote Laura, 'but said Dad's & mine would follow later. However he could not contain himself & said we may as well have them – but they would not be in effect till January 8/64. I think he was as thrilled to give as we were to receive a cheque for £50 each. It is wonderful & I am so glad he is giving us some of the benefit of his good fortune.'[66] Three days later he left Bradford on the 7 a.m. train to London on the first leg of what was to be a great adventure. '. . .a thought for David,' mused Laura, 'a thankfulness that his work which is also his pleasure has brought him success & thankful that he has shared his financial gains in all our lovely gifts. Only I pray will he keep good & use his gifts for the world's good.'[67]

On 30 December, Hockney left London for New York, secure in the knowledge that he had enough money to allow him to spend a year in America. The Kasmin show had also been a sell-out, netting him a couple of hundred pounds. 'I knew I had a star on my hands straight away,' Kasmin recalls, 'though David did not have a big head. He was neither a boaster nor did he expect things. He took it all with great ease and grace. It didn't go to his head. It's not as if he stayed at home and lapped it all up. Instead he went off to work in a foreign city where he wasn't known at all, where he wasn't treated as a star, and where he didn't know the ropes.'[68]

CHAPTER SIX

A HOLLYWOOD COLLECTION

In the autumn of 1963, Hockney had begun an affair with Ossie Clark, Mo McDermott's friend from Manchester, that was to have huge significance in his life. Extrovert and charismatic, Clark exuded confidence. He was just into his second year and starting to blossom under the tutelage of the brilliant Professor Janey Ironside, head of fashion design at the Royal College of Art. Clark had been a precocious stylist even back in Manchester, which in those days was provincial compared to London. 'He wore flares he'd made himself and 13-inch winklepickers, a trilby hat and a long black ex-army coat; his hair was dyed black, meticulously cut short in the fashion of the day, remembers Jane Normanton, a fellow student at the time, who recalls thinking, "Wow, you can do that in London, but not here! He was determined to go places."'[1]

Though he was quite openly gay, Clark was in a relationship with Celia Birtwell, who had followed McDermott down from Manchester and was working as a waitress in the Hades coffee bar. Theirs was a friendship which, stimulated by a shared interest in fashion and design, as well as by a certain physical attraction, had drifted into an affair, and they were living together in Notting Hill, in a tiny flat above a bicycle shop on Westbourne Grove. When Clark met Hockney, however, the combination of his sexuality, charm and seeming innocence, not to mention his star being in the ascendant, was too much, and Clark was immediately seduced.

'Taken up seriously by DH,' Clark noted in his diary for 1963. 'He was giddy, effeminate, mad and exaggerated,' Hockney recalls, 'and I liked the personality immediately. He didn't have a northern accent

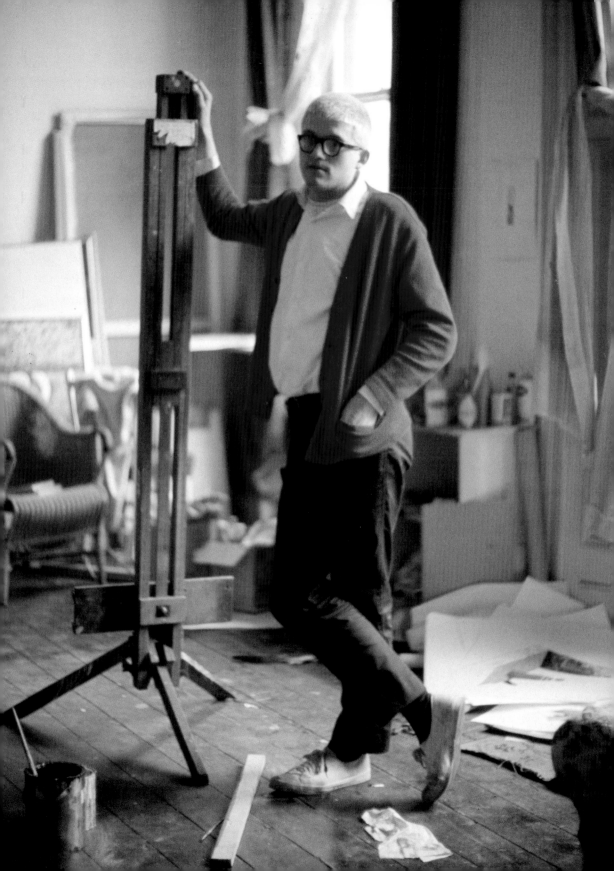

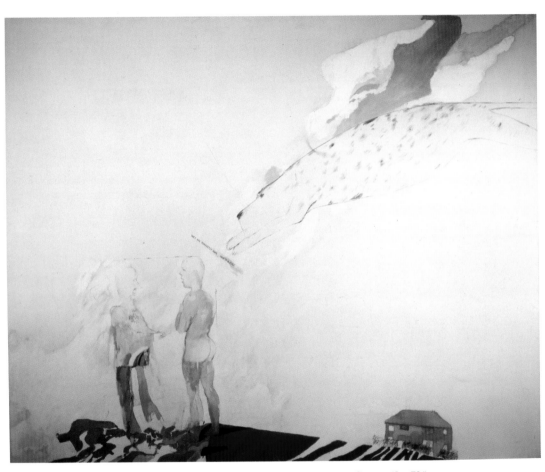

Picture Emphasizing Stillness, **1962**. Oil and Letraset on Canvas, 62 × 72″

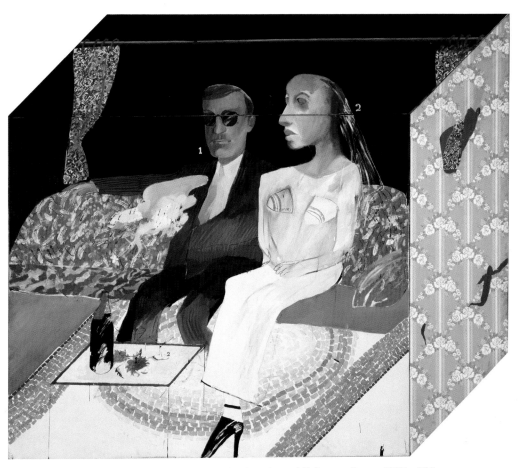

The Second Marriage, **1963**. Oil, Gouache and Collage on Canvas, 77 ¾ × 90″

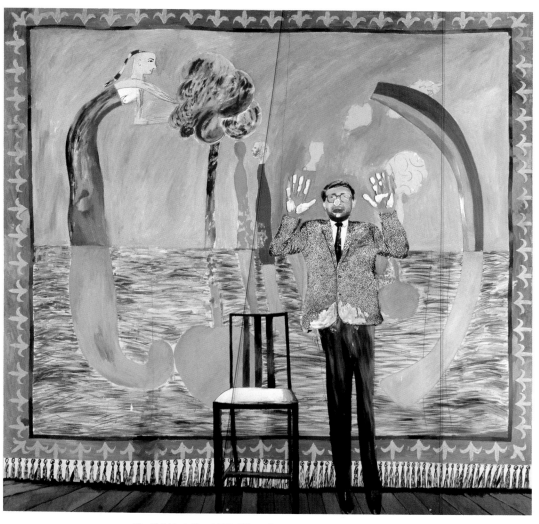

Play Within A Play, **1963**. Oil on Canvas and Plexiglass, 72 × 78″

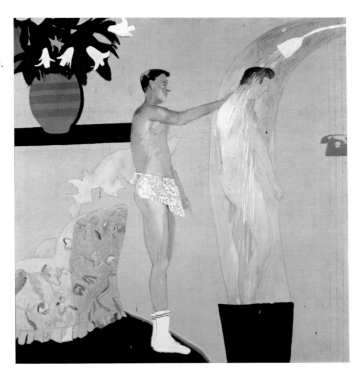

Domestic Scene,
Los Angeles, 1963.
Oil on Canvas,
60 × 60″

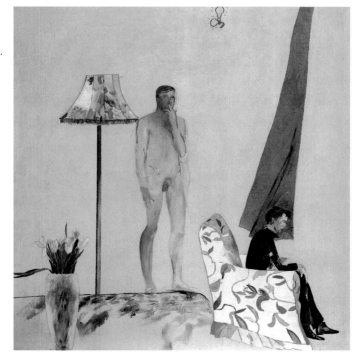

Domestic Scene,
Notting Hill, 1963.
Oil on Canvas,
72 × 72″

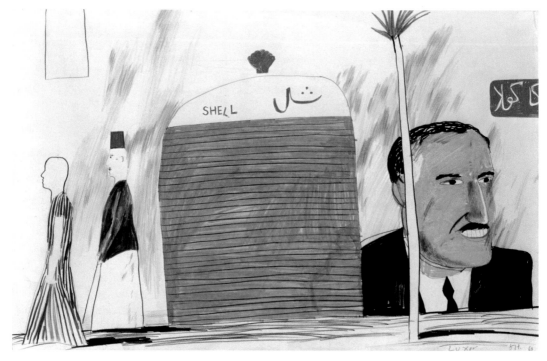

Shell Garage, Luxor, 1963. Colored Crayon, 12 ¼ x 19 ¼″

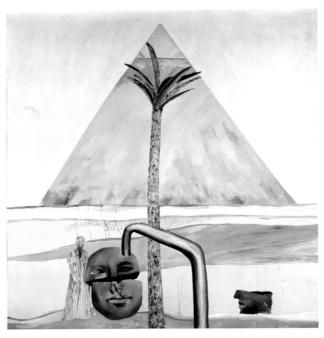

Great Pyramid at Giza with Broken Head From Thebes, 1963. Oil on Canvas, 72 x 72″

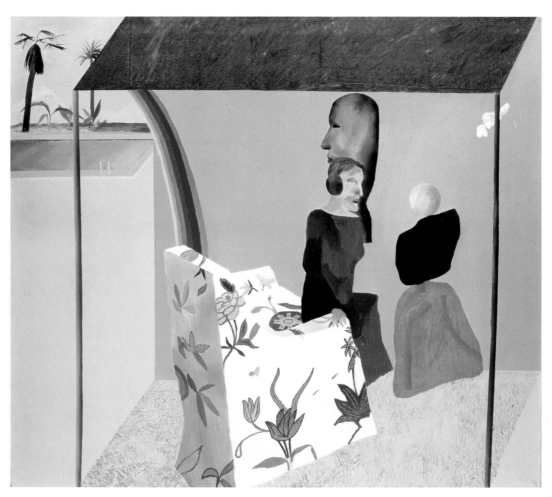

California Art Collector, 1964. Acrylic on Canvas, 60 × 72″

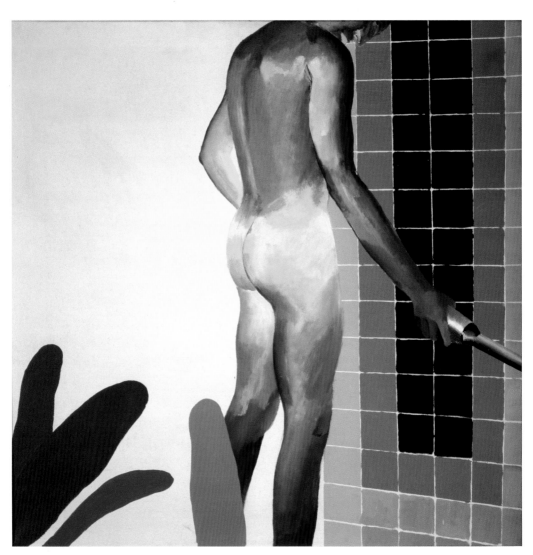

Boy About to Take a Shower, 1964-69. Acrylic on Canvas, 36 x 36"

because he'd taken elocution lessons.' They were young, free from their parents, ambitious and keen to try out new experiences. 'Mo used to organise sexy evenings at Powis Terrace. We enjoyed playing around, we enjoyed sex. When it came to sex and drugs and rock 'n' roll, everybody was at it, though I was never into rock 'n' roll. Sex and drugs certainly. It was a potent combination.'[2]

When Hockney embarked on the longed-for US trip at the end of December, flying first to New York, Clark agreed that he would visit during the college holidays. Hockney stayed with Mark Berger and visited the Pratt Institute where he completed and sold two etchings, *Edward Lear* and *Jungle Boy*, the latter, which portrays a very hairy man under a palm tree staring at a large snake, being inspired by Mark who was extremely hirsute and kept snakes as pets. These earned him a princely sum, $2,000, good pocket money for his trip to LA. He also visited the New York dealer Charles Alan, who had seen Hockney's work at the Kasmin Gallery, and was keen to give him a show at his gallery on Madison Avenue. It was agreed that Hockney would exhibit pictures from his California trip in the autumn.

As they discussed the next stage of the trip, Alan discovered how limited Hockney's knowledge of Los Angeles was. In fact, he was so worried when he found out that not only did Hockney not know a soul in LA, but that he couldn't drive either, that he tried to persuade him to go to San Francisco instead. But Hockney was adamant he was going to LA. Part of its glamorous appeal was sex, or the perceived availability of it, not just the perfect bodies he had yearned after through the pages of *Physique Pictorial*, but the sleazy, homoerotic side as portrayed in John Rechy's *City of Night*, his novel of hustlers in New York, Los Angeles and New Orleans. It is easy to understand from the vivid LA section how exciting it must have made the city seem to a relatively innocent young man eager to widen his experiences. 'This is clip street, hustle street – frenzied-nightactivity street: the moving back and forth against the walls; smoking, peering anxiously to spot the bulls before they spot you; the rushing in and out of Wally's and Harry's: long crowded malehustling bars.'[3]

As Hockney was leaving the gallery, Alan said, 'But if you don't drive, how on earth are you going to get into the city?' When Hockney replied, 'I'll just catch a bus,' Alan realised how clueless he was about the place, with its hundreds of square miles of suburbs, and contacted one of his artists, an LA-based sculptor called Oliver Andrews, to ask if he would meet Hockney at the airport.

Approaching Los Angeles airport Hockney became more and more excited. 'I remember flying in on an afternoon, and as we flew in over Los Angeles I looked down to see blue swimming pools all over, and I realised that a swimming pool in England would have been a luxury, whereas here they are not, because of the climate. Because you can use it all the year round, even cheap apartment blocks have pools.'[4] Oliver Andrews was waiting for him in his Ford pickup truck, and drove him to the Tumble Inn, a small motel at the bottom of Santa Monica Canyon. 'David immediately sent a telegram back to Charles Alan,' Andrews later wrote, 'telling him he had safely arrived, and said "Venice California more beautiful than Venice Italy."'[5]

Hockney was even more thrilled arriving in LA than he had been on his first trip to New York. 'I was so excited,' he wrote. 'I think it was partly a sexual fascination and attraction . . . I checked into this motel and walked on the beach and I was looking for the town; couldn't see it. And I saw some lights and I thought, that must be it. I walked two miles and when I got there all it was was a big gas station, so brightly lit I'd thought it was the city. So I walked back and thought, what am I going to do?'[6] The solution came to him in a flash – a bicycle – so when Andrews came round the next day to check on him, they went off to a cycle store.

Since the only knowledge Hockney had of Los Angeles was derived from *City of Night*, he decided to visit Pershing Square to try and experience first hand the sleazy, sexy, hot nightlife so evocatively described by Rechy, the world of 'the nervous fugitives from Times Square, Market Street SF, the French Quarter – masculine hustlers looking for lonely fruits to score from . . . the scattered junkies, the small-time pushers, the queens, the sad panhandlers, the lonely exiled nymphs haunting the entrance to the men's head, the fruits with the hungry eyes and jingling coins; the tough teenage chicks – "dittybops" – making it with the lost hustlers . . . all amid the incongruous piped music and the flowers-twin fountains gushing rainbow colored: the world of Lonely America squeezed into Pershing Square . . .'[7] Checking on a map, Hockney saw that Wilshire Boulevard ran from close to the Tumble Inn, ending a few blocks from Pershing Square, so he jumped on his new bike. There were two things, however, he had failed to take into account. The first was the distance, which was nearly seventeen miles, and the second was the fact that the real Pershing Square might be different from that described in the novel.

'I started cycling,' he later wrote. 'I got to Pershing Square and it was deserted; about nine in the evening, just got dark, not a soul there. I thought, where is everybody? I had a glass of beer and thought, it's going to take me an hour or more to get back; so I just cycled back and I thought, this just won't do, this bicycle is useless.'[8] When Oliver came round the following morning, religiously keeping up his promise to keep an eye on Alan's protégé, he was lost for words when Hockney told him he had cycled to Pershing Square. Nobody *ever* went to downtown LA, he told him, and suggested to Hockney that they should go out and buy him a car. The fact that he couldn't drive would not be a barrier, he promised, as he would give him some lessons. As for the licence, obtaining one in California was easy.

Over the next few days Oliver gave Hockney some instruction in his pickup truck, before taking him off to get a licence. This procedure consisted of filling in a form and answering a simple written test, with questions like 'What is the speed limit in California?' whose multiple-choice answers required little more than common sense to answer correctly. In the driving test, when they asked him where his car was, he pointed to the truck. The instructor, who by now thought he was quite mad, drove around with him for an hour or so, failed him on four points, but awarded him a provisional licence anyway. 'How easily I got it terrified me actually,' he recalls. 'I thought, "So this is all they do here to get one?" I mean, in England they deliberately fail a lot of people. In the end I just thought, "Well, that's the kind of place it is."'[9] With plenty of money in his pocket, Oliver then took him to buy a

car, and for $1,000 dollars Hockney became the owner of a white Ford
Falcon with a bright red stripe down the sides.

He now set out to practise on the local roads, heeding Oliver's
one piece of advice, which was 'Avoid the freeways'. Needless to say,
on his second day behind the wheel he found himself on a freeway by
mistake, an experience that both thrilled and frightened him. 'Once I
got on,' he remembers, 'I didn't know how to get off it, so I just kept
going, and the sign said San Bernadino, and then Las Vegas, another
250 miles, and I thought I might as well just drive through the desert.
It would be good practice and it would give me confidence. So I drove
to Las Vegas. I even went to the casino there and won some money,
about $80, on my first trip to a casino.' Travelling back on the old
road through the desert, he passed through the Mojave Desert city of
Barstow, and when he stopped for gas they gave him canvas bags full of
water in case the car overheated. 'Of course I loved all that,' he recalls.
'I felt it was like the Sahara I was crossing.'[10]

Finding a studio and somewhere to live in LA was not difficult
in those days. Taking the advice of Oliver Andrews and of Bill Brice,
another artist Charles Alan introduced him to, he just drove around
looking at 'For Rent' signs, and soon found rooms for $90 a month in
a Santa Monica apartment house which looked like the superstructure
of a 1930s ocean liner, as well as a studio on Main Street in Venice,
overlooking the ocean, for $80. Within spitting distance he also
discovered a small shop that sold some imported foods, including
Marmite and his favourite cereal, Weetabix. When he asked for bloater
paste, however, he was told they did not import it since it was not
considered fit for human consumption. 'Within a week of arriving . . .
in this strange big city, not knowing a soul,' he noted, 'I'd passed the
driving test, bought a car, driven to Las Vegas and won some money,
got myself a studio, started painting all in a week. And I thought: it's
just how I imagined it would be.'[11]

One day a week, usually on a Monday, he would take out his car and
cruise the big wide boulevards of LA, just to look at what was around
him. He was endlessly thrilled by what he saw and took inspiration from
everything – palm trees, banks, squares and avenues, office blocks, not

to mention the weird and wonderful variety of domestic architecture, the Spanish haciendas, the mock-Tudor villas, the castellated mansions, the Swiss chalets, all sitting alongside futuristic buildings like John Lautner's Garcia House on Mulholland Drive, or his Chemosphere on Torreyson. 'Los Angeles is the only place in the world,' he says, 'where the buildings actually make you smile when you drive around.'[12]

'There were no paintings of Los Angeles,' he told Melvyn Bragg, in an interview in the *Listener* in 1975. 'People then didn't even know what it looked like. And when I was there they were still finishing some of the big freeways. I remember seeing, within the first week, a ramp of a freeway going up into the air, and at first it looked like a ruin and I suddenly thought, "My God, this place needs its Piranesi; Los Angeles could have a Piranesi, so here I am!"'[13] So, rather than his own ideas or things he'd seen in a book, Hockney began to paint the things he saw around him.

The first picture Hockney painted in Los Angeles, *Plastic Trees Plus City Hall*, shows a large palm tree in front of a cloudy sky with the City Hall skyscraper in the background. It was also the first painting in which he successfully used acrylic paint. This was a medium he had tried once before, back in London, but had abandoned because the textures and colours of the paints he could get hold of were not very good. Finding only American equipment in an LA art store, however, he discovered that their acrylic paints were vastly superior and started to use them. 'It was what a lot of the American artists were using,' he remembers. 'It is different from oil paint because it dries very quickly, and you have to paint in certain ways with it.'[14] Other characteristics of acrylic, such as its regular consistency, allowing it to be applied thinly while retaining its full brilliance of colour, go a long way to explaining the changes in Hockney's painting style during this period. His paintings became flatter and much more about image and colour than about texture. 'When you use simple and bold colours,' he later wrote, 'acrylic is a fine medium; the colours are very intense and they stay intense . . .'[15]

Until arriving in LA, Hockney had been quite ignorant about the existence of a Californian art scene. Yet he had happened on a golden age in LA, a period when art was all about art and artists, not institutions and money.

There was a thriving scene based in and around La Cienega Boulevard, where Felix Landau, given the title of the 'Tastemaker of La Cienega' by the *LA Times*, had opened his gallery in 1951 to show established greats like Rico Lebrun and Jack Zajac; his was the first Los Angeles gallery to show Francis Bacon. Landau eschewed pop art, leaving that to galleries such as the Rolf Nelson, and the Ferus, the latter where Irving Blum had given Andy Warhol his first solo exhibition, and his first exhibition of the Soup Cans, and among whose leading representatives were Billy Al Bengston, Ed Kienholz and Larry Bell, the self-styled 'Studs' who would saunter into Barney's Beanery, a bar at the top of the street, as if they were members of some Hell's Angels gang.

The Beanery was the premier LA art-world hangout, as much for the fact that Barney was willing to carry a tab as for its prime location so close to all the galleries. It was dimly lit, the drinks were cheap, the bartenders friendly, and it adjoined an inexpensive diner where artists could afford to eat. It became so popular that in 1965 Ed Kienholz turned it into a work of art, a tableau called *The Beanery*, which, when you looked into it, gave you the odour of beer, and the sound of clinking glasses and bar-room chatter from an audiotape.

La Cienega Boulevard was also the scene of an LA cultural imperative: the Monday Night Art Walk. This was a tradition that had begun in 1961 when two dealers decided to hold simultaneous openings in the hope of attracting bigger crowds. Other galleries soon joined them, until it became a regular occurrence. 'Monday night on La Cienega,' wrote the correspondent for *Time* magazine in July 1963, 'is quite possibly not only the best free show in town but also one of the most popular institutions in Los Angeles County . . . Last week the 22 exhibitions ran the gamut of modernism, from a show of Arp and Henry Moore sculpture at the distinguished Felix Landau Gallery to paintings by pop artist Billy Al Bengston at the Ferus Gallery.'[16] There was op art at the Feingarten Gallery, kinetic art at the Esther Robles Gallery, and if it was the weird and wonderful you were after then you needed to go no further than Cecil Hedrick and Jerry Jerome's Ceeje Gallery, which showed the work of the renegades and mavericks.

'On a Monday I would go to La Cienega,' Hockney recalls, 'and I would walk up and down and I would tell them I was a young artist from England, and like that I got to know artists quickly.'

He soon added Ed Ruscha, one of Irving Blum's young stars, to his list of new friends. Another friendship he struck up at this time was with Christopher Isherwood, the writer whose *Berlin Stories* had so intrigued him, and to whom the poet Stephen Spender had given him an introduction. Isherwood had emigrated to the United States at the outbreak of the Second World War, where he had lived happily in California, first with the photographer Bill Caskey, and latterly with the artist Don Bachardy. Bachardy was thirty years younger than Isherwood and had such youthful looks that when they set up home together in 1953, when Bachardy was eighteen, the rumour went round that Isherwood had taken up with a twelve-year-old. In many ways the success of their relationship lay in the father-and-son aspect of it, and Isherwood actively encouraged Bachardy to go to art school to study painting seriously, and was immensely proud when he became successful.

Hockney had found out that the house in which Isherwood lived, 145 Adelaide Drive, was just up the hill from the Tumble Inn. 'Stephen Spender had bought etchings off me in 1961,' Hockney remembers, 'and he certainly had written to Christopher Isherwood, because he knew that I was coming to LA. So I phoned him up and he simply invited me over for dinner.'[17] Bachardy was away so Isherwood, slightly panicked at the idea of having to entertain a complete stranger on his own, rang his close friend Jack Larson, a screenwriter, librettist and actor, and asked him and his lover, the writer and director Jim Bridges, to come over and join them. 'David arrived on a bicycle,' Larson remembers, 'with this portfolio of drawings from *A Rake's Progress*. The work was extraordinary and unlike anything I'd ever seen, and I could see immediately how talented he was. Frank O'Hara used to take me around places and explain in a lucid and dynamic way why Jackson Pollock was extraordinary, or why Kline was extraordinary and it

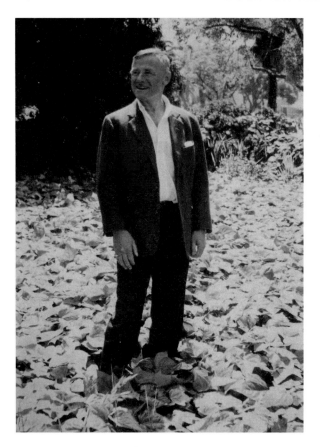

Christopher
Isherwood

turned out that he was almost right about everything, whether it was poetry and literature or painting. I learned from him to look at something and trust my judgement, and right away I saw that these drawings of the *Rake's Progress* were real, and that David was the real thing, original and interesting. They looked like something that could have been on the wall of a pharaoh.'[18]

Isherwood hit it off with Hockney straight away, initially for the simple reason that he fell in love with the way he spoke. 'Chris called me up,' Bachardy remembers, 'and told me that he'd met this quite extraordinary young Englishman with bleached blond hair and glasses with a wonderful Yorkshire accent that he fell for immediately because it was the same accent that he would have had if he hadn't been sent off to public school.'[19] Isherwood had been born at Wyberslegh Hall, on the borders of Cheshire and Greater Manchester, where he spent much of his childhood, before being sent off to prep school in Surrey, and then to Repton in Derbyshire. Even after years of living in America, he still had strong feelings of nostalgia for his childhood: meeting Hockney brought back a whiff of home.

A week later, Bachardy also met and immediately liked Hockney. 'He was so easy to get to know,' he recalls, 'and he and Chris had already established a friendship. And I saw straight away that he was inner-directed. He was a young man with a purpose.'[20] Initially a little in awe of Isherwood, Hockney soon relaxed around him and found common ground in their love of reading and literature: it was the beginning of what was to be one of the key friendships of his life. As Isherwood was to tell him later on, 'Oh David, we've so much in common: we love California, we love American boys, and we're from the North of England.'[21]

Scarcely had Hockney settled into his new life than Kasmin arrived from London, another Los Angeles virgin, now looking to his young client to show him the ropes. 'David had found me a room in a place which he thought was very swanky called "Gene Autry's Hotel Continental",' Kasmin remembers. 'It was on Sunset, very close to Schwab's Coffee House, where girls used to go for coffee and hope to be picked up by casting directors. David lived in a rented room in Santa Monica, and he decided he would come and share the room with me. To his amazement I had no idea who Gene Autry was, and so it seemed to him a waste that I should be staying there.'[22] One thing about the hotel that puzzled Hockney was the fact that the elevators were always filled with serious-looking men in dark suits, a mystery solved when they discovered that the hotel was the business headquarters for the local branch of the Mafia. Any qualms Hockney may have had about the discovery of this piece of information were, however, made up for by the swimming pool on the roof, where he spent many happy hours tanning himself.

Ever since he had arrived in LA, Hockney had been planning to pay a visit to the offices of AMG, the Athletic Model Guild, the publisher of *Physique Pictorial.* He was intrigued by the fact that though many of the storylines were set indoors, in a bathroom for example, there was often the strong shadow of a palm tree across the bath, suggesting that the pictures were in fact shot outside. He both wanted to see where this happened and buy some of the photographs, so he took Kasmin to the studios, which were on downtown 11th Street in a house which the founder of the AMG, a photographer called Bob Mizer, shared with his mother. The city jail, situated close by, provided quite a few of the models for the magazine, in the way of drunken sailors and similar types who were in the can overnight, while the rest were usually young men who were killing time while searching for the Hollywood Dream. It was their way of earning a quick ten bucks.

'We went down to a suburban backstreet,' Kasmin remembers, 'to an innocent-looking house in nowhere-land, and pressed a bell on a door in a sort of privet hedge, and we were let in. David told them he'd come from England and that he was an admirer of the magazine. We found ourselves in a perfectly ordinary house, which had a lean-to in the back garden near a pool.'[23]

Surrounding the 'tacky' swimming pool were a series of Hollywood ancient-Greek plaster statues, and the lean-to constituted the studio where they would create the shower, bathroom or living room which they needed for their shoots. There were notices everywhere warning people not to touch anything, because Mizer knew that as soon as they weren't being watched, the models would steal everything and run off. 'The studio only had two walls,' Kasmin recalls, 'so they could move the camera around, and this was where his idea of paradise was created, where the boys stood taking their showers. We both thought it was hilarious and were amazed at the roughness of it all, and the fact that you could make glossy dreams out of such shabby bits of plywood, while they were astonished at the idea of anyone wanting to come to their offices.'[24] Mizer's answer to anyone who criticised the quality of the sets was to say, 'Remember we are AMG, not MGM.'[25]

The photographs which Hockney bought on that first visit to AMG were the inspiration for a series of voyeuristic paintings featuring showers, the first of which was *Boy About to Take a Shower*, based on a shot of a fourteen-year-old boy, Earl Deane, which had appeared in the April 1961 issue. Standing in a shower cubicle, he is handling the spray with water cascading down his back. The painting omits both his head, which is visible in the photograph, and the water, while emphasising the shower head and the lines of his naked body, creating an overtly sexual image. The shower paintings which followed this, *Man in Shower in Beverly Hills* and *Man Taking Shower*, both made much use of the water. 'Americans take showers all the time,' Hockney says. 'I knew that from experience and physique magazines . . . Beverly Hills houses seemed full of showers of all shapes and sizes – with clear glass doors, with frosted glass doors, with transparent curtains, with semi-transparent curtains . . . The idea of painting moving water in a very slow and careful manner was, and still is, very appealing to me.'[26]

When Hockney returned to London at the end of the year and was asked by Richard Hamilton to give a lecture at the ICA, he chose the subject of gay imagery in America, basing his talk around *Physique Pictorial*. With enormous glee he regaled his audience with his account of visiting the AMG studio, showing slides from the magazine alongside clips from soft-porn movies with titles like *Leave My Ball Alone*, in which a Greek statue comes to life and indulges in a bout of nude wrestling with a young boy who has stolen his ball. While delivering a thought-provoking lecture, he also had the audience in stitches with his witty and mischievous comments on the contrived scenarios.

The gay scene in LA may still have been underground, but to Hockney it certainly seemed more accessible. 'Nowadays people are used to an organised gay scene,' he says, 'but in those days things were very different, and it was only here that I found a scene that did not exist elsewhere. I suppose I was like a child in a sweet shop. The California beach was like heaven. The boys are very good-looking and they look after their bodies.'[27] He admits to having been thoroughly promiscuous for the first and only time in his life. 'I used to go to the bars in Los Angeles and pick up somebody. Half the time they didn't turn you on, or you didn't turn them on, or something like that. And the way people in Los Angeles went on about numbers!'[28] One drawing from this period, *Two Figures by Bed with Cushions*, brilliantly evokes the urgency of such sexual liaisons, showing two men apparently hurriedly undressing in preparation for an encounter of which, after it was over, as Hockney later recalled, the only memory would be the appearance of the bed. Kasmin, a somewhat unwilling companion on these trips to gay bars, often had to be protected from unwanted attention by Hockney saying that he was his date and dragging him onto the dance floor. 'Neither of us were very great dancers,' he recalls, 'and Californians are all so big. On one occasion David took me to a bar, and they refused to give me a beer because I didn't have my passport on me and they thought I was underage. I was David's dealer aged twenty-eight, and David said, "Oh, don't worry! Just give my young friend a glass of milk. He'll be quite happy.'"[29]

The true reason that Kasmin had come to LA was to further spread the word about Hockney among serious collectors. Meeting people was never a difficulty for Hockney, because they almost always loved him as soon as they met him. He was open and funny and, particularly to the Americans, he was exotic. They loved his clothes and his accent. Likewise, he thought Americans were hilarious, as well as being thrilled to meet actors he had admired since he was a boy, such as Vincent Price, who invited him and Kasmin for a drink at his home, where he had a library built into a disused swimming pool and served them cocktails from a coffin-shaped cabinet.

Most important were collectors such as Betty Asher, the daughter of a wealthy pharmacist, who had been collecting contemporary art since the late fifties and owned important works by Rauschenberg, Warhol, Ruscha and Lichtenstein; and Betty Freeman, who had trained as a concert pianist and who collected abstract expressionist paintings and was a patron to many composers. It was Jack Larson who introduced them to Betty Freeman. 'He told me he'd got this new friend,' Kasmin recalls, 'who was *avant-garde*. "The stuff on her lawn looks like grass," he said, "but it's more like watercress."'[30]

California Art Collector, which was based on these and other meetings, was the second painting completed by Hockney in LA, and included domestic imagery common to the type of collector he had visited. Since all the houses had big comfortable armchairs, the collector, a woman, is seated in one, on a big fluffy carpet, admiring a sculpture by the Scottish artist Bill Turnbull, then sculptor of choice to the nouveau riche. A striped painting, possibly by Morris Louis, hangs on a pink wall; there is a primitive stone head, while outside there are palm trees, a view of the Santa Monica Mountains – and, most significantly of all, a swimming pool, the first to appear in Hockney's paintings.

*

Though Hockney had begun *Man in Shower in Beverly Hills* in Santa Monica, it was actually completed in Iowa City, where, in the summer of 1964, he was offered a six-week job teaching at the University of Iowa, in the heart of the Midwest. The invitation came from Byron Burford, the dean of the university art department, and a painter himself. Never having experienced the American interior, Hockney accepted the post eagerly, and a salary of $1,500. He took the painting off its stretcher, rolled it up, put it in the boot of his car and, deciding to go via Chicago, set off on Route 66. 'I drove through Arizona, New Mexico, Kansas, Missouri and Illinois,' he remembers, 'picking up hitchhikers all the way. The freeway wasn't done, so I took the old road. I drove on my own and I stayed in Chicago for five days and looked at the big museums and things, and then drove west to Iowa City.'[31] All the while he was nervous about what was in store on his first major teaching post, not just because of what was expected of him, but because of his appearance. Somehow he didn't feel he looked serious enough. Somewhere en route, he happened to pass an optician's with a pair of heavy round horn-rimmed spectacles in the window, which he decided were just what was needed to give him a more professorial look. He ditched his National Health spectacles, and wearing his new 'owl' pair, he drove confidently into Iowa City, and straight through it from one end to the other, in the mistaken belief that he was just passing through its suburbs.

Iowa was a real culture shock for Hockney. He found it stiflingly dull. The landscape was boring and flat, with mile after mile of identical houses stretching into the distant skyline, and the only occasional excitement was to be found in the form of huge electrical storms and massive fast-moving cloud formations. The faculty was very conservative, and when he took his first drawing class he was shocked to find that most of those attending were doing so not out of a desire to learn to draw, but because they got paid more money as a teacher if they were known to have attended this particular class. 'There were three nuns in the class,' he remembers, 'and I thought that maybe they were in it for the drawing, but no, it was the same thing. They wanted to get money from teaching.'[32]

One advantage of the lack of a social life in this small city – there was one bar he liked, but it was as much a bohemian hangout as a gay bar – was that Hockney devoted almost all his spare time to painting. He completed *Man in Shower in Beverly Hills*, and four other pictures, *The Actor*, *Arizona*, *Cubist Boy with Colourful Tree* and *Iowa*, a landscape, depicting farm buildings beneath a dramatic cloudscape, to remind him of a place he had little intention of returning to. His routine was to paint at night, and then go swimming in the local pools, which didn't close till two in the morning. '. . . perhaps it was three or four till I got to bed,' he told Cecil Beaton, 'so I couldn't get up at eight o'clock, so I'd go in at ten thirty and stay till one, but no one seemed to care.' Because none of the students could paint a sphere, he set his class to paint a door. 'They all got canvases the size of a door and painted as realistically as possible, and we had an exhibition of all the doors down a corridor. It looked nice.'[33] When Patrick Procktor came to teach in Iowa the following year, Hockney recalls, 'he found out that they didn't consider me as having been too respectable. He was much more willing to spend evenings with the art history faculty after hours. I didn't really care. I think Patrick was a little more polite than me, and he did tell me later that they wouldn't employ me there again.'[34]

When the six weeks were over, Hockney had the paintings all shipped to Charles Alan's gallery in New York, and set off to meet Ossie Clark in Chicago, the plan being that they would drive together to New Orleans. It turned out to be the beginning of an epic road trip. Clark had won a competition for shoe design and had used the £150 prize money to fly first to New York, where, on a night out on the tiles, he had met Brian Epstein, the manager of the Beatles. 'Introduced to Eppie in a gay bar . . .' he wrote in his diary. '. . . going down in a lift with BE.' When Clark told him he was heading west to meet Hockney, Epstein had given him a note which he had promised would get them access to the Beatles' upcoming concert at the Hollywood Bowl in LA. Later that evening, Clark was refused a beer at PJ Clarke's, as the barman thought he was underage. '"What's a beer please?" (I'D AVOID EYE CONTACT.) "Alright, you've caught me out, I'll have milk,"' and someone took a dislike to his long hair. '"Fucking long-haired faggot! Listen buddy, this is a tough town and if I were you I'd leave.'"[35]

He flew to Chicago to meet Hockney, who was under the impression they were heading for New Orleans. 'No, we're going to California to see the Beatles,' said Clark. 'I realised,' Hockney remembers, 'that as Ossie couldn't drive, I would be doing all the driving, and it's a very long way, about two thousand miles. I remember saying to him, "Well, we'll have to drive long, long hours, so can you keep me entertained?" In those days you couldn't pick up that much music on the radio. It was mostly apple pie recipes and things like that so I asked him to make up gossip, anything to keep me awake, which he did for the most part, though there was one moment driving through Nevada when I fell asleep and we ran off the road. Well, we got there and then I found out that he didn't have tickets, just this note, and I thought, "This is the Hollywood Bowl. Will we get in?"' Epstein's note worked: they did get in, and saw the Beatles in style. 'We were sitting in the front row, and it was terrific.'[36]

Derek Boshier was living in San Francisco at the time, and after the show, Hockney called him and asked if he would like to join the trip, to which Boshier readily agreed. While they waited for him to arrive, Hockney showed Clark the sights. 'Disneyland,' Clark noted in his diary; 'mistaken for a Beatle on a trip to the moon to escape the excitement of the Beatles at the Hollywood Bowl. Bette Davis in the flesh; Mrs Dennis Hopper; Beach Boys, Surf City; art hype; The Tumble Inn Motel, Santa Monica; Hard Days Night – 6 no 1 hits, The Beatles.'[37]

Three days later, the trio set off, their first stop being the Grand Canyon, where Hockney did a tiny drawing in a notebook, *Ossie and Derek in Grand Canyon*, which he gave to Boshier. In 1964, the US counterculture hadn't spread much beyond the big cities, so both Clark and Hockney had to put up with ridicule throughout the 1,300-mile drive, particularly in the more redneck areas. This was especially true of Clark. 'I remember that wherever we went,' says Hockney, 'whenever we sat down in a restaurant, everyone thought Ossie was a woman, because he had long hair, and nobody had long hair in those days. None of us really cared when they made fun of us. We thought it was quite amusing and we gave up on it.'[38] Clark also had a penchant for wearing crushed-velvet coats and chiffon scarves, and in the Neiman Marcus store in Houston, where the gang had stopped to buy mirrors which looked like the front cover of *Time* magazine, the assistant who served them said she didn't need their addresses to ship the mirrors: 'Don't worry, I'll just send them to Camelot.'

As they drove through the Deep South, they saw another side of life in America. 'We passed through terrible areas of rural poverty,' Boshier recalls, 'and it was very noticeable that all the blacks we saw had their heads bowed.' When they finally got close to New Orleans, and passed the sign welcoming them to the city, they did what had become routine which was to switch on the radio to the local station so that they would get the music of the area. 'So we turned the radio on when we saw the New Orleans sign,' Boshier remembers, 'and the first song that came on, which had just been released that very week, was the Animals singing "There is a house in New Orleans", the opening lines of Bob Dylan's "House of the Rising Sun". I'll never forget that. The New Orleans sign was there and the record was playing, and I thought that was great.' Here Boshier decided it was time to part company. 'I said to the others I was going to go off and find some girls, and I was going to leave them to do whatever they wanted.'[39]

After a short stay with Ferrill Amacker in New Orleans, Hockney and Clark drove to New York, where Hockney had his first American show at the Alan Gallery, selling all the paintings he had completed in Los Angeles as well as *Iowa*, *Arizona* and *Cubist Boy with Colourful Tree*, which were painted in Iowa. Clark, on a permanent high, was thrilled to meet Paul Newman, Diana Vreeland, then editor of American *Vogue*, and Andy Warhol at the opening. He also hung out with the band of the moment, the Velvet Underground, got an appointment with John Kloss, one of the hottest young designers in New York, and met the artist Robert Indiana, who gave him a bolt of cloth printed with his own op art design, which he was to use to great effect in his degree show the following summer.

Hockney used the time to consolidate his friendship with Henry Geldzahler, who took him round the galleries and amused him with tales of his various adventures, which had included starring in one of Warhol's films, in which he had to sit on a sofa in the Factory smoking a cigar and staring at the camera for hours while Andy busied himself making phone calls, occasionally returning to check that the camera was still running.

Yet despite the excitements of the trip, when Hockney and Clark finally returned to London in early October, they were barely speaking. 'I think he found David very difficult to be with all the time,' Celia Birtwell recalls. 'I think he didn't like the fact that the trip was very much on David's terms. He had won £150, and that was all the money he had, so after that ran out he really had to do what he was told.'[40] He called Birtwell and begged her to come back to him, telling her how much he had missed her and how tired he was of the lifestyle he had been leading. Within a few weeks he had moved in to the flat she was renting in St Quintin Avenue, where they were to enjoy their happiest months together. Hockney returned to Powis Terrace, which he set about smartening up in expectation of an imminent visit from his parents, whom he had not seen for nine months.

Kenneth and Laura Hockney had two reasons to visit London in November 1964: firstly to meet Margaret, off the boat from Australia, where she had been visiting Philip, who had emigrated there. Secondly, Ken had a demonstration to attend. 'We found David's flat beautifully decorated,' wrote Laura in her diary on 12 November; 'unfortunately heater not fixed in lounge – but kitchen was complete and warm.' Over the next few days, while awaiting Margaret's arrival, she filled her time shopping in the Portobello Road, visiting the Commonwealth Institute, attending the Lord Mayor's Show and engaging in her customary maternal tasks. 'After meal, gathered up David's washing & took to launderette – what a wash! Guess he's been so busy decorating, no time to launder.'[41]

When Ken and Laura departed to met Margaret at Tilbury Docks,

Hockney got back to work in his Powis Terrace studio on a picture that would remind him of what he was missing. It was *Picture of a Hollywood Swimming Pool*, and was based on drawings that he had done on his return to California after Iowa, when he had become fascinated by the squiggly lines created by the reflections of water in swimming pools and the problems of how to paint water. 'It is a formal problem to represent water,' he wrote, 'to describe water, because it can be anything – it can be any colour, it's moveable, it has no set visual description. I just used my drawings for these paintings, and my head invented.'[42] He was happy to admit that in these first paintings of water, when struggling to work out the best way to depict it, he was influenced by some of the later work of Dubuffet, and by what he referred to as Bernard Cohen's 'Spaghetti Paintings', such as *Fable* and *Alonging*. This influence is also clearly seen in another pool painting, *California*, with its squiggles and jigsaw-like shapes.

While his fascination with swimming pools was to become a major theme of Hockney's work, at this very moment he was temporarily distracted by a niggling anxiety that his work might not be considered sufficiently contemporary. Though this was partly just the insecurity of the young, it was also boosted by the fact that he only had to look at Kasmin's other artists, such as Kenneth Noland, Frank Stella, Jules Olitski and Anthony Caro, to see that he was the only figurative artist in the stable. 'I have never thought my painting advanced,' he commented, 'but in 1964 I still consciously wanted to be involved, if only peripherally, with modernism.'[43] So he fleetingly flirted with abstraction, beginning with *Different Kinds of Water Pouring into a Swimming Pool, Santa Monica* and following on with a series of still lifes, such as *Blue Interior and Two Still Lifes* and *Portrait Surrounded by Artistic Devices* in which he explored the different possible interpretations of Cezanne's famous remark that he wanted to 'treat nature by the sphere, the cylinder, the cone'. 'The "artistic devices",' Hockney wrote, 'are images and elements of my own and other artists' work and ideas of the time . . . All these paintings were, in a way, influenced by American abstractionists, particularly Kenneth Noland, whom I'd got to know through Kasmin who was showing him. I was trying to take note of these paintings. The still lifes were started with the abstraction in mind, and they're all done the same way as Kenneth Noland's, stained acrylic paint on raw cotton duck, and things like that.'[44]

A second series of still lifes, titled *A Realistic Still Life*, *A More Realistic Still Life* and *A Less Realistic Still Life*, was completed in Boulder, Colorado, in the summer of 1965, where Hockney had been invited to teach at the university. He flew first to New York, accompanied by Patrick Procktor, who was fresh from his second one-man show at the Redfern Gallery and on his way to follow in Hockney's footsteps teaching in Iowa. Patrick was a flamboyant figure, an eighteenth-century dandy transported into the twentieth century. Born in Dublin, the son of an accountant for Anglo-Iranian Oil, he chose to do his national service in the navy, where he learned to speak Russian. He eventually graduated to becoming a Russian interpreter with the British Council, in which post he was quite happy to indulge the fantasies of those of his friends who thought he was a spy. Openly homosexual and a talented artist, who studied at the Slade under the landscape painter Kyffin Williams, he was immensely tall, with gangly legs, a long sensitive face, expressive hands and slim fingers which he used to eloquent purpose, and a sharp fantastical wit. Hockney had found him stimulating company since they first met at the Young Contemporaries show in 1962. They were part of the same bohemian circle, and Procktor was the occasional lover of Michael Upton, now married to Hockney's great friend Anne McKechnie. 'The thing that I loved about Patrick was his flamboyance,' Hockney remembers. 'I also liked him because he could mock the art world. He felt he was a bit more outside it than I was, and anybody who mocks pomposity I'm attracted to.'[45]

It was Patrick's first trip to New York, which he initially hated. 'It seemed hideously ugly, hard and rude,' he later wrote, 'and their art was repulsive to me . . . Apart from looking at art, David and I rushed through a lot of low life, downtown.'[46] They stayed with Mark Berger in his apartment in the Bowery, a loft with enormous rooms to paint in, and Hockney gave Procktor a four-day whirlwind tour, visiting all the museums, meeting artists and eating out a lot – they were constantly hungry as Mark had nothing in his refrigerator but macrobiotic food.

Patrick Procktor

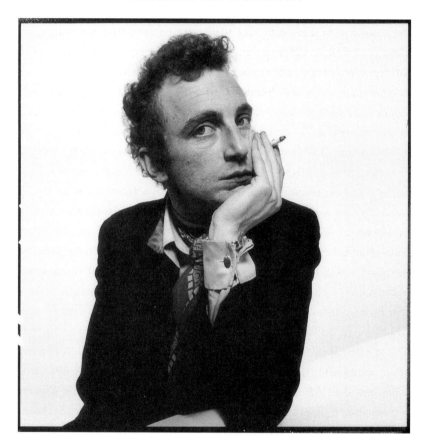

Hockney sold some etchings to the Museum of Modern Art and used the money to buy another car, a plum-and-cream Oldsmobile Starfire convertible with polychrome metallic plum upholstery, the Falcon having been ditched the previous autumn. 'It was about six or seven years old,' Hockney remembers, 'an enormous car with a seven-litre engine. It did about twelve miles to the gallon, but since gas was only thirty cents a gallon then, that didn't matter, and it had an electric roof and electric windows, which in 1965 was very rare.'[47] 'It was rather an outrageous car,' wrote Procktor, 'and got some stares by the time we reached rural Iowa where we were asked, "Why are you driving that flash *nigra* car?"'[48]

After dropping Procktor off in Iowa City, Hockney made his way to Boulder, which turned out to be a much bigger and livelier place than Iowa. The university, founded at the same time as the state of Colorado in 1876, had a spectacular setting against the background of the Flatirons, a range of impressive rock formations which run along the eastern slope of Green Mountain, with the Rockies rearing up behind. Though the faculty had given him a large studio in which to work, to Hockney's amusement it had no windows, something that immediately reminded him of his trip to Italy with Michael Kullman, trapped in the back of a van. 'Here I am surrounded by these beautiful Rocky Mountains,' he recalled, 'I go into the studio – no window! And all I need is a couple of little windows.'[49] His typically witty response was to paint *Rocky Mountains and Tired Indians*, a picture entirely invented from geological magazines and his own romantic ideas, there being no Indians within three hundred miles of Boulder. The plastic and metal chair in the painting was put in for compositional reasons, and, to explain its presence, he dubbed the Indians 'tired'.

Hockney enjoyed his time in Colorado. He found himself a lover, a nineteen-year-old American student called Dale Chisman, who, after a car accident, was lucky enough to have been exempted from the Vietnam draft. This dark cloud hung over all male students of eligible age in 1965, a year in which the number of ground troops deployed to Vietnam rose dramatically from 3,500 to 200,000. 'Dale became a friend because he was lively,' Hockney remembers, 'and anyone who was lively was someone you hooked up with. Students like Dale made the place, so I would be hanging out with them outside the college.'[50] His friend Norman Stevens came to stay, and there was also a visit from another of Kasmin's artists, Colin Self, who was in the US on a painting trip. When Procktor's residency in Iowa was over, he too drove over to Boulder, with his own student lover, Dick Mountain, whose ambition was to go to San Francisco and become a drag queen. They spent a few days in Boulder, exploring the Rockies, where Hockney gave Dick the nickname 'Pike's Peak' after one of the higher mountains, and driving up to Central City, an old gold-mining town near Aspen. At the end of the trip, all five, together with Dale Chisman, piled into the Oldsmobile, which had bench seats, making for plenty of room, and drove to San Francisco, a thrilling journey taking in mountainous twisting roads, broad highways and numerous motels. When they reached San Francisco they stayed at the Embarcadero YMCA, which was cheap, if not to the taste of Stevens and Self, who found it much too gay.

After a few days enjoying the sights of San Francisco and its gay bars, Hockney and Procktor left the others and drove down to LA, where Procktor had to fulfil a commission from Joan Cohn, the wealthy widow of Harry Cohn, former head of Columbia Pictures, to paint a mural for the cinema in her home in Beverly Hills. This had come about through his friendship with her lover and soon-to-be husband, the actor Laurence Harvey, star of such films as *Room at the Top*, *Walk on the Wild Side* and *The Manchurian Candidate*. Harvey was a bisexual who strung along his long-term lover and manager, James Woolf, through three career marriages, and once confessed to Jack Larson that he considered women to be 'extortionate creatures'. He had befriended Procktor the previous year while he was appearing onstage in London in *Camelot* at the Drury Lane Theatre, and had bought some of his paintings from the Redfern Gallery. Patrick was suitably impressed. 'Laurence Harvey was at the height of his fame,' he wrote, 'and a darling.'[51]

To begin with they stayed at the Tumble Inn, where they were eventually joined by Stevens and Self, who stayed for a few days, dining with Isherwood and Bachardy, going to see Bob Dylan at the Hollywood Bowl and hanging out at the beach. 'We didn't have that much money but it was all very exciting,' Hockney recalls. 'I remember we were on this beach in Santa Monica, just up by Santa Monica Canyon. It was a high school beach, and there was this very pretty California girl lying on the sand. Colin was looking at her and he told me that she had inspired him for a work he was going to do called "Nuclear Victim". I couldn't see the connection. Anyway, he did her as a shrivelled-up corpse.'[52] Eventually Stevens and Self took the Greyhound bus back to New York, leaving Hockney and Procktor to move into a guest house which Joan Cohn had lent them in the grounds of her home. Hockney immediately nicknamed it the 'Little Grey Home in the West'. Soon after their arrival there, they were invited up to dinner in the main house, where they enjoyed a real Hollywood evening. 'The dining room looked wonderful: the waiter wore white gloves, the knives and forks and even the dishes were gold,' Procktor recalled. 'The food was hamburgers. Joan smiled and said she hoped we thought that this was typically American, and she added that the steak had been flown in from Maine. After dinner they played a gramophone record of Larry's, where he read love poetry over a romantic orchestral accompaniment, for an hour. They were so very much in love.'[53]

While Procktor was working on his painting, Hockney was approached by Ken Tyler, a printmaker, who had his own atelier, Gemini Ltd, on Melrose Avenue. Tyler had attended the Art Institute of Chicago, and studied lithography at the John Herron School of Art in Indiana, graduating with a masters degree in 1963 and then studying with the French master printer Marcel Durassier, who had worked with both Picasso and Miró. He opened Gemini in 1965 and his strong emphasis on the importance of technique soon began to attract many of the greats of the American art scene, such as Josef Albers, Jasper Johns and Robert Rauschenberg. His approach to Hockney was for a series of lithographs with a Los Angeles theme. The only problem was a lack of finance, as his backer had just pulled out leaving him high and dry. Hockney, who had immediately liked Tyler and been greatly impressed by the quality of his work, called Paul Cornwall-Jones in London and had little difficulty in persuading him to agree to pay for and publish the edition.

What Hockney came up with was a typical example of his subversive wit, a set of six prints that poked fun at the kind of Beverly Hills collectors who bought art either for social prestige or financial investment. He called it *A Hollywood Collection* and it was his idea of an instant art collection, pre-packaged for a Hollywood starlet, and because Gemini was situated behind a framer's shop, he drew appropriate frames as part of the prints. Each lithograph is an imitation of a framed picture representing a particular genre. The titles speak for themselves: *Picture of a Still Life that has an Elaborate Silver Frame, Picture of a Landscape in an Elaborate Gold Frame, Picture of a Portrait in a Silver Frame, Picture of Melrose Avenue in an Ornate Gold Frame, Picture of a*

Simply Framed Traditional Nude Drawing and *Picture of a Pointless Abstraction Framed under Glass*. Once again his versatility and his fertile imagination triumphed.

Hockney encouraged Procktor to come up and have a look at Gemini, resulting in him producing his first lithograph, *Seated Crowd on the Grass*, featuring portraits of himself, Hockney and Rolf Nelson, whose gallery on Santa Monica Boulevard was at the cutting edge of the avant-garde. He also introduced him to Barney's Beanery, and to his friends Ed Ruscha and Dennis Hopper. When Joan Cohn and Laurence Harvey left on a trip to Europe, Procktor had to move out of the guest house, so Hockney arranged for them both to stay at Jack Larson's. With *A Hollywood Collection* finished and delivered to Gemini, he was preparing to return to London for his second show with Kasmin, when he got involved in a fateful distraction. Hanging out in his favourite gay bar, the Red Raven, he was introduced to a boy called Bob, known locally as 'Princess Bob'.

'Ten days before leaving for London,' Hockney remembers, 'I met this kid who I thought was Mister California Dish. His name was Bobby Earles and I said I was just going back to England, why not come back with me? He was an incredibly sexy boy. He was everything that California was about. But the thing is, it was simply lust on my part, and lust doesn't work for too long.'[54]

That night he told Procktor that he was in love, and that he was taking Bob back to England with him. This beautiful blond Californian boy, Hockney's perfect fantasy made real, had never left California before, so the first thing they had to do was get him a passport. Then the three of them drove to New York, with Procktor and Hockney arguing all the way. 'He said, "You've gone mad",' wrote Hockney, '"you're crazy." I said, "Never mind, we'll make up for it at night, it's all right."'[55] When they reached New York, Earles thought it was a terrible place, but Hockney told him that he was going to love Europe. Leaving Procktor to get to know New York a little better, they boarded the liner SS *France*, the flagship of the Compagnie Generale Transatlantique, to sail to Southampton. With an interior designed and built by the finest French craftsmen and artists, and 80 chefs on board, giving its Grill

Room the reputation of being the best French restaurant in the world, the *France* was the fastest and most luxurious ship afloat. All this was wasted on Princess Bob, however, who only wanted to sleep and have sex, a memory of which was beautifully captured in the patently erotic post-coital study *Bob, France 1965*.

In a postcard to Mo McDermott from LA in early October, Hockney had written, 'I will be back in London about noon on November 1 at Waterloo Station from the S.S. France. I am bringing back a marvellous work of art, called Bob.'[56] So McDermott, Kasmin, Clark and a few others knew what to expect when they formed a welcome-home committee at Waterloo early that morning, a meeting that was captured on camera by the film director Henry Herbert, who was shooting a film about Kasmin for the BBC.

Unsurprisingly, Earles was less than impressed with London. He thought Powis Terrace was a 'dump', bemoaned the fact that there were no gay bars, and showed no interest in anything other than having sex, and wanting to meet the Beatles and the Queen. 'He's a dumb blonde bleached whore,' said Clark, who gave him the nickname 'Miss Boots'.[57] The only thing that excited Earles in the ten days he spent in London was sitting at a table next to Ringo Starr at the Scotch of St James's nightclub. 'He was very dumb,' wrote Hockney. 'He'd no interest in anything . . . After a week I said I think you should go back . . . And I put him on a plane and sent him back. There is a drawing . . . of a marvellous pink bottom, and that's all he had in his favour I suppose.'[58] The story of Princess Bob did not end happily. Hockney saw him two years later working as a go-go dancer on Laguna Beach, and a few years after that, he heard that he had died from a drug overdose.

Hockney's second show at the Kasmin Gallery opened in December 1965, with the title *Pictures with Frames and Still-Life Pictures*, the prints being shown simultaneously at Alecto Editions. There was the usual opening party attended by the cream of society, and this time enlivened by the arrival of Sheridan Dufferin's flamboyant mother, Maureen, Marchioness of Dufferin and Ava, and her third husband,

Judge John Maude, a notoriously old-fashioned and right-wing judge. 'He was famously anti-homosexual,' Kasmin recalls, 'and was always sentencing gay people to hard labour. There was a lot of activity going on in the back room, boys kissing all over the place and people smoking dope, and he came up to me and asked, "Those people down there, aren't they homosexuals?" He was in a state of some nervous interest at watching all the forbidden actions going on.'[59]

The show was a sell-out, the average price for Hockney's work having risen to £500, with the largest canvas in the exhibition, *Rocky Mountains and Tired Indians*, going for £750 to the Peter Stuyvesant Foundation.

The critics were unanimous in their praise. 'Most of David Hockney's latest paintings . . . are the outcome of a trip to California,' wrote John Russell in *The Times*. 'They are certainly among his best so far.'[60] Writing in the *London Magazine*, Robert Hughes noted that 'Hockney's art has lost its exotic heroes. The magicians, generals, hot-gospellers and Ku Kluxers of his earlier paintings have now disappeared; what fascinates him is the face of Los Angeles, which he paints . . . as a flat, glaring, overlit, antiseptic madhouse in which nothing happens.'[61] In *Studio International*, Edward Lucie-Smith wrote: 'The paintings, drawings and prints in the new exhibition are the product of a much longer residence in and around Los Angeles, and are a great commitment to America itself. By comparing them to Hockney's earlier work, it is possible to see how astonishingly sensitive he is to atmosphere. Chameleon-like, he has become a Californian . . .'[62]

Robert Melville, in the *New Statesman*, pinpointed the swimming-pool painting as being of particular merit. 'The best picture in the exhibition is about the best he has ever done. Called *Two Men in a Pool, LA*, it depicts two sun-bronzed figures with pale bottoms at the far end of a rippling, sunlit pool that is treated as an intricate curvilinear pattern in blue and white, and it is far and away the most imaginative and pictorial use to which Art Nouveau has been put since its revival. I doubt if any artist of his generation has produced a better picture.'[63]

Once again Hockney waited till after the opening was over to invite his parents to see the show. They arrived on Laura's birthday, 10

December. 'I had asked David on the phone,' she wrote in her diary, 'to have his place clean – & it was – but I had a lovely surprise, on turning bed covers down to find new sheets and new blankets. Now! I said it feels like home & hugged him. They were tomato red sheets and p. cases – & next morning David asked if I would like some for my birthday – well of course – so off we went to Barkers & I was presented with two sets.'[64] Laura was happy to be introduced to 'many artist friends', who included Patrick Procktor, Michael Upton, Peter Blake and his wife Jan Haworth, and Dale Chisman, who had come over from Colorado, and the show filled her with pride. 'I think David's exhibition was very pleasing & very wonderful,' she wrote, '– some of the drawings I could understand & more so after reading the many write-ups in several papers. I'm glad it is a success – there were many people there when we went. He has done very well indeed.'[65] Her joy at having him back in England was, however, to be short-lived.

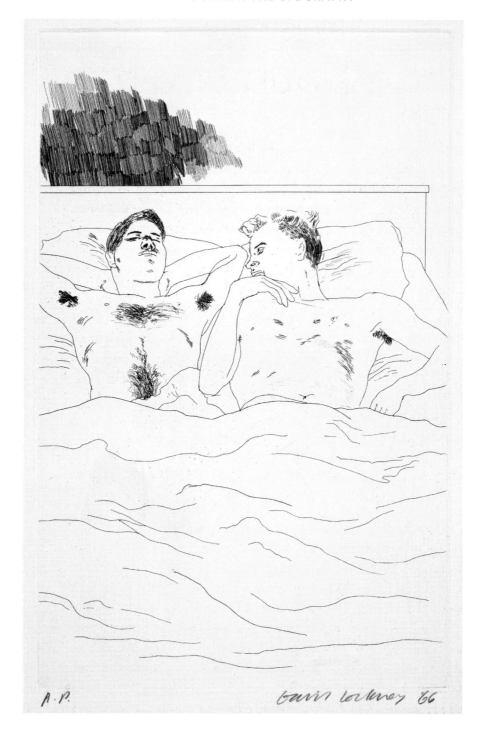

A.P.   David Hockney 66

CHAPTER SEVEN

IN THE DULL VILLAGE

'POP ARTIST POPS OFF' ran the headline in the Atticus column in the *Sunday Times* on 9 January 1966, followed by the story that 'David Hockney, Britain's brightest young artist, has decided to leave Britain.' It described him wandering around his flat deciding whether or not to sound off about his feelings in a letter to the *Daily Mirror*.

> I want to know why the Government is trying to get everybody into bed by eleven o'clock. Why else do all the pubs close at eleven and the telly shuts down at twelve? It makes me fed up, so I'm going to America. Life should be more exciting, but all they have is regulations stopping you from doing anything. I used to think London was exciting. It is compared to Bradford. But compared with New York or San Francisco it's nothing. I'm going in April. I'm going to teach for two months in Los Angeles, then I'll just stay on and paint. I'll come back now and again to see my dealer and my parents, but I doubt if I'll ever stay here again. I feel more lively there so I work better. That's all it is.[1]

That Hockney's outwardly sunny nature concealed a streak of rebellious anger did not come as a surprise to his mother, though she confessed to having been 'rather shocked' by this outburst when she read it. 'I know it is the side of David we do not see,' she wrote, 'but he does not hide it. So different from our way of life. I should like to talk with him about it.'[2] In spite of the fact that he was living in a period when class barriers were beginning to break down among the young, when fashion designers and pop stars, photographers and artists, largely from the working class, were mixing freely with the upper and middle classes, dining with lords and ladies and partying with royalty, Hockney felt

In the Dull Village, 1966-67

a strong solidarity with his working-class roots. He was angry for the workers. 'It's . . . to do with the class system; it's still to do with the fact . . . that drinking after eleven costs more because you have to join a club,' he wrote. 'The poor workers, they're supposed to go to bed and get up to work. It's very undemocratic.'[3]

It was this sense of righteous indignation that Hockney put to good use when it came to propaganda on behalf of gay rights. In September 1957, Sir John Wolfenden's famous report had recommended that homosexual behaviour between two consenting adults should no longer be considered a crime, a suggestion that had earned it the nickname the 'Pansy's Charter' from the *Daily Express*. Yet the Macmillan government had chosen to ignore its advice, despite a plea in a letter to *The Times* signed by thirty-three eminent public figures from the worlds of politics, the Church and the arts, including Lord Attlee, J. B. Priestley, Bertrand Russell, the Bishops of Birmingham and Exeter, and Stephen Spender, that the government should 'introduce legislation to give effect to the proposed reform at an early date'.[4] Even Hugh Gaitskell, leader of the Labour Party, and Harold Wilson, the man who was to succeed him, were nervous of supporting the Wolfenden Committee's recommendations, believing that to do so would cost them six million votes. They may have had a point. When a proposal was made in Burnley, Lancashire, that the town should allow the opening of a club for homosexuals, a leading Labour activist commented, 'There'll be no buggers club in Burnley.'[5] On the whole in 1966, public attitudes to homosexuality were still largely hostile, and sex between men was illegal and punishable with a prison sentence, which made David's openness about his sexuality all the more courageous. He just didn't care. 'I don't think,' wrote Roy Strong after first meeting him, 'that I'd ever before encountered anyone so overtly homosexual.'[6]

Among the young, however, whose attitudes to sex were becoming more liberal, tolerance was generally more widespread, as it was among the upper echelons of society where it was often openly tolerated and defended. Indeed, it was the House of Lords which first declared in favour of reform, when in October 1965 it passed the Sexual Offences Bill, introduced by the Liberal peer the Earl of Arran, though not without some opposition from peers like Lord Dilhorne who thundered that such a bill would not only legalise sodomy, but encourage male prostitution. It was a brave move on Arran's part, who, like many social reformers before him, was to be the victim of abuse, contempt and ridicule. The bill suffered a stormier ride through the Commons, steered by the maverick Labour MP Leo Abse, and it was to be nearly two years before it passed on to the statute books.

It was against this background that Hockney began work on his next project, a series of etchings based on the work of Constantine Cavafy, whose poems had previously inspired several paintings – *Waiting for the Barbarians*, *Kaisarion with All His Beauty* and *Mirror, Mirror on the Wall*. Ever since his Egypt trip in 1963, Hockney had harboured a secret desire to illustrate a series of Cavafy's poems, an ambition he mentioned to Paul Cornwall-Jones, who immediately encouraged him to go ahead. Discovering that Cavafy's translator, John Mavrogordato, was still alive and living in London, Hockney went to visit him in Montpelier Walk, behind Harrods. A pacifist, like Hockney, he was described as 'a generous, courteous, charming, and modest man . . . a philanthropist, genial companion, conversationalist, connoisseur, talented amateur artist . . . and collector of books and art'.[7] It was a fruitless trip, however, because by the time of the visit the former professor of Byzantine and Modern Greek Language and Literature at Oxford was eighty-four years old, suffering from dementia and had completely lost his memory.

When Hockney recounted this tale to Stephen Spender, asking for his advice, he introduced him to a young Greek poet called Nikos Stangos, and it was decided that the two of them should provide a new translation of the poems to go with Hockney's drawings. A year younger than Hockney, Stangos had studied philosophy at Harvard University and was working as a press officer at the Greek Embassy in London; as a fellow homosexual who shared Hockney's socialist principles, and who spoke perfect English, he was the perfect collaborator.

On his Egypt trip in 1963, Hockney had visited Alexandria, the home city of Cavafy, who had lived in a second-floor apartment above a brothel in the Rue Lepsius. From the balcony Cavafy could see both a hospital and the Church of St Saba, which had prompted him to comment, 'Where could I live better? Below, the brothel caters for the flesh. And there is the church which forgives sin. And there is the hospital where we die.'[8] Hockney's mind had been alive with the descriptions he had read of Alexandria in Lawrence Durrell's *Alexandria Quartet*, but instead of the bustling cosmopolitan and bohemian city of his imagination, where generations of immigrants from Greece, Italy and the Levant had settled to take advantage of its position as a centre of commerce, he found a dull modern port almost totally devoid of any Europeans. Realising that he would get no inspiration there, he decided instead to travel to Beirut, then considered the Paris of the Middle East. 'I didn't know anybody there,' Hockney remembers, 'but I thought I'd just go there to get atmosphere. I went for about a week. I carried a sketchbook wherever I went, drawing the buildings, the Arabic signs and exploring the seedy parts. It was a good destination then, a stopover if you were heading to the east, and a very cosmopolitan city, much more cosmopolitan than Cairo or Alexandria, and it also had a reputation for being rather racy.'[9] On his return he called his mother to tell her about it. 'David phoned in the evening,' she wrote in her diary. 'He has had a marvellous time as usual and done a lot of work. Visited Damascus and Lebanon. Lucky boy! How wonderful.'[10]

Cavafy's poems can be divided into two categories: the poems about historical Alexandria and mythology, and the sensual poems set in modern Alexandria, lyrical musings on love and eroticism, mostly concerned with furtive and often doomed love between young boys. 'I suppose that because I know more about love than about history, I chose to do those,' says Hockney. 'Of course they are about gay love, and I was quite boldly using that subject then. I was aware that it was illegal, but I didn't really think much about that at the time. I was living in a bohemian world, where we just did what we pleased. I wasn't speaking for anybody else. I was defending my way of living.'[11] In creating the illustrations for the book, Hockney worked from three sources: his own drawings, photographs which he had either taken or bought, and drawings which he etched straight onto the plate from life. *Two Boys Aged 23 or 24*, for example, is based on a photograph of

Mo McDermott and Dale Chisman lying in bed, while *According to the Prescriptions of Ancient Magicians* was copied onto the plate from *Boys in Bed, Beirut*, an ink drawing made in London using two more friends as models.

The etchings made for *Illustrations for Fourteen Poems from C. P. Cavafy*, rather than being exact illustrations of the contents of each poem, were largely intended to parallel them, suggesting to the reader an experience similar to that described. Whereas Cavafy's young men were often tormented and fugitive, David's had a defiance about them, a feeling of indifference to what the world might think. As they climb into bed and prepare to make love they look the viewer straight in the eye. With 'his etchings for the Cavafy poems', wrote his contemporary Derek Jarman, 'he produced vital new images that pulled away the veil behind which the work of older painters had had to hide. The Cavafy etchings were particularly powerful. With his fine line he produced images of boys in bed that resembled Cocteau – but without a trace of the sentimentality which so often bedevils gay art.'[12]

In October 2010, Neil McGregor, the director of the British Museum, included in his radio series *A History of the World in a Hundred Objects* the Hockney etching *In the Dull Village* as an example of art as propaganda. The figures, he commented, 'could be American or British, but they inhabit the world of the poem, which is about a young man trapped by his circumstances, and who escapes his dreary surroundings by dreaming of the perfect love partner . . . a boy imagined rather than actually present in the longed-for flesh. Cavafy's poem reads as modern verse, but looks back to an ancient Greek world in which love between men was an accepted part of life. They are poems of longing and loss, of the first meetings of future loves, and of intoxicating passionate encounters and they were exciting fodder for Hockney, material that he could use for his own art as an example of how an artist could make a public statement out of such private experience.'[13]

in the boring village where he's waiting out the time—
he goes to bed tonight full of sexual longing,

all his youth on fire with the body's passion,
his lovely youth given over to a fine intensity.
And in his sleep pleasure comes to him;
in his sleep he sees and has the figure, the flesh he longed for . . .

Hockney took a deliberately realistic approach in making these etchings, which he felt suited the subject matter, and they were among his first ventures into line drawing with ink, an enterprise whose sheer difficulty excited him. 'I never talk when I'm drawing a person,' he wrote, 'especially if I'm making line drawings. I prefer for there to be no noise at all so I can concentrate more. You can't make a line too slowly, you have to go at a certain speed; so the concentration needed is quite strong. It's very tiring as well. If you make two or three line drawings, it's very tiring in the head, because you have to do it all at one go, something you've no need to do with pencil drawing . . . you can stop, you can rub out. With line drawings you don't want to do that. You can't rub out line, mustn't do it. It's exciting doing it, and I think it's harder than anything else; so when they succeed they're much better drawings, often.'[14] Unlike his previous etchings, which relied much more on the use of aquatint, the Cavafy illustrations are almost entirely line drawings and they are undoubtedly one of his greatest achievements. 'I have just seen the first pulls from some of the plates,' wrote Edward Lucie-Smith in *The Times*, 'and thought them not only the best work I have seen by the artist, but probably the finest prints seen in England since the war.'[15]

Alecto Editions was by now operating out of premises in Kelso Place, South Kensington, which was large enough to incorporate the entire production process. Along with Mike Rand, an assistant in the etching studio at the Royal College, they took on Maurice Payne, with whom Rand had studied at Ealing Art School. Payne was young and eager to learn and, equally important, took to Hockney and his coterie from the very start. 'It was a fun and interesting time,' he recalls. 'What interested me in meeting this gay crowd was that people could be so different. Personally I found straight guys boring to be with because it was all about who's got the girls and who hasn't, that whole competitive thing. When I was at school I was very good at sports and football and things like that, and I remember when I met Mo and Ossie the first time, there was an occasion when they were crying together about something, and I remember thinking, "Straight guys would never show any emotion. Great, it's OK to cry."[16] Payne was to be David's assistant on the Cavafy project and for many years to come.

Since Hockney was already a skilled printer himself, most of the initial work was done at Powis Terrace. This consisted of preparing the copperplates by covering them with a film of wax, drawing onto them with a sharp steel-tipped 'pen', and the actual etching process itself, in which the completed plate is placed in a bath of acid, mixed with potassium chlorate to speed up the process. Because the acid bath produced such strong unpleasant fumes, this procedure took place on the balcony where most of the vapours would blow away into the street. It proved impossible to eradicate all traces of the stink, however. 'The fumes creep everywhere,' Hockney told James Scott, who was making a film about the Cavafy etchings for the Arts Council, 'and I couldn't sleep so well because of them, so I had to keep getting up early and keep working on them. That was very good really.'[17] When the plate had been in the bath long enough, it was then washed under the shower until all traces of the acid were washed away. Once the plates were cleaned up and polished they were ready to be taken over to Kelso Place to be pressed in one of their huge cast-iron printing presses.

At the same time that he was working on these etchings and beginning to develop a more naturalistic way of realising the human figure, Hockney was approached by the actor Iain Cuthbertson, an associate director of the Royal Court Theatre, to design a play which he was about to direct. The suggestion had come from the artistic director of the Royal Court, Bill Gaskill, a founding director of the National Theatre and a fellow Yorkshireman, born in Shipley. 'I had never done anything in the theatre,' Hockney recalls, 'but I was consciously interested, and had seen a lot of theatre in the early sixties. I remember seeing *Waiting for Godot*, and stage versions of *Under Milk Wood*, and Mo

knew the theatre and he might get us tickets for things. I didn't know
the play but I was sympathetic to it immediately.'

The play was Alfred Jarry's *Ubu Roi*, one of the first works of the
Theatre of the Absurd, which at its premiere in Paris in 1896 had so
offended the audience with what they saw as its vulgar and obscene
nature that they almost rioted. The version that was to play at the
Royal Court had been translated by Cuthbertson and was to be co-
directed by him and Gaskill. It was the first time it had ever been
performed in England, and it was to be presented as a comedy, with
the lead being taken by the great music-hall star Max Wall.

Initially Hockney was resistant to the idea. 'After all,' he said,
'in paintings before that, I had been interested in what you might
call theatrical devices, and I thought that in the theatre, the home of
theatrical devices, they'd be different, they wouldn't have quite the
same meaning as they do in painting, they wouldn't be contradictory —
a theatrical device in the theatre is what you'd expect to find.'[18]

Fear of failure, however, was not something that was ever to loom
large in Hockney's life, and his eventual decision to take on the project
was indicative of a lifelong willingness to try out new mediums. He was
attracted by the surreal humour of the play, by the way the action raced
along, but most of all by the written instructions of the playwright to
eschew traditional scenery. 'I designed it based on Alfred Jarry saying
"Don't bother with the scenery,"' he recalls, '"just put a notice up
saying Parade Ground." So I took that up and for the Parade Ground
people just walked on with a letter in their hands, and put it down and
when they walked off it just read Parade Ground, and things like that.'
The Polish Army was represented by two people with a banner tied
round them, which simply read 'Polish Army'.

In the end Hockney had a lot of fun working on *Ubu Roi*, designing
both the sets and the costumes, which were painted on sandwich
boards and carried around by the actors. Jack Shepherd, as Mère
Ubu, had bosoms sewn onto the outside of his dress, with red nipples
which lit up, while Max Wall wore a pear-shaped body suit and
sported a green bowler hat. 'My own first entrance in the play,' Wall
reminisced, 'was made from beneath the stage as I was hauled up to

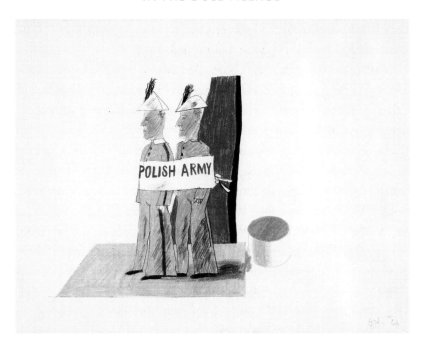

stage level on a lift while sitting on a toilet that matched up with the backdrop on which was painted a cistern and lavatory chain.'[19] The sets themselves were like large paintings, a garish series of poster-paint backdrops, suspended from the flies by ropes, which dropped down when required, 'like a joke toy theatre' as Hockney remembered it. 'Hockney's hair was bleached,' wrote Bill Gaskill in his memoirs, 'and with his huge glasses and not dissimilar features he looked like the ghost of George Devine as he peered from the back of the circle at the recreation of his brushstrokes on the backcloth. "I didn't think they'd copy it exactly."'[20]

In June 1966, as soon as his work on Ubu was completed, Hockney set off for California where he had been asked to teach for six months at the University of California, Los Angeles (UCLA). He left England with one major worry on his mind: his father's health. Kenneth had been diagnosed with diabetes three years previously and had twice recently gone into diabetic comas – a problem of his own making, as he had stopped taking the pills that had been prescribed for his mild form of the disease. This led to him being taken into hospital just before Christmas, where, refusing even to contemplate taking insulin, he was put back on his tablets and after two weeks spent as a 'difficult' and 'aggressive' patient, signed himself out of the hospital against the opinion of five doctors.

'Kenneth is very confident he can cure himself,' wrote Laura on 17 January 1966, 'and is taking tablets regularly.' But ten days later, he began to deteriorate again, mulishly refusing, day after day, to see a doctor. 'And so it went on,' wrote Laura in despair, 'he getting worse and worse – yet fighting against it with all his might – so sure he could cure himself right up to Sunday morning when he had to give in.' He 'gave in' only because he had fallen into a coma, and had to be rushed to hospital where they eventually managed to bring him round. Within a fortnight, however, he was in a coma again, this time for twenty-four hours, an event that finally left him in no doubt that he had to follow doctor's orders. On 10 February, Laura was able to observe: 'Now getting proud of the fact that he can inject himself – a good sign he is better.'[21]

In New York, meanwhile, Hockney picked up his new car, an open-topped Triumph which had been shipped over from England, and drove it across America to California, fantasising all the way about his forthcoming job. '. . . as I got further and further West,' he wrote, 'I became more and more excited, imagining my class would be full of young blond surfers.'[22] When he finally arrived in LA, he went to stay in a small apartment in Larabee Drive, off Sunset Boulevard, belonging to a young dealer, Nick Wilder, whom Hockney had met the previous year.

Openly gay when he first set up shop on La Cienega, the 28-year-old Wilder stood out from the rest of the leather-jacketed, macho art types because of his preppy appearance. 'He seemed like a Yale man in a suit,' Jack Larson recalls, 'very proper and reserved, but he wasn't like that at all.'[23] The youngest of three children of a scientist who had been one of the inventors of Kodachrome, Wilder had attended Amherst College in Massachusetts, where he got himself a job at the

university museum as projectionist for art history slide lectures, and
had graduated at Stanford in art history. Bitten, like so many of his
contemporaries, by the California bug, he had opened his gallery on
La Cienega after establishing a reputation as a *wunderkind* dealer at
the Lanyon Gallery in Palo Alto, which was regarded as the leading
Bay Area gallery. Rumours were soon flying around that he was heir
to the Kodak film fortune and had bottomless funds to support and
promote artists. 'In fact, I started the gallery by leaping in, in this
naive, monomaniacal, underfunded way,' Wilder recalled. 'I often
didn't know where the rent was coming from. I didn't have enough
money but people thought I was rich because of the way I looked.'[24]

Hockney and Wilder shared a passion both for art and the bohemian
way of life. 'Nick was about my age, quite intellectual,' Hockney
recalls, 'and I instantly got on with him. He was only just opening his
gallery, where he showed very radical artists for the time. He was a bit
disorganised, but very driven, and he loved the arts and the artists.'[25]
Wilder was to discover many great, then unknown, local talents, like
Ron Davis, Bruce Nauman, Robert Graham and Tom Holland, and
the Nicholas Wilder Gallery soon flourished, with a number of big-
name East Coast painters like Kenneth Noland, Helen Frankenthaler,
Cy Twombly, Jules Olitsky and Barnett Newman eventually joining.
Despite Wilder's conventional appearance, he remained an out-and-
out bohemian, the large living room at his West Hollywood apartment
furnished solely with a huge yellow sculpture by John McCracken that
was often draped with his underwear. 'The tiny kitchen,' Hockney
remembers, 'contained a refrigerator which never had anything in it
other than pickles and sauces because if we wanted food, we would just
call up Chicken Delight and somebody would deliver chicken or pizza
or stuff like that. There were just mattresses on the floor for sleeping,
and you would have gone to bed and some boy would come in and get
on the mattress with you. It was a life that we liked. You never knew
what was going to happen any night and I thought it was terrific. I was
young and free and this is what we all did.'[26]

The class at UCLA to which Hockney had been assigned turned
out to be a disappointment, because far from being full of the young

blond surfers, it was, just like in Iowa, peopled with would-be teachers who were there solely to get credits that would give them better pay. There were not even any keen students of art whom it might have been a pleasure to teach. Then, just as he was beginning to despair, in walked a young student who was to be one of the great passions of Hockney's life, Peter Schlesinger. 'I took one look at him,' Hockney remembers, 'and I thought, "That looks like a real young Californian." He was just the kind of person I'd been hoping to meet in my class.'[27]

Schlesinger was the eighteen-year-old son of a life-insurance salesman, the second of three brothers from the San Fernando Valley, better known to Angelenos as 'the Valley'. The family had moved when he was ten to Encino, a small town which lies on the northern slopes of the Santa Monica Mountains, where they lived an ordinary middle-class life, and the boys had a liberal Jewish upbringing. From the age of seven or eight, Schlesinger had known that he wanted to be an artist, an ambition in which he was encouraged by his parents, and every Saturday during his high-school years, his father used to drive him all the way to UCLA to take art courses. In 1965, a dreamy time when the hippy movement was just beginning, he was enrolled at the University of California in Santa Cruz. It had no art classes, however, so in the summer of 1966 he came back down to live with his parents and take a drawing course at UCLA. 'On the first day of class,' he recalled, 'the professor walked in – he was a bleached blond; wearing a tomato-red suit, a green and white polka-dot tie with a matching hat, and round black cartoon glasses; and speaking with a Yorkshire accent. At that time, David Hockney was only beginning to become established in England, and I had never heard of him.'[28]

It could be said that fate threw them together, since it later turned out that Schlesinger shouldn't have been in the Hockney class, which was for advanced students only. Hockney, however, assured the faculty that in his opinion Schlesinger was quite advanced and showed considerable talent, and so he was allowed to keep him. 'I could genuinely see he had talent,' says Hockney, 'and on top of that he was a marvellous-looking young man. I was always looking for lively young people and he was intelligent and he was curious, and a far cry

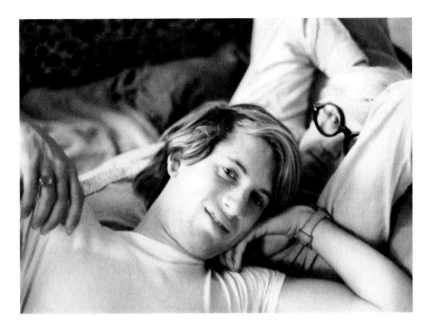

Peter Schlesinger
and David Hockney

from Bobby Earles.'[29] Schlesinger was equally taken with Hockney. 'I was drawn to him because he was different,' he remembers. 'He was teaching life drawing. He was a good teacher who loved teaching and giving his opinion. He was also fun and lively and amusing and I was quite shy in those days and I liked hanging out with older people rather than my own age group.'[30]

It wasn't long before Schlesinger was spending all his spare time away from class with Hockney, who couldn't wait to introduce him to his friends. 'One day David came by,' Jack Larson recalls, 'and he brought this young student, Peter. He was very sweet, and quite observant, but I suppose he was very innocent. We all went out to dinner, and there was no doubt in my mind that David was absolutely smitten with this wonderful-looking, quite charming young boy who wasn't a Beverly Hills swinger, but a boy from the Valley.'[31] That Hockney was in love was equally clear to Don Bachardy who recalls that 'it was clear right away that there was something going on between them'.[32]

Owing to Schlesinger's shy nature and an innocence about his sexuality, what was actually going on at this stage was nothing physical, merely the gradual process of them falling in love. 'I didn't really consider whether or not I was gay at that time,' says Schlesinger, 'because I guess I didn't really know what it was. I didn't identify it till I actually did it. We just hung out together and nothing else happened for two or three months.'

Schlesinger was still living with his parents, and he waited till they were away for a weekend before asking Hockney over to the house. They spent the day by the pool, where he did some drawings of Schlesinger sitting in a deckchair in his swimming trunks reading a book. The moment that the affair was finally consummated took place just before the end of term, when Schlesinger was faced with having to return to Santa Cruz and the realisation that this would take him away from David, who had to stay in LA. For David, to have finally found a soulmate was the realisation of a dream. 'It was incredible to me,' he later told the art historian Marco Livingstone, 'to meet in California a young, very sexy, attractive boy who was also curious and intelligent. In California you can meet curious and intelligent people, but generally they're not the sexy boy of your fantasy as well. To me this was incredible.'[33]

When the term was over, Hockney flew to London for a few days, courtesy of the Royal Court, to attend the opening of *Ubu Roi* on 21 July. Unable to find the time to get to Bradford, he persuaded his parents to come to London to see the play. 'Ken and I . . . went to the Royal Theatre to see the play,' wrote Laura in her diary. 'Not quite our cup of tea – tho' we knew what to expect.'[34] Critically, too, the show had a lukewarm reception, the main gripe being that in choosing to present it as 'something between a Christmas pantomime and an exhibition of child's art',[35] Iain Cuthbertson had deprived the play of its main virtue, which was to outrage the public. Max Wall was criticised for simply playing himself. 'Ubu may be an international figure,' wrote the drama critic of *The Times*, 'but wherever he goes and however he changes his appearance, he must remain unmistakably a monster . . . Of this there is not a trace in Mr Wall's performance.'[36] It was generally agreed that 'visually, at any rate, it is great fun',[37] though Hockney was not asked to do theatre design again for about ten years, leading him to assume that he was simply no good at it; the *Ubu* sets represented a last gasp for his working in a highly stylised and artificial manner.

To tie in with the Royal Court opening, Kasmin put on a show of the original drawings for the sets and costumes, described by Paul Overy in the *Listener* as being 'gay, witty and lightweight'.[38] He combined it with the first exhibition of the Cavafy etchings, which certain people found perplexing. Hockney was in the gallery one day when two old ladies came in, and they asked him to explain to them why two men were sitting on the bed in the same room. 'The thing is,' Hockney replied mischievously, 'they are very hard up and they have to share a room.' The Cavafys were generally admired, although, given the subject matter, they were slow to sell, but, as Overy pointed out, 'Hockney concentrates on presenting homosexual liaisons as something completely normal and acceptable. To do this requires a courage one must admire . . . '[39] It was to be Hockney's last show with Kasmin for a while, because when he flew back to California at the end of the month he was not to return to England for a whole year.

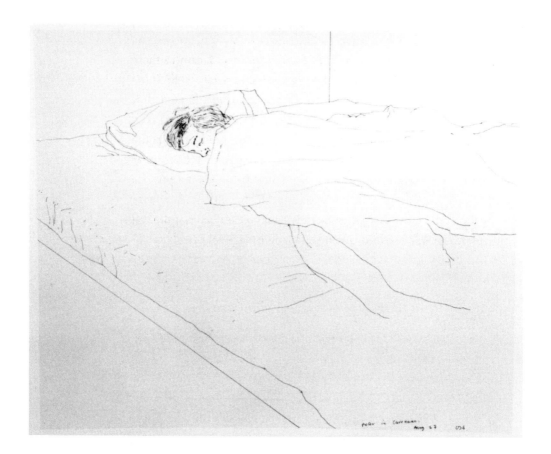

CHAPTER EIGHT

A BIGGER SPLASH

Hockney's first move on his return to LA was to find himself an apartment of his own, where eventually he might also live with Peter Schlesinger. The place he found, in a very seedy part of the city near to the junction of Pico and Crenshaw Boulevards, was a run-down little house that had been converted from a garage. Dirt cheap, it had concrete floors, a bedroom, a tiny kitchen and bathroom, and a room at the front to use as a studio. When the gas stove was lit, cockroaches dived for cover. There was no phone. Instead Hockney took a leaf out of his father's book. 'It had a telephone booth right outside,' he remembers, 'and I just kept all my quarters and dimes so I could make phone calls. I didn't have that many phone calls anyway. People didn't in those days. I just went to see people in person.'[1] It was in this scruffy little studio/apartment, in one of his most prolific periods, between the summers of 1966 and '67, that Hockney painted some of his most iconic paintings.

The first of these was *Beverly Hills Housewife*, an enormous twelve-foot-long picture which, the studio being so tiny, had to be painted on two canvases and which, as Hockney remembered, 'I could never get more than about five feet away from . . .'[2] It is the modern-day equivalent, as Henry Geldzahler later described it, of those 'grandes machines' from the heyday of the Paris Salon in the nineteenth century, 'impressively large paintings grandly conceived to show the artist's strength'.[3] The subject was Betty Freeman, the daughter of a chemical engineer, Robert I. Wishnick, who had made a fortune in Chicago. Inspired by the example of her father who gave away large amounts of his money to hospitals and educational establishments, she dedicated her life to supporting people in the sphere of the arts which she loved most, contemporary music, and over the years commissioned works

Peter in Carennac,
1967

from many of the world's most famous modern composers, such as
John Cage, Pierre Boulez, Harrison Birtwistle and Steve Reich.

She and Hockney had been introduced by Jack Larson during his
first visit to LA. 'She used to have these kind of concerts on Sunday
afternoons,' Hockney recalls, 'and sometimes they were almost like
a joke. I remember one afternoon when there was this event which
consisted of just one note going on and on and on for hours and hours
and people just sat there and didn't really know what to do. I think
it was by Harry Partch, a composer she had rescued off the streets.
Then Betty would come in and say, "You can talk if you want to." If
you did, it then just sounded like there was a washing machine going
on in the other room. I was very amused by this of course, but I loved
Betty because she was interested in painting and music.'[4] Still in the
throes of his love affair with the very newness of Los Angeles, he first
asked Mrs Freeman if he might paint her very glamorous swimming
pool. When he arrived at her house to do some preliminary sketches,
however, he found himself seduced by her entire surroundings – the
open-plan inside-outside house, the lush plants, the perfect lawn, and
the belongings (already hinted at in his entirely invented *California Art
Collector*) which included a William Turnbull sculpture, the head of an
antelope bagged by her husband and a Le Corbusier chaise longue. Since
Hockney was carrying an early Polaroid Land camera, he persuaded
Betty to pose for him in front of the house.

This was one of the first instances of Hockney using the camera
as a tool to help compose a picture. Though he had previously taken
many photographs, using a tiny Kodak Instamatic, they were mostly
holiday snaps. From this out-of-focus, rather badly lit black-and-white
print, he composed an extraordinary painting which, though it does
not name the sitter, was his first naturalistic portrait for many years,
and the first of a series of paintings which, to millions of people, were
to be *the* evocation of California. Betty Freeman loved the finished
work and liked to joke that she was 'just one of the artistic objects on
display'.[5]

*

Hockney's image of California as a carefree land of sunshine, affluence and leisure is indicated in the series of paintings featuring swimming pools on which he now embarked. He saw the swimming pool as the embodiment of the foreigner's view that he had of the country, and he began meticulous observations of the water in the pools he saw. 'Water in a swimming pool is different from, say, water in the river, which is mostly a reflection because the water isn't clear. A swimming pool has clarity. The water is transparent and drawing transparency is an interesting graphic problem. I noticed that with the sun on the pool you got these dancing lines, so I would sit watching the surface of the pool and draw what I saw and then I would go and paint it. I drew with coloured pencils, or I would just work with an ordinary pencil. The problem is, how do you represent water in the pool graphically?'[6]

Though there was no photography used in the swimming-pool paintings, because the camera 'freezes' water, which was not the effect he was after, he did continue to use it as an aide-memoire, typically in one of his first paintings featuring Schlesinger, *Peter Getting Out of Nick's Pool*. 'I didn't ever pose in the pool,' Schlesinger remembers, 'which is why the painting looks a little weird, especially the legs underwater, because I was actually posed against the hood of my car. Then he put two paintings together.'[7]

Photography was used in a similar fashion in another important painting of this period, *Portrait of Nick Wilder*. Hockney's friend Mark Lancaster, an English artist who had worked for Andy Warhol, took photographs of Wilder standing in his pool as studies for what was to be Hockney's first explicit portrait since that of his father, painted in 1955. The picture, which shows the upper torso of Wilder emerging from the pool like a Roman bust, perfectly captures the Californian light, with the overwhelming brightness of the sun creating extremely dark shadows. For Hockney it was something of a breakthrough. 'To me, moving into more naturalism was freedom,' he wrote. 'I thought, if I want to, I could paint a portrait; this is what I mean by freedom . . . I could even paint a strange little abstract picture. It would all fit into my concept of painting as an art. A lot of painters can't do that . . . To me a lot of painters were trapping themselves; they were picking such a narrow aspect of painting and specializing in it. And it's a trap. Now there's nothing wrong with the trap if you have the courage to leave it.'[8]

The more closely Hockney observed water, the more fascinated he became; but it was a photograph that inspired his next depiction of the subject. While leafing through a book about the construction of swimming pools which he found on a Hollywood news-stand, he came across a photograph of a splash, and immediately thought what a good subject it would be for a painting. 'What amused me was the fact that the splash only lasts a very, very short time,' Hockney recalls, 'and a photograph can freeze it, and that's not what it's like. When you paint it, you can make it flow. That is the difference, and that is what I was doing.'[9] The first painting of this series, *The Little Splash*, was a tiny picture, two foot by one foot, and was painted quite quickly, in a couple of days. It was closely followed by *The Splash*, which was a bit bigger and more fully realised, giving more emphasis to the background. With hindsight, Hockney decided that this version was too fussy, with the background, in which you can see the landscape, detracting from the subject, so he now chose to paint an even bigger, eight-foot-square version, using a simpler building and very strong light.

A Bigger Splash turned out to be one of Hockney's most enduring images, a painting securely established as one of the masterpieces of twentieth-century art. It is a mesmerising depiction of order and chaos. On a hot, still, cloudless day, with the sun at its highest in the sky, the heat at its most intense and the surface of the water in the swimming pool mill-pond calm, a diver has leapt from the diving board and disappeared into the depths of the pool, gone for ever, his existence marked only by a violent eruption of water that is in complete contrast to the ongoing stillness of the scene. To emphasise this contrast, Hockney put the paint on using rollers, except for the splash. '. . . the splash itself is painted with small brushes and little lines,' he wrote. 'It took me about two weeks to paint. I loved the idea, first of all, of painting like Leonardo, all his studies of water, swirling things. And I loved the idea of painting this thing that lasts for two seconds . . . the effect of it as it got bigger was more stunning.'[10]

*

In the summer of 1966, Schlesinger had returned to Santa Cruz to continue his studies, and Hockney would visit him there at weekends, trips which were immortalised in a series of beautiful drawings, such as *Peter in Santa Cruz*, which demonstrate his ever-increasing skill with a line. Among these, perhaps the most sublime is *Dream Inn, Santa Cruz*, a touching portrait of Schlesinger asleep on a bed, the tranquillity and gentleness of which says everything about the happiness of the relationship. It is a remarkably accomplished drawing, in which he breathes life into his lover's body with an astonishing economy of line. Hockney didn't have to wait long for them to be permanently reunited, since Schlesinger was becoming increasingly disenchanted with the lack of any art teaching at Santa Cruz, and was missing Hockney. At the end of the term he made the decision to transfer down to UCLA, which he was able to do quickly thanks to the help of Hockney's friend Bill Brice, an influential teacher there who pulled a few strings.

So at the beginning of 1967, Schlesinger moved into the Pico Boulevard apartment and began his art course. He had to explain his new living arrangements to his parents, to whom he was close. 'I was living with David,' Schlesinger recalls, 'but I pretended to my parents that I wasn't. Then they found out what was going on, and there were fights and arguments and they eventually said I had to go and see a psychiatrist. They sent me to see someone I knew, and I went for a while, but I hated doing it because I didn't feel I had a problem that needed changing.'[11] These sessions kept his parents off his back, but amounted to little more than hours of gossiping about mutual friends. The person who helped Schlesinger most was Nick Wilder. 'My father once went to see Nick to say he was worried about me, and Nick said to him, "Your son is with a very wonderful person and would you rather have him hustling on Santa Monica Boulevard?" and that was one thing that helped my father see my relationship in context, because Nick, being naturally drawn to the underworld of LA, knew all of that scene of hustling.'[12]

Although Hockney had shared apartments before, this was the first time that he had ever lived with a lover and it was quite a steep learning curve, since Hockney was a self-confessed slob, and Schlesinger was naturally neat and tidy. For Hockney, it was a blissful period. With

Schlesinger out at school, he would paint all day, then go out in the evenings to eat, returning home to a bed which was as much a place to read as to sleep or make love. Unable to go to bars since Schlesinger was underage, they kept the fridge stocked with Californian white wine. Sometimes they would go to Nick Wilder's for a swim, and hang out with the young and beautiful boys who were invariably to be found there. They went to the cinema a lot, and visited friends, in particular Christopher Isherwood and Don Bachardy, and Jack Larson and Jim Bridges, Hockney regarding both of these couples as role models when it came to successful gay relationships. 'The six of us spent many hilarious evenings together,' wrote Schlesinger, 'often at a little Japanese restaurant where they would sneak me sake, illicitly.'[13] 'Looking back on it,' Hockney wrote, 'it was certainly the happiest year I spent in California, and it was the worst place we lived in.'[14]

In the first few months of 1967, Hockney worked on *A Bigger Splash* and *Peter Getting Out of Nick's Pool*, as well as new paintings such as *A Lawn Sprinkler* and *Four Different Kinds of Water*. Then he went off to teach three days a week of the summer term at Berkeley, the oldest part of the University of California, on the east shore of San Francisco Bay. Here they gave him a studio and put him up in a hotel on Telegraph Avenue. It was quite a different experience from his previous posts, because he was teaching graduates, who proved to be an interesting group, and included Joel Perlman, who went on to become a successful sculptor, and the painters Alan Turner and Mary Heilman. In addition, it was an extraordinary time to be in the San Francisco area, then at the centre of the phenomenon that has come to be known as the 'Summer of Love'. This had its origins in the Golden Gate Park, where on 14 January 1967, tens of thousands of young people came together on a glorious sunny day to celebrate a Gathering of the Tribes, a Human Be-In, at which Timothy Leary addressed the crowd and encouraged them to 'Turn on, tune in, drop out'. By the summer, the message had reached 100,000 people, who had variously made their way to San Francisco in a haze of marijuana, LSD and flower petals.

Although he was aware of it, the counter-culture affected Hockney very little, though he did occasionally attend anti-Vietnam War meetings. He was too busy teaching, painting in his studio and flying back at the weekends to see Schlesinger. Occasionally he would stray from the path of true love. 'Sometimes I can remember I would have gone to bed in my hotel and then woke up thinking, "I'm feeling a bit horny." and I'd get up, get in the car and drive over to San Francisco and check into the Embarcadero YMCA, which is cheap, and it was an amazing place. All you had to do was check in and you got this tiny little room for about three dollars, and if you went for a shower and it was three in the morning, as soon as they heard the shower going, there would be two or three other guys who'd come and join you and you got what you wanted pretty quickly. I just thought this was amazing. This is America.'[15]

Hockney completed *A Bigger Splash* in Berkeley, before beginning a new work, another painting featuring Schlesinger. Leafing through the *San Francisco Chronicle* one day, he had come across an advertisement for Macy's department store, which used a colour shot of a room to advertise furniture. 'The photograph caught my eye,' he wrote, 'because it was so simple and such a direct view, although it's got angles in it . . . I thought it's marvellous, it's like a piece of sculpture, I must use it.'[16] Directly transcribed to the canvas, it showed a room furnished with a single bed, a side table and a rug, with the light coming from an open window in the top right-hand corner. Hockney's next thought was that there should be someone on the bed, so he summoned Schlesinger to fly up to Berkeley for the weekend and photographed him lying on a table at the correct angle, naked from the waist down. The two images were then put together.

The finished work was named after the town where Edgar Rice Burroughs lived and wrote the Tarzan books. 'He called the painting *The Room, Tarzana*,' Schlesinger recalls, 'because I was from Encino and Tarzana was the next-door community. I didn't want him to call it *The Room, Encino* as I thought my parents might see it and recognise it as being me. David was of course quite oblivious to any of these fears and couldn't care less what my parents thought or anything.'[17] Since the painting is undeniably erotic, presenting him as a sex-object lying face down on the bed, passive, his eyes open and buttocks bare, wearing nothing but a T-shirt and a pair of white sports socks, Schlesinger's caution is understandable. Though many people have cited *Reclining Girl*, Boucher's 1751 portrait of the child-courtesan Marie-Louise O'Murphy, as an obvious reference for this painting, Hockney denies this, saying, 'I knew the painting, of course, but it wasn't in my mind at the time.'[18]

The Room, Tarzana is important because of the way Hockney used light and shade to create perspective. There are no shadows in *A Bigger Splash*, nor in *Portrait of Nick Wilder*, though there are hints of shadow in *Beverly Hills Housewife*. '. . . because of this light dancing around,' he wrote of this painting, 'I realised the light in the room was a subject and for the first time it became an interesting thing for me, light. Consequently I had to arrange Peter so the light was coming from the direction of the window . . . I remember being struck by it as I was painting it; real light; this is the first time I'm taking any notice of shadows and light. After that it begins to get stronger in the pictures.'[19]

In the early summer, with his teaching contract at an end, Hockney ended his tenancy in Pico Boulevard and decided to give Schlesinger the treat that he wanted more than anything else, which was to make his first trip to Europe, and to travel by sea. They sailed cabin class on the RMS *Queen Elizabeth*, then the largest passenger ship in the world. Schlesinger was entranced by the decor, with its wood panelling and curved surfaces, which he labelled 'Dowdy Deco', and was thrilled when they passed the Queen Elizabeth's sister ship the *Queen Mary* mid-ocean, with much sounding of horns. In the dining room they shared a table for the whole journey with a Mr and Mrs Wally Warwick from Allentown, Pennsylvania. 'They didn't say much,' Hockney recalls, 'but I remember that he collected wooden decoy ducks. They said they were coming to Europe and going to go to Switzerland. I said I'd assumed that they would go to Italy as I thought all Americans went to Italy, and Mrs Warwick said no, she didn't like Italy because of what the Italians did in the war. She said they were no respecters of authority. Well, I told her that as far as I was concerned, that was one of their more charming characteristics.'[20]

Schlesinger was thrilled to arrive in England to a welcoming committee of friends, including Patrick Procktor, fresh from a successful show at the Redfern Gallery, John Kasmin and Ossie Clark, all eager to meet Hockney's new lover. They drove off to Powis Terrace, which did not particularly impress Schlesinger. 'It then really only consisted of two big rooms, and I remember thinking it was kind of filthy. Of course David smoked heavily, and I had never smoked, and I didn't particularly like the cigarette ash in the bed.'[21] Hockney's first big sacrifice for Schlesinger, a demonstration of the strong feelings he held for him, was to give up smoking. It was a privation that also delighted his mother. 'I am so glad about that,' she confided to her diary '– he is a good boy, only different . . . he has his own ideas of life but I'm so happy about him and very thankful.'[22]

Once they had settled into Powis Terrace, the unsophisticated boy from Encino had to deal with the enormous social circle in which Hockney moved. 'It was a little scary,' Schlesinger recalls, 'because I was only nineteen and shy and I didn't know anybody. Swinging London was in full swing and I was a little suburban Californian.'[23] Hockney may have been little-known in America, but in London he was a star, one of the glittering group of young artists, musicians, designers and photographers that had put London on the cover of *Time* the previous year. Antonioni had come to London to film *Blow-Up*, the Rolling Stones and the Beatles ruled the world of popular music, it was a must to be seen in the pages of *Vogue*, and the Scotch of St James, Sibylla's and the 100 Club lit up the night scene. Society revelled in its new 'classlessness' and its leading hostesses fell over themselves to invite Hockney and Schlesinger to their houses. 'There was a big garden party at Lindy and Sheridan Dufferin's,' Schlesinger remembers, 'and Princess Margaret was the guest of honour. Nothing could happen until she arrived, and when she arrived she had to go around and shake everybody's hand, and somehow, being the least important person there, I was the last person for her to meet and I didn't have a clue what to say. I was left speechless. Everyone was wearing silver, and I was sitting at a table with Lord Snowdon, and at one point in the evening he threw a glass of wine at Princess Margaret.'[24]

Hockney's fame was well attested when he was one of the sixty-four signatories of a full-page open letter in *The Times* on 24 July, paid for by the Beatles, calling for the legalisation of marijuana; others included Jonathan Miller, George Melly, Tom Driberg MP, David Bailey and David Dimbleby. Though this letter was to achieve nothing, other than to elicit a few splutterings of horror from Middle England, a few days previously a far more important piece of legislation had been passed by Parliament that was to transform Hockney's life and the lives of countless other homosexuals.

On 21 July 1967, royal assent had been finally granted to the 1965 Sexual Offences Bill, which gave exemption from prosecution for homosexual acts committed between consenting adults in the privacy of their own home. It was a huge step forward, even though outside this exemption homosexuality continued, technically speaking, to be a punishable offence, a situation that was not to change until 2003. 'The Earl of Arran,' reported *The Times*, '. . . said that because of the Bill perhaps a million human beings would be able to live in greater peace. "I find this (he said) a truly awesome and a truly wonderful thought."'[25] Cecil Beaton wrote, 'A great event in history that this should have been achieved.' Had it happened a century earlier, he mused, 'Oscar Wilde could have given us half a dozen more *Importances* and early life for so many of us made less difficult.'[26]

At the end of July, Hockney decided to whisk Schlesinger away from the social whirl and take him and Patrick Procktor on a tour of Europe. Hockney loved to drive, and this was the first of many similar trips, dubbed 'Mr Whizz's Tours' by Christopher Isherwood, and done entirely on Hockney's terms. The drive to Paris passed without event, though it was a little slow, since Hockney's brand-new Morris Minor convertible, which he nicknamed his 'district nurse's car', had a 900cc engine and was incapable of overtaking. In Paris they stopped at a little art materials shop on the corner of Boulevard Saint-Michel and Rue Saint-André des Arts to buy watercolours and paper, as the most practical painting medium for travelling.

The next stop was to be Uzès, near Nîmes, where Douglas Cooper, the celebrated collector and friend of Picasso, lived in the Château de Castile. Famously obstreperous and a cultivator of quarrels, he was not a man who took kindly to people turning up uninvited at odd hours. 'He wasn't expecting us,' Schlesinger recalls, 'and we just rang his bell and the servant came out and said, "I'm not waking him at five in the morning," and we had to sleep in the car until Mr Cooper could be awakened and he was not pleased. David just used to arrive at people's doorsteps with three other people thinking they would be pleased to see him . . . Douglas did actually allow us to stay one night there.'[27]

From Nîmes they headed to Italy, stopping off in Lucca to visit the American art critic Mario Amaya, and visiting Ferrill Amacker in Florence. After a short spell on the beach in Viareggio, they ended up in Rome. As they travelled, they painted, but while Patrick discovered a true love of the immediacy of watercolour, Hockney could not persevere with it. 'It was the first time I properly tried watercolour, but in the end I preferred coloured pencils,' he says. 'With watercolour, you have to follow certain rules otherwise you are in the soup. For instance, you have to move from light to dark because you can't put a light colour on top of a dark, and generally you can't put more than three coats on otherwise the colour would begin to get nondescript and muddy. There are techniques you have to follow and I got into it a bit but I didn't get into it enough for me to want to carry on.'[28]

After Rome, they drove back to France to stay with Kasmin who had rented a house for the summer, the only actual invitation they had. For Procktor and particularly Schlesinger, the trip had been a steep learning curve. 'There was no plan; there was no map,' he remembers. 'We didn't know where we were going. There were no reservations anywhere. If you stopped somewhere and the inn was full, you'd have to spend the night sleeping in the Morris Minor. That wasn't too comfortable even for me but for Patrick, who was so tall, it was an absolute nightmare.'[29]

Their destination was Carennac, a medieval village of breathtaking beauty that lay right on the banks of the River Dordogne. John and Jane Kasmin had first visited it in 1961, taking rooms in the chateau, which had been turned into a hotel. Carennac's romantic history appealed to the poet in Kasmin, its ancient priory having been for many years the home of François Fénelon, the seventeenth-century Catholic theologian, who was said to have written there his famous work *Télémaque*, a saga of the adventures of the son of Ulysses and Penelope. When the chateau finally shut up shop as a hotel, the Kasmins decided to rent it every August during their sons' school holidays. The painter Howard Hodgkin and his wife Julia joined them in this enterprise, and over the next few years, Carennac was to be the setting for a number of idyllic summer holidays for them and their families and friends.

On this first visit, Hockney and Schlesinger coincided with the Cornwall-Joneses and Jane Kasmin's mother, the fabric designer and painter E. Q. Nicholson. The long, carefree days, filled with sunbathing, sightseeing and reading, were immortalised in drawings such as *Carennac, Vichy Water and 'Howards End'*, *Jane in a Straw Hat* and *Kasmin in Bed in His Chateau in Carennac*, while the evenings generally passed in a haze of delicious food, wine and marijuana. 'It was a lovely place, with loads of bedrooms,' Hockney remembers. 'In the evenings we played word games. I remember one game where somebody said a word and the next person had to say a word that either rhymed with it or made sense with it . . . It got interesting as it started to get faster because the words seemed to get quite revealing and if people kept it going, it was very good. Mo [McDermott] was good at it because he simply said the first word that came into his head, even if it had no relationship to the word that was spoken. I never remember him stopping the game. It was Kasmin who was the one who usually stopped the game because he was trying to think up something clever.'[30]

This European tour convinced Schlesinger that he 'was born on the wrong continent in the wrong century', and that he had to move to London. However, when he applied for a place at the RCA, Hockney's connection with the college did not work in his favour. 'I took along a portfolio of drawings I had done at UCLA,' Schlesinger recalls, 'and

I was turned down. I heard later that it was because they thought David had done the drawings for me.'[31] Disappointing though this was, Patrick Procktor then suggested that he should apply to the Slade, which eventually accepted him, to begin his course in September 1968. As it turned out, being a much smaller school, it was to suit Schlesinger better.

Both Hockney and Schlesinger were prolific photographers and they returned to England with rolls and rolls of film. Hockney's prints and negatives usually ended up being chucked haphazardly into a box, never to be looked at again. On this occasion, however, after Schlesinger had returned to UCLA, Hockney had a clear-up and came upon several boxes of his own photographs from the previous five years. 'I realised then that if you put them away in boxes and you can't see them, they just get lost and you have to be able to see things. So I made a decision to just stick everything into books.'[32] He immediately went to Harrods and bought a large green photograph album into which he stuck all his snapshots from the previous five years. Inspired by this, and by the belief that he could take photographs just as well as anyone elses, he also bought his first good camera, a 35mm Pentax. From the moment he started his next album, the quality of the images got better and better.

After Schlesinger had returned to UCLA, Hockney turned his hand to another portrait, this time of his old friend Patrick Procktor. It was the first of a series of portraits he was to paint over the next ten years, in which he sought to re-educate himself as a draughtsman and test his powers of observation. In *The Room, Manchester Street* he further developed his use of perspective, to create an illusion of space, and used backlight effectively to show off the figure of Procktor, standing, campily holding a Sweet Afton cigarette in his left hand. The shadows on the floor and the patterned carpet created by the cool silvery light pouring through the venetian blinds are also beautifully subtle. Made from a mixture of drawings, photographs and life, the painting depicts Procktor's London home and studio at 25 Manchester Street, which the artist André Gallard described as being 'rather like going into a film set: as if you had stepped back into 1880'.[33] In fact, as Hockney described it, you never really knew what you were going to find there. 'In 1967 Patrick's studio looked clean, neat and office-like. The next year it looked like a den in the Casbah – it seemed to change as often as Auntie Mame's.'[34] In the portrait, which brilliantly captures Patrick's theatrical bearing and extravagant hand gestures, it has the former appearance. Though honoured to have been the subject of such an important painting, Procktor never really liked the portrait, which he considered to be unflattering.

While Hockney was still working on this painting, one of his other portraits won him the most prestigious art prize in England, the publicity for which took his fame to a new level. The John Moores Prize for Contemporary Painting was held biennially at the Walker Art Gallery in Liverpool. First awarded in 1957, when it was intended to be a one-off event, it was the brainchild of John Moores, the founder of the Littlewoods department store and the football pools company, who was a keen amateur painter, and who wanted to celebrate the best of modern art in Britain. Open to all, its subsequent success ensured that it was soon regarded as the country's leading showcase for avant-garde art. In its tenth year, Hockney won with *Peter Getting Out of Nick's Pool.* 'Preview at John Moores Exhibition at Liverpool,' wrote Laura in her diary. 'We were very proud and pleased to see David on Television he being first prize-winner at the Exhibition. Almost all the papers had write-ups with photos of both David and his picture. We had many congratulations around.'[35] In a typically generous gesture, Hockney put half the considerable prize money of £1,500 towards a trip to Australia for his parents, to visit his brother Philip.

The Room, Manchester Street was completed in January 1968, just in time to be included in his fourth one-man show at the Kasmin Gallery, a striking exhibition of seven large canvases, which he called *A splash, a lawn, two rooms, two stains, some neat cushions and a table . . . painted.* It hung alongside *A Bigger Splash*, *The Room Tarzana* and four other new pictures, *Two Stains on a Room on a Canvas*, *A Neat Lawn*, *Some Neat Cushions* and *A Table.* 'David's exhibition is wonderful,' wrote Laura of her and Ken's

visit to it '– only 7 huge pictures – but he does improve and his work is
so perfect in detail. It seems a huge success and there have been more
than 2000 visitors in 9 days.' Writing in *The Times*, Guy Brett described
'images which are permeated with Hockney's feeling for Los Angeles.
These new paintings are sharper and neater and broader in scale than
earlier ones; the brittle subject matter and Hockney's dry shallow paint
surface are very elegantly matched.'[36]

With the show over, Hockney flew to New York with Kasmin,
staying at the Stanhope Hotel on Fifth Avenue, across the street from
the Metropolitan Museum. The plan was to return to LA to spend
six months with Schlesinger prior to his course at the Slade, but not
before undertaking another epic road trip across America, this time in
a Volkswagen brought over from Europe by a friend of Schlesinger's.
After much cajoling Hockney persuaded Schlesinger to take a few
days off school and fly up to join them. He arrived at the Stanhope
soon after midnight and at five in the morning the three of them set
off, driving through Pennsylvania, Ohio, Iowa, Nebraska, Colorado
and Utah, everything recorded in hundreds of photographs taken by
Hockney with his new Pentax camera. '. . . it was like an *Easy Rider*
in a Volkswagen,' he wrote. 'Nice pictures of Colorado when it was
snowing.'[37]

    While Hockney had been in London, Schlesinger had moved in
with friends who lived on 3rd Street in Santa Monica. In a 1934 art deco
apartment building across the street – which in LA was considered
historic – there was a tiny penthouse for rent, where Schlesinger and
Hockney could live, while using a small spare room in the friends'
house as a studio. It was a perfect arrangement. 'It was like being on
the *Queen Mary*,' wrote Hockney, 'with the mist in the morning, in
Winter . . . and it was very nice. They were very happy times; once
we were in the house, I didn't care if I went out to see anybody or not,
whereas before that . . . I was a roamer, I had to go out. It was because
of Peter. Why should I go to a bar and roam around? There was no
need for it.'[38]

Again Hockney was to prove that an artist does not need a large studio to paint a big picture, for in the very small room in this old wooden house he produced three seven foot by ten foot paintings. In the first of these, he challenged himself to attempt something he'd never done before: his first double portrait. The painting was quite different from any of his previous works containing two figures, such as the marriage pictures and the domestic scenes, in that those were painted from his imagination rather than from life; and the subjects he settled on were Christopher Isherwood and Don Bachardy, two of his most intimate friends who also happened to live conveniently close by.

Hockney was fascinated by the dynamics of their relationship and began by hanging out with them and working up preliminary drawings. 'The trouble with drawing people you don't know,' he told the art historian Anthony Bailey, 'is that you never really know what they look like. You spend a lot of time just trying to get a likeness. Whereas if you know them well you know there are several faces there. You can draw one of them, a face that belongs to a certain day.'[39]

He also took lots of photographs of the two men, observing that when he asked them to relax, Isherwood would always sit with his right foot across his left knee looking at Bachardy, while Bachardy would look straight at Hockney. That gave him the pose, and the 'story' – in this case an older man's worries about his much younger lover. 'If a picture has a person or two people in it,' he said, 'there is a human drama that's meant to be talked about. It's not just about lines.'[40] Though the setting for the portrait is the living room of their house, Hockney never took his easel and paints down there, preferring to work on it in his little studio. While Isherwood would often come and sit for him, he relied mostly on photographs for the figure of Bachardy. 'I remember that when the painting was almost finished, he was still dissatisfied with the painting of my head,' Bachardy remembers. 'If you look at the painting you can see that the paint on my head is much more built-up than it is with Chris, where the paint is very fresh, very first time, whereas he really laboured over me.'[41]

Part of the problem was that just when Hockney was quite far into the portrait, Bachardy left LA to go and live in London for two months, a situation that did not make Isherwood particularly happy. 'Three-thirty in the afternoon and raining hard in heavy gusty showers,' he wrote in his diary on 1 April. '. . . Just the right weather for the situation in this house, which is that Don took off at noon for London. We neither of us quite knew why he was doing this. Chiefly because David Hockney has lent us his apartment and since I still have no reason to go there it seemed as if Don had better use it.'[42] Since he was lonely after Bachardy had left, Isherwood got into the habit of dropping round to Hockney's studio most days, either to sit for him or just to talk about books, California or life. 'He'd talk about Don being in England,' Hockney recalled. 'I do remember he said, "Oh David, don't ever get too possessive about your friends; let them feel free." Later I think he was a bit hurt that Don stayed away a long time. Still, it was good advice.'[43] Eventually, dissatisfied with not being able to paint from life, Hockney rolled up the canvas and took it to London, only to find that Bachardy had left the previous week. The result was that it was completed without another sitting. 'When I saw the picture,' Bachardy remembers, 'it was quite clear that Chris looked much fresher, and I don't think that David was ever satisfied with the version of me. I know better than to complain, and in the end what does it matter? We were flattered and pleased to be among the subjects for those wonderful double portraits.'[44]

About a month after he had started work on *Christopher Isherwood and Don Bachardy*, Hockney began a second double portrait, of the wealthy art collectors Fred and Marcia Weisman. Marcia Weisman was the daughter of Meyer Simon, of Portland, Oregon, the creator of the Hunt Wesson Foods empire. In the early 1950s she and Fred began to build up what would become one of the best contemporary art collections in the country. Their first purchase was *Self Absorbed*, a sculpture by Jean Arp, which they followed up with works by Willem de Kooning, Andy Warhol, Barnett Newman, Clyfford Still, Ed Ruscha and others, until they owned over a thousand major pieces, including Jasper Johns's iconic *Map*. On meeting Hockney, she asked him if he would paint her husband. He declined, since he did not like taking on commissions; but after seeing their house he offered to paint them as a couple.

American Collectors is a characteristically witty portrait in which the Weismans are portrayed, rather like Betty Freeman, as further objects in their collection. 'In the Weisman portrait,' he wrote, 'there's a Turnbull sculpture, a Henry Moore sculpture, other things, all part of them. The portrait wasn't just in the faces, it was in the whole setting.'[45] On the left Fred stands bolt upright as if carved from a piece of wood, his hand clenched so tight that an accidental drip, which Hockney chose to leave on the canvas, almost appears to have been squeezed out by him. To his right stands Marcia, echoing a huge totem pole behind her, her mouth frozen in the same rictus grin as the face on the pole. 'It really had a similar look,' wrote Hockney. 'I couldn't resist putting that in.'[46] Marcia was not amused. In fact, the Weismans hated the picture so much that they decided to take it out of circulation by buying it and donating it to the Pasadena Museum, with the stipulation that it should be kept in the basement.

Hockney completed one more large painting, *California Seascape*, which depicts a window and sea view in the home of the artist Dick Smith, in Corona del Mar, before returning to London with the unfinished portrait of Isherwood and Bachardy. Had it not been for Schlesinger starting at the Slade, though, he would almost certainly have remained in California and travelled back and forth. His mother was delighted. 'David is back again in London,' she wrote at the beginning of July. 'He came home just for a few days. Met the people who are to judge the "First Biennale of Prints" in Bradford at Cartwright Hall. My washer has broken down – but David went in to town with me and bought a brand new Servis Super Twin. He is so kind to me, indeed to us. He gave Ken money, but he never spends it wisely.'[47]

His return home turned out to be timely, as in September, on a trip to Bradford to judge the work sent in for the Print Biennale, he was able to see at first hand just how ill his father was and what Laura had to cope with. '. . . in the odd hour we had together we talked of Australia. Dad was late in and David kept going to bus stop to meet him and back again to find he had not come. We started our meal but could not enjoy it. Had just picked up phone to call Infirmary when Mr Holloway came to back door. He had picked Ken up in Harrogate Road. Again in coma – he had kept on the bus to the terminus at Ravenscliffe and walked back half dazed – dared not cross road and slumped by wall. David tried to impress the fact he must come straight home – or there would be no Australia . . . I was getting so ill with worry night after night.'[48]

Schlesinger arrived in London in September, ready to take up his course at the Slade. Foreign students were not given their own painting area on the premises, so one of his first moves was to buy himself a bike in order to cycle each morning to the school, in Gower Street, Bloomsbury, and from there to Regent's Park, where he had temporarily rented studio space off Kitaj. As a result, Schlesinger never quite fitted in, because he would have to leave after classes, while the other students hung around to paint. It didn't help either when word got out that he was David Hockney's boyfriend, and he was considered a bit of an oddity. 'I would flit in and out of the Slade,' he recalls, 'but I had this whole other life with David, a very un-studenty life. I raised a few eyebrows at the Slade, especially when I arrived in my Ossie Clark snakeskin jacket. I didn't really take part in the student life there.'[49]

At least Hockney was supportive. 'He certainly took an interest in my painting,' Schlesinger remembers. 'He was respectful of my work without critiquing my pictures. He didn't like to carry on in a professorial way, but he certainly encouraged me, and he hung some of my work up on the wall in Powis Terrace.' The closest he came to giving Schlesinger any kind of tutorial was allowing him to watch and draw alongside him while he worked on a portrait. 'I drew Cecil Beaton a couple of times with David,' Schlesinger recalls, 'and I drew while David was drawing John Gielgud and Rudolf Nureyev.'[50] On another occasion, Lindy Dufferin had managed to persuade Sir Frederick Ashton to allow her and Hockney to draw the Royal Ballet in rehearsal. They took Schlesinger along, but since only two of them were allowed in the rehearsal room at once, he had to stand and watch from the door. Here he caught the eye of Wayne Sleep, one of the company's up-and-coming young dancers. 'During my breaks, I chatted to him there,' Sleep wrote later, 'and he asked if I would be willing to be drawn. This led to an invitation to join them that day, with Sir Fred, at

Lindy's house in Holland Park for lunch. Sir Fred and I posed together for the artists, he in a chair with me (naked) sitting at his feet.'[51]

While Hockney's sitters usually had no objection to Schlesinger being brought along, there was one notorious occasion when the subject was extremely unhappy about it. In October 1968, the music critic of the *Observer*, Peter Heyworth, suggested to Hockney that he might like to do a portrait of W. H. Auden, who happened to be staying with him. Since he longed to meet Auden, Hockney cast aside all his usual doubts about commissions, and said he would love to. Without asking, he decided to take Kitaj and Schlesinger with him, reasoning that Auden was probably not unlike Chris Isherwood, who was always cheered up by the sight of a beautiful young boy. How wrong he turned out to be. 'Auden was a bit grumpy about having three people there,' wrote Hockney, 'and my impression of him then was that maybe he was playing a role, the grumpy man, because he complained all the time about pornography. He talked all the time. He said every time he went to the railway station in New York to make a journey and he wanted to read detective novels, it was all pornography now, all pornography. He gave me the impression of being rather like the headmaster of an English school.'[52] The documentary maker and author Peter Adam, who was involved in filming Auden at the time, put it more strongly: 'Auden was furious . . . he kept on about "the manners of people who have no manners and the invasion of his privacy".'[53] In spite of the bad atmosphere, the drawings Hockney made were a success, beautifully capturing the craggy lined landscape of the poet's face. 'I kept thinking,' Hockney said, 'if his face looks like this, what must his balls look like?'[54]

In between putting the finishing touches to *Christopher Isherwood and Don Bachardy*, and planning a new double portrait, Hockney was typically industrious, going on a trip down the Rhine in September to take photographs of castles, as references for a new illustrated *Grimm's Fairy Tales*, as well as paying a visit in October to a friend who had a house in the south of France, the film director Tony Richardson. Hockney had first come across the flamboyant and complex Richardson while working on *Ubu Roi* at the Royal Court and they had struck up an instant friendship. They had a Yorkshire background in common,

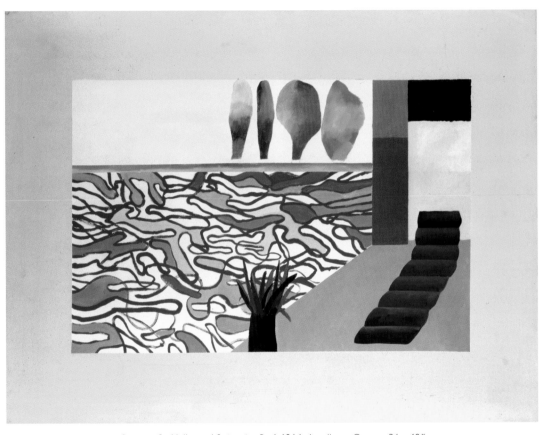

Picture of a Hollywood Swimming Pool, **1964.** Acrylic on Canvas, 36 × 48˝

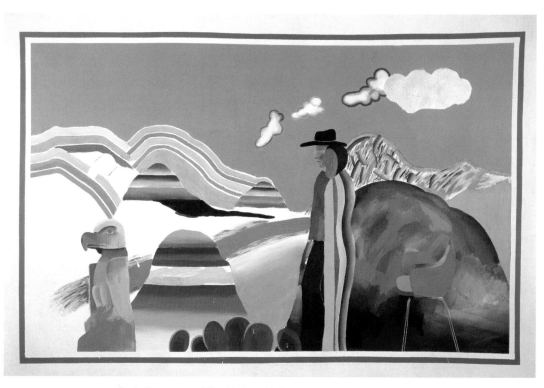

Rocky Mountains and Tired Indians, **1965.** Acrylic on Canvas, 67 x 99 ½″

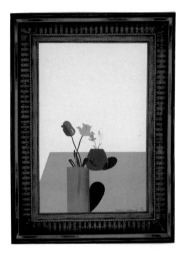
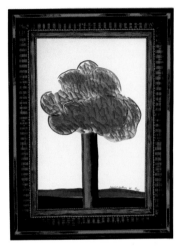
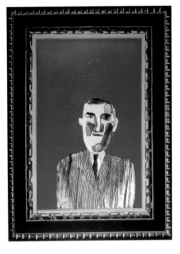
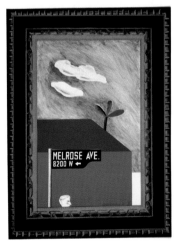
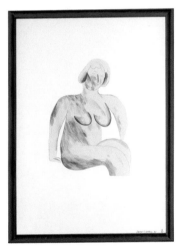
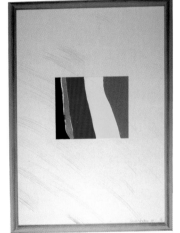

A Hollywood Collection, 1965

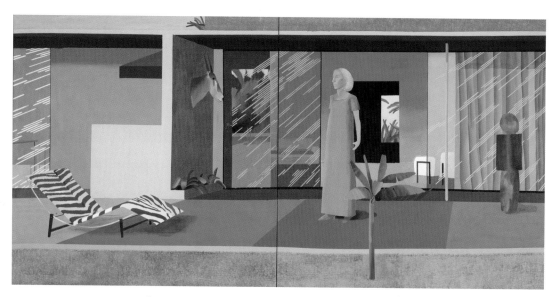

Beverly Hills Housewife, 1966-67. Acrylic on Canvas, 72 x 144″

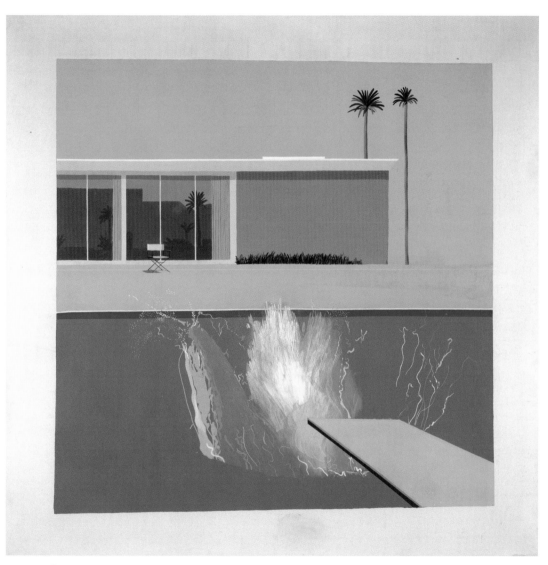

A Bigger Splash, **1967.** Acrylic on Canvas, 96 x 96″

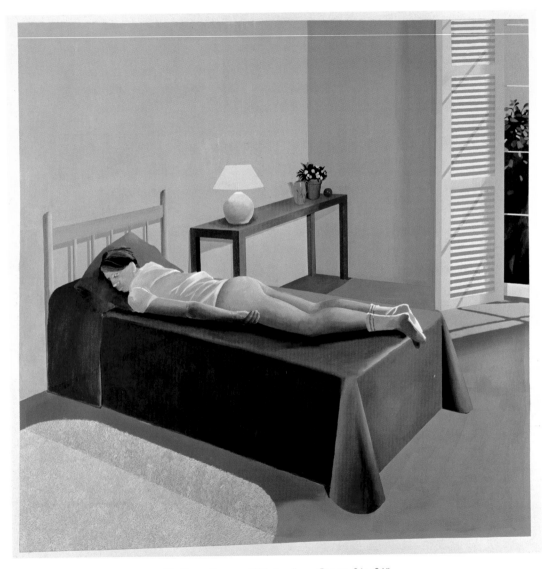

The Room, Tarzana, 1967. Acrylic on Canvas, 96 × 96″

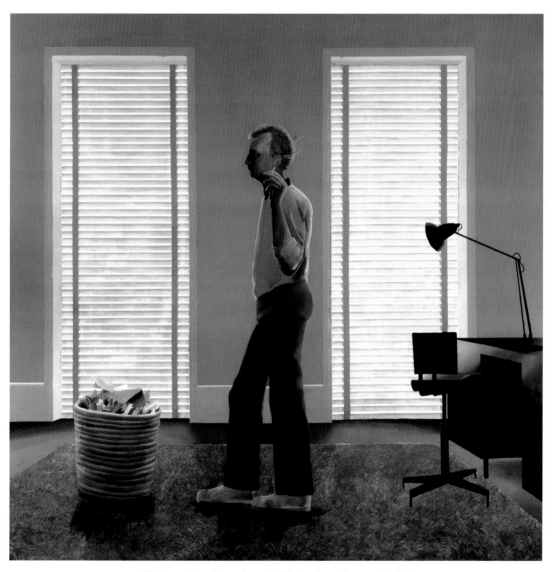

The Room, Manchester Street, 1967. Acrylic on Canvas, 96 x 96″

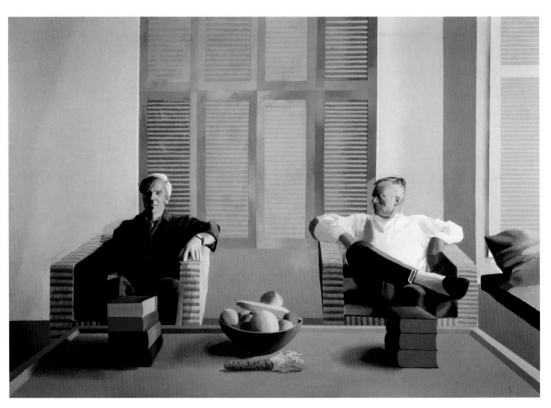

Christopher Isherwood and Don Bachardy, 1968. Acrylic on Canvas, 83 ½ × 119 ½″

Richardson, the son of a pharmacist, having been born and brought up in Saltaire, just outside Bradford, and educated at Ashville College, a minor public school in Harrogate. By the time they met, Richardson had had a distinguished career, firstly in the theatre with the English Stage Company, putting on the first productions of *Look Back in Anger* and *The Entertainer*, and latterly in films, as the director of two successful social realist productions, *A Taste of Honey* and *The Loneliness of the Long-Distance Runner*. Having made a fortune from his latest film, *Tom Jones*, to which, along with John Osborne and Albert Finney, he owned all the rights, he had used part of the money to buy an extraordinary property in the mountains above St Tropez, just outside the town of La Garde-Freinet.

Le Nid de Duc, 'the nest of the night owl', was a hamlet in which two or three families had once eked out a living harvesting cork from the cork-oak forest which was the only real source of revenue in the area. Abandoned since the 1950s, it was almost entirely in ruins when Richardson first came across it, and he fell instantly in love with it, seduced as much as anything by the profusion of wild flowers that flourished there throughout the seasons, 'the wild mimosa . . . the wild tree heather, white and purple; the scarlet poppies; the violets and blue periwinkles; the purple and yellow flags; orchids of every colour; white starwort and daisies; gold celandine and ragwort; green spurge; and the red and orange berries of the arbutus'.[55] By the time Hockney paid his visit – the first of many over the next few years – it had been restored with the help of local craftsmen. There were six houses habitable and, precariously cantilevered out of the sloping hillside, a brand-new swimming pool, which was later to form the setting for another of his most iconic paintings.

Richardson was a wonderful and generous host who mixed and matched his guests regardless of class or sexual preference, so long as they amused him and were prepared to bend to his whim. 'When you are at his mercy,' wrote Christopher Isherwood, 'he can drive you absolutely nuts. You have to do exactly what he says every moment of the day. If you refuse he asks "Are you alright?" as much as to suggest that your refusal is the first sign of an oncoming mental breakdown.'[56] The six houses could accommodate twenty or thirty people, usually artists, musicians, actors and writers, with any children sleeping in one huge room, and everybody gathered together for meals, which were taken outside on a long table set beneath a huge tree, around which ducks and peacocks wandered. Delicious Provençal food was provided, while wine flowed, loosening tongues and encouraging gossip. Guests needed their wits about them, especially if Richardson decided to play one of his 'truth' games. 'He once asked a man,' wrote Isherwood, '"How long was it after your marriage before you started sleeping with boys again?" And the man hesitated and then replied, "Four months," and his wife cried out and got up and left the room, and soon afterwards they were divorced.'[57] After years of experiencing similar behaviour, John Osborne, his partner in Woodfall Films, used Richardson as the model for the character of KL, the tyrannical film producer from whom the three couples are escaping, in his play *The Hotel in Amsterdam.*

Richardson loved games, not all of them quite so sadistic. He 'organised games, picnics and theatre evenings; treasure hunts could last the whole day. He would always make sure that the most unsuitable couples or the most unconventional ones were teamed up together. One never knew what one would find: bottles of champagne hidden in a stream with glasses, or a book with pornographic photographs.'[58] In the evenings there would be charades, or murder in the dark, and sometimes elaborate theatrical productions put on by Natasha and Joely, Richardson's children from his marriage to Vanessa Redgrave. The one thing that was expected of the guests was that they should join in, and woe betide those who didn't. 'He could be cruel or incredibly charming,' Schlesinger recalled, 'directing the house party as he would one of his plays or movies, and he loved guests who performed well. No extrovert, I failed the audition and he took a great dislike to me.'[59] Hockney, who refused to join in the games, was told by people, 'Well, he'll never invite you again', but because he was always seen to be drawing and observing, he got away with it and was asked back many times.

*

On his return to London, and with *Christopher Isherwood and Don Bachardy* finally completed, Hockney was preoccupied with thinking about a new double portrait of his close friend Henry Geldzahler and his partner Christopher Scott, whom Hockney had drawn once before, in 1967, in the lithograph *Henry and Christopher*, which shows Henry seated in an armchair and Christopher lying on a sofa in the Chateau Marmont. Each print in the edition of fifteen was customised: one, for example, has hand-painted multicoloured lines connecting their mouths, as if to signify a conversation taking place between them even though their mouths are closed. Hockney was intrigued by what made the relationship work between the gregarious and witty Geldzahler and the younger and rather dour Scott and, believing them to be perfect material for a new large oil, he flew to New York in November to stay with them, in the Wyoming Building on Seventh Avenue. In his role as curator of twentieth-century art at the Metropolitan Museum, Geldzahler was putting the final touches to *New York Painting and Sculpture: 1940–1970*, a landmark show that was to open the following year, and give the Museum of Modern Art a run for its money.

Geldzahler was a man Hockney truly loved, who made him laugh more than anyone else, and who introduced him into the New York art world where, as well as the Warhol crowd, he encountered artists such as Frank Stella and Ellsworth Kelly. With a great eye as well as a vast knowledge of art, Geldzahler was not afraid to criticise, and he became one of the few people from whom Hockney got critical feedback about his work. But like many a man of formidable intellect, Geldzahler could also be temperamental and difficult, and he had a voracious sexual appetite in which not even Hockney's boyfriend was off-limits. 'I first met Henry,' Schlesinger recalls, 'when I was in the little house in Santa Monica. He was a little chubby thing, but very amusing. At one point David had to go out to get some cigarettes, and at that moment Henry pounced on me. He literally did it in a matter of seconds. Once he'd established that I wasn't interested in going along with his desires, he immediately lost interest in me entirely. Of course that didn't apply to David, because he was famous. To get on with

Henry you had to be useful to him and you had to serve his ego in some way.'[60] Geldzahler's wit was legendary. On one occasion he managed to browbeat Andy Warhol into painting his portrait for free. When Warhol had completed it, he delivered it to Geldzahler, who had a good look at it before handing it back. 'You've left something out,' he told him. 'Whaaat?' drawled Warhol, in his soft, barely audible voice. 'The art!' replied Geldzahler.[61]

He could also be quite cruel. 'There was this old society lady called Violet Wyndham,' Hockney remembers, 'and she used to give lunches in Trevor Square. When I took Henry to lunch with her, I told him that she was a rather marvellous old lady whose mother was called Ada Leverson and was a very loyal friend to Oscar Wilde. She met him when he came out of prison and he said to her, "Only you, Ada, would know what hat to wear on an occasion like this." This was all explained to Henry before we went to lunch. Violet was pretty deaf, and when we arrived at her house and she greeted us, Henry turned to me and said loudly, "Now let me get this straight. Oscar Wilde was her mother." Of course I couldn't stop laughing, and Violet was saying, "What? What?" and I thought, "You are cruel, Henry, but you are very, very funny."'[62]

In New York, Hockney began the portrait of Geldzahler and Scott by doing some preliminary sketches. 'He did a few drawings on the spot,' Geldzahler later recounted, '– of my face, of Christopher and of the scene out of the window behind the couch, which was a scene out of the window in another room of the apartment. That was something he decided to do in order to let in more air, I suppose, more space to the picture.'[63] Scarcely had he started work, however, than Hockney was struck down with flu at a time when Geldzahler's doctor was on holiday in Florida. 'For the last four days of his stay,' Geldzahler recalled, 'he tried every home remedy in patent medicine that he had ever heard about. He also made the point over and over again that in England you can reach a doctor over the weekend. That has not been my experience.'[64]

In spite of being ill, Hockney still managed to get enough drawings done, and the painting was completed once he was back at home in

Powis Terrace. It was on this return journey to London, however, that he became involved in an incident which was to have profound significance, and which was to gain him almost heroic status within the homosexual community.

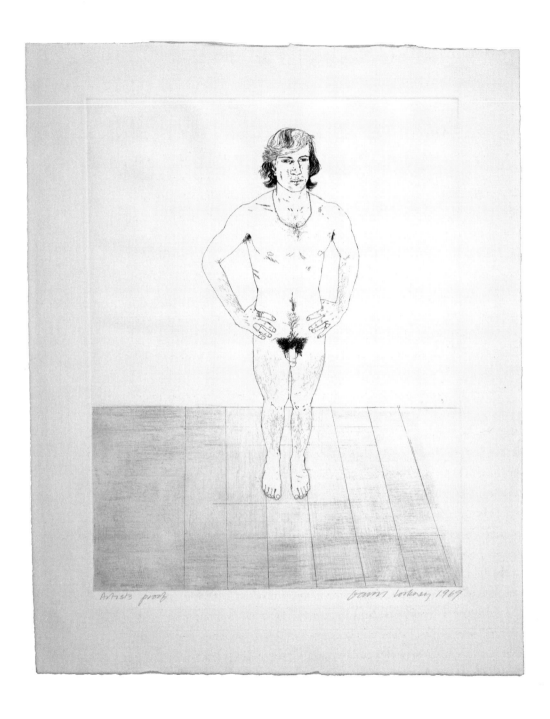

Artist's proof   David Hockney 1969

CHAPTER NINE

PETER 1969

Before his return to London at the beginning of December 1968, Hockney had been down to 42nd Street to stock up on the latest male physique magazines. With titles such as *Golden Boys*, *Teenage Nudist* and *Champion*, they were among the first American magazines to feature naked men full-frontal. As he passed through customs at Heathrow, a very young officer stopped him and asked him to open his bag. 'I'd put the magazines on top of my clothes,' Hockney recalls. 'They weren't very sexy. They were pictures of naked men posing in sylvan glades, that sort of thing.'[1] The customs officer took the magazines out of his bag, had a good look and told him he was confiscating them because they were pornographic. 'I said, "You've got the wrong person today. I'm not a little businessman who's going to run off. I'll see you in court if necessary."'[2]

Peter, 1969

When Hockney told Kasmin that he was prepared to fight the case, Kasmin suggested that it would be cheaper to fly back to New York and buy some more magazines. '"That's maybe what you'd do, Kas," I told him, "but I've got some principles."'[3] Hockney's first step was to telephone HM Customs and Excise's head office, where he was passed from official to official, each of whom told him that the magazines certainly qualified as pornography. 'Finally I got to the top guy,' he recalled, 'and he said, "Yes, we're seizing them, they're pornographic . . . in one of the pictures the boys have painted their genitals with psychedelic colours." I cracked up laughing on the phone and thought, if he doesn't think it's funny, I can't communicate with him at all . . . I told him I would see him in court.'[4] Hockney's confidence that he could win a court case was bolstered by his knowledge that in the USA, as a result of a series of Supreme Court rulings passed in 1962, similar photographs of nude men were not considered pornographic.

Next, he contacted the National Council for Civil Liberties who put him in touch with the prominent civil rights lawyer Benedict Birnberg, an outspoken defender of the rights of homosexuals. 'I had a call from Martin Ennals, the general secretary of the NCCL,' Birnberg remembers, 'asking me if I could help this young artist, David Hockney, who then came to see me in my office at London Bridge. He was artistically dressed, and he smoked prolifically. The legal atmosphere of the 1960s was still pretty repressive, with a lot of archaic legislation being enforced, so it was no surprise to me that Customs and Excise had seized these perfectly innocuous little magazines which they alleged were pornographic. They were just pictures of nude young men. So what? Quite frankly it was a ludicrous case. All I could really do was to raise hell over it, which I did as best I could.'[5]

Birnberg wrote to Customs and Excise threatening legal action if the magazines were not returned. Simultaneously Hockney was marshalling his own big guns, first persuading Sir Norman Reid, the distinguished director of the Tate Gallery, to write to them explaining that Hockney was an artist with a renowned international reputation who needed the magazines for his work, and then getting the art historian Sir Kenneth Clark, author of *The Nude*, to agree to testify for him should the case come to court. As the fuss intensified, the press took up the story. 'The wicked censor strikes again,'[6] wrote a correspondent for the *Guardian* under the headline 'POP CUSTOMS', which led to Laura Hockney getting wind of it. She was supportive. 'Isn't it awful,' she said in a telephone call, 'when you need them for your work?'[7] Before long the story had reached the ears of the Home Secretary, James Callaghan, who, having more pressing problems to deal with, such as the emerging conflict in Northern Ireland and the passing of the Race Relations Act, decided that prosecuting David Hockney would be more trouble than it was worth and instructed HM Customs and Excise to return his property. This they did, though without apology.

'I remember they were delivered back in a large brown envelope,' says Hockney, 'that had OHMS written on it. There was a list of everything they'd taken, which had all been written down by the customs man in this incredibly repressed handwriting. I think they were frightened that if I took it to court I would win. I defend my way of life. I was prepared to defend myself because I thought, "If I don't do it, who will? And if nobody does it, they just rule."'[8] It was an attitude that won him many admirers and made him something of a hero to the blossoming gay rights movement. 'It really was quite an important little case,' says Birnberg. 'It was a blow for liberation for David Hockney himself and it all contributed to the wave of emancipation that was going through at that time.'[9]

While Hockney was fighting Customs and Excise, he kept himself grounded by working on the portrait of Henry Geldzahler and Christopher Scott. The American poet and art historian David Shapiro, closely following the progress of this picture for an article he was writing for *Art News*, gave an atmospheric description of Hockney's studio in Powis Terrace, which, he wrote, 'serves as both beehive, arsenal and coffee-mill: a few oils, finished and un- against the wall (. . . photos taped to the canvas); T-fluorescents above; three windows to the west; a draftsman's desk; copperplates; radio; Rowney stacking palettes; cans and rags; Vibo French curves; electric heater; Black and Decker finishing sander; The Splendour of Brass (Telemann *Overture in D Major*); Lyons pure-ground coffee filled with pencils; Eagle prisma colour and other acrylics; on the floor, telephone, stapler and knives; Rowney bristle series, photos of Henry Geldzahler, Christopher Scott and the work-in-progress against the wall; also pliers, paper, palettes, rubber rollers; on another wall a photo of the New York skyline, and the Duchess of Kent arriving to open St Thomas's; Richard Hamilton's poster of the Stones; Hokkers green Liquitex; an Ashai Pentax; Lepage's gripspreader; a jar of pennies . . .'[10]

With the recently finished *Christopher Isherwood and Don Bachardy*, Hockney had broken new ground. His use of perspective draws the viewer into the picture, creating a triangular relationship between the subjects and the spectator. Isherwood frowns rather worriedly at Bachardy, reflecting his real-life concern that he had gone off to London for two months, while Bachardy smiles directly at the spectator, as if in some conspiratorial dialogue with the artist, a man of his own age. Though he preached a philosophy of sexual freedom between partners, once telling Hockney, 'I have the greatest respect for lust',[11] Isherwood was prey to the fear that one day his much younger lover might leave him for someone else.

Hockney was developing the portrait as drama, and this is nowhere better realised than in *Henry Geldzahler and Christopher Scott*, a picture that is awash with tension. In the middle of the canvas, on a huge pink sofa, sits Henry, jacketless, his formal waistcoat and tie suggesting that he has just returned from the office. Staring straight ahead at the spectator, he looks relaxed, and brimming with confidence, the very image of the important museum curator. To his left stands the slim figure of Christopher Scott, dressed in a raincoat and standing stock-still, gazing into the distance in a rather vacant fashion. Hockney liked to joke that it was 'St Henry radiating light, visited by an angel in a raincoat',[12] and it has often been compared by critics to traditional Annunciation scenes. 'Christopher looks rather as if he's going to leave,' Hockney later told Mark Glazebrook, the director of the Whitechapel Gallery, 'or he's just arriving. He's got his coat on. That is how I felt the situation was . . . that's all intended in the picture.'[13]

The involvement of the viewer in this picture is made all the more real by the sense that one is seated in a chair behind the glass table in the forefront. This was complicated to achieve. 'It took me about two or three months to paint,' wrote Hockney. 'To draw the floor I laid tapes from the vanishing point, which is about two inches above Henry's head, to the bottom of the canvas. At one point in the work there were twenty or thirty tapes radiating from his head. I photographed the picture then – it looked like an incredible radiant glow from a halo round his head.'[14]

Though his large double portraits are among his greatest work, there is a glaring omission in the *oeuvre*. No painting exists of Hockney himself with Peter Schlesinger, the love of his life, though a drawing does exist depicting Schlesinger sitting cross-legged on a sofa with

Hockney in profile walking towards him from the right. 'The closest
we ever came to a double portrait featuring myself and Peter,' Hockney
recalls, 'were photographs we took with each other in the photograph.
I might have been thinking about doing a painting but we broke up, and
it would never have happened after that.'[15]

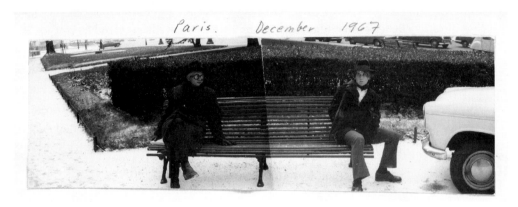

For the time being, however, life was rosy. 'We set ourselves up in
Powis Terrace in quite a domestic way,' wrote Hockney. 'It was very
happy, very nice. I painted away there, and Peter had a little studio
round the corner in Notting Hill where he did some very big paintings;
they were quite ambitious.'[16] This domestic harmony was a big change
in London lifestyle for David, who had been used to going out almost
every night with Patrick Procktor.

Powis Terrace was being transformed by Schlesinger from the
'dirty and messy and cold' flat that Don Bachardy had found when he
had stayed there the previous April.[17] His efforts did not go unnoticed
by Ken and Laura, when they visited in early October. 'David's flat
is beautiful,' wrote Laura, '– newly decorated in white walls and
carpeted – large wall wardrobe with mirrored doors all around one
bedroom. Kitchen modernised and very pleased I was to find he had a
"help", a Mrs Miller who is to come in three times a week.'[18] There is
no mention of their having met Peter, though they did meet on other
occasions. 'I met David's parents several times,' Schlesinger recalls,

Paris,
December 1967

'but we didn't talk because they didn't know what to say to me and I didn't know what to say to them.'[19]

The new 'help', Mrs Miller, was a Jamaican, a little older than David, who, when she wasn't cleaning, worked as a film extra. She was interested in art – as a young girl, she told them, she had modelled for Jacob Epstein – and Schlesinger thought she was probably too elegant for cleaning. She spent much of her time sitting cross-legged on the kitchen table drinking endless cups of tea and smoking. 'We were always hanging out,' he says, 'smoking joints and discussing the paintings with Patrick, Ossie and Mo.'[20] Hockney doted on her and never failed to ask her opinion on his work, while McDermott and Clark liked to tease her after Clark claimed to have found her in the kitchen putting talcum powder on her face in order to lighten her skin. She was a valuable addition to Powis Terrace, which, thanks to Schlesinger's influence, was beginning to acquire some new furnishings, including a glass table from the über-fashionable contemporary furniture store Aram, on the King's Road, and a huge new leather sofa bought from Harrods for the princely sum of £750. 'I had never paid anything like that for a piece of furniture,' Hockney recalls, 'so Peter went to Kasmin, who said, "Oh, David could afford three sofas like that." It was a terrific sofa and people could sleep on it.'[21] Though his attitude to money was that he was rich if he had sufficient to do what he wanted, it still pricked Hockney's conscience that the sofa cost more than his father earned in a year.

Schlesinger also enjoyed combing the antiques stalls on the Portobello Road on a Saturday morning. 'We had very different tastes,' says Schlesinger, 'because I liked finding old things in Portobello Market, while he just preferred things that were all new. I would buy a vase for a pound. He considered a lot of the stuff I bought as being junk.'[22] Among the antiques he bought were a Charles Rennie Mackintosh chair, some Lalique lamps and a rococo sledge, which were interspersed with a small forest of coloured cut-out trees, made and painted by Mo McDermott. With all the surfaces painted white, the room looked very striking. 'Peter made that lovely big room really beautiful,' Celia Birtwell remembers, 'with the Mackintosh chair and the glass table, the big leather sofa and the Lalique lamps. He had a hi-fi system in three sections with speakers on either side of the wall, very expensive, but really the business then. It was his way of making his mark. He pulled the flat together and transformed it.'[23]

Birtwell was one of the first close friends that Schlesinger made in London. Her father was an estimating engineer in the textile business, and her mother a seamstress, making wedding dresses in Manchester; they brought up three daughters in a house full of books and flowers. She was the eldest and arty, and she always knew that what she wanted from life was new experiences. At Salford Art School, studying textile design, she met the rebellious young Mo McDermott, who in turn introduced her to 'this really mad boy' called Ossie Clark, who was a student at Manchester College of Art, and another friendship was born. When Birtwell took him home, her mother immediately recognised his genius. 'He liked my mother very much,' recalls Birtwell, 'because she was extremely patient (unlike myself); she'd show him how to sew a collar or put a seam in. She had hours and hours of patience. She used to say to me, "He's really special," or [of his clothes] "It's a work of art, Celia."'[24]

When, after Salford, Birtwell came down to London, her job as a waitress at the Hades coffee bar soon reunited her with Clark, since it was one of the favoured hangouts of the students from the Royal College. 'D'ya like my fucking frills?' he remembered her saying to him. She was 'dressed like BB, blue jeans and Victorian blouse, boots with a lavatory heel'.[25] It was not long before they became an item, bound together by creative brilliance, her talent for textile design and his for cutting, not to mention a certain physical attraction. From the start, Birtwell's friend and fellow lodger, Pauline Boty, warned her against him. 'He could be a lot of trouble for you,'[26] she said.

It was Boty who first pointed out Hockney to Birtwell while they were walking near Hennekey's pub on the Portobello Road one Saturday morning. 'I saw this extraordinary-looking guy with long hair wearing a maroon corduroy jacket,' Birtwell remembers, 'and I said, "Who's he?" and she told me, "He's one to watch and he's at the Royal College and he always gets up in the social studies class and gives a lecture to the other students. He's really smart.'[27] She finally met him when Hockney took up with Clark, though at first, probably out of shyness, he had little time for her other than the occasional 'Oh, hello, love' when he would visit their flat in Blenheim Crescent. But this all changed in 1968. 'One day we were round at Patrick Procktor's,' says Birtwell, 'and David came round and he had this rather attractive boy with him called Peter Schlesinger who was quite a gentle character, and he and I immediately got on really well. It was Peter that brought me and David together as friends because he couldn't ignore me any more.'[28]

Schlesinger's friendship with Birtwell blossomed because they were two of a kind, gentle, artistic and rather shy: Birtwell even thought that they looked alike. They were both less gregarious than their respective partners. 'I moved to Linden Gardens to a first-floor flat in 1968,' she remembers, 'and that's really where I first began to see Peter a lot . . . Peter would come round and visit me in the evening and we'd sit and chat while David was out at parties, and then David would come round to pick him up to take him home.'

At weekends the two couples established a tradition of holding tea parties, invitations to which quickly became sought-after. 'I like tea parties because they're not like dinner,' Hockney used to say, meaning that people would leave after tea, allowing him to get back to work. Organised by Schlesinger, they had to be done in Hockney's style, a throwback to his mother's teas when he was a child, with a proper china tea service, and cakes and sandwiches. Invitations would go out to between ten and fifteen people, of whom there was a core group consisting of Patrick Procktor, Mo McDermott, Anne Upton, Maurice Payne, Kasmin and his wife Jane, Lindy and Sheridan Dufferin, Mark Lancaster and the Clarks, to which was added a cosmopolitan mixture of people Hockney might have run into during the week or was working with at the time, or who just happened to be cruising the Portobello Road on a Saturday. 'Powis Terrace tea parties,' wrote Clark in his diary in 1969. 'EVERYBODY THERE.'[29]

It was not long before these gatherings got out of control. 'What happened later,' says Melissa North, a girlfriend of Tony Richardson, 'was that after the flat was enlarged and all glammed up, it became a destination for collectors and smart American hostesses and people like that when they came to London. They would go to David Hockney's for tea, and as the tea parties had always been very open, they suddenly went from being the same twelve people to being forty people and he didn't like it any more.'[30] '. . . the last one I gave,' he told Gordon Burn in 1971, 'I invited about . . . well I invited thirty-two, but you know, people bring other people, so about sixty turned up. Well it was chaos! Not everybody could have a cup of tea, so I stopped giving them.'[31]

As they saw more and more of one another, Hockney and Birtwell gradually became friends too. 'I soon discovered the great thing about her is that she is very funny,' he recalls, 'and within ten minutes of meeting each other we were always laughing, and that's what I loved about her. They say that laughing clears the lungs and I said to Celia, "That's it. People who shouldn't smoke are people who never laugh." So we became great friends.'[32] It also suited Birtwell to have two kind gay men in her life at a time when life with Clark was becoming increasingly difficult. Clark's career had taken off in 1965 when Alice Pollock, the owner of the fashionable boutique Quorum, on the King's Road, had signed him up exclusively, and he was soon dressing the rich and famous at a time when London was seen as the most swinging city in the world, as well as designing stage costumes for the Beatles and the Rolling Stones. He had no qualms about throwing himself full pelt into the lifestyle that accompanied fame, but he had no backup, and this was to be his downfall. 'Ossie was a terrific person,' says David, 'but his tragedy was that he needed somebody to organise him, like I had Kasmin. But he didn't have anybody who could do that for him at that point. The problem was simple, in that he used to work very hard to produce an incredible collection, and the moment he had some money, then he would stop. He was a rock 'n' roller and he always wanted to go off to the rock 'n' roll parties.'[33] As the fame and the money went to Clark's head, he started taking too many drugs, became sexually promiscuous, and was often violent to Birtwell, who leant on Schlesinger and Hockney for support.

When Hockney went home for Christmas that year, he left Schlesinger, who couldn't afford to go home to America, behind in London. Though Hockney was only away for two days, they were not happy ones for Schlesinger. 'The first Christmas I spent in London I spent on my own,' he says. 'I wasn't invited anywhere, and it was rather bleak.'[34] Meanwhile, Laura recorded: 'David came Christmas Eve and we had Pork and Christmas Pud etc.' He arrived home with a welcome and generous gift: the money for their trip to Australia. 'Ken and I received a cheque for £800, with more to follow promised . . . What a day we had!!!' When he left Bradford on Boxing Day to return to London, she wrote: 'Always feel flat when David has gone – but it has been lovely . . . I did ask if the trip was to cost him more than he expected, but he said not to worry – "money is to use".'[35]

By this point in his life, Hockney could easily afford to send his parents to Australia. Since his first show with Kasmin, his work had fetched more year after year, and his large pictures were now fetching between £1,000 and £2,000, at least a fivefold increase since 1963. 'I had to keep adjusting the prices,' Kasmin recalls. 'They never stayed still. There were many more people wanting paintings than there were paintings, and not just people who came to me as clients asking to buy one, but also people who had art galleries who wanted to have shows. Trying to work out how to ration out the paintings was one of the hardest jobs I had as an art dealer.'[36]

In 1968, Hockney had had one-man shows not only with Kasmin in London, but also at the Galerie Mikro in Berlin and the Museum of Modern Art in New York, not to mention appearing in group shows such as the Venice Biennale and *Young Generation: Great Britain* at Akademie der Kunst in Berlin; and in February 1969 the prestigious Whitworth Art Gallery in Manchester gave him a mini retrospective, showing twenty-eight paintings together with a selection of prints. His ever growing international reputation now meant that his pictures were selling as fast as he could produce them, and his earnings were commensurate with this.

Much of his money came from the lucrative sale of his prints, and in March 1969, he began work on his next major set of etchings, a project that was to take up the rest of the year, to the exclusion of any painting. In December 1962, he had made his limited edition etching of Rumpelstiltskin, the strange gnomish character from *Grimm's Fairy Tales*, which he had loved as a child, giving them away as Christmas presents to his family and friends. Ever since then, he had wanted to illustrate a selection from the fairy tales, and eventually he suggested the idea to Paul Cornwall-Jones, who had by now split from his partners in Alecto to start a new imprint, Petersburg Press. Cornwall-Jones was only too happy to work with Hockney again and immediately started setting up the structure for the publication, bringing in Gordon House, who had designed the catalogues for the Kasmin shows, and the typographer Eric Ayers as the design team. 'David wanted new original translations from the German,' Cornwall-Jones recalls. 'He first suggested Isherwood should do it, so I went to see him but he didn't want to do it. He then suggested asking Wystan Auden, but he wasn't interested either. So I commissioned Heiner Bastian, a German who had been working at City Lights Bookstore in San Francisco, and he worked on it with me and my wife Tammy.'[37]

Hockney found the tales entrancing. After reading all 239, and researching various illustrated editions, notably those by Arthur Rackham and Edmund Dulac, he initially chose twenty stories, of which fifteen were translated and twelve made the final list. He picked the stories, a number of them quite obscure, entirely for the vividness of the images they conjured up for him. 'Old Rinkrank', for example, begins: 'A King built a glass mountain and announced he would give his daughter to the first man who could climb it without falling.' Just as Hockney was fascinated by painting water, so he was with the equally difficult technical problems of representing glass. He had always loved the verse from 'The Elixir' by the mystical poet George Herbert, which runs:

> A man that looks on glass,
> On it may stay his eye,
> Or, if he pleaseth, through it pass,
> And then the heav'n espy.

'That's why . . . I chose the story of Old Rink Rank, about the glass mountain,' he told Mark Glazebrook in an interview. 'I liked the problem of how to draw and represent a glass mountain. That was a nice little problem to give myself.'[38] While trying to solve it, he made six or seven versions of the mountain, breaking up a large sheet of glass in the process and piling it up in the studio to draw it jagged. His eventual solution was to use the technique of reflection, revealing the king's palace through the mountain, which also magnifies what it reveals.

It is clear from the work that Hockney derived enormous enjoyment from this project, drawing not just from the depths of his own vivid imagination, but on his great knowledge of the history of art, enabling him to reference the work of artists ranging from Leonardo to Magritte. This starts with the frontispiece depicting Katarina Dorothea Viehmann, the elderly German widow who gave the Brothers Grimm many of their stories, who is drawn in the style of Dürer. In 'Rapunzel', the story of a couple who give away their baby to an enchantress in exchange for some rapunzel flowers, he imagined that the reason the enchantress, whom he drew with a beard, had no children of her own was that she was so ugly no one would sleep with her. Because she was a virgin, he based the drawing of her with the baby on her knee on the Madonna in Hieronymous Bosch's *The Virgin and Child and the Three Magi*. The prince who eventually comes to rescue the child, by then a beautiful maiden with long golden locks, was lifted from Uccello's *The Hunt in the Forest*. In 'The Boy Who Left Home to Learn Fear', the ghost which 'stood still as stone' is reminiscent of one of Magritte's 'stone age' paintings, a series of 1950s works depicting organic objects turned to stone. It amused Hockney when distinguished art historians would write to him as if his references were their discovery, when to him it seemed obvious that he was quoting from a particular artist.

Not all the drawings are referenced from the past. Mo McDermott posed for some of the images in 'The Little Sea Hare', for example, while 'The Boy Who Left Home to Learn Fear' opens with a picture of a comfortable armchair, a perfect representation of the security of home, which is lifted directly from a drawing he had once made of an armchair in the library at Clandeboye House in Northern Ireland, the home of Sheridan and Lindy Dufferin. In addition, photographs he had taken of castles on his Rhine trip the previous October proved valuable.

Though to begin with Hockney made preliminary drawings, particularly where the subject had some technical problem, as work progressed, more and more of the etchings were drawn straight onto the copperplates on special tables set up in Powis Terrace, before being placed in acid baths on the balcony, under Maurice Payne's supervision. Since leaving Alecto, Cornwall-Jones no longer had a printing studio, so when the plates were ready, Payne took them down to the print department at the Royal College, where his friend Mike Rand let him proof them in the studio. Again a number of stories had to be culled. 'I got carried away,' Hockney told Glazebrook, 'and I did so many for some stories that if I had done twelve stories the book would have been so thick and so expensive that we couldn't go on.'[39] He had still completed eighty etchings before he knew he had to stop.

It was decided that the initial book would contain six stories, with a possible second volume if the first was a commercial success. When the time came for the paste-up, Cornwall-Jones thought Hockney might be interested in getting involved. 'When I first showed him a paste-up,' he recalls, 'he said, "Why are you bothering me? I'm painting and drawing." Anyway, with great reluctance he came round the next day to St Petersburg Place, and he was grumpy because he felt he didn't want to get involved in organising a book. In fact he started getting involved straight away, saying, "Oh, we don't want to do this, we should do that," and he spent about a week reorganising the whole thing.'[40] Hockney was determined that this should not be an 'art' book with loose pages, but a real picture book in which on every page the image would be seen before reading the text it was illustrating. This would mean printing an etching on the back of an etching, a problem that was solved by simply doubling over the paper, an idea taken from Japanese books. *Six Fairy Tales from the Brothers Grimm* took over a year to produce and was published at the end of 1970. As a flyer for the book, a miniature version was published by the Oxford University Press, in a planned edition of 2,000: it ended up selling 150,000 copies.

In the canon of Hockney's work, there is no doubt that *Six Fairy Tales* is right up there with the Cavafy poems, not just because of the superb quality of the etchings, but equally because of the sheer inventiveness and wit of his imagery. Hockney certainly considers it to have been a major work, not just for the time he spent on it but also for what he learned while doing it. 'They're more complex than my previous etchings,' he wrote. 'First of all, instead of using aquatints to get tone I decided on a method of cross-hatching, which I used throughout. I just stumbled across it, and thought it was quite a good way to do it. And then I found that you can get very rich black by cross-hatching, then etching, then putting wax on again, and then drawing another cross-hatching on top on another, on another; the ink gets very thick . . . it was a step forward for me in etching techniques.'[41]

Though Hockney's concentration on the Grimm project meant that no further paintings were completed in 1969, it was not to the exclusion of any drawing, and in May he took Schlesinger off to stay with Cecil Beaton at Reddish, near Salisbury in Wiltshire, whose portrait he was doing for an article in *Vogue*. Beaton had been one of Hockney's earliest patrons, and he adored David. 'We could not be further apart as human beings,' he wrote in his diary, 'and yet I find myself completely at ease with him and stimulated by his enthusiasm. For he has the golden quality of being able to enjoy life. He is never blasé, never takes anything for granted. Life is a delightful wonderland for him; much of the time he is wreathed in smiles. He laughs aloud at television and radio. He is the best possible audience, though he is by no means simple. He is sophisticated in that he has complete purity. There is nothing pretentious about him; he never says anything he does not mean. In a world of art intrigue, he is completely natural.'[42]

The only other guest that Whitsun weekend was another bright young man, the flamboyant 34-year-old director of the National Portrait Gallery, Dr Roy Strong. The year before, he had shaken up this previously stuffy institution by mounting a massive exhibition of Beaton portraits, a turning point in the gallery's history and so successful its run had to be extended twice. His invitation to a quiet weekend turned out to be exactly that as Beaton, preoccupied with the portrait sessions, paid Strong little attention, abandoning him to paint watercolours in the conservatory and garden, as well as to waspishly observe his host. 'Cecil is nothing if not vain,' Strong wrote in his diary, 'so there was much coming and going with piles of hats from which Hockney could make a choice for Cecil to wear. David's early attempts didn't go down at all well, hardly surprising for his graphic style highlighted every wrinkle on Cecil's face.'[43]

Beaton studied Hockney meticulously while he was being drawn and perfectly described how, like a monkey, Hockney squinted and grimaced up at him and then down again to his drawing pad. Beaton was impressed by how tireless Hockney was and by the infinite care and precision he took over his work, marvelling as he sharpened his pencils for the hundredth time. About the results, however, Beaton was not so happy, particularly the early attempts. 'To begin with,' he wrote, 'I was utterly appalled, having remained in some romantic but extremely uncomfortable pose for a great deal too long, when I saw an outline in Indian ink of a bloated, squat, beefy businessman. He laughed. No, it wasn't very good, and he embarked upon another which turned out to be just as bad. About eight horrors were perpetrated while the days advanced until, finally, something rather good emerged. He was encouraged. He was enthusiastic. Would I sit again tomorrow all morning and then again after lunch. He eventually decided to draw me in pencil rather than ink and the result was different and better.'[44]

While Hockney was working on the portrait, Schlesinger was either doing his own sketches of Beaton, or taking photographs, demonstrating a great skill in capturing those fleeting moments that define an era, much in the same way as did his hero, the great French photographer Jacques Henri Lartigue. One such image, taken in the conservatory, shows Beaton and Hockney seated in basketwork chairs. The former, dressed like an Edwardian dandy in a green velvet suit, yellow socks and a large velvet floppy hat, is leaning back, eyes skyward, his legs wide apart, with his camera placed strategically between his legs. David, sitting cross-legged and gazing affectionately at the photographer, brings the dandy right up to date in all his sixties glory, wearing a pink plaid suit, the ubiquitous odd socks in bright green and red, deemed a 'retina irritant' by Beaton, and his trademark black spectacles 'as large as bicycle wheels'.[45]

On their last night at Reddish, Beaton took them to dinner with Richard 'Dickie' Buckle, the ballet critic of the *Sunday Times*, who had designed his exhibition at the National Portrait Gallery and whose Wiltshire cottage was the setting for Hockney's painting *Domestic Scene, Broadchalke, Wilts*. After dinner Hockney regaled the company with his philosophy, showing that the idealism of the sixties had not quite passed him by. 'David talked of the coming of the Golden Age,' Beaton wrote in his diary. 'He had read many philosophers, and has thought a great deal. In the next forty years all will change. The computer will do away with work; *everyone* will be an artist. No need to worry, all the leisure in the world, everything will be beautiful. There will be no private property, or need to own anything. Everyone will be ecstatically happy. It was marvellous to see this white-skinned, champagne-topped, dark-glassed young man in pale pistachio green with bronze boots, orange and yellow alternate socks, holding forth with such vehemence.'[46]

Though the weekend was a success, the drawings he did were not among Hockney's best, as was often the case with his commissions: Beaton was not someone he knew well, whose changing moods and emotions he had observed on a daily basis. He told Henry Geldzahler, for example, that the reason his portrayal of Christopher Scott in the double portrait is slightly wooden is that he hadn't really known him or been sure how long he was going to be around. His drawings of Schlesinger on the other hand – sleeping, reading, swimming, clothed, naked – breathe flesh and blood into him so that the viewer feels he knows him. Somehow Hockney manages to convey his strong attraction to his lover. Nowhere is this more true than in a striking three-foot-high etching of Schlesinger naked in 1969, which employs two sets of perspective: one for the lower half of the body, in which he is viewing it from above, thus foreshortening the legs; and another for the torso and the head, seen on the level. The result gives the impression that we, like the artist, are admiring Schlesinger's body from the feet upwards.

Hockney's drawings of Schlesinger occupy a special place in his art, and are a record of his most precious relationship during one of the happiest times of his life. They also represent a travelogue of all the places they visited together – California, Paris, Marrakesh, Rome, Carennac, Vichy, to name a few – as well as Le Nid de Duc, Tony Richardson's house, which was the setting for the iconic painting *Portrait of an Artist*. In the summer of 1969, he and Schlesinger made up a party there with Geldzahler, Kasmin, Clark and Birtwell. Richardson, who was in Australia filming *Ned Kelly* with Mick Jagger, had lent his house to Hockney for a month, leaving his girlfriend Melissa North to make sure things ran smoothly.

North was in her early twenties, a girl about town from London who, along with her friend Celia Brooke, used to be invited by Richardson to spice up dinner parties at his house in Egerton Crescent, South Kensington, where they would encounter the likes of John Gielgud, Ralph Richardson, John Mortimer and other theatrical and literary giants. On one such occasion she found herself sitting next to David Hockney, who invited her to tea. They subsequently struck up a friendship, and when Hockney came to Le Nid de Duc in 1969, she fell completely under his spell. 'I'd always had a weakness for him,' she recalls, 'and that summer I fell madly in love with him so that if he spoke to me I would just sweat and blush and crumple. It sounds pathetic, I know. I found him very, very attractive, and I loved his work and I loved the way he was drawing all the time and the way he organised expeditions. He was always going to look at something, either the Miró Foundation or a show, and we'd all follow. He never stopped drawing, and then he started drawing me. It was absolute agony because I was having to sit there with him looking at me, and me thinking, "My nose is too big. I'm so plain. How embarrassing that he's drawing me to be kind," and as I had this mad obsession with him, this attention was almost too much to bear. I was up there sweating and all my clothes would start sticking to me and I would get more and more humiliated. I think he must have sensed this sort of passion and he was very, very sweet to me.'[47]

*

Soon after their return to England, Clark and Birtwell asked Hockney to be best man at their wedding. The marriage took place in August and was doomed to failure; it might never have taken place had it not been that Birtwell was pregnant and had received a letter from her father as good as ordering her to get married. 'So we just went out and got married,' says Birtwell, 'and we dragged David along as best man. He turned up looking like an old wreck, so I said, "You could have just dressed up a little bit!" so I think he put a carnation in his lapel, and we went off to the registry office.'[48] The only other person present was Clark's sister Kay, a nightclub chanteuse whom David had loved ever since she had told him, 'What I love in the morning is a cup of coffee, a good cough and a cigarette.'[49]

The wedding took place at Kensington Registry Office with Birtwell dressed in a beautiful chiffon dress by Clark decorated with Birtwell's trademark 'Mystic Daisy' print. As they tumbled out after the ceremony, they stopped a vicar who was passing by and asked him if he would take their wedding photograph. He refused, no doubt because Birtwell was seven months pregnant and showing it. 'Then we all went back to Powis Terrace, and had tea, and then the next day Ossie just buggered off with Chelita Secunda.'[50] In his diary Clark noted nonchalantly, 'Married Celia. Tears. "Tell me what you want, I'll get you whatever you want" – Hockney, Kay a witness. DH promised Kay an etching she never got . . . honeymoon with another woman.'[51] Hockney remembers that 'we laughed at the time. We thought it was an odd way to start, but Ossie was an odd person.'[52]

Over the next few months Hockney completed a large number of drawings of the newly-weds in preparation for a proposed wedding portrait, trying both figures in different positions and with different looks on their faces. He also took many photographs recording the details he might use, of the vase, the book, the telephone, the lamp and the table. Peter Webb, author of *Portrait of David Hockney*, recounts Clark's version of the moment Hockney found the perfect composition. 'Ossie remembers . . . he had only just got up and so had no shoes on. He slumped into a chair with a cigarette, and Blanche, one of their

white cats, jumped onto his lap. Celia was standing on the other side
of the window with her hand on her hip, and Hockney said, "That's
perfect." He later added their Art Deco vase and lamp, and called the
cat Percy, the name of Blanche's son, because it sounded better.'⁵³ The
actual painting would have to wait for the time being, there being no
room to work in the studio as every available inch of space was taken
up with etching equipment.

Hockney also had plans for another large painting inspired by a
trip he had made in September to the French spa of Vichy. This pretty
town in the Auvergne had been known since the sixteenth century for
its mineral baths and drinking waters, whose restorative powers were
later made famous through the letters of the Marquise de Sévigné,
who claimed that they had cured her of a paralysis in her hands. Its
blossoming fortunes made it a centre of fashion, with a casino, new
streets and villas, and even an opera house; up till the outbreak of the
First World War, it had been the summertime music capital of France.

Hockney took Schlesinger and Clark with him to stay at the chic
old Pavillon Sévigné hotel, in order to take the waters, and they drove
down in a Triumph Vitesse, bought on the advice of Keith Vaughan
with whom he had dined a few days before leaving. 'The more I see of
D.H. the more he impresses me,' Vaughan wrote of the occasion. 'He
has all the best qualities of his generation. Modest and self-confident,
honest in speech, unconcerned with impressing yet considerate
and well-mannered, impatient with all fraudulent or compromised
behaviour, ardent, curious, warm hearted, uncorrupted (and probably
uncorruptable) by success . . . he does what he says he will. Months ago
. . . talking about special issues of stamps which I did not know about
he said, "Oh, but they're marvellous, haven't you seen them, I'll send
you some." And two days later I get a postcard covered with about 8s
6d worth of special issue stamps. And the last time I saw him . . . just
before he was motoring to the S. of France in his convertible Morris
. . . I said, "You ought to get a Triumph Vitesse – they're better than
a Morris for long journeys." "Maybe I will. It's an idea. I'll go and buy
one tomorrow morning. There'll just be time." And he did.'⁵⁴

Vichy was the first spa that Hockney visited to take the waters, the drinking of which took place in a lovely art nouveau building and involved a degree of ritual which was amusingly described by Wayne Sleep, on one of his visits there during a stay at Carennac. 'When you arrive at the spa itself,' he wrote, 'you are given your own glass cup in a string bag. Ladies in nurses' uniforms ladle the water from the spring into your cup – and you then drink it. The sulphur content made a loo immediately necessary. It is very good for the system but the stink of rotten eggs can be hard to take. At dinner that evening I noticed that the majority of the guests looked half dead. So much for the water, I thought.'[55]

Le Parc des Sources, in the middle of the town, created in the time of Napoleon Bonaparte, had fascinated Hockney since he had first seen it the previous year, because of the way the trees had been planted in the form of a triangle in order to create a false perspective, making it look much longer than it really was. It reminded him of a sculpture, and gave him the idea to create a new painting based on one of his favourite themes, that of the picture within a picture. Taking three plastic chairs, he placed them at the edge of the park, and got Clark and Schlesinger to occupy the two right-hand ones as if they were watching a film or a play, leaving the left-hand one empty to signify where the artist had been sitting. He then took photographs of the scene from behind, which he would later use to create the painting. 'I wanted to set the three chairs up for the three of us,' he wrote, '. . . then I'd get up to paint the scene. That's why the empty chair is there – the artist has had to get up to do the painting. It's like a picture within a picture; I was going to call it *Painting within Painting,* like *Play within a Play.* That gives it the strong surrealist overtones.'[56]

While Hockney had been engaged on the Grimm project, Kasmin had had to be patient. 'It was always tricky with David,' he recalls, 'because there weren't that many paintings a year. There were plenty of drawings, but people always wanted paintings.'[57] He was not idle, however, always thinking of new ways to further his artists' reputations. When Charles Alan had to close his New York gallery for reasons of ill

health, Kasmin pulled off a coup by persuading André Emmerich, one
of Manhattan's leading dealers in contemporary art, to take Hockney
on. Emmerich was a soft-spoken, very straight businessman, who had
a great interest in pre-Columbian art and a strong feeling for American
abstract painting. He represented many of the artists Kasmin liked,
and had shown Kenneth Noland, Helen Frankenthaler and the estate
of Morris Louis in London, as well as Anthony Caro in New York.
'He was a believer in order,' says Kasmin. 'He had well-run galleries
with well-spoken staff and was used to dealing with rich people.
He was without any peculiarities of character at all, except that he
was addicted to sweets . . . and his idea of generosity was to share a
shoeshine with you in the office. Instead of saying, "Let me take you to
lunch," he would say, "Let me buy you a shoeshine." He had a lovely big
gallery and he always had at least one young gay man there, someone
that David could talk and joke with. It was already the most important
place to have a show in New York, and David benefited from being
with a gallery that was primarily non-figurative.'[58]

Emmerich's first show of Hockney paintings, in November 1969,
included the three great double portraits, *Christopher Isherwood and Don
Bachardy*, *Henry Geldzahler and Christopher Scott* and *American Collectors*.
Kasmin had pointed out to him that he should not sell to European
dealers, who would simply take the work back to Europe to sell at
twice the price, but try and find buyers in New York. One painting
was already sold, however. *Christopher Isherwood and Don Bachardy* had
been bought by an English lawyer, Sir John Foster, for $6,000 as a gift
for his close friend, Marguerite Littman. Mrs Littman, a Southern
belle who lived in a grand house in Chester Square, had established
herself as one of London's leading society hostesses. Said to have been
Truman Capote's model for Holly Golightly in *Breakfast at Tiffany's*,
she was a confidante of Tennessee Williams, and had been Elizabeth
Taylor's voice coach on the film of *Cat on a Hot Tin Roof*. She was once
with the great playwright beside the swimming pool of the Cipriani
Hotel in Venice when, looking at a particularly thin girl in a bikini, she
turned to him and said 'Look, anorexia nervosa,' to which he replied,
'Oh, Marguerite, you know everyone!'[59]

Isherwood was among her circle of friends, and, after seeing the picture in Hockney's studio, she had made it known to Sheridan Dufferin at one of her numerous lunches that she would love to own it. Its subsequent history is of interest, because it was a painting that meant a great deal to the artist, and it shows how easy it is for a picture simply to slip out of circulation. 'David loved the picture because Chris and Don were friends of his,' Kasmin remembers, 'and I was keen for it to go to the National Portrait Gallery as David is an English painter and Isherwood an English writer. Sheridan, however, put pressure on me to sell it to Marguerite. So it was bought by John Foster and on his death in 1982 the picture was sold to an English dealer, who sold it to a Texan billionaire for a great deal of money, a flash Harry who flew around the world in pastel-coloured aeroplanes. Hockney was broken-hearted about this. He literally wept. I couldn't believe it had happened.' From the Texan it went to the Manhattan art dealer Andrew Crispo, who was later jailed for tax evasion, and from there it ended up belonging to the financier Gilbert de Botton who gave it to his wife Jacqueline as part of divorce proceedings, and with whom it still resides, its value having leapt from $6,000 in 1969 to several million today.

When Hockney returned to London after the Emmerich show, he began work on *Le Parc des Sources, Vichy*, the first picture he had painted for ten months, which was the longest period he had gone without painting in ten years. 'I'd gotten to the point,' he wrote, 'where I didn't seem to care about the painted mark that much . . . Somehow a kind of painting block took over. Probably in the end acrylic paint did it, the burdens of it.'[60] Getting back into painting proved difficult, since the new picture was large, as big as the double portraits, and he struggled with it. 'I began working on it in January,' he wrote, 'and it took me much longer than I expected . . . I think the difficulties stemmed from the acrylic paint and the naturalism, the fight to achieve naturalistic effect, the difficulty of blending colour, things like that.'[61] The result is a masterful picture, surreal and strange, that fills the viewer with unease, posing the question as to what is going on psychologically with these two figures, lost in their own thoughts, Clark's perhaps of his descent into chaos, Schlesinger's of whether he might be becoming a prisoner in one of Hockney's canvases. Hockney eventually completed it just in time for it to be included in the biggest exhibition of his work so far, a retrospective at one of the most influential galleries in London, the Whitechapel.

Always at the forefront of showing contemporary art, in 1938 the Whitechapel had been the first London gallery to show Picasso's *Guernica* in an exhibition protesting at the Spanish Civil War. Its landmark show, however, and a milestone in the history of British post-war art, was *This is Tomorrow* in 1956, which consisted of a series of installations assembled by various artists to represent their vision of the future. The director at that time was Bryan Robertson, who transformed the place into London's most exciting exhibition space, opening British eyes to the work of American abstract expressionists such as Jackson Pollock, Robert Rauschenberg and Mark Rothko. In spite of this, it was starved of funds and by the time Robertson retired, his successor, Mark Glazebrook, one of the founders of Alecto Editions, found the gallery's finances in a parlous state.

One of Glazebrook's first decisions was to invite Hockney to mount a retrospective of the past ten years. Glazebrook had, after all, been in the vanguard of Hockney admirers, having spotted him as a serious talent while he was still at the Royal College, and been the purchaser of what Hockney considered to be the best picture in his first exhibition, *Play Within a Play*. The Whitechapel exhibition, curated by Kasmin and Hockney, occupied the entire gallery, even overflowing into the foyer and back into previously unrevealed side chambers. It included forty-five paintings, from *Doll Boy* to *Le Parc des Sources, Vichy*; his complete graphic work, comprising 116 items; and forty-seven drawings. The enormous cost of mounting the show was partly defrayed by David, who, to raise money, made a special lithograph, *Pretty Tulips*, in an edition of two hundred, which was a sell-out.

Hockney left the hanging, which he always claimed he was no good at, to Glazebrook and Kasmin, and went away with Schlesinger and Christopher Isherwood to stay at Le Nid de Duc, only returning the day before the private view on 1 April. 'We . . . went to the opening like everybody else; so it was a surprise to me,' he wrote.

'. . . just a few days before we came back, I began to think Oh my God, all those early pictures which I haven't seen in ten years are going to look terrible. When I saw them, though, I thought, they do stand up; they're not that bad . . . I could see the way things progressed, how I'd taken one aspect of a painting and developed it in other pictures so that it changed quite visibly . . . It dawned on me how protean the art is; it's varied, with many aspects, many sided.'[62]

His parents visited the show on 17 April, along with his brother Paul and family. They left Bradford at 5.30 a.m. on a very hot train and Paul's children, Lisa and Nicky, were both sick. 'Went from King's Cross by tube to Whitechapel,' wrote Laura, 'where David met us at the Gallery. There for an hour pre-opening time we viewed at leisure his wonderful exhibits of ten years work.'[63] The critics were impressed. Guy Brett, writing in *The Times*, singled out the California pictures. 'Many of Hockney's recent paintings have been about California. So much so that one easily identifies his qualities, his whole painting style, with the vision he has given us of that place. Describing "California" one describes a Hockney.'[64] The *Spectator* critic Paul Grinke loved the portraits, 'an area in which Hockney works with great feeling largely because he almost invariably paints personal friends or lovers, which is a good way of putting his sitters at ease and also gives us a more than usually intimate glimpse of their personalities. Of the recent portraits, the 1968 painting of Christopher Isherwood and Don Bachardy . . . is a most accomplished work.'[65] In *Apollo*, James Burr wrote: 'His ability to parody the good manners of picture-making is brilliant,' ending his review: 'This decade of Hockney's achievement is erratic, but nevertheless recalls his humorous satirical gifts at their sharpest and most alert . . . It seems to have reached a point of development that looks ominously like a cul-de-sac, but no doubt by some unusual act of visual agility he will extract himself and continue his distinctively eccentric painting progress without which English painting would be markedly the poorer.'[66]

For Hockney, it was a remarkable end to the decade.

CHAPTER TEN

MR AND MRS CLARK
AND PERCY

There was one significant painting missing from the Whitechapel show, listed in the catalogue as number 70.2, *Untitled*, 'A Portrait of Ossie Clark and Celia Birtwell, Unfinished'. The proposed wedding portrait as yet only existed in the form of countless photographs and a few drawings. Writing long after the wedding in August 1969, Clark remembered, 'Married Celia . . . DH gave picture for wedding present – *Mr and Mrs Clark and Percy*, later sold to pay deposit on house,'[1] which was a case of his memory playing tricks on him. Not only did Hockney never give this work to the Clarks, but he did not even begin work on it till April or May 1970, and he was not to complete it till May 1971.

Though *Mr and Mrs Clark and Percy* fits well in the canon of traditional English wedding portraits, such as Arthur Devis's *Mr and Mrs Atherton* and Gainsborough's *Mr and Mrs Andrews*, it also defies convention by having the man seated and the woman standing, swapping the customary position of the figures, which immediately makes it stand out. 'Because it is the reverse of normal,' says Hockney, 'people read things into it, but I just thought it looked better that way, and Ossie must have done it naturally as I don't tell my sitters to do too much. I just watch them.'[2] The picture does tell a story, however, of two people together but apart; she stands, serene and beautiful, looking directly at the artist, a slight look of sadness in her eyes, while he slouches rather sullenly in a chair, a cigarette in one hand, his right foot buried in the shagpile carpet, his thoughts perhaps drifting in the same direction as those of the cat sitting on his lap, staring out of the window. To model Percy, 'they borrowed a stuffed white cat from a taxidermist, which was brilliantly funny', recalls Birtwell. 'People read all sorts of things

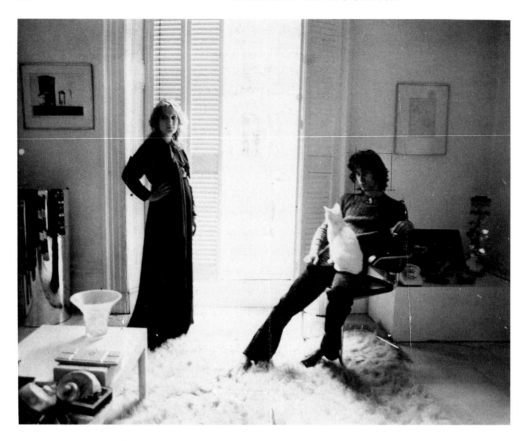

Mr and Mrs Ossie
Clark, Linden
Gardens, London,
1970

about us from looking at the painting. They said they could see that the writing was on the wall, but it wasn't. How could they know? David didn't even know us that well.'[3]

'It turns out now,' Hockney says, 'that it is quite a memorable painting, but when you're doing it you don't know that. I have no idea what makes a memorable picture. If I did there would be more of them.'[4] Part of what makes it so striking is its size, ten foot by seven foot. Hockney made the picture so big because he wanted viewers to feel that they were in the room with the couple, but making this seem natural presented enormous problems, and he put blood, sweat and tears into the work in order to overcome them. The setting of the painting is the Clarks' flat in Linden Gardens, which was painted first; Clark and Birtwell then came to Powis Terrace on numerous occasions during which Hockney attempted to paint them directly onto the painting of the room, an exercise made even more tricky by the fact that it was contre-jour. 'The figures are nearly life-size; it's difficult painting figures like that, and it was quite a struggle,' he wrote. 'They posed for a long time, both Ossie and Celia. Ossie was painted many, many times; I took it out and put it in, out and in. I probably painted the head alone twelve times; drawn and painted and then completely removed, and then out in again and again. You can see that the paint gets thicker and thicker there.'[5]

Living with Schlesinger and working on a painting of this size made Hockney only too aware of the limitations of the Powis Terrace flat. He had lived there since 1962, and it had proved a perfect set of rooms for a single artist, but since the arrival of Schlesinger in his life, space had been at a premium, and when the lease of the adjoining flat came up, Hockney bought it and employed a young, very handsome architect, Tchaik Chassay, to create a lateral conversion. Fresh out of the Architectural Association, Chassay was living with Melissa North, Tony Richardson's former girlfriend. He had ambitious plans for the new annexe, including a large dining room, a library and a beautiful new bathroom. In order to keep disruption to a minimum, it was agreed that the conversion work would go on quite separately, and only when it was complete would the builders break through to join the two flats together.

Schlesinger was excited about the new plan; he was beginning to find life in London a little claustrophobic in more senses than one. He worked hard at his painting and wanted to be thought of as an artist in his own right, but wherever he went he was always known as 'David Hockney's boyfriend'. He longed for his own identity, and the more Hockney painted and drew him, the more he felt that to most people he only existed as a sex object in his lover's pictures. He yearned to be cherished emotionally as well as physically, but was unable to grasp that living with a great artist it was inevitable he would always come second. 'At some point,' he says, 'I began to feel a bit smothered. David is an overwhelming person, and with his painting there was not much room for me in that world.'[6]

Hockney was blissfully unaware of all this, either struggling with the problems presented by *Mr and Mrs Clark and Percy*, during which time he would scarcely have even noticed Peter, or travelling with him and various other companions around the spas, museums and picture galleries of Europe, which made Schlesinger feel he was just part of the gang. In fact, when Schlesinger wasn't around, such as on a trip to Vichy in August when he visited his parents in California instead, Hockney missed him dreadfully. He just didn't tell him. 'I am here getting cured again with Wayne, George and Mo,' he wrote to Henry Geldzahler on 7 August. 'I must admit I can't stand Peter being away much longer. His absence has made me very melancholic. It's so pretty and he complements the surroundings so that it seems worse here than the more familiar Powis Terrace. Anyway he will be back in fourteen days. He sounds as though he quite enjoyed California. I thought he might, as this is the first time he could use the bars and night life.' After asking Geldzahler to telephone Schlesinger to give him his love and kisses, he added a PS: 'I can't phone him as his mother may answer.'[7]

When Hockney returned home from Vichy on 3 September, it was to face some worrying news about his own mother. Laura's health had been poor for most of the year, starting with attacks of rheumatism and arthritis that had caused her constant pain and left her feeling tired and depressed. While Ken had done his best to persuade her to try acupuncture as a cure, Hockney had taken her to Harrogate to enquire about spa treatment, unfortunately to no avail. 'I thought it had closed down,' she wrote in her diary on 20 May. 'Found I was right . . . no spa waters on sale now. The pond room is turned into a Museum where we visited & also went down to see the well where water springs, which used to be used for healing. Had a glass of it which just tasted salty.'[8] When an abdominal pain was diagnosed as a tumour on her bowel, she had an operation on 1 September; Hockney rushed up to Bradford to find her tired and sore, but on the mend, and living on a diet of soup and junket. He presented her with a bottle of spray perfume, which cheered her up immensely. His visit was short but sweet. 'David came again and has now gone back to London & his travels,' she reported on 5 September. 'His exhibition in Belgrade opens this week.'[9]

The exhibition, at the National Gallery in Belgrade, was the final stop on a European tour of his Whitechapel retrospective, which he and Schlesinger followed, first to Rotterdam and then Hanover, travelling by train, boat and bus – 'getting about that way,' he said, 'was much more fun than flying.'[10] Writing to Henry Geldzahler, he described how beautiful the trip had been, in particular Marienbad and Karlsbad, both spas in which they took the waters. In Karlsbad he loved the 'pine forests on the steep hills above the town. We took a little railway ride up one hill and walked back down through the pine forest in a marvellous rain storm. It really gave the place some Gothic gloom which I'm sure I've told you before, I love.' Schlesinger, however, seems to have got somewhat on his nerves. He 'was a little disappointed at the lack of pretty trinckets [*sic*] and merchandise. Anyway on the drive back to Prague I gave him one of my sermonettes that seemed to put things right in his pretty little mind.' For the final leg of their trip, they took a Russian boat from Bratislava to Belgrade. 'It was quite fantastic,' Hockney reported. 'You must do it one day. It glides along the Danube at about 15 miles an hour. We had a cabin with a large window on the deck with the water only about three feet below. The whole experience is so placid you really get a rest.'[11]

The last three months of 1970 saw Hockney spending more time than usual in Bradford. Laura's recuperation was a slow and painful process. She spent three weeks in hospital, then came home, to find Margaret had cleaned the place from top to bottom, much to her delight. 'It just looked lovely,' she wrote in her diary on 19 September, And there was more: 'Ken had a VERY BIG SURPRISE – a coloured Television. He has wanted one for a long time & thought I would like it too. It is a lovely piece of furniture and the colour is good.'[12]

Hockney didn't see her till the beginning of October because he was working to finish a commission: to design a poster for the 1972 Olympic Games in Munich. Out of twenty-nine international artists approached by the organising committee to produce posters representing the intertwining of sports and art worldwide, he was one of five from Great Britain, the others being Allen Jones, Ron Kitaj, Peter Phillips and Alan Davie. He chose water as his theme, and his design showed a diver breaking the surface of a typical Hockney swimming pool, its surface a myriad of swirling dappled ripples.

On his return from Munich to deliver his design, he drove up to Bradford for the day and took Ken and Laura to Ilkley for a short blow on the moors, followed by a quiet meal together. 'It was good to see David,' she wrote. 'He is so anxious to arrange for a holiday and recuperation.'[13] A fortnight later, on 14 October, he was back, bringing Celia Birtwell, who was staying with friends nearby, and the following day they all went on a trip to Fountains Abbey, one of Laura's favourite places. After that, work kept him away till December when he came up for his Aunt Audrey's wedding, bringing Laura a beautiful Ossie Clark blouse as a gift. He then, wrote Laura, 'suggested we should go & buy a dress I had seen & liked but too expensive. He bought dress, coat and hat for my birthday. I'm thrilled with dress and hat . . . felt like a Duchess.'[14] A few days later, on 10 December, her seventieth birthday, he sent her two dozen red roses, as he had on every one of her birthdays since he had left home.

Work on Powis Terrace progressed slowly, but it was an excuse for Schlesinger to start shopping again, which kept him involved in David's life. Before Christmas they went off together to Munich, where Hockney had to sign an edition of his Olympic posters. 'We came back through Paris,' wrote Hockney to Ron Kitaj on 2 January. '. . . I really like it more and more indeed I think Paris is going to have a great revival. People look so beautiful there. They either look chic, which is nice, or scruffy in a marvellous "La Boheme" way . . . Of course Peter always loved Paris . . . Work is progressing slowly on the flat. In Paris we bought a table and fourteen chairs for our dining room, made in 1925 for a Mme de Courcel who had a lot of classical sculpture in her house. Its [sic] quite beautiful . . .'[15]

Laura was well enough to come to London at the end of January to see off her daughter-in-law Alwyn, John's wife, who was on her way back to Australia, where they, following in the footsteps of Philip Hockney, had emigrated in 1968. Hockney booked her and Ken into the Strand Palace Hotel and took them for dinner at one of the most fashionable restaurants in London, Odin's in Devonshire Place. 'Met

David's friend,' wrote Laura, 'who cooks all the food himself, & getting our order left us to go and cook it . . . Ken had steak and fried onions & David a foreign dish! . . . Brought back souvenir menus which David and Patrick Procktor had drawn. Later our friend the cook said he would toast Alwyn in Champagne.'[16]

Alwyn got off lightly with just a toast, as 'the cook' was the renowned restaurateur Peter Langan, who had taken over and turned round the fortunes of Odin's after its original owner, James Benson, was killed in a car crash in 1966. Langan was a legendary drunk, and lecherous with it. 'He was a womanizer,' said the artist Bruer Tidman, who worked at Odin's in the late sixties. 'He would go round asking the girls to get their tits out – but there wasn't much he could do most of the time because he was so out of it.'[17]

Odin's was run as a restaurant in which the proprietor would have liked to dine himself, and woe betide anyone Langan took a dislike to. 'When my old brown bitch, Susie, was recovering from a hysterectomy in 1968,' the art critic Brian Sewell recalled, 'he invited her to dinner, wore a jacket and ate with her. She sat on the opposite chair confronted by all the panoply of a place-setting, and ate a dish of diced steak, very slowly, savouring each cube, and gazing about her as though she wished to see and be seen. At a neighbouring table four boisterous Australians objected; their complaints began indirectly, with such remarks as "Jesus, now we've seen everything", and grew to a grumble about not paying the bill in such a filthy, unhygienic restaurant. Peter ignored them for some time . . . but at last he could bear it no longer and, without rising from his chair or raising his voice (and taking care not to disturb Susie's poise), he addressed them with, "I own this joint. I don't care a damn about hygiene. I'd rather have this restaurant full of dogs than Australians – as you can see for yourselves, they have better manners."'[18]

Langan was also a genuine lover of art and artists. A close friend of Patrick Procktor, he encouraged artists to trade art for food, a mutually beneficial arrangement he called 'eating it down'. 'To find a restaurant close at hand,' wrote Procktor, 'which was not only welcoming but extremely good, and, to boot, that bought one's paintings in exchange for food, was a thrill both for David and for me. David introduced Ron Kitaj . . . and Peter's career as the most successful restaurateur of our time began. Odin's became quite a place for artists and their friends . . . and some of those ate their way through the price of pictures acquired by Peter.'[19] In this way Langan procured the services of Hockney and Procktor to design his menus, and Procktor's watercolours and Hockney's drawings and prints were soon among the dozens of works of art, hung like postcards, which adorned the walls. One of the first pictures Hockney traded in this way was *The Enchantress with the Baby Rapunzel*, an early pull from the *Six Fairy Tales from the Brothers Grimm*, made before the set went on sale officially. There are many drawings of Langan himself in the tiny airless kitchen, wearing his stained bum-freezer chef's jacket, with knife in hand or cradling his favourite large brandy glass filled with Löwenbräu lager, as well as a delicate portrait in coloured crayons of him seated wearing a blazer, nursing a glass of wine.

There was a period in the late sixties and early seventies when Hockney went to Odin's almost every night with a group of his friends, among whom were usually Schlesinger, Procktor, Kirsten Benson, who was James Benson's widow, Wayne Sleep, the brilliant young ballet dancer, and his boyfriend, George Lawson, a highly intelligent and very amusing antiquarian bookseller who worked at Bertram Rota Booksellers on Long Acre in Covent Garden.

Hockney met George Lawson through Kasmin, who had taken him into the shop, and they immediately hit it off because his camp, rather wicked sense of humour made him laugh. Likewise, George fell easily into David's milieu, taking a particular liking to Ossie Clark and Mo McDermott. 'I liked Ossie enormously,' Lawson says, 'because David had this entourage who just waited to see what he was going to do or say, so if he said, "Look, the sky is very green today," then everyone would say, "Yes, the sky does look a bit green," or if he said, "I'm going to the cinema," then they would all go to the cinema. But Ossie never did. He would do the opposite, and that is what I liked about him.'[20] Lawson took to McDermott because he was so funny and quick-witted. 'I remember once David and I were running down the stairs at Powis Terrace, and Mo knocked on one of the doors and ran away, and David said, "You shouldn't have done that, Mo, because the lady who lives there is blind," and Mo said, "Well, she'll never know we weren't there." This kind of thing used to make David crack up.'[21] It was Kasmin who had introduced him to Wayne Sleep, who soon moved into Lawson's flat in Wigmore Place, behind Harley Street. It proved to be the beginning of a long and happy relationship. 'We all became inseparable for a while,' Lawson recalls, 'and would see each other every day. Because we didn't have a kitchen, every meal was in a restaurant. We would all go out to dinner every night, usually to Odin's where we would have the back table. Wayne, David, Peter, Patrick Procktor and me more or less lived there.'[22]

The morning after their dinner at Odin's, Ken and Laura went to see Chassay's renovations at Powis Terrace. 'Looked around David's flat,' Laura recorded on 26 January, 'which is going to be very beautiful & hopes to be ready in six weeks, tho now it is chaos.' Celia was there discussing the bathroom tiles, which she was designing, and she took Ken and Laura to her shop to try on some shirts and blouses. 'David got some too,' Laura wrote, 'and we were most amused when Dad tried on "with it" coats nearly to floor shaped & <u>no pockets!!</u> He did look comical. Poor dad was like the dog with the bone – but tho the cupboard was full, he got <u>none</u>.'[23]

If there was ever an *annus horribilis* in David's life, then it was this year, 1971. He was struggling to finish *Mr and Mrs Clark and Percy*, there was the constant noise of the builders next door, and he had compounded his problems by breaking one of his own golden rules, which was not to undertake portrait commissions. Yet when Sir David Webster, the general administrator of the Royal Opera House, had asked him personally if he would paint his retirement portrait, Hockney initially said he might consider doing a drawing, then ended up agreeing to a painting. Sir David, often referred to as 'Daisy' by those in the music world, was a Scot with a background in the retail trade, who since the war had succeeded in turning Covent Garden from an impoverished venue with no permanent company and a rather provincial image into one of the leading opera houses in the world. He approached Hockney because he knew that he loved opera.

'A lot of pressure was put on me by Dickie Buckle and a few other people in the opera world,' David recalls, 'and I explained that I didn't really want to do it. There are problems painting portraits of people you don't know and I didn't really want to spend time doing that.'[24] He ran into problems even before he started the painting, unable to decide what the setting should be despite endless visits to Webster's house off Harley Street. 'Then they began to natter me,' he wrote, 'when will it be ready, he's retiring on this date, and so on. And in the end I thought, all I can do is paint him in my studio. So that's the setting; the table and chair and flowers are in my studio.'[25]

As soon as he was settled in the tubular chair that Hockney had chosen for him to sit in, Webster would fall asleep, making it tricky to capture his personality. No longer the vibrant energetic man he must have been when young, Webster was a sick old man, who, it turned out, was at death's door. While he was sleeping, Hockney did lots of drawings of him, and when he was awake, he took as many photographs as he could. He just couldn't get the mood, and his problems were compounded by the fact that the painting had been commissioned by a major institution and had to be completed by a deadline, something he was not used to and which filled him with fear.

Before he could begin, however, *Mr and Mrs Clark and Percy* had to be finished, and on the day he completed it, 15 February, the first person he called was his mother. 'David phoned – he has finished his picture,' she wrote. 'Takes his <u>first driving test in England</u> tomorrow – do hope he passes. He is so kind – in spite of depression went to bed with a thankful heart for his thoughtfulness and generosity – we are certainly blessed in our family, even if we ourselves are difficult.'[26]

Hockney was also facing a much more significant difficulty: after nearly five years together, his relationship with Schlesinger was beginning to founder. 'I met Peter when he was eighteen,' he says, 'and we had certain things in common. We could travel around museums together, for example, but I realise now that there were a few things we didn't quite have in common. I don't think he ever had much of an ear for music and I probably took him to too many operas. Then he always wanted to stay in London, whereas I wanted to be in California. Another thing was humour. He could be quite funny, but only a little bit, whereas I would tend to mock things more.'[27]

Sexual boredom had also set in, and in order to try and inject a little romance into their life, as well as to get away from the Webster portrait for a while, Hockney took Schlesinger and Birtwell to Morocco for a fortnight. They stayed in Marrakech at La Mamounia, famed for its twenty acres of lush gardens and its decor in a mixture of art deco and Moroccan styles. The hotel's many associations appealed to David. Churchill and Roosevelt had stayed there during the war when they attended the Casablanca Conference. Josef von Sternberg filmed *Morocco* there with Marlene Dietrich, while Alfred Hitchcock not only used it in *The Man Who Knew Too Much*, but got the inspiration there for *The Birds*, when he opened the door onto his balcony and was assailed by a flock of pigeons.

'The Hotel in Marrakech,' Hockney wrote to Henry Geldzahler, 'was rather like the Beverly Hills Hotel only of course more Moroccan . . . When we arrived we bought some high quality Kief and every evening we sat on our large wooden balcony completely stoned. Each afternoon I did a large coloured drawing of a scene in the hotel or Celia or Peter (with a Palm Tree in the background). And in between I took the usual 300 photographs.'[28] Hockney and Schlesinger had a large bedroom with a beautiful balcony and view, and one of the drawings he did was a rear view of Schlesinger standing on the balcony 'gazing at a luscious garden and listening to the evening noises of Marrakech'. This drawing, inspired by *The Balcony, Macao* by the nineteenth-century artist George Chinnery, was later worked up into a painting, *Sur la Terrasse*, which Hockney began work on when he returned home.

While Schlesinger found it hard to control his mounting irritation that all Hockney wanted to do at the hotel was to arrange him in poses to draw and photograph, Hockney was equally irritated by Schlesinger's demands that they should indulge in some social life. 'There was a terrible row,' Celia recalls, 'and David said to Peter, "The trouble with you, Peter, is you just want to be in Marrakech,

Kensington, and I've come away from all that," and they had to take a pile of Valium to calm down. Peter was getting excited by the fact that "the Gettys were living just over there!"[29] Things improved a little when they made a detour to Madrid on their way home to visit the Prado, David's first trip to Spain. They arrived in a blizzard, and the snow-covered city reminded him of Berlin and Vienna. His agenda had been to look at the Velázquez pictures, but he ended up being much more impressed by the Goyas. 'All those rooms full of Goyas,' he wrote to Geldzahler, 'they're fabulous; about six rooms in the Prado, beginning with the early works, when he painted pretty pictures of people dancing in sylvan glades, happy pictures, beautifully painted . . . and finally those marvellous pictures he did in his old age, almost like Bacons. Marvellous!'[30]

On his return, Hockney had to face the deadline for his portrait of Sir David Webster. As usual, Powis Terrace was full of people coming and going and for the first time they became a distraction. Hockney told everyone to leave – Schlesinger went off to Paris for a few days – and locked himself in the studio, working on the picture for eighteen hours a day until it was finished. He later admitted to Anthony Bailey that he actually spent longer on the tulips in this picture than he did on Webster. It had been an unhappy experience: he didn't like the finished work, in spite of the fact that it was considered a great success by both the sitter and those who commissioned it. 'I was also terrified then,' he says, 'of being asked to do a hell of a lot of portraits . . . I didn't regret doing it afterwards, but I certainly didn't want to do any more, otherwise they'd be turning me into a society portrait painter and I didn't want that.'[31]

The Webster portrait was completed at the same time that *Mr and Mrs Clark and Percy* went on show at the National Portrait Gallery, in an exhibition called *Snap* which explored the idea of likeness, and it vexed Hockney that the Webster was generally thought to be a better picture. Writing in *The Times*, Guy Brett found the portrait of the Clarks 'unusually bland and lacking in tension',[32] while Marco Livingstone has described the surface of the picture as being 'murky and uninviting'.[33] Henry Geldzahler's pertinent comments about it got right to the root of Hockney's fears. 'If David, aged 32, 34 or 36, had decided to devote the rest of his life to painting pictures like this, he would have become a latter-day Pre-Raphaelite – an English painter really of very local interest. He would have been a mystifier, a prestidigitator, somebody who could do the impossible with paint – and yet something would have fallen out of the content. And that something is the element of risk, of doubt.'[34]

He decided to take a much-needed break from portraiture. He found his new inspiration in a hand-tinted postcard that Kasmin had given him depicting a small island in the Inland Sea in Japan, a country he had a strong desire to visit. Just as *Domestic Scene, Los Angeles* had been based entirely on preconceived ideas, so in *The Island* Hockney wanted to see how close to the mark he might be about Japan, before actually going there. 'The postcard attracted me for many other reasons: the problem of depicting the sea because of the inlet, the connections with landscape (or seascape) painting and with Monet, and, not least, that it looked like a piece of cake.'[35]

Scarcely had he started work than he received a call from Jack Hazan, a young cameraman and film-maker, which was to be of immense significance in his life. Ever since filming the paintings in Hockney's Whitechapel retrospective show, Hazan had been trying to convince Hockney to be the subject of a feature film. 'I was immediately wowed by this show,' Hazan recalls, 'because of the double portraits. I'd never seen any of his canvases before, and I thought the possibilities were enormous. I got very excited because the subjects were alive, and I could possibly gain access to them, and maybe, I thought straight away, I could film them in the same poses. I could possibly make something dramatic out of it and produce some kind of mystery. The paintings are very compelling. The film was never intended to be a documentary. I wanted to make something cinematic.'[36]

A few months previously, Hazan had persuaded Hockney to view some earlier films he had made for the BBC, one about an artists' colony in Camden, and the other about the Liverpudlian artist Keith Grant. He made it quite clear that this was with a view to Hockney possibly participating in a film himself. But though polite and civil about it, Hockney did not like what he had seen. Not quite straight documentaries, Hazan's films required the participants to act a little, rather than just talk to camera. 'David recognised that,' says Hazan, 'and the first thing he said to me when he came out was, "I'm not going to act, Jack," and then I heard nothing from him. So I just kept ringing him and ringing him and he was never encouraging.'[37]

One day, however, he suddenly said yes. 'Jack started nattering me,' Hockney remembers, 'and I was always putting him off, and then he came back to me and nattered again, and finally I agreed to do it to get rid of him.'[38] Hazan turned up at Powis Terrace the following day with two assistants, a couple of lights and a 16mm Cameflex movie camera, a type much favoured by the French *nouvelle vague* film-makers because of its portability and unforbidding appearance. 'When I arrived there,' he recalls, 'he was rebuilding Powis Terrace and there were a lot of Irish builders around. I filmed him painting the Japanese island picture a bit, and because I'm fairly skilled and confident I did it very fast. I think he liked the light I provided as well, which was daylight done by using redheads with blue filter paper. I was excited when I left, and the next day, when we got the rushes, it looked marvellous, and he was very photogenic, with his bleached blond hair and his rugby shirt.'[39] For his part, Hockney was only too glad to see the back of Hazan, and had few worries about having agreed to take part. 'There were three people with one camera,' he remembers, 'and I just kept thinking, "Well, this will be slightly out of focus, and it will play one or two nights at the Academy Cinema in Oxford Street with the Polish version of *Hamlet*, and then it'll be gone."'[40] He could not have been more wrong.

Since the return from Morocco, things had begun to unravel between Hockney and Schlesinger. In Paris in February, Schlesinger had met Fred Hughes, Andy Warhol's young business manager, a keen Anglophile and stylish dresser who bought his suits and shoes in London. When Hughes came to London with Picasso's daughter Paloma to see *Death in Venice*, which hadn't yet opened in Paris, and invited Schlesinger and Hockney to join them for dinner at the fashionable Chinese restaurant Mr Chow in Knightsbridge, Schlesinger accepted the invitation. On the night, David didn't want to go. 'He said he was going to stay home and work,' Schlesinger remembers. 'He told me to go, saying, "I'm not interested in meeting Paloma. If it was Pablo, I'd go."'[41]

The evening turned out to be more significant than Schlesinger could ever have imagined. He turned up at the restaurant to find Paloma's guests already there, the Spanish designer Manolo Blahnik, who designed shoes for Zapata, a trendy boutique, and Eric Boman, a strikingly beautiful young Swedish illustrator and fabric designer. Hughes and Paloma had misjudged the length of the film and were an hour late for dinner, giving Schlesinger plenty of time, over a number of Screwdrivers, to get acquainted with the two strangers. Schlesinger was almost instantly infatuated with Boman, and the attraction was mutual. 'It was a *coup de foudre*,' says Boman, 'or certainly lust at first sight. We had a huge attraction to each other. It happens, and from then on we saw each other every day.'[42]

With the Webster portrait completed, the builders about to break through the wall to complete the lateral conversion, creating chaos and dust in the flat, and his relationship with Schlesinger rocky, Hockney decided to take off to California for a couple of weeks 'for some adventure'.[43] He stayed with Nick Wilder, and hung out with their mutual friend Arthur Lambert, whom he had met in 1968. 'When I first went to see Arthur,' Hockney recalls, 'Nick Wilder had told me he was a banker, which immediately put me off a bit. When I went to his house, however, and he opened the door and I saw this unbelievably dishy boy standing behind him, I thought, "Well, he's no ordinary banker."'[44]

Lambert was a 34-year-old financier, who had moved down from Washington to take over a company that ran answering services, much used by Hollywood stars, and the dishy boy was his much younger lover, Larry Stanton, a painting student. 'I remember the night David came over,' says Lambert, 'because I was wrestling with a very complicated recipe, a French dish with goose and beans called Cassoulet, and making it was practically causing me a nervous breakdown. But David was immediately obviously very attracted to

Larry, so things went really well from that point, and our friendship began.'[45]

In the days before there were exclusively gay bars in LA, Lambert's house off La Cienega Boulevard, which had a vast living room on the first floor with great views over the city, became a focal point for the gay community. 'The police were very aggressive then,' he says, 'and were constantly arresting people for touching each other. You couldn't dance, or anything like that, so we used to have dances at my house and it was always full of the most beautiful young boys.'[46] It was not long before word of Lambert's lifestyle drifted back to his employers in Washington, who immediately fired him, their excuse being that they needed a 'family man' to run the company. He kept Hedges Place on, however, and when Hockney arrived at the end of March 1971 he was able to spend blissful hours there drawing and enjoying the company of boys such as Paul Miranda, of whom he did two fine line drawings, one of him stretched out on a sofa, the other, which is signed 'for Arthur', of him seated on the edge of a table.

'David was going off to LA,' Schlesinger recalls, 'and having little affairs, which I wasn't aware of until I saw the drawings he had done of the various boys.'[47] These dalliances meant nothing to Hockney, however, who still believed he and Schlesinger had something strong enough to be able to overcome their difficulties. He told the journalist Gordon Burn: 'I have a relationship with this boy that's as complete as two people could have.'[48] Even when Schlesinger admitted to carrying on an affair, which Hockney must have suspected, since Boman was coming round to Powis Terrace every day, he convinced himself that it was just a fling that would soon be over. 'At first I was a bit hurt,' Hockney wrote, 'and then I thought, well there's nothing I can do about it really. After all, I'd just been to California to release myself, as it were. And I thought it's probably temporary . . .'[49] He retreated into work, specifically on *Sur la Terrasse*, a picture tinged with a curious melancholy as the remote figure stares into the middle distance.

Resisting the demands of others was becoming more and more of a problem as Hockney's fame increased. Nikos Stangos, for example, with whom he had worked on the Cavafy project, was trying to revive

Sir Kenneth Clark's *Penguin Modern Painters* series, which had run from 1944 to 1959, and aimed to bring the work of modern artists to a wider public outside the art galleries. 'I get nattered to death here,' Hockney wrote to Henry Geldzahler in June, 'and just wish at times that only a few people liked my work. Still it's made me get a bit tougher. I actually refuse to do things that people ask now, and just sit and paint. If I allowed everybody with some scheme or other to take up my time, I would never get anything done at all. I'm sure Nikos will be a little disappointed but the real truth about those little books is that they are not that interesting. When Penguin originally did there [*sic*] modern painter series . . . nothing like the books existed. Now my catalogue from the Whitechapel is really better and more interesting . . . than the Penguin book format will be, so I don't care about it, and I suspect nobody else does other than Nikos . . .'[50]

By the middle of June, Schlesinger was spending more and more time alone in his studio and it was becoming increasingly clear to Hockney that the affair with Boman was serious. Jack Hazan noticed the tension between them when he went to film in Powis Terrace for a second time – no mean achievement, given Hockney's new tougher stance on his time. 'The fact that I'd had my foot in the door,' Hazan says, 'did not allow any further entrance. Every time I actually gained access to his studio or to him, I had to negotiate specially, which was very wearing on my nerves.' Hazan turned up at the studio and after a very short time, Hockney suddenly said, 'Let's get Peter.' 'I had no idea who Peter was. Anyway, Peter came, and arrived looking very angry, and he looked at me in a very hostile way. He sat down on this stool and David painted him. You could have cut the atmosphere between the two of them with a knife, as Peter plainly did not want to be there, and I realised then that David had got him there on the pretext of drawing him just to have him in front of him. There was huge tension and David was furiously painting and he knew he had to do it rapidly because Peter's patience was wearing thin.'[51]

When Hazan showed the rushes to his business partner, David Mingay, an assistant editor at the BBC, he saw at once that the key to the film lay in the story of the break-up between Hockney and Schlesinger.

Unbeknown to Hockney, that is the road they decided to go down. Because they had no script and no agreement with Hockney, it was a question of making it up as they went along, shooting any footage they could get which might possibly be relevant: Ossie Clark's fashion show at the Royal Court Theatre, a glamorous event at which Twiggy, Amanda Lear and Alice Ormsby-Gore were among the models who sashayed down the catwalk in Manolo Blahnik's first collection of shoes, Hockney and Celia Birtwell in the front row, with Schlesinger and Boman turning up wearing identical sailor suits; Kasmin in his gallery, pretending to ring Hockney to complain that he had forgotten to turn up to a meeting; and endless shots of Mo McDermott in Powis Terrace. 'The story was slowly evolving,' says Hazan. 'We had scores of scenes all marked out on the glass partition in the editing room, small scenes, which we'd shot. There were no computers then and we didn't know where the scenes fitted, so we would just scrub one out and put it higher or lower on the glass partition, or wherever it seemed to fit.'[52]

Work on Powis Terrace was completed in the early summer, and the small flat was transformed into a large, light and airy space with lots of room to breathe. There was a library panelled with cedarwood, a state-of-the-art bathroom featuring a circular shower lined with Celia Birtwell's dark blue tiles, and, at the end of the main corridor, an open-plan dining room in which stood the table and fourteen chairs bought in Paris. The truth was, of course, that this beautiful place had been created with Schlesinger in mind, and now that it was finished, he was leaving. There was a sadness and a sterility to it, which was picked up on by the artist and film-maker Derek Jarman, who dined there one night. 'The Art Deco blight has taken over David's home. Lemonade is served in precious Lalique glasses. There's a dining-room table that would seat the boardroom of the Chase Manhattan bank and David has the food brought in from Mr Chow's. The flat now parodies his painting. There are huge bunches of tulips in yet more Lalique vases dotted around like wreaths. The place is antiseptic, a waiting room for the good life . . . When I first came to Powis Terrace you could lounge around, but now the decoration dwarfs and depresses . . . David, who seems the same on the surface, has become a tortoise

within a decorator's shell.'[53] Hockney felt his life unravelling and
made desperate attempts to pull things together, taking Schlesinger
off on a trip to Le Nid de Duc, for example, though this was hardly
the best atmosphere in which to give him attention. When Hockney
was lonely and miserable, there was always Bradford to escape to, and
thinking about his parents took his mind off himself. 'Yesterday I had a
delightful day with my parents in the English lakes,' he wrote to Henry
Geldzahler, 'visiting Wordsworth's cottage and house by the lake at
Grasmere. I'd forgotten how beautiful it really is. The drive from
Bradford is through bleak moorland scenery, and quite spectacular.
Although it's June the weather was like November. It's all very Gothic
up there – and I love Gothic places. We must go when you next come
to England – it's only five hours drive and in my new car with steario
(forgive my atrocious spelling) it should be very pleasant.'[54]

Everything came to a head in the high summer. 'David went to
LOT in France for a month,' wrote Laura on 28 July, 'with his friends
and John Kasmin.'[55] The holiday was to be spent with the Kasmins
at Carennac, and the group consisted of some of his inner circle –
Clark and Birtwell, who was six months pregnant and working hard
to make her fractured marriage work, Mo McDermott and Maurice
Payne – together with George Lawson and Wayne Sleep. Hockney had
pleaded with Schlesinger to come, and to begin with everything was
calm. The weather was warm and sunny, the food was delicious, and
everyone lazed around reading, swimming in the river and sunbathing
and falling under Carennac's magical spell. Hockney worked, having
arranged before he left London for Payne to bring down a carload
of etching plates, and among the drawings he completed was a
particularly charming one of Birtwell sitting in a green garden chair,
exuding feminine beauty and grace. A postcard he sent to Ron Kitaj on
18 August – 'The weather is beautiful, I am working slowly and Peter
is reading Proust' – makes everything sound idyllic, but the truth by
then was somewhat different. 'In Carennac,' he later wrote, 'Peter and
I hadn't been getting on well at all, and I was getting very miserable
about it. We'd had one very pleasant day when we drove down the
Gorge de Tarn . . .'[56]

This scenario is supported by George Lawson's version of events. 'Peter was already going off on his own,' he recalls, '. . . on long bicycle rides in the countryside and we wouldn't see him throughout the whole day. He was just wandering around on his own. He just didn't want to be with David.'[57] Not even a trip to Barcelona to visit the Museum of Modern Art and the Picasso Museum could calm things down. Eventually Schlesinger said he would like to go to Cadaqués, a town on the coast of Catalonia, famous for its associations with artists like Marcel Duchamp, Joan Miró and Salvador Dali. Richard Hamilton had a summer home there, and through him Mark Lancaster had rented an apartment from 'Teeny' Duchamp, Marcel's widow, and invited Schlesinger and Hockney to stay.

Unfortunately Lancaster was not up to speed on what was going on between them, and had also invited Eric Boman. 'Mark had invited me and David to visit him in Cadaqués,' Schlesinger recalls. 'David said no, but I said I was going anyway, because I wanted to meet Eric there. When I said this, he said he would drive me there.'[58]

Arriving in Cadaqués to find Boman in residence did little for Hockney's state of mind. Nor did the fact that it was the height of the summer season and the town was crawling with tourists, including a large group of English gilded youth who were guests of the brewing heir Jonathan Guinness and his wife Sue who had a house up in the hills. The Guinnesses had invited Lancaster to bring his party to a picnic they were holding on top of a rock down the coast, to which they would all be travelling by boat. When Hockney heard about this, he went into a sulk. 'I'm not going,' he said. 'It's too social and there are too many Hoorays.'[59] Lancaster, Schlesinger and Boman paid no attention and went down to the harbour, followed by an increasingly agitated Hockney.

'There was a screaming match at the dock,' Boman remembers, 'when everyone was on the boat, and it was leaving for the lunch. Peter was on it and David was standing on the dock in tears. He was making an ultimatum, which was, "If you go on this picnic, you can't come back."' At that point, Schlesinger says, 'Everyone was getting involved. Richard Hamilton was shouting and David was crying. He said, "I'm leaving. Come with me." And I said, "No, I'm staying here," and he shouted "Fuck off" and left.'[60]

Completely distraught, Hockney jumped into his car with the intention of driving back to Carennac alone, but got no further than the medieval town of Perpignan, just north of the Spanish border, where he decided to stay the night in the Grand Hotel. As much to his surprise as theirs, he encountered George Lawson and Wayne Sleep there, en route from Barcelona where they had been staying with the Spanish sculptor Xavier Corberó. 'David was in a state and on his own,' Lawson remembers, 'so we had to go and sit by his bed. Then as we were sitting there was an earthquake, and the chandelier began to shake, and the bell of the clock tower crashed to the ground. The next morning we said to him, "What a night! What a night!" and he said, "What do you mean? I'm very upset." And we said, "David, there was an earthquake. The whole hotel was shaking," and he just said, "Oh, I'm very upset with Peter." He was having an internal earthquake, which had quite overwhelmed him.'[61]

Arriving back at Carennac, Hockney burst into floods of tears at the sight of Clark and McDermott, totally disconsolate at what he had done. To top it all he got an unexpected and unwelcome surprise. In the excitement of the last few months he had completely forgotten about Jack Hazan who was still anxiously pursuing him and, hearing that he was going to be staying with Kasmin, had decided to drive down there on the off chance of getting some more film in the can. After arriving with his sound recordist to find no sign of David, he had decided to stick around anyway and film whatever was going on. 'We concocted a scene together,' Jack recalls, 'with Mo and Ossie playing around in the chateau. I was filming that, when who should arrive but David, and he came in and saw me. I turned the motor off and he looked at me and said, "Oh my God!" and was really upset and left. I didn't speak to him until that evening when we were having dinner and it was made quite clear to me that I couldn't do any more and I had to leave the next day.'[62]

Remorse now set in and Hockney began to regret his behaviour towards Schlesinger. 'I thought, I've been really cruel to Peter, what a rotten thing I've done. So I said I must phone up and apologise, and say I didn't mean to be bitchy if I was bitchy.'[63] Since reaching him by telephone was complicated, and ultimately involved leaving messages, he decided to drive back to Cadaqués, speak to Schlesinger in person and then leave, hopefully on less of a sour note. As it happened, Clark was planning to drive to Nice the following day to stay with Mick Jagger at the Villa Nellcôte, where the Stones were recording their album *Exile on Main Street*, so he said he would take Hockney there. Maurice Payne and Mo McDermott decided to go along too. 'I drove down there with Mo,' Payne remembers, 'and David drove with Ossie in his huge Bentley. When you're losing somebody you pull out all the stops and I think David was absolutely distraught.'[64]

When Hockney reached Mark Lancaster's, however, he was the last person Schlesinger wanted to see. 'Peter said, "I don't want you to stay here, get out of this town" . . . I said, "I've just driven back, I'm not going to leave now; I'm going to stay a day, I'm going to rest" . . . Richard Hamilton was quite amused by it all. He said, "The border police must know you very well, David."'[65] Hamilton offered to put them up and Hockney spent the time making a marvellous etching of him sitting in a chair holding a cheroot in his right hand. Not even the most profoundly emotional state could prevent him working. When he had finished, he returned to London, feeling a little better in the belief that he had made it up a bit with Peter. But it was the beginning of the end.

After all the drama, Schlesinger and Boman had no desire to stay any longer in Cadaqués, so Clark offered to take them with him to Mick Jagger's, an idea they jumped at. Schlesinger suggested that they should stop the night en route with Tony Richardson at Le Nid de Duc, but when they arrived there unannounced, Richardson, out of loyalty to Hockney, made it quite clear they were not welcome. So they drove straight on to the Villa Nellcôte, arriving in the early hours of the morning to find everyone asleep, and making themselves unpopular by eating an entire Paris-Brest pastry that had been intended for the next day's lunch. The two boys crept into a maids' room at the top of the house, and later that day, Clark drove them to the station where they boarded a train for Paris. It was standing room the whole way.

'The end came,' Schlesinger says, 'when I went to Greece with my parents right after all this, like a week later. We were in Athens first and then we went to stay with Mary North on Lindos. In Athens I got really mad at my father, and called him David. I never went back to David after that. When I got back to London, I told him that I was moving out.'[66]

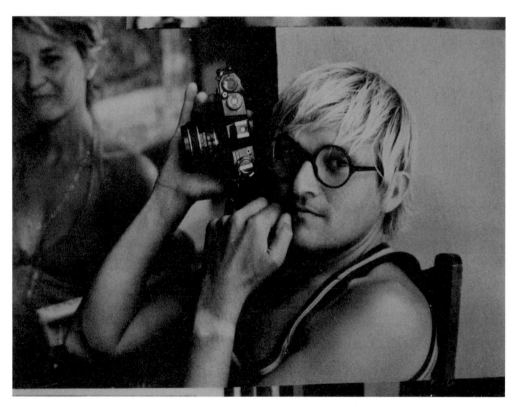

David Hockney with Pentax

CHAPTER ELEVEN

PORTRAIT
OF AN ARTIST

Hockney's break-up with Schlesinger was the first really painful thing that had ever happened to him, and he took it very badly. He returned to London and his beautiful new flat, in which almost everything reminded him of his lost lover: the dining-room table and chairs, the leather sofa, the Lalique lamps, his paintings on the walls, and in the studio, on the easel, the almost completed *Sur la Terrasse*, a picture that exudes melancholy and nostalgia. They filled him with a deep sense of emptiness. He had no appetite for going out, or for staying in. 'It was very traumatic for me,' he wrote, 'I'd never been through anything like that. I was miserable, very, very unhappy. Occasionally I got on the verge of panic, that I was alone, and I started taking Valium . . . It was very lonely; I was incredibly lonely.'[1] Things got worse when Schlesinger returned to London and was living just round the corner in his studio in Colville Terrace. 'David never really accepted it,' Schlesinger recalls. 'He was always asking me to a party or inviting me to dinner and asking me to do this and that, and there were tears and him asking me to move back in, pleading and pleading. And of course he was asking everybody for advice and they were giving it. Henry said, "Buy him a ring," and somebody else said he should buy a building with two studios so I could have a separate life. This all went on for some time.'[2]

If it can ever be said that there was a silver lining to this dark cloud, it was that Hockney soon discovered that the solution to his unhappiness was to throw himself into work, initially for fourteen or fifteen hours a day, the result being that over the next year he was to produce an enormous volume of work. The ghost of Schlesinger haunts many of these paintings, not least *Sur la Terrasse*, a ravishing picture in blues and greens. It must have been hard for Hockney to put the finishing touches to it. There is an air of loneliness too about *Pool and Steps, Le Nid de Duc*, which shows a pair of Schlesinger's sandals lying beside a swimming pool that is otherwise deserted. It is a painting that successfully makes use of a stain technique, favoured by American abstract artists such as Helen Frankenthaler and Morris Louis, to depict the water, in which acrylic paint diluted with detergent and water is stained into the weave of the canvas. The fact that the picture was started in May 1971, while Hockney and Schlesinger were still living together, does not detract from the suggestion in the finished work of a relationship with somebody who is no longer there.

A new painting, which Hockney began in September, was *Still Life on a Glass Table*, in which he revisited the favourite theme of painting transparency. In 1967, he had made an ink drawing, *A Glass Table with Glass Objects,* in which he tentatively explored this subject, but while that was a rather clumsily executed and naive sketch, the 1971 work is a masterpiece, 'a virtuoso display', wrote Marco Livingstone, 'of Hockney's recently acquired perceptual conviction in dealing with the refraction of light through glass, the reflections off it and the modifications of surface through it; yet through all this transparency he manages to endow the subject with a credible sense of weight and mass'.[3] Though Hockney saw this as a fairly straightforward painting, various friends pointed out that all the objects on the table either belonged to or were particularly loved by Schlesinger, which led him to question whether unconsciously he might have chosen them to reflect his emotional state.

The only painting he made at this time that can be said to have had no associations with Schlesinger was *Rubber Ring Floating in a Swimming Pool*, a very simple picture which on first sight could be taken for a Max Ernst abstract, and which was based entirely on a photograph taken in Cadaqués. 'It's almost copied from it,' wrote Hockney. 'I was standing on the edge of the pool, the pool water was blue and there was this red ring, and I just looked down and pressed the shutter . . . At first glance it looks like an abstract painting, but when you read the title the abstraction disappears and it becomes something else.'[4] To Henry Geldzahler, this painting was an indication of how Hockney was still interested in modernism, even if he had chosen to distance himself from it. '. . . he's interested in modernism, he's interested in goofing on it, he's interested in learning from it, he's interested in painting now, he's interested in the whole panoply.'[5]

The most important painting which he began work on at this time was a portrait of Schlesinger inspired by the accidental juxtaposition of two photographs lying on the studio floor. 'One was of a figure,' he wrote, 'swimming underwater and therefore quite distorted . . . and the other was of a boy gazing at something on the ground; yet because of the way the photographs were lying, it looked as though he was gazing at the distorted figure. The idea of once again painting two figures in different styles appealed so much that I began the painting immediately.'[6] Schlesinger is the subject of *Portrait of an Artist*, dressed in a pink jacket and looking down into a pool with an underwater swimmer in it. He painted the swimmer first, using the same thin acrylic wash technique that he had employed on *Pool and Steps, Le Nid de Duc* in order to emphasise wetness. He then, however, coated the rest of the canvas with gesso, the traditional mixture of glue, chalk and pigment used to prepare surfaces, which prevented his altering either the position of the pool or the figure, and immediately got him into difficulties. 'The figures never related to one another,' he recalled, 'nor to the background. I changed the setting constantly from distant mountains to a claustrophobic wall and back again to mountains. I even tried a glass wall.'[7]

He made occasional trips to Bradford and, though he never shared his unhappiness with his parents, was able to do things for them that took him temporarily out of himself. 'David arrived at 11am,' wrote Laura on 5 October, '& we went to Leeds where we visited shops whilst David called at Leeds Art Gallery . . . then we went on to Harrogate. In Harrogate we bought gloves and a lovely suit for me (Ken's choice) & some shirts and bow ties for Kenneth. What generosity & how I enjoyed shopping amongst beautiful things with no restraint – but most of all I love David's kindness of heart – the pleasure he gets from giving I can understand as from what he gives me, I can now give to others.'[8]

On their return home she recorded: 'David took several photographs of Ken & I for a picture he is going to paint.'⁹ This is the first mention of Hockney's intention to paint a portrait of his parents, an idea conceived while Laura had been in hospital, but which was not to come to fruition for another three years. These photographs were the basis for drawings he completed early in 1972, notably *The Artist's Father, 1972*, which shows Kenneth slumped in the corner of a sofa, wearing a three-piece suit, a bow tie, and with a different watch on each wrist, a habit he had fallen into in case one of them might be wrong. He looks crumpled and ill at ease, quite in keeping with his character, in contrast to the two drawings of Laura, both titled *The Artist's Mother*, in which she looks completely relaxed, her attention entirely focused on her son. Of these two, one in ink and the other in coloured crayon, the latter was worked into a small oil painting, *Mother in a Wicker Chair*, which remained unfinished.

When Mark Lancaster returned to London from Cadaqués in late October, he found Hockney deeply depressed. 'David was completely heartbroken,' he recalls, 'so I suggested to him that one way to deal with this was to do something he'd never done before, to go somewhere fabulous he'd never been and forget about everything. I said, "Why don't you go to Japan?" and he said, "That's a good idea," and the next day he called me up and said, "Do you want to come with me?" It is clear, however, from a postcard Hockney wrote to Henry Geldzahler a few days later that he was not yet ready to give up on Schlesinger. 'I leave November 8 for Japan with Mark Lancaster. I think Peter and I will work it out by Christmas. I admire his stubbornness and love him very much so it [*sic*] must. I have been working very hard. Why don't you come to London for Christmas . . . Give my regards to Broadway and all the boys on 42nd St . . .'¹⁰

Lancaster jumped at the prospect of a trip to Japan, and joined Hockney in California a fortnight later, where he had been visiting Christopher Isherwood and Don Bachardy and pouring his heart out to them. 'Peter and David both confided in us about the break-up of their relationship,' Bachardy remembers, 'and we did our best. But what more can you do than give your ears? Peter was very determined. I don't think he really understood what real artists are like, that they are obsessed by their work. David just didn't pay enough attention to Peter. That is the truth, and in the end Peter was independent enough to say it wasn't good enough. We were so sympathetic towards David, who was hurting so much more than Peter.'[11] But Hockney was also secretly angry with Isherwood for having advised him to give his younger lover his wings, anger which he expressed in late-night calls to Jack Larson and Jim Bridges. 'At a certain point,' Larson recalls, 'David started phoning Jim and me late at night just weeping that Schlesinger had left him and he blamed the advice that Isherwood had given him. Isherwood said you could only have a long-term relationship with a younger man if you left them free to have affairs with other people. Otherwise you just couldn't keep them.'[12]

'Mr Whizz's Tour' of Japan began in the St Francis Hotel on Union Square, San Francisco, on 11 November, its first day commemorated with a pen-and-ink drawing of Lancaster asleep in his bed, a familiar subject for Hockney. He made hundreds of drawings of his friends sleeping, who often woke to the sound of the scratch of a pen nib on cartridge paper, or the whirr of the electric pencil sharpener. From San Francisco they flew to Honolulu for two days, staying in the Royal Hawaiian Hotel on Waikiki Beach, known as the Pink Palace, where the spirit of Peter Schlesinger caught up with them. 'Mark had a shirt,' Hockney wrote, 'exactly like one Peter had been wearing once when I'd drawn him; I didn't know this until one morning I woke up and the shirt was lying on a chair, and I drew it, early in the morning.'[13] This drawing later became the painting *Chair and Shirt*, another melancholy evocation of lost love.

Hockney's initial impressions of Japan were not good. 'Kenneth Clark was really right about Tokyo,' he wrote to Henry Geldzahler, 'it makes Los Angeles look like Paris. After the first day and the excitement wears off, I realise what a mess it really is. When it was rebuilt after the war they forgot to plan parks in it, so apart from the Imperial Palace grounds, which no one can enter, there are no Parks in the centre of the city. The air is twice as bad as New York. People walk around wearing masks all the time. I'm assuming it's to filter the air.'[14]

Nor was he impressed by the art he saw there, which he described as being like 'Woody Alan's [sic] versions of Japanese versions of Pop Art'.[15]

Their next stop, however, was the ancient imperial city of Kyoto, whose status as an artistic and cultural centre had meant that it had largely escaped bombing raids in the war, and its superb temples, parks and buildings had mostly survived. Hockney loved it, and immediately missed Schlesinger. 'It's very beautiful here,' he wrote to Geldzahler, 'and I think because of that I miss Peter enormously. It's knowing he would love it so that makes me a little depressed he's not here. Also I'd love to suck his cock.'[16] In another letter written on the same day, he told Ron Kitaj, 'Mark is an enjoyable and intelligent travelling companion who likes what I do and of course shares an interest in seeking out the night life, but its [sic] not like travelling with Peter and I know its unfair of me to expect it to be, but I can't help it really. It sure is the real thing I've got and I suppose if Peter stays away I'll suffer for quite a long time . . .'[17]

In the Municipal Gallery of Kyoto, Hockney found some Japanese art that he really admired, in a show called *Modern Painters in the Japanese Style*, and was fascinated to find that all the artists were old men in their seventies. 'There was a beautiful painting on silk,' he told Geldzahler, 'called *Osaka in the Rain*, done in 1935. The nearest thing in my cogniscance [sic] was Dufy – but it was really a lot better than that.'[18] As for the Japanese boys, 'they are as exquisite as the Zen gardens. I have done a few drawings and taken eight hundred photographs . . . and really have been turned on so much that if I never left Powis Terrace for five years I've enough in my head to keep me going.'[19]

Staying at a hotel in Kobe two days later, Schlesinger telephoned at midnight, and there was a row when he reiterated that he had no intention of ever moving back into Powis Terrace. 'He said he enjoyed living in his studio alone,' Hockney confided to Geldzahler, continuing, 'I'm not sure what to do now . . . I must have some physical affection from him on my return or I must seek it elsewhere, and while I can't abandon him, if I actually find someone to share things with, my loyalties I have for Peter for what he gave me will be transferred.' Seeking advice, he broached the subject of his difficulty in meeting Peter's sexual needs. 'The way I look at our problem is one of Peter's lack of confidence and his apparent envy of mine. Yet he knows the truth about mine. I only have confidence about one thing – my work. Therefore I make it important to me. I really don't have sexual confidence any more and I'm sure Peter knows that. That's what makes me sad as I think he is using that knowledge in a cruel way . . . I am perfectly prepared to accept the differences between us as individuals, it seems to me he has the difficulty doing that. I am a gregarious Yorkshireman and he is a rather quiet Californian. Surely the two can be compatible if they like each other? Or should I have another gregarious Yorkshireman as a friend?'[20]

For Hockney, the highlight of this trip was Macau, the Portuguese colony south-west of Hong Kong. 'Macau is divine,' he told Geldzahler. 'You must go there . . . you'd love it. It's a combination of the Orient and old crumbling faded Europe. Very very beautiful . . . We had lunch at the Bela Vista Hotel on the Verandah looking over the South China Sea. It was very romantic . . . and it made the food terrific. The set lunch was believe it or not written in English and was "Green Pea Soup with Croutons", a "Fish Cutlet", braised ox tongue with white sauce and for a moment I thought I was on British Railways going to Bradford, so we washed it down with Mateus Rose, to help the starving Portuguese.'[21] They also attended an opera in the Macau casino, during which, he reported happily, 'you can sit and have a Chinese lunch, walk about and smoke while it's on – you can't do that at the Met'.[22]

Their next stop was Bangkok, the highlight of which was a visit to a male brothel, even though 'afterwards I did have terrible guilt about it – you know decadent westerners exploiting the natural beauty of a lovely country etc.'.[23] His guilt was not strong enough, however, to stop him returning on their last night in Bangkok. 'We put on our new Hong Kong made white suits, went to the brothel, asked for two skilful boys and just sat and watched them do all their tricks. It was like a Francis Bacon painting – I must admit though I think it was genuinely decadent, as when we got up to rush to the airport the boys immediately stopped. Silly romantic me thinking they would ignore us and go on having fun.'[24]

The last port of call in the Far East was Burma, where they stayed in the Strand Hotel in Rangoon, a city that appealed to him because 'unlike most cities of South East Asia it's completely untouched by America, therefore full of crumbling colonial British buildings, most of them with the signs still on – Barclays Bank etc. Like most Communist countries all there was for sale in the shops was toilet rolls and crude soap. Nevertheless the Strand Hotel . . . seemed to ignore all this and everyone acted as though it was 1925. There was a fat lady pianist in the Palm Court with a rather seedy violinist alternating with a small swing orchestra. I loved it all.'[25] Hockney depicted this scene in a drawing of Lancaster sitting in a chair in the very grand Palm Court, titled *Mark, Strand Hotel, Rangoon 1971*.

The original itinerary had been to fly from Burma to India, and from there to travel to Afghanistan, but this was cut short with the outbreak of war between India and Pakistan on 3 December so the intrepid travellers found themselves instead in Istanbul, which was bitterly cold, and finally in Rome. From here Hockney wrote to Geldzahler expressing his continuing indecision as to what he should do about Schlesinger. Celia Birtwell, in whom he was increasingly confiding, had advised him to forget Schlesinger, on the grounds that he was behaving in too cruel a fashion. 'It saddens me,' he admitted, 'but I think I'll have to. I'll just leave him completely alone and see what he does, although the moment he appears lost, I'll possibly cave in as usual. He did write me a rather naive letter about how he's not left me, although if he hasn't I don't know what it is he has done.'[26]

With hindsight it is easy to understand Peter's apparent indecision. 'I was being a little equivocal,' he recalls, 'because I was trying to spare his feelings. I was twenty-three and muddled and all his friends were putting pressure on me, saying things like "How can you be so mean to him?" and "You're ruining his life" and "You're so cruel".'[27] For this reason he made the mistake of agreeing to meet Hockney on the day he returned, a reunion that did not go well. 'I suppose it's all over,' Hockney wrote to Geldzahler. 'It is painful and I am unhappy as I've really had to tell him that I can't really see him for a while, as it's too difficult for me. You see I think it's a bit unfair of him to welcome

Eric with open arms and sex, and me with a rather nervous coldness. He then refuses to stay saying I was too stoned – having not smoked for five weeks, Ossie's joint handed me at the airport had really made me high. Anyway Henry it's too difficult if he won't let me express my love in any way now, and so all I can do is try and forget and see how he feels in two or three months . . .'[28]

Hockney returned to London bearing two sketchbooks filled with drawings and a tight schedule ahead of him, as he had an upcoming show with André Emmerich in New York. 'I must really get down to painting now,' he wrote, 'as the show is in April and although I have Mo as an assistant I actually have to do the paintings myself, which do take some time, and I must begin my Japanese pictures.'[29] Curiously the first of these, *Mount Fuji and Flowers*, a painting that uses the same stain technique as *Pool and Steps, Le Nid de Duc*, is a very romantic view of Japan, as far removed as one could imagine from a country in which, as he put it to Kitaj, there was 'hardly a patch of land that could hold a factory that has not got one'.[30] Considering he saw little of Mount Fuji and did no drawings of it, it is a fantasy, inspired by the traditional woodcuts of nineteenth-century Japanese artists such as Hokusai, its images sourced from a postcard and a Japanese flower-arrangement manual. Henry Geldzahler considered it 'a very beautiful and perfect picture'[31] and later bought it for the Metropolitan Museum.

A mark of Hockney's ever increasing fame was his being asked to appear on BBC Radio 4's *Desert Island Discs*, whose deviser and presenter, Roy Plomley, interviewed well-known people and asked them to choose the eight records, plus one book and one luxury, they would take with them if forcibly stranded on a desert island. For Hockney, who had been brought up in a house in which the radio had played such an important part, and who was still an avid listener, painting and relaxing to the sound of the radio, it was incredibly exciting, and he made his appearance on 5 February 1972.

His choices, mainly classical, were spur of the moment, and would, he said, have been completely different had he made his choice on another day. He began with Beethoven's 5th Symphony, not the orchestral version, but the Liszt transcription for the piano, played by Glenn Gould, because when he had first heard it at George Lawson's house, it had made him laugh. This was followed by another piano piece, Erik Satie's 'La Belle Excentrique', played by Aldo Ciccolini, which romps along in the manner of a piano rag. Then his favourite composer, Richard Wagner, made his first appearance with the great German bass-baritone Theo Adam, singing 'Verachtet mir die Meister nicht', an aria all about art from *Die Meistersinger*. Following this came a section from *Les Biches* by Francis Poulenc; then 'San Francisco', from the film of the same name, and sung by its star, Jeanette MacDonald. He chose it because 'it's about California and a very pretty song, and really I like it because it used to be sung by a marvellous drag queen in a bar . . . and he actually looked like her in the film and swung out into the bar on a swing – it was really terrific'.[32]

Record number six was the Monte Carlo Opera Orchestra playing the overture to *Fedora*, 'a marvellous corny opera' by Umberto Giordano, which Hockney told Plomley he liked to play once a month while working. Then came Marilyn Monroe singing the 'very affecting' 'I'm Through with Love' from *Some Like It Hot*, while his final choice was back to Wagner with the 'Liebestod' from *Tristan und Isolde*, which he described as being 'almost the same thing . . . it's just high art form', and which he picked as the record he would take with him if allowed only one out of his eight choices. Not surprisingly, his luxury turned out to be 'some paper and some pencils and a battery-operated pencil sharpener', while his book, to accompany the Bible and the complete works of Shakespeare, was a pornographic novel, *Route 69* by Floyd Carter, author of such titles as *Battle of the Bulges*, *Big Joe*, *Camp Butch* and *Forbidden Fruit*. He chose it to stop himself fantasising too much. 'I think it was written in a back room on 42nd Street,' he said, 'and it's full of bad grammar and spelling mistakes, but quite touching in its way, and it covers a great number of interesting things.'[33] Not surprisingly, his mother was slightly perplexed by this choice. 'Listened again today at the usual time,' she wrote, '– his choice of book to take was most unusual – was he joking – just one of his "cheerfully disrespectful"

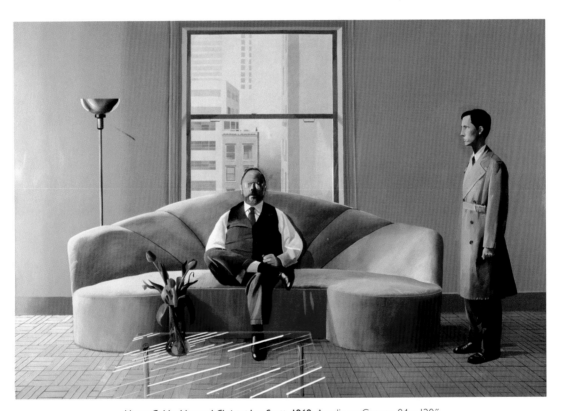

Henry Geldzahler and Christopher Scott, 1969. Acrylic on Canvas, 84 × 120˝

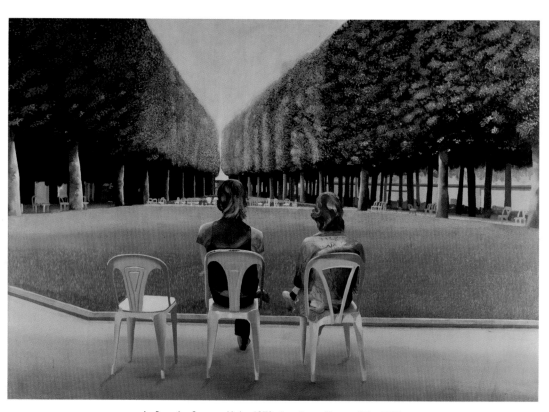

Le Parc des Sources, Vichy, **1970.** Acrylic on Canvas, 84 × 120″

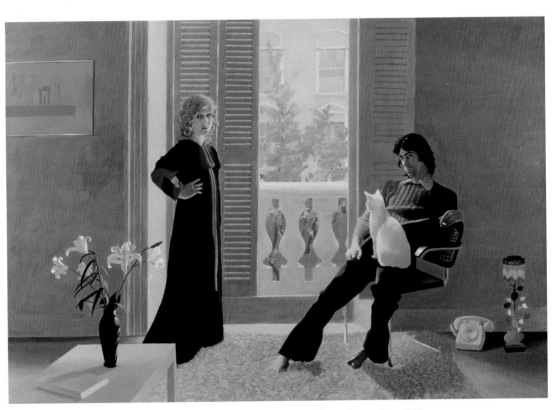

Mr. and Mrs. Clark and Percy, **1970-71.** Acrylic on Canvas, 84 × 120″

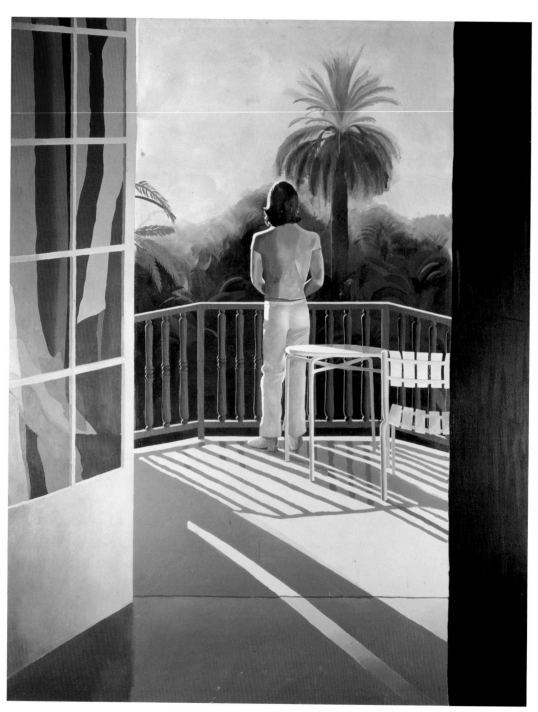

Sur La Terrasse, **1971.** Acrylic on Canvas, 180 x 84″

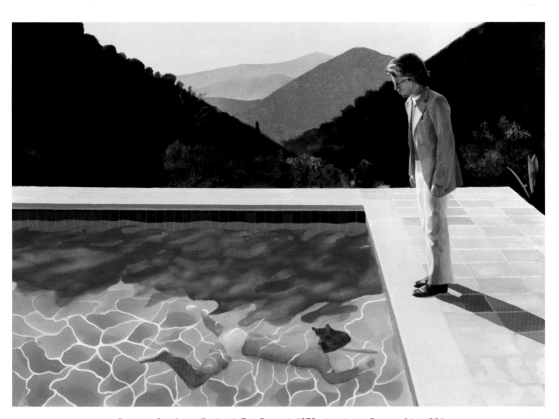

Portrait of an Artist (Pool with Two Figures), 1972. Acrylic on Canvas, 84 x 120˝

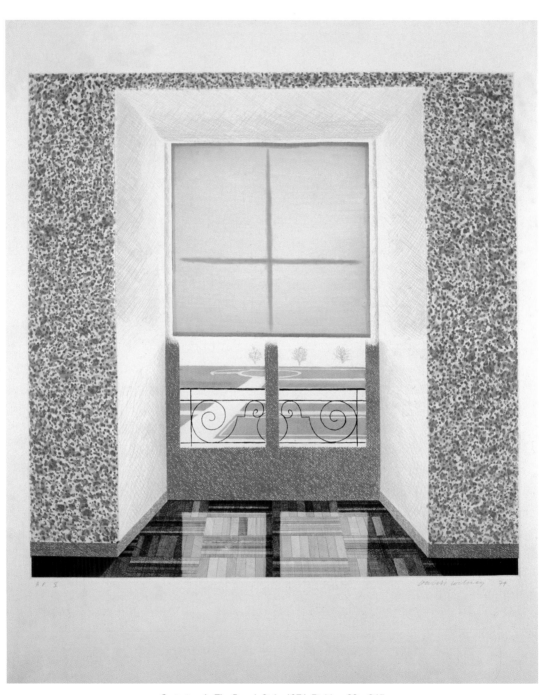

Contrejour In The French Style, **1974.** Etching, 39 × 36″

*Celia in a Black Dress
with Red Stockings*, 1973.
Crayon on Paper,
25 ½ × 19 ½″

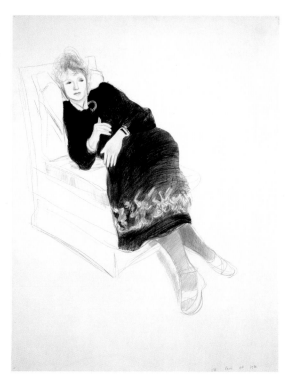

Celia Half Nude, 1975.
Crayon on Paper,
30 × 22″

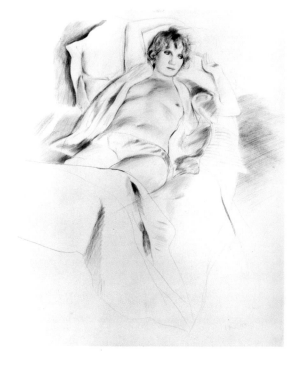

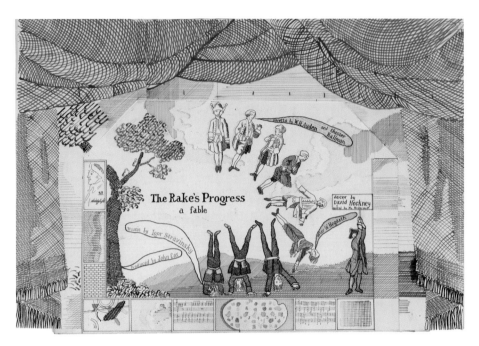

Drop curtain for The Rake's Progress.
From *The Rake's Progress*, 1975-79. Ink and Collage on Cardboard, 14 × 20 ½″

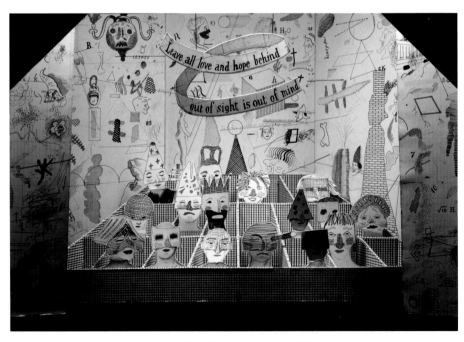

Bedlam. From *The Rake's Progress*, 1975.
Ink on Cardboard, 16 × 21 × 12″ (model)

idioms . . . I love him very much. I know he loves the life he lives and is very lucky to be able to do as he pleases & thereby earn a living.'[34]

After this brief distraction, he was back in the studio with *Portrait of an Artist*, with which he was still struggling. 'The longer you work on a painting,' he wrote, 'the more you're loath to abandon it, because you think throwing away six months is terrible. So I struggled on and on and fiddled on with it, realizing it didn't work, couldn't work . . . it was the angle of the pool which was causing me all the problems. I couldn't alter the water section and it was impossible to adjust it, so I decided to repaint the picture completely.'[35] He also took the decision to destroy the first version of the picture, so it would be out of his mind, but, because parts of it were well painted, he cut the canvas up very carefully, removing one portion depicting a plant growing from the edge of the pool, which he later framed and gave to the Clarks as a late wedding present.

By the time he had made up his mind to start the picture again, it was late March and the Emmerich exhibition was due to open in May. Even though Kasmin told him he was mad, Hockney was confident he could repaint it in two weeks, since he knew what he had done wrong and how to make it right second time around. In need of more references to work from, he decided to make a trip down to Le Nid de Duc. He was, however, unable to ask Schlesinger to accompany him because, unbeknown to him, he had flown out to California with Jack Hazan, who had persuaded him to film some swimming pool sequences for his movie. Instead he took Mo McDermott as his stand-in, along with the pink jacket Schlesinger was wearing in the picture, and a young photographer, John St Clair, to be the underwater swimmer.

They spent several days at Le Nid de Duc, where Hockney posed McDermott by the edge of the pool and St Clair swam back and forth beneath the surface for hours on end. 'To get different kinds of distortion in the water,' he wrote, 'I had John swim underwater in different light conditions . . . and with different water surfaces . . . and I had Mo gazing at him with the shadows in differing positions.'[36] While this was going on he took hundreds of photographs using a brand-new Pentax Spotmatic II, a fully automatic camera that allowed him to shoot much more quickly and get much better exposures. On their return to London they took the film straight from the airport to a processing lab in north London so that it would be developed within twenty-four hours. With the exhibition due to open in New York in a few weeks, time was running out.

Somewhat ironically, Jack Hazan, whom Hockney had been trying to avoid for so long, contributed to helping him finish on time. At the beginning of 1972, feeling a little guilty about France the previous summer, Hockney had tentatively allowed him to do some more filming, capturing him painting in his studio, as well as in conversation with Henry Geldzahler, Patrick Procktor, Celia Birtwell and Joe MacDonald, a young male model from New York. When Hazan, who had witnessed the destruction of the original, heard that he was going to repaint the portrait, he asked if he could film it. 'I said Oh my God, no,' Hockney recalled, 'I'm really going to work eighteen hours a day on this with Mo. Mo's going to do all the spraying to keep the paint wet. The last thing I want is somebody interfering.'[37] Hazan's solution to this was, in return for occasional access to film, to offer to lend him a set of daylight lights for a fortnight, which would enable him to work in the right lighting conditions at night as well as during the day. 'And I agreed,' said Hockney, 'just so that I could have the lights and work night and day . . . painting it only took about two weeks, but every single day I think we worked eighteen hours on it.'[38]

Schlesinger returned from LA just in time to agree to pose for some photographs for Hockney, who was having difficulty because all the shots he had were of Mo, while any drawings of Schlesinger were done for the previous version of the painting. 'I had to do it in the same light as the south of France,' Hockney wrote. 'Of course London, which is farther north, does not have the same light. Capturing the shadows the right way, trying to recreate the same light, meant going out early in the day. I photographed Peter in Hyde Park on an early Sunday morning.'[39] The image he actually used to paint the figure was one of his earliest composite photographs, in which a number of the images were glued together in order to provide more detailed information than could be obtained from the enlargement of one negative. The first one, taken in Paris in 1969, had been a jokey image of Hockney and Schlesinger seated on a park bench, in which they had each taken a shot of the other and pieced the two prints together. These composite photographs, which were later to gain in complexity and become a major part of Hockney's work, were initially fairly simple and were often used to deal with architectural subjects on his travels, where he was having a problem with perspective. 'I did try using a wide-angle lens,' he told Marco Livingstone, 'but I didn't like it much. Its distortions were extremely unnatural . . . I thought, "Why don't you just take many and glue them together?" It would be more like the real thing than a wide-angle lens which makes the verticals go this way and that way . . . I don't like distortion in photography.'[40] But they were also used for portrait subjects, such as in a sitting he did with Rudolf Nureyev in November 1970, at his house in Richmond.

Portrait of an Artist was completed just in time to be sent to New York for the exhibition. 'I varnished it,' wrote Hockney, '. . . and the next morning we got up at six o'clock to begin rolling it. At eight-thirty the men came to collect it to send it off on a plane to New York, and it got there just in time . . . I must admit I loved working on that picture, working with such intensity; it was marvellous doing it, really thrilling.'[41] Though the finished work is an impressive painting by any standard; it was also of great importance both to Hockney as an expression of his loss and to Schlesinger as a measure of self-esteem. 'In titling the painting *Portrait of an Artist*,' Henry Geldzahler commented, 'David is giving Peter his birthright, his mess of pottage – he's calling him an artist. It's very difficult to have your progeny learn to fly. And I think for David this is a very important painting psychologically because it gives Peter dignity, allowing him to be the artist that he is . . .'[42]

In gratitude for all his hard work, Hockney took Mo McDermott to New York with him for the opening at André Emmerich. They stayed with Geldzahler on 7th Avenue, where Hockney did a coloured crayon drawing of his host sitting in an armchair, wearing a loud Hawaiian shirt and smoking one of his trademark cigars. Geldzahler told him afterwards that it was the best drawing ever done of him. At the time he was involved in raising money for the Phoenix House Project, a non-profit organisation that aimed to provide help for the victims of drug and alcohol abuse, and had asked various artists such as Joseph Cornell, Jim Rosenquist, Adolph Gottlieb and Alex Katz to provide an original work of art for him to sell on behalf of the charity. When Hockney offered another portrait, Geldzahler recalled telling him, '"You really can't because I am fund-raising for them. It would look a little funny." So he said, "Well," and just sat down with an etching plate and in about an hour, he did my jacket, my hat, my pipe and my iced coffee. I like that print because it's a portrait of a subject with the subject missing.'[43] It was this etching, *Panama Hat*, which Hockney gave to him to sell.

The exhibition, *David Hockney: Paintings and Drawings*, opened on 13 May with *French Shop*, painted in September 1971, on the cover of the catalogue. It was taken from a photograph of a grocer's shop in the French spa town of Miers, 'one of those little French towns', wrote Hockney, 'where, occasionally, when they build a shop, they try and blend it in with the old ones. Its architecture seemed so simple that it could almost have been erected by a builder, not an architect . . . this little building had a purity that I found very attractive.'[44] The show also included *Pool and Steps, Le Nid de Duc, Chair and Shirt, Still Life on a Glass Table, The Island* and *Sur la Terrasse*, but its star was undoubtedly *Portrait of an Artist*. The circumstances of its sale, however, caused Hockney some grief.

Kasmin did his utmost to try and prevent Hockney's work falling into the hands of speculators, and had already warned André Emmerich about this. Hockney was happy that the Philadelphia Museum had shown an interest in *Portrait of an Artist*. Unfortunately, while they were biding their time coming to a decision, a man walked in off the street, an American, apparently with money to spend, who gave the impression that he was a friend of Hockney's and who seemed to know the painting well. Assuming him to be bona fide, Emmerich agreed to sell him the picture, the most expensive in the show, for $18,000. Within a few months the painting was with a London dealer, who took it to an art fair in Germany, and it ended up being sold to a London collector for nearly three times its New York price. When

Hockney found out he was very upset. 'The guy had been sent by some dealers in London to buy the picture tricking both André and myself,' he recalled. 'Within a year people had made far more on that picture than either Kasmin, André or I had. Considering the effort and trouble and everything that had gone into it, it seemed such a cheap thing to do . . .'[45]

It was not the money that was at the heart of Hockney's annoyance about the fate of this painting, but the fact that he had put the better part of six months of both his emotional and working life into it only to find it whisked away from under him. Though money took away the stress of having to churn out work in order to survive, it had never been that important to him, other than as a means of paying for materials, giving him freedom to travel anywhere and allowing him to go to a restaurant without worrying about how he was going to pay the bill. He called himself 'restaurant rich'. 'If you're an artist,' he wrote, 'the one thing you can do when you get money is use it to do what you want in art. That's the only good thing you can ever do for yourself. As an artist, what do you need to live on? As long as you've got a studio and a place to work in, all you're going to do is paint pictures all day long.'[46]

On his return to England after the Emmerich show, Hockney had two portraits in mind. The first was another double portrait, of his old friends George Lawson and Wayne Sleep. Since Sleep was a dancer and Lawson played the clavichord beautifully, it seemed obvious to give the painting a musical setting. After making a number of drawings and taking numerous photographs, he decided to pose them in George's tiny mews house in Wigmore Place, with Lawson at the clavichord and Sleep standing in the doorway listening to him playing. 'The pose was interesting,' Lawson recalls. 'Wayne was looking at me at the keyboard, standing and listening. I think it was a nice conceit that he had a ballet dancer not moving just listening. I wanted the painting to be called "A Flat", because I was actually playing the note A flat.'[47]

From the very start, however, Hockney struggled with this painting, becoming increasingly obsessed with making it more and more naturalistic. 'Six months I worked on it,' he wrote, 'altering it, repainting it many times . . . I kept taking photographs, thinking it was

finished myself, and then deciding it's not right, no, that's not right. I
drove Mo mad. He thought it was wonderful at times, and then he'd
think, oh my God, he's at it again . . . Looking back now, I can see that
the struggle was about naturalism . . .'[48] At one point he made a cut-out
of George which he took to his studio to help him decide the placement
of the figure. 'I would draw on it and cut it and move it about on the
painting, then draw it back in.'[49]

To distract himself from these problems, he began to prepare for
the other painting he was considering, a portrait of himself with his
parents, which Henry Geldzahler had suggested. 'I said that it would
be very important for him to know how he felt in relation to his
parents,' he wrote, 'and how he felt they feel about each other. "Get
all three of you into a painting," I said. "You are going to have to do
some very hard thinking in visual terms."'[50] On 1 July he drove up
to Bradford. 'Today David is coming,' noted Laura, '& hopes to take
photographs for a large picture he is going to paint.'[51] Unfortunately he
arrived home to find his father 'writhing and groaning' on the floor,
after an apparent diabetic fit. He was rushed into St Luke's Hospital,
where the doctors thought it was possible he might have suffered some
kind of stroke. When he eventually came round, dazed but able to
recognise the family, Hockney took a photograph of his bedside table,
complete with vase of flowers, water jug and tumbler, an invitation to
the Emmerich exhibition, and a small plastic box bearing the legend
'BEST DENTURES'.

Kenneth spent two weeks in St Luke's recovering from what
turned out to be a condition related to his diabetes, so the preliminary
work on the new portrait was postponed till Hockney returned to
Bradford at the beginning of August, after two weeks with Henry
Geldzahler in Corsica. 'David arrived at 12 noon,' Laura wrote on 2
August. 'I was showered with gifts . . . I had no flowers – so David
went off to get some – (he wants some in the picture) & returned
with two dozen carnations white & pink & 8 gladioli. Oh! They are
so gorgeous – the roses in my garden (after the rain) would not have
supplied such an array. We cleared up while he was out so room was
ready. He preferred back room & took many photographs, and both of

us sat for drawings.'[52] Further sittings took place in London ten days later, when Laura noted: 'I feel so tired when "sitting" for David – he must find it difficult & I do not feel at my best.'[53]

In the latter half of 1972, Hockney had another concern: Kasmin was pressuring him to produce enough pictures for a show in December. Jack Hazan had filmed Kasmin for his documentary ringing Hockney from the gallery to complain that he had a queue of people wanting paintings and nothing to offer them. Though this scene was entirely invented, with Kasmin talking into thin air, it reflected the truth. The ongoing problem was that as Hockney had become more successful, there was less need for him to churn out pictures, and he had the luxury of being able to spend more time on individual pictures. 'In the past the only reason I didn't was that I couldn't,' he wrote. 'As an artist who was earning his living by painting I needed the money. The pictures were cheap. I had to do a few . . . just to keep going. There's nothing wrong with deciding that, since the pictures cost so much, you only need to paint ten a year to keep yourself going . . . I work it out and think, I don't need to paint more than this unless I want to.'[54]

The upcoming show was of particular importance to Kasmin and Sheridan Dufferin as it was to be the last show at their gallery. They had taken the decision to close for a variety of reasons, not least because the lease had only two more years to run and there were plans to redevelop the whole section of Bond Street in which it was situated. Deep recession was looming in America, the most severe since the end of the Second World War, and they were fearful of a global financial crisis. 'At the same time,' Kasmin remembers, 'Sheridan's interests were beginning to move elsewhere. He was taking more of an interest in British sporting pictures, and Indian miniatures, and was buying pictures of India by Daniell and other English artists. I was also not having a happy time personally and I was running out of steam.'[55] To tide them over they took out a lease on a new premises in Clifford Street, further down Bond Street.

What made it even more important that Hockney should finish

the double portrait of George Lawson and Wayne Sleep in time for this show was that he had relatively little other work to offer, apart from his Japanese paintings, and one or two from his travels in Europe. 'We both thought the picture would be ready,' he recalled. 'It looked as though it was finished in October . . . but I struggled on and on, and in the end I wouldn't let him show it. I said, "No, I can't, because it's not right."'[56] This was disappointing, not just for Kasmin but for McDermott, who had been so encouraging, and for Sleep and Lawson, who had given up so much time to pose for it. 'It didn't get finished,' Lawson remembers, 'and my belief is it was because Wayne and I were getting on terribly well, and Hockney had broken up with Peter, and I think his inability to complete the picture reflected what he was thinking, and that was, how annoying it was that he had, in his mind, introduced us, and there we were having a nice time and he wasn't. He said there were problems with the vanishing point or something like that, but I think that the real reason was an emotional thing. It's a pity because if he had been able to paint listening, I think it would have been wonderful.'[57]

Without *George Lawson and Wayne Sleep*, Kasmin's final exhibition, which opened on 11 December, was a bit of a damp squib, with a smattering of small canvases, including the Japanese paintings, *Mount Fuji* and *Japanese Rain on Canvas*, which were outnumbered by drawings from his travels, together with various studies of Schlesinger, Birtwell and his parents. 'By comparison with the one in New York,' Hockney commented, 'this looked rather a wishy-washy show, really. I wouldn't normally have shown small pictures like that, without showing a big painting as well.'[58] The critics were largely unimpressed, Guy Brett's review in *The Times* being typical. He referred to Hockney's 'refined technique', which he 'to judge from his new exhibition at Kasmin, has been exercising . . . without much to say. In his new paintings he continues with his liking for commenting on the strategies and stage-craft of other artists past and present, but they lack his customary edge. It is left to the drawings to fill us in with Hockney's meandering itinerary from hotel to swimming-pool in the company of his friends.'[59] Though the reviews were unmemorable, an unfitting end to a relationship with a remarkable gallery, the gallery itself went out with a bang. 'After the gallery closed,' Kasmin recalls, 'we all went to a great big dinner-dance at the Savoy, all the artists worldwide that Sheridan and I represented, the whole lot. It marked the closing of the gallery and made an event of it.'[60]

At the beginning of 1973, feeling tired and not a little depressed, Hockney decided to spend some time in California, where he was sure the sunshine and the boys would give him a much needed shot in the arm. He planned to create a new series of works on the theme of weather, which would reunite him with Ken Tyler and Sid Felsen at Gemini. He settled into the Chateau Marmont and was soon writing to Ron Kitaj, 'California has been very pleasant so far. I should have come here 6 months ago. I'm sure it's partly because I'm working in a new environment and a new medium but I'm enjoying it enormously . . . I haven't taken Valium since I've been here and the temptations of grass have only occurred twice. I arrive at Gemini at 8.00am much to the surprise of the printers who tell me that the artists don't usually show up till 11 . . . Ken is such a good printer. It's terrific getting into complicated lithography again. There's no one in London can print like him. Every little thing I put on a stone really appears. I've almost completed the first four, Rain, Mist, Sun and Lightening [sic], and hope to do four more – Snow, Frost, Wind and a Rainbow . . . I feel quite marvellous and in excellent health. Early bed is doing wonders for my energy.'[61]

At the beginning of February he rented a beach house in Malibu belonging to the actor Lee Marvin, and Celia Birtwell came out to visit him with her two boys, Albert, aged three and a half, who was nicknamed 'Chappie', and George, aged one and a half, and a nanny. 'Living with two chicks and two brats is not what you're used to,' she told him, 'but don't worry.'[62] In the past six months, she had become very close to Hockney, partly because of her link to Schlesinger and partly by their mutual unhappiness. Clark was at the height of his fame, his clothes all the rage not just in London, but in Paris and

New York. Celebrity had gone to his head, however, and his constant desire to party with the jet set, his affairs with both men and women, combined with his massive intake of drugs, had put enormous strain on his marriage. 'We had some really nice times very early on,' Celia recalls, 'but then as he became more famous he lost the plot. I think he felt he could get away with having his own life, and having me in the background, planted there as a homebody, keeping it all together. I was quite prepared to do that, but not on those terms. Sometimes he would come back for two days, bringing a friend so I couldn't shout at him, probably some gorgeous woman who he knew I would like, and playing those sorts of games. It was a nightmare really.'[63]

Birtwell's gentle feminine side strongly appealed to Hockney, and when he saw that she was hurting emotionally just as badly as him, he opened up to her, finding at last the perfect shoulder to cry on. 'I think he found we spoke the same language about his unhappiness and his broken heart,' she says, 'so he used me as his confidante.'[64] As they licked each other's wounds, he began to transfer all the feelings he had felt towards Schlesinger onto her. Having her with him in California made him begin to feel calm. '. . . I'm getting used to life here,' he told Kitaj. 'At first it was very strange but Celia was so marvellous. She understood my moods and why I seemed so distant. She likes it here, although I think it's mainly the change, and the fact that she hasn't cried for a month . . . I think I'm better off staying out of England for a while. I think of Peter of course . . . and I have received a few letters from him, but I just don't want to return to that lingering pain, and staying here with Celia is finally getting rid of it.'[65]

It was close to being a happy time for him. He immersed himself in the work, revelling in the technical difficulties involved in the creation of the weather lithographs, which were to be a follow-up to *The Hollywood Collection* he had previously produced for Gemini. These were entirely inspired by prints of the weather he had seen in Japan and were to prove a welcome break from the constraints of naturalism he had been experiencing in his portrait work. The resulting prints are both playful and clever. Of the six in the series, *Snow* is the one most obviously based on Japanese woodcuts, *Rain* the most abstract, memorably depicting the experience of rain by using highly diluted lithographic ink which literally runs off the page, while *Wind* has the wit, depicting four of the prints being blown through the air past a street sign for Melrose Avenue. One just knows that the artist had fun making them. Hockney also immortalised Ken Tyler in a full-length lithograph, which in tribute he titled *The Master Printer of Los Angeles.*

At the end of each day he drove the forty miles back to Malibu to enjoy a semblance of family life with Celia, Albert and George, whom he was teaching to walk. 'That's when I really got to know Celia,' Hockney remembers. 'She is very, very sympathetic and she knows how to make me laugh. She plays with words, which I like, and she has a sense of the absurd. We got very close and I suppose I was in love with her.'[66] It was a love that was never physically consummated. 'He slept in the same bed as me a few times,' Birtwell says, 'but it was just cuddling like friends. I think David was very frightened physically, and I don't think it was easy for him to have a physical relationship. You can't be closer than being in bed with somebody, but he was very shy with me like that, and nothing was ever said. Then Ossie came down like a bloody boomerang and ruined the whole thing.'[67]

Hockney too blamed it all on Clark. 'I did consider having a physical relationship with her in California,' he says, 'but then Ossie turned up with a massive amount of drugs and got her to go off to Palm Springs for a weekend with the children, and he told me to stay behind.'[68] It is a version of events he shared with Ron Kitaj, writing that he was 'snuggling up to Celia' and 'Ossie must have judged the time this would take and arrived to break it up. At first I didn't know what to do so I retreated and took up my usual position of observer, but living with them closely I see what Celia really has to put up with. The experience has made me much closer to Celia, and further away from Ossie. I confess I don't really understand him, but he really is terrible to her . . .'[69]

Clark had been offered a free flight back to New York on board the private jet of Ahmet Ertegun, the president of Atlantic Records, and insisted that Birtwell and the children fly with him. Hockney turned down the opportunity to travel with them, and chose instead to leave

Malibu for LA where he spent some time with Nick Wilder, now his official dealer in California. In 1970 Nick had moved his gallery from La Cienega Boulevard to Santa Monica, into the then rather seamy area between La Cienega and North Robertson, which was known as Boys Town, because of the largely gay community that resided there. The move fitted the 'bad boy' image he had cultivated in the late sixties when he had participated wildly in the sex and drugs scene after losing a handsome lover, a ranked tennis pro, to suicide. 'I ran around a lot after that to fight off depression,' he recalled. 'I went to the bars and the clubs . . . no orgies, just a different partner every couple of weeks or months. I was living such a fly-now-pay-later existence nobody wanted to be my boyfriend . . . I never thought of myself as promiscuous because all the while I was looking for Mister Right.'[70]

By the time Hockney was visiting in 1973, Wilder had long since found his 'Mr Right' in the person of Gregory Evans, a boy some twelve years his junior who had been born and brought up in Tulsa, Oklahoma, and had run away from home in 1967, at the age of fifteen, to become a hippy in the Haight-Ashbury district of San Francisco. 'I ran away from a typical middle-class American upbringing,' Evans remembers. 'I was attracted to San Francisco – 1967 was the Summer of Love, and I just knew that I belonged there. I fell into sex, drugs and rock 'n' roll and living in communes.'[71] He went to LA three years later with some friends of his who were performing in the musical *Hair*, and eventually met Nick Wilder and began to hang out at his gallery. Within a month of their meeting they became lovers. 'Nicholas was totally unique and passionate about art,' Evans says. 'He liked to talk about it, to explain to you exactly what he did love about pictures and what he thought made pictures good. I liked that. And he made me feel liked. He was very engaging and he liked being with you and he made you feel that. He was also extremely funny with a sharp wit. He knew all the jokes, all the nasty jokes. I always had a sense of humour, and water seeks its own level.'[72]

Gregory Evans was already friends with Peter Schlesinger, whom he had met with Wilder in LA in the summer of 1970, and he had first met Hockney in 1971 when he and Wilder had been passing through

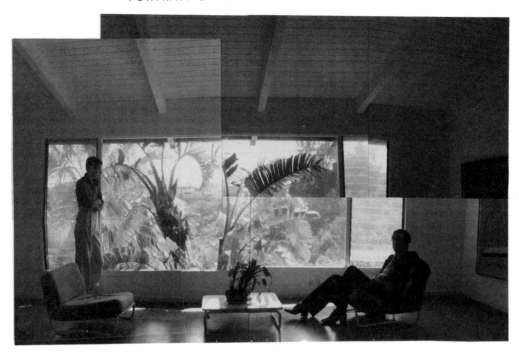

London and had briefly stayed in Powis Terrace. Now he had the opportunity to get to know him better. 'Nicholas had *The Hollywood Collection* of prints in storage in the gallery, and I remember him showing them to me and I knew they were unique. But that's all I knew about David. I didn't know any of the other work. He was very successful, but he was always friendly, and loved talking about himself and what he was doing and this is the enthusiasm he's maintained for ever.'[73] Hockney was likewise attracted to this handsome young boy with a wry sense of humour, and being intrigued by the relationship between him and Nick, considered painting their portrait.

At the turn of 1973, Wilder and Evans were living in a house in the Hollywood Hills on Appian Way, and Hockney executed a number of drawings and photographs of them there. 'What attracted me in this Hollywood house,' he recalled, 'was the window, like a big aquarium – it looks wonderfully exotic to an English person.'[74] Sadly the painting was never realised, which at the time Hockney put down to the same problems with naturalism he had experienced with the portrait of George Lawson and Wayne Sleep. He did, however, create a 'joiner'

Gregory Evans and Nicholas Wilder, Appian Way, Hollywood, 1973 out of six photographic prints that gives an idea of what the double portrait might have been like, showing them in their living room, with Wilder seated and Evans standing by the picture window.

Both to escape from Schlesinger, whom he was still missing dreadfully, and the dramas surrounding the Clarks, he came to the decision to spend some time in Paris. 'I began to think of Peter,' he wrote to Kitaj on 1 April, 'and so I have written to him telling him that the real reason I'm going to go to Paris is that I really don't want to see him. I realize I must make an effort and try and get the last bit of that affair out of my head . . .'[75] He also saw it as an opportunity to regroup. 'I was in a state of confusion and I felt I had to get away from London . . . I had been struggling with the paintings, like the one of George Lawson and Wayne Sleep . . . There was something wrong in what I was doing and I had to find out what it was and I needed peace and quiet. It was always hard to get peace and quiet in London. There were always people asking, would you do this, would you talk on that, would you do a television programme, would you do the other?'[76]

He left California a week later, on 8 April, a day that was to be etched into his memory for the rest of his life. En route to visit the famous French film director Jean Renoir, the news came on the car radio that Pablo Picasso had died. This came as a terrible shock to Hockney, who had thought of Picasso as invincible, the immensely powerful life force that he was. It was the first time Hockney had felt the loss of someone he deeply respected, but when he arrived at Renoir's house and broke the news, the elderly Frenchman merely commented, 'What an un-Picasso thing to do.'[77] For Hockney, however, as his closest friend Henry Geldzahler noted, it represented 'loss of innocence, the realization of death's inevitability'.[78]

CHAPTER TWELVE

CONTRE-JOUR IN THE FRENCH STYLE

When Hockney visited Bradford on his return to England, his mother found him 'rather quieter than usual somehow – tho' I don't know where or why'.[1] He had got back to London to find that most of his friends were out of town, and he didn't have Celia Birtwell to talk to as she had her parents staying. Only Mo McDermott was left, who had just moved into the renovated basement of Powis Terrace, but he immediately brought back memories of Peter. 'The basement is almost finished,' Hockney told Henry Geldzahler, 'and is quite beautiful. Mo is quite delighted, although he tells me Peter is very jealous. I must admit – rereading what happened to poor Emma Bovary made me think of him a little – or is that very unFreudian of me?'[2] Hockney's decision to escape to Paris made sense in light of the fact that, as he also told Geldzahler, 'I do notice . . . a strange feeling, and I'm almost ready to reach for the Valium again.'[3]

Before he left, he ran into Peter Schlesinger in London, a meeting that helped clarify his feelings. 'I did see Peter for about an hour,' he wrote, 'but there is so much bitterness between us still, that I think it's best to forget him for a year or two.'[4] In addition to seeing it as a convenient haven, Hockney had another good reason to visit Paris. For some time, the Berlin publisher Propyläen Verlag had been encouraging him to produce a print for a portfolio called *Homage to Picasso*, in which seventy artists had been asked for their own tribute to Picasso. Though it was never intended to be published posthumously, the artist's death was the catalyst that finally persuaded Hockney to agree. The only person he wanted to work with was the man who had been Picasso's etching printer for twenty years: Paris-based Aldo Crommelynck.

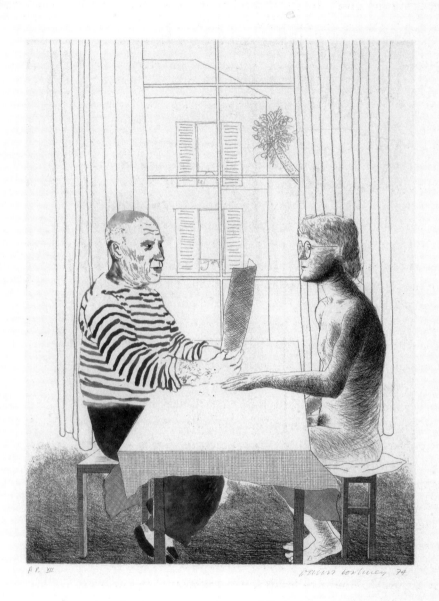

Crommelynck was a mesmerising figure – tall and gaunt, with long spindly fingers usually stained with ink and nicotine. Apprenticed at seventeen to the French printmaker Roger Lacourière, he worked not only with Picasso, but with other great artists such as Léger, Miró and Matisse, and he soon emerged as the principal creative force in the studio. With his brother Piero, he opened his own atelier in Montparnasse in 1955, attracting major talent such as Le Corbusier, Giacometti and, notably, Braque, and when in 1963 he heard that Picasso needed a printmaker close to where he lived, he established a studio in a former bakery in Mougins and began a partnership that was to last until the artist's death. During these ten years Picasso produced some 750 intaglio plates, including the notorious 'Series 347', an edition of largely erotic etchings showing Raphael and Rembrandt painting and coupling with their models, which, in 1968, the Art Institute of Chicago deemed 'unfit for public consumption'. After Picasso's death the brothers returned to Paris and opened a studio on the Left Bank, in the Rue de Grenelle.

Artist and Model, 1973–1974

Hockney used to joke to his friends, 'I can now afford a garret in Paris,'[5] and, if it didn't exactly fit the description, the apartment he moved into at the beginning of May, borrowed from an artist friend, was both tiny and uncomfortable: he described it as 'pretty horrible – not even a chair to sit and read in'.[6] To make himself feel at home, he began a small painting of his mother in oil paint. 'Mo says he loves the smell,' he commented. 'So do I.'[7] He loved these first few months working with Crommelynck who, though they had never met, already knew about his work from Richard Hamilton, another of his clients. 'It was thrilling,' Hockney recalls, 'to meet somebody who'd had such direct contact with Picasso and worked with him such a lot. He taught me marvellous technical things about etching.'[8] One of the things that Hockney so admired about Picasso, and could identify with, was the fact that he made all his own prints in the traditional way, working on the plates himself, scratching, cutting, chipping or whatever was required.

He threw himself into his studies with the great printer, who taught him how to master two important techniques. The first was the 'sugar lift', an established process using a saturated sugar solution mixed with poster paint that allows the artist to paint what he wants to etch directly onto the plate, just as he would onto canvas. Once the sugar has dried, a very thin layer of acid-resistant varnish is painted over the plate. The plate is then put into a bath of warm water and, once in the bath, the sugar begins to dissolve, eventually pulling completely away from the plate to leave an open area that can be aquatinted, etched and printed. It was a technique that Hockney knew, but had struggled with. 'Every time I'd tried it in London,' he wrote, 'I'd had to chip the varnish away and the sugar didn't come off. Or, if it came off, it lifted off lots of other varnish as well.'[9] When he had finally mastered this process, he couldn't wait to tell Maurice Payne, who already knew it well, and in his excitement he made a picture to demonstrate what he had learned, *Showing Maurice the Sugar Lift.* 'Maurice at first was a bit offended by the title, because he said, "People'll think I don't know about sugar lift." I said, "Nobody knows what sugar lift is." And I explained, "Look, Maurice, it sounds like the name of a song: Showing Maurice the sugar lift, cha, cha, cha."'[10]

More important still was that Crommelynck taught him to do coloured etching, using a method that he had invented himself which allowed the artist to draw from life in colour on one plate, dispensing with different plates to register the colours. 'This was very, very ingenious,' says Hockney. 'Before this method, the trouble was that it was impossible to be spontaneous with etching if you were using colour. You had to plan things very carefully, but this allowed spontaneity. I was quite thrilled with it.'[11] So excited was he when Crommelynck first told him about this technique that he immediately dropped the portrait of Gustave Flaubert he was working on, and insisted they try it out that very afternoon. The result was the Picassoesque *Simplified Faces*, a series of four heads created entirely from geometric elements. Other prints followed, including two of windows in the Louvre, and, later, a portrait of Gregory Evans in red checked shirt and blue jeans. This was done in London when he was hungover after a night out and was drawn straight from life. With his tousled hair and far-away look, it captured exactly how he must have been feeling. 'People are always amazed when they see the prints,' Hockney commented, 'and are very surprised they're etchings; they think they're lithographs and all kinds of things.'[12] Picasso himself never actually tried out the technique, which was invented just before he died, making Hockney the first artist to make serious use of it, a source of pride for both him and Crommelynck. Hockney recalled, 'He said to me after I'd been there a while and we got to know each other, "It's a pity you didn't come earlier, you'd have really liked Pablo . . . and he'd have really liked you."'[13]

After a few nights in his uncomfortable apartment, Hockney moved into the Hôtel Nice et Beaux Arts in the Rue des Beaux Arts, a short walk from Crommelynck's studio. He wrote to Henry Gelzahler, 'I'm sat in a small room looking at the roofs of Paris . . . I have started work on two etchings – homage à Picasso . . . The exhibition opens in Berlin on July 15, so as usual I should just get them done in time . . . Paris is lovely and peaceful, after London that is. It just gets so emotionally hectic for me there.'[14] Picasso would surely have been charmed by these etchings had he lived to see them. The first, titled *The Student – Homage to Picasso,* shows an older, rather professorial version of Hockney carrying a large portfolio of his work, smartly dressed in jacket, spotted bow tie and broad-brimmed hat and seeking the approval of a much younger-looking Picasso, depicted as a head perched on top of a column, at the age he might have been when he was being lionised as the inventor of cubism. It is a throwback to Hockney's earlier works that were drawn entirely from his imagination, and were the first sign of an attempt to move away from naturalism.

The second etching, *Artist and Model,* even echoes *Myself and My Heroes,* the 1961 etching in which Hockney portrayed himself admiring Gandhi and Walt Whitman, in this case Picasso being the figure of hero worship. It is a touching image in which he sits naked before the maestro's piercing gaze, his nudity defining him not as a fellow artist but as a model and innocent disciple who lays no claims to his greatness. 'We are witness to a meeting of apprentice and master,' Geldzahler pointed out, 'the innocent and uncorrupted showing his work to the great artist of the century.' He went on to comment that the special joy of the etching for him was 'the intrusive palm tree that pridefully bursts forth on a line directly above the young man's genitalia, masked as they are by the table'.[15] Hockney pooh-poohed this as being another example of Henry's obsession with Freud.

For some time, Geldzahler had been toying with the idea of doing a book on Hockney, a project with which the artist was fully prepared to cooperate, and for the purpose of which he had rented Casa Santini, Mario Amaya's Italian villa outside Lucca, for the summer. 'Mario's house is definitely OK for August,' Hockney wrote, 'and I have been to see Phaidon about the book. I think you might be able to get some expenses for the summer immediately.'[16] The idea was that they should hole up together for a few weeks and thrash out the form the book would take. It was suggested that Henry should fly to Paris, and they could then leisurely drive to Italy, stopping off for a few days at the Grand Hotel, Vittel, to get them healthy and in a working mood. He asked Geldzahler to find out from Mario 'a. how to get to the house from Lucca. b. Is there a telephone. c. Is there a record player (I know they have real opera in Italy, but a bit of music would not be amiss, would it?) etc. etc. etc.'[17] He ended the letter saying that Kasmin had broached the subject of royalties, adding, 'I told him I didn't care what my share was, as I don't make my living from books, so I'm sure whatever you suggest will be O.K.'[18]

They arrived in Italy at the beginning of August, and were soon settled into the villa, a lovely old Italian farmhouse with a large covered terrace, from where Hockney wrote to his parents on 3 August, 'It's beautiful here, but rather remote (45 minutes drive to the nearest town) therefore very good for work. Every morning Henry and I write notes for the book and then in the afternoons I draw or read . . . It's wonderful having no telephone (in London it seems to ring about 60 times a day) and the slight inconvenience we soon get used to. It also encourages letter writing . . .'[19] Inside there was a living room furnished with huge yellow 1930s sofas and chairs and a cast-iron stove. There was also a shower, where Hockney one day took photographs of a visiting American friend, a young photographer called Don Crib. 'It was a simple room, tiled, with no curtain,' he recalled. 'I love showers.

A shower is more ideal than a bath for showing off the body. The sight was beautiful with the figure and the water flowing.'[20]

Immersed in the peace and quiet, with not a hum to be heard, and only the occasional car horn to disturb the silence, Hockney felt the cares and tensions that had been assailing him slip away. 'We write every morning on a terrace overlooking a pleasant valley,' he wrote to Kitaj, 'a lady from the village comes and cleans (Henry) and makes us lunch, and the afternoons are spent drawing or reading. We usually go out in the evenings for dinner . . . Henry and I get on extremely well – no emotional hangups, which makes me feel calm and rested . . .'[21] He enjoyed the writing, which he found easier than he had expected, telling his mother that it was 'obviously a habit one can get into',[22] and completed a number of drawings. These included a charming study of his bedroom mirror, draped with scarves and bow ties, and a number of studies of Henry, usually engaged in his favourite pastimes of reading and smoking cigars.

For two weeks the days drifted by until their idyll was rudely interrupted by the unexpected arrival of Kasmin, who had fled in a hail of pots, pans and glasses from his holiday home near Carennac, after driving his wife, Jane, from whom he had separated, incandescent with rage by telling her that he had fallen in love with his new girlfriend, Linda Adams. He arrived exhausted after driving at speed with only one overnight stop at Arles, accompanied by two white-faced passengers, the architect and designer of the new Clifford Street Gallery, John Prizeman, and the rather eccentric figure of Eugene Lambe.

A striking-looking Irishman with a full red beard and more than a passing resemblance to Lytton Strachey, Lambe was the oldest of four brothers, the rest of whom were high-flyers in the British Army. He was the opposite, a vegan, who dressed entirely in canvas and cotton and wouldn't wear leather in case it had come from a slaughtered animal. Immensely well read, he had abandoned a law degree to move in with George Lawson and Wayne Sleep who were now living in Powis Gardens, in the capacity both of a friend and a gentleman's gentleman. 'He certainly used to do the laundry,' Lawson recalls, 'and I would often find myself saying, "Lambe, Lambe, where are my shirts?" Because he looked like a professor, we always called him Doctor Lambe, though the Doctor was a bit spurious. He had been at Trinity for ever and knew absolutely everybody and everybody knew him because he was so striking-looking.'[23]

Hockney was immediately intrigued by him, and made a fine drawing of him in coloured crayon, sitting on the terrace wearing a cotton smock and a wide-brimmed hat. 'I watched him doing the big, finished drawing,' said John Prizeman, 'sitting in front of Eugene, staring at him intently. He started at the top of the blank page, slowly filling in Eugene's hat, and working down the page, like unrolling a curtain.'[24] With their work interrupted, Geldzahler and Hockney felt compelled to entertain their guests, one day taking them for a swim at the magnificent Renaissance palazzo, Villa Reale, the home of the Pecci-Blunt family, one of whom, Camilla, was married to an LA art dealer, Earl McGrath, and photographed Hockney among the statuary and the group dancing on the lawns. Then, after Kasmin and the others had left, Hockney and Geldzahler visited another great villa, La Pietra, outside Florence, celebrated for its beautiful gardens and statues and the great collection of art and books it housed. It was home to the legendary aesthete and man of letters Harold Acton, the model for the character of Anthony Blanche in Evelyn Waugh's *Brideshead Revisited.* John Pope-Hennessy, the director of the Victoria and Albert Museum, took them, and Hockney wrote to Ron Kitaj: 'The house and garden are so beautiful and I thought he was charm itself, and quite genuine . . . just the four of us had lunch in that enormous dining room . . . We had a pasta to start with and Henry was served first. He just couldn't get it out of the dish properly and as I began to laugh, Henry said he felt like Charlie Chaplin. J P-H and Harold Acton politely tried to ignore it which made me laugh all the more as it made Henry really look like Charlie Chaplin . . .'[25]

By the end of the month, they were both ready to leave and get back to their normal lives, if with some trepidation. 'The other evening we had been to Lucca for dinner,' Hockney told Kitaj, 'and arrived back about 11.30. I made some tea and we sat ourselves on the porch in our regular seats. As Henry poured I fiddled with the radio to get the BBC World Service on the short wave. Henry then announced we

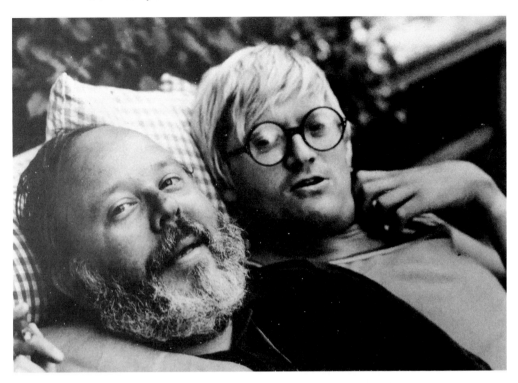

had only six cigars left and I said we were like a couple of old rubber
planters whose only worry was when the next shipment of tobacco
would arrive. We laughed but it did seem true. I think Henry dreads
the return to New York as much as I do to London.'[26]

Henry Geldzahler
and David Hockney

Hockney dreaded the old distractions, chief among which was
the continuing soap opera of the lives of Clark and Birtwell. When
Birtwell had returned to London in April, their relationship was at a
low ebb, Clark's recent behaviour having been less than satisfactory.
'I flew back in Ahmet Ertegun's private jet to New York,' Birtwell
remembers, 'and I got the most terrible, terrible backache in the plane.
We arrived in New York and we stayed in a basement flat belonging to
Henry Geldzahler, and Ossie immediately wanted to go off with Mick
Jagger and Bianca and I was stuck in his basement flat with the babies .
. . I was in terrible pain and I just couldn't wait to get back to London.
Ossie couldn't care less and he whooshed off for three days to be with
Mick and Bianca. By then I had had absolutely enough.'[27]

Clark saw things differently. On a whim, with the idea that it might save his marriage, he sold Kasmin the picture Hockney had given them for £7,000, and put a deposit on a large house in Cambridge Gardens, which he intended to do up as a family home. 'I was quite hurt . . .' Hockney wrote to Henry Geldzahler. 'I know he needed money very quickly for his house, but somehow it made me a little sick that my sentimental gesture had been turned so quickly into something else. Celia does not talk about the house. I think she has no plans to live in it. She says she would like to be alone for a while in Linden Gardens if only Ossie would leave. I don't think he will, but I think the crunch is coming shortly.'[28]

Hockney did have a good reason to return home. Paul Hockney was now sitting as a Liberal councillor in Bradford and he was therefore able to invite his parents to the city hall when, on 8 September, J. B. Priestley was made a freeman of the city. 'All parties – Conservative, Labour & Liberal gave speeches of welcome,' wrote Laura in her diary. 'Paul represented his party (alone) & was very funny & very good – we are very proud of him.' There was more, she recorded: 'J.B.P is to have a portrait done by David commissioned by the Corporation.'[29]

When originally approached with this commission by John Thompson, the director of Bradford City Art Gallery, Hockney had once again been extremely reluctant to agree. Thompson had then asked Paul to act as intermediary, making it difficult for him to say no. The result was a compromise. Hockney would agree to a drawing, but not a painting. 'We thought it would be good,' Thompson told *The Times* correspondent, 'if Bradford's most famous artist could draw the city's most famous author . . . It will go into our collection and we shall probably make it the centrepiece of a special exhibition. It will be our first Hockney original.'[30]

The sitting took place in London on 14 September at Priestley's flat in the Albany, off Piccadilly, and the result was a series of three pen-and-ink drawings, in two of which Priestley is sucking on his pipe, while in the third, the one ultimately chosen by the gallery, he holds the pipe in his hand while looking intently at the artist. According to Hockney, there was little conversation between them. 'He just sat there, looking big.'[31]

Hockney found himself dreaming of his idyllic holiday, writing to Henry Geldzahler, '. . . the Summer was fabulous, without a doubt it was the nicest summer I have spent since 1966. Thank you. At the time I loved it, in retrospect it seems to get better every day . . . London seems very gloomy.' He cited Birtwell's absence as one reason for this, and also Mo McDermott's very low spirits. 'I notice he stays up here more and more,' he wrote, 'and at times he even looks as though he is about to Panic.'[32] What Hockney did not realise, and was to remain unaware of for another year, was that McDermott was using heroin. 'This started in the early seventies,' Celia Birtwell remembers, 'but he lied to everybody and he just got thinner and thinner.'[33]

For myriad reasons McDermott had become an integral part of Hockney's life. To begin with he was stylish and had an eye for what was good. 'I once took Mo to visit Freddie Ashton,' Hockney recalls. 'He saw two marble obelisks on Freddie's mantelpiece. The next day I was at his flat in Ladbroke Grove and I saw these two obelisks, and when I got close to them I noticed they were made of cardboard . . . He'd just copied them. Mo could make anything and I quickly saw that.'[34] He was extremely practical, if occasionally a little undisciplined, and a talented artist himself, which made him a valuable studio assistant. He had also created his own business making and selling decorative trees and flowers cut out of wood and hand-painted, a number of which would, at any one time, be dotted about Powis Terrace. 'Mo could even clean up quickly, even if he was a totally "sweep it under the carpet" person. I remember once when my mother came,' Hockney recalls, 'and he had put my pornographic magazines under the sofa and I saw my mother sitting on the sofa and the pornographic magazines sticking out from under it, and I thought, "Good old Mo!"'[35]

He could make Hockney laugh to boot, a trait required of anyone who might wish to join his circle, and Hockney also admired his self-confidence when it came to his sexuality, which McDermott had no inhibitions about. 'He could be a little whore,' Hockney says, 'with one fantastic talent, which was that he could fuck anything and it

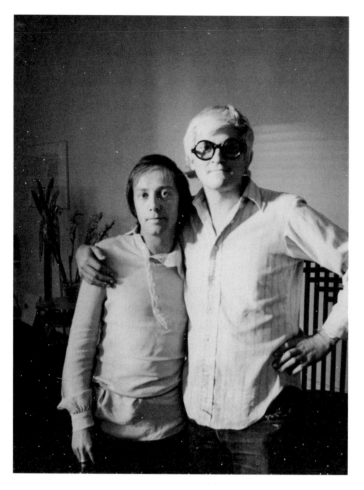

David Hockney and
Mo McDermott

didn't seem to matter to him. I said to him that it was a talent I didn't have. Sometimes he used to say to me, "What will happen to me in my old age?" and I used to tell him, "There'll always be someone looking for the comforts that you can bring them, Mo."[36] For some time he enjoyed an arrangement with Peter Coats, the erudite and gentlemanly gardening editor of *House & Garden*. 'We called him "Mr House & Garden",' Hockney recalls. 'He would say to Mo, "Tell me about the Beatles," and Mo would say, "I don't know the Beatles," and he would say, "Well, pretend you do." Mo knew what to do for the gentlemen. He was very sharp like that."[37]

In the mood Hockney was in, it is not surprising that he even began to consider giving up Powis Terrace and moving elsewhere. He had heard that the painter Rodrigo Moynihan was selling his house in Argyll Road, Kensington, and expressed an interest in buying it. He particularly loved the garden. 'I do think that eleven years in the same place is about enough,' he wrote to Geldzahler, 'and somehow Powis Terrace isn't the same as it used to be with Mrs Evans gone and Joan the dry cleaners.'[38] Not even Birtwell's eventual return could lift his spirits. 'Things haven't been so good since the Clarks returned,' he wrote a few days later. 'Ossie seems terrified as if his world is about to collapse tomorrow, and while it frightens Celia a little she does have sympathy for him now . . . I think that's very sweet and natural.'[39]

He tried to get back into work, starting a new version of *George Lawson and Wayne Sleep*, but he got nowhere with it, and realising that there was nothing to keep him in London any longer, made the decision to return to Paris for at least a year. He told Clark, who had finally been kicked out by Birtwell, that he could move into Powis Terrace. 'I am leaving London Thursday evening,' he wrote to Geldzahler. 'Maurice is driving me and a lot of equipment . . . I'm looking foreword [*sic*] to it, I think, more than my first trip to California. The relief of getting out of London and being able to work all day long will ease my life so much . . . It's all very well having excitement or turbulence in one's life, but then one needs a period of reflection to sort it out. That's why I look foreword to Paris so much. I hope to work it all out on canvases.'[40] Working on the oil painting of his mother had made him fall in love with oils again, and he decided to abandon acrylic for the time being. 'Oil painting is such a delight again. One doesn't have to hurry, or keep bits of colour with labels on etc etc.'[41]

Hockney was to spend the better part of the next two years in Paris, living in a beautiful apartment in the sixth arrondissement rented from Tony Richardson. 3 Cour de Rohan was a romantic place, hidden away behind the Rue Saint-André des Arts and accessed through iron gates, behind which lay a series of three connecting courtyards, parts of which dated back to the fourteenth century. The French painter Balthus had once had a studio in the same building, and Hockney too soon fell under the spell of its ivy-clad walls, ancient trees and cobbled surfaces. It was close to L'Odéon Métro station; he used to tell would-be visitors, 'Just pass the statue of Danton and you will find me.'[42] He arrived on 4 October, and was soon settled in, writing to Geldzahler, 'Paris is very pleasant. For the first time in years I can have eight hours a day painting alone with no disturbances. The telephone only seems to ring two or three times and it's usually only friends arranging dinner.

I've started a few french lessons but my progress is slow, and after a hard day painting it's a little hard to concentrate, but I intend to slog at it.'[43]

He soon established a routine. 'I used to have my breakfast out at the Café de Flore and read the papers,' he recalls, 'and then after that I'd come back to the flat and paint. I might go out to lunch at one of the little places on the corner – there were loads of places – and then I'd work in the afternoon, and about five or six o'clock I'd walk down to the Café de Flore or Les Deux Magots. At first I thought that old bohemian Paris had gone and then I realised that in fact I was living in the last bit of it. The Left Bank was still cheap. There were a lot of hotels which you could live in for not that much money, so I was always meeting all kinds of people. I lived on cash and I used to walk everywhere. I could walk to the Louvre. I could walk to the Pompidou, to the Opéra, to the Coupole. I hardly ever took a taxi. I really liked my routine. If I didn't want to go to the cafe I didn't, I just worked.'[44] The apartment consisted of one large room with a high ceiling, which he used as a studio, a kitchen and two or three bedrooms. 'I've got settled in and started a painting of the mirror in my room at Lucca,' he wrote to Geldzahler. 'As it seems a time for reflextion [sic] in painting, I thought it a good subject. I only brought oil paints here, and it's very exciting using them again. I'm quickly adapting my techniques to it.'[45]

Hockney was at a crossroads in his life. 'I was thinking about many things and about certain attitudes to painting I felt were dead,' he wrote. 'I was trying to break out of something . . . of what I called obsessive naturalism . . . Usually when I get into that state I have to do something, so I just sit and draw in some way or other. At that time I felt almost as though I should go back to drawing skeletons, as I did when I was a student at the Royal College of Art, thinking, what shall I do?: I'll make a study of the skeleton; what should I do?: I'll make some drawings of my friends; I'll make them slowly, accurately, have them sit down and pose for hours.'[46]

One of the first to be drawn was Celia Birtwell, who came over to Paris on a number of occasions in November. 'The whole point of going was to be drawn by him,' she recalls, 'so I always took a pile of things with me . . . One day I had met this woman in Earls Court who had a trunkload of the most marvellous pieces of silk lingerie, and I took them with me to Paris. That's when he drew me in all those pretty clothes, and in the dirndl skirt with the flowers on it. If I was there for a week he would do several drawings. They were done in pencil, and each took about four or five hours to draw. The best drawings he ever did of me were done in those three months.'[47] These, notably *Celia in a Black Dress with Red Stockings*, *Celia in a Black Dress with White Flowers*, *Celia Wearing Checked Sleeves* and *Celia in a Black Slip, Reclining*, are more than just beautiful drawings, for they also reveal the artist's feelings. Indeed, they might be the work of an ardent lover, in that they imbue the model with a sensual warmth and femininity. They are sexy. 'In the French drawings, when we were very close,' she told the art historian Paul Melia, 'there was something going on between us which I think he portrayed through those drawings. He said to me that this was his way of expressing how he felt about me.'[48]

Just as he had cultivated an entourage of friends in London, so in Paris Hockney moved among an eclectic mix of Europeans and Americans, many of whom appear in his drawings from this period. Chief among his French friends was Jean Léger, a young designer for Helena Rubinstein, who Hockney liked to say 'works in a lipstick factory'.[49] A good-looking, highly cultivated Parisian, always impeccably dressed, with a quiet sense of humour and a twinkle in his eye, he had met Hockney in London in 1967. An etching of 1971, *Rue de Seine*, shows the view from the Paris apartment Léger shared with his lover Alexis Vidal, an interior designer, where Hockney often used to stay; it was published in an edition of 150 by Petersburg Press to raise money for the National Council for Civil Liberties. Léger, the subject of a large and affectionate drawing, *Portrait of Jean Léger*, spoke fluent English and, according to Celia Birtwell, acted as a kind of chaperone to Hockney, whom he was thrilled to have living in his home city.

Gregory Evans was also living close by, in the Rue de Dragon off the Boulevard Saint-Germain, having split up with Nick Wilder and come to Paris with the intention of studying fashion. He had turned up after a period of floating around Europe and getting into a number of scrapes, including being refused entry to the UK by Customs and Immigration at Gatwick airport after arriving on a flight stoned out of his head. 'In Los Angeles,' Evans recalls, 'I had been to the George Trippon School of Fashion Design to learn technical aspects of pattern-making and cutting, and I had this fantasy while I was there of going to fashion school in Paris, and I did none of it.'[50] Instead, supported by a private income, he set about having a good time. It was a great moment to be in Paris, a time of change, as the last breath of the post-war society of poets, actors, artists and musicians combined with an influx of a young international set of models and designers connected with the fashion industry. 'I didn't even speak French and wasn't fluent enough to go to any kind of serious school, but I have to say it was probably the best time of my life. I loved Paris. It was a fantastic time. It was so new and exciting and thrilling. The first year I lived there I probably never went out before four o'clock in the afternoon and I never went to bed before seven or eight in the morning.'[51]

Since his apartment was only two minutes' walk from the Café de Flore, Evans would amble down there in the early evening and seek out the familiar figure of Hockney, who stood out from the crowd with his colourful rugby shirts, red braces and odd-coloured socks, and often wearing a panama hat or even a beret. They would drink white wine, and talk about life, and a true friendship slowly developed. 'I went to the opera with David,' he says. 'We travelled. I used to love spending time with him watching him paint. Occasionally David and I would lunch and then we would go to the Louvre in the afternoon. We'd go in the side door and there would be nobody there.'[52]

Among the other regulars at the Flore was another of Hockney's friends, an American painter called Shirley Goldfarb, whose curious appearance also singled her out. 'She was a most extraordinary woman,' Jack Hazan remembers. 'She always dressed as a beatnik with long black dyed hair. She had massive bulging eyes all mascaraed up and she always wore the same clothes – a roll-neck black sweater and jeans with high-heel clog boots.'[53] Goldfarb had come to Paris to fulfil her romantic dream of being an artist living against the backdrop of the city of artists. She had taken a tiny studio in the Rue Liancourt in

Montparnasse, where she lived with her husband, Gregory Masurovsky, a graphic artist, and a wiry little Yorkshire terrier which accompanied her everywhere. Here she would work on large abstract-expressionist paintings executed using a brush/palette-knife technique. 'I paint a square every day,'[54] she used to say, speaking French with a strong American accent, by which she meant a one-inch square of paint on the canvas. For twenty-five years she sat every day at the Café de Flore, in her latter years writing a journal, posthumously published as *Carnets Montparnasse, 1971–1980*. Though her intensity and her social ambition made most people run a mile, Hockney adored her.

'I thought she was funny,' he recalls. 'She liked mocking things, and we became quite good friends. I used to dine at the Coupole a lot and Shirley would come looking for me, and when she found me she'd sit down at the table and if she ordered lobster I knew I would have to pay for it. People used to think she was taking advantage of me, but I said, "Well, if I was in her position I would do the same." She had no money and in those days you could live in Paris like that. She told me sometimes she would sit down with no money at all and somebody would come along and pay for her. She and Gregory lived very modestly, but she thought they were privileged living in the most beautiful city in the world.'[55]

Fascinated by their relationship, Hockney naturally saw them as a subject for a new double portrait. They had lived in two tiny little rooms for over twenty years, Gregory, who was very quiet and reserved, having the windowless back room, out of which he could not go without passing through Shirley's room at the front. 'Their relationship is a weird subject,' Hockney wrote. 'He can't go out of the building without her seeing, but she can. They are married but they are apart.'[56]

Shirley Goldfarb and Gregory Masurovsky, painted in acrylic after a drawing, showed their curious living conditions, with Shirley seated on a chair in her studio, while Gregory perches on the edge of a single bed in his cubicle.

Another eccentric woman who fascinated Hockney was the stage and costume designer Lila de Nobili, an Italian from a grand family, whose designs had included the celebrated Visconti production of *La Traviata* with Maria Callas. 'The set . . . was of such refinement and elegance,' wrote the television producer Peter Adam, 'that it made reality look shoddy.'[57] Her appearance was less refined than her creations, however, dressed as she always was in rather shabby shawls and stockings. Hockney met her through Tony Richardson, with whom she had collaborated on *The Charge of the Light Brigade*, and she had also designed both *Ondine* and *Sleeping Beauty* for Frederick Ashton at the Royal Ballet, where she was known to the company as 'Knobbly Lil'.[58] When she first came to tea at the Cour de Rohan, she had just come out of retirement to design *Manon Lescaut* for Visconti at the international festival in Spoleto in Italy.

De Nobili lived in just the kind of Paris garret that Hockney used to joke about owning. 'One afternoon we went to her tiny little apartment,' Celia Birtwell recalls, 'which was right at the top of this staircase that went up for ever . . . And there was this little flat, with a minute kitchen – I remember it had a Belfast sink and there was this great big box of Persil sitting there. She had cats and it was just the perfect scenario – this highly regarded, rather marvellous-looking woman living in this tiny flat.'[59] She had no telephone, and only one teacup, which particularly amused Hockney. A shy and quite reclusive woman, he perfectly captured these elements in his beautiful and touching drawing, *Lila de Nobili*. 'She had an almost masochistic humility,' wrote Peter Adam, 'and a closed nature at odds with all those inflated egos in the world of theatre and opera, like a strange bird who had fallen out of a nest.'[60]

In December, Andy Warhol, over in Paris to discuss an upcoming show of his Mao portraits at the Musée Galleria, visited Hockney at the Cour de Rohan. 'David took a couple of Polaroids of him,' Celia Birtwell recalls. 'David was talking about all these portraits he was doing, and he had all these palettes all over the floor covered with different-coloured paints and I remember Andy Warhol saying, "Oh, I really like those palettes," and I thought, "Trust you to look at the palettes rather than the picture he was painting." Then we all got into a cab with some Frenchwoman, and she started talking in French to someone else, and Warhol said sharply, "Stop speaking in that language. Speak in English." That was typical of him. He had real command and wanted everything done his way.'[61] The Polaroids were later used as the basis for a coloured crayon drawing of Warhol.

Among a number of handsome young men in Hockney's drawings from this period were Randy Hunt, a friend of Henry Geldzahler's; Carlos, whom he met through Lila de Nobili; Mark Lippscombe, a friend from LA; and the exotically named Jacques de Bascher de Beaumarchais, a lover of Karl Lagerfeld, and nicknamed by Hockney 'Jacques de Quelque Chose'. A French aristocrat, who claimed to be descended from the author of the Figaro plays, he was slim and good-looking, with a pencil moustache. Hockney made several drawings of him, including one of him wearing a sailor's suit. 'He was extremely stylish,' he recalls, 'and obviously based himself on a kind of Proustian figure. I remember one of his parties. He would have all these unbelievable French soldiers, big butch soldiers, lining up to fuck him. There were some marvellous orgies organised in Paris. They were really well done because the French pay tremendous attention to detail.'[62]

Among all the young men, however, there was only one serious lover. Writing to Henry Geldzahler in January 1974 about a proposed trip to New York, Hockney announced, 'Yves-Marie has entered my life. I asked him to come to New York with me, although it's a bit difficult with his mother and school etc., so I don't know if he'll come, but don't be surprised if he arrives with me.'[63] Yves-Marie Hervé, always referred to as 'Yves-Marie de Paris', was a young student at the École du Louvre to whom Hockney was attempting to teach some English. 'He was a very pretty boy with masses of dark hair falling forward,' Kasmin remembers. 'He was a gay man's dream boy, nice-natured, willing, not at all camp; he looked like someone who needed to be loved. It was impossible not to like him. He was desirable even if you weren't gay.'[64] To Celia Birtwell he was 'super French, and he had this wonderful draped hair. I can see why David liked him; he looked marvellous, he was a wonderful poser and he knew how to dress. He was petite, like a toy.'[65]

Just as with Peter Schlesinger, their relationship was that of teacher and pupil, and Hockney spent many hours introducing him to his favourite museums and exploring the little back rooms at the Louvre, where the supposedly less interesting pictures were hung. At the Museé d'Art Moderne, he took him to Brancusi's studio. 'I loved that room,' he wrote, 'with the dust on it, the pieces in it and that marvellous atmosphere. Next door was that other terrific room with the González sculptures, which have always affected me. He was a wonderful sculptor. So I was, in a way, looking at art of the long past, and at early modern art, which of course was made in Paris . . .'[66]

Naturally Hockney also wanted to introduce Hervé to the work of Picasso, which involved a trip down to Avignon, where the late works were being shown in the Musée du Petit Palais. Hockney arranged for them to stay just outside Uzès with Douglas Cooper, whose great collection of cubist art, built up since the 1930s, included the work of Braque, Léger and Juan Gris, as well as Picasso. Hockney found Cooper enthralling company, if infuriating. 'He was quite a fascinating person,' he says, 'but he had the emotional age of somebody of about seven. There was a mad side to him which I rather liked.'[67] Cooper's twenty-year friendship with his great hero and neighbour, Picasso, had ended on the fateful day in 1970 when he dared to tell the artist that it was time he recognised his illegitimate children, Paloma and Claude. Losing his temper at this reminder of his mortality, Picasso threw Cooper out of his studio. 'There was a steep flight of stairs leading down from Picasso's villa to the front gate,' his partner John Richardson later recalled, 'and poor Douglas paused on every step, kneeling and weeping and grovelling and begging to be forgiven! It did him no good at all.'[68]

In spite of the fact that Cooper had made it quite clear that he thought the late Picassos were 'terrible', when Hockney and Hervé went to Avignon he insisted on accompanying them. 'We arrived there,' Hockney recalls, 'and he goes in and starts telling me immediately how dreadful they are. So I said to him, "Can I just have a short time looking at them by myself?" Then I did say to him, "Well, I can see one thing anyway, which is that they are about being an

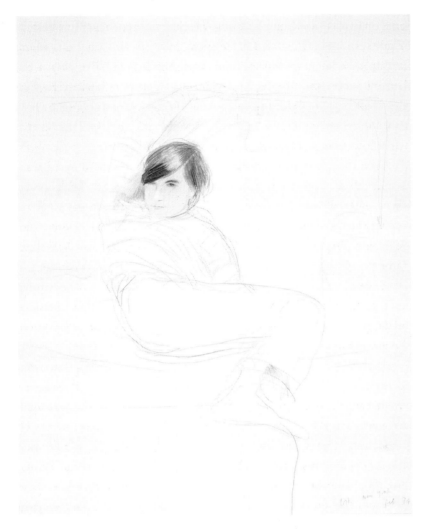

Yves-Marie, New York,
1974

old man. Perhaps you've not seen that." I started taking a few digs
at him, because he was trying to give me the impression that from
the moment he was banned from Picasso's studio, all his paintings
went to rack and ruin.'[69]

On their trips away together and in Paris, Hervé became the subject
of numerous drawings – lying on a sofa in the Paris studio reading
Jean Cocteau, curled up seductively in Henry Geldzahler's New York
apartment, sitting on a chair reading in the garden of Le Nid de Duc.
Spending so much time in Hockney's company meant that his English

came on in leaps and bounds. Not so Hockney's French, partly because he put very little effort into his lessons, and secretly rather played on speaking the language with a thick Yorkshire accent. 'I've been a bit slack with mon francais,' he wrote to Geldzahler on 17 January, 'as I've been working hard painting and looking after my parents here for a few days. I drew them, but we also saw a lot of Paris, they said they had a marvellous time so I feel quite good.'[70]

Even though it was only for a few days, for Kenneth and Laura their trip to Paris was a welcome break from the hardships back home, where Edward Heath's government had brought in a three-day week to combat the problems of rising fuel prices. 'In England,' Hockney told Geldzahler, exaggerating just a little, 'there is no electricity gasoline trains or TV, but Celia says everybody is having a good time (Isn't it lovely, just like the war). I do think people love to suffer collectively, don't you?'[71] Among the drawings Hockney executed of his parents during their four-day trip was a touching study of Kenneth in coloured crayon, sitting in a chair with his arms folded.

As well as showing his parents the sights, another distraction from his French lessons was dealing with a visit from Clark, who was on best behaviour with his new landlord. 'Ossie came for the weekend last week. He was charm itself. Making the tea, sweeping the floor, entertaining visitors for tea etc. but he did want something from me. He has now moved into my studio to make his dresses (Mo is converting the large sitting room back to a studio) and I'm told I wouldn't recognize the place. I now tend to read actions in your Freudian way and see it as a way to keep me away from London and Celia, for underneath all his activity here I did detect a fear.'[72]

Hockney was working on three oil paintings that were intended for a show which the British Council was putting on in Paris in October at the Musée des Arts Décoratifs. The first was the double portrait *Shirley Goldfarb and Gregory Masurovsky*, while the other two came about directly from his endless expeditions to the Louvre. *Contre-jour in the French Style — Against the Day dans le Style Français* — a typical playful Hockney title — was inspired by a window in the Pavillon de Flore, at the south-west corner of the Louvre, which was showing an exhibition of French drawings from the Metropolitan Museum. 'The first time I went,' he wrote, 'I saw this window with the blind pulled down and the formal garden beyond. And I thought, oh it's marvellous! marvellous! This is a picture in itself . . . So I took some photographs of it, made a drawing, and started painting.'[73] Consciously drawing on a traditionally French style, the pointillist technique of the neo-Impressionists, helped him to loosen his brushwork again, and from the start the painting went well. The result beautifully depicts the light passing through the translucent blind and its reflection in the parquet floor. The picture that followed this, *Two Vases in the Louvre*, echoed the print of Jean Léger's apartment, *Rue de Seine*, with the window looking out onto a view across the courtyard to the Rue de Rivoli.

However much Hockney loved his Paris life, there were times when he found the French quite exasperating. He wrote to Henry Geldzahler in February still fuming about 'a story of Paris and French rudeness', which had occured two days previously when he had taken Shirley Goldfarb and her husband to dinner at Maxim's to celebrate their twenty-first wedding anniversary. 'Shirley comes in a dress and Gregory in his leather jacket and tie. As the Maitre D is showing us to our table he says – feeling Gregory's jacket – that it's not pretty (joli) enough for Maxims. I couldn't believe my ears and assumed I'd heard it wrong. The place of course was full of businessmen in hideous suits (that didn't fit them).'[74] They went on to Régine's nightclub, for which Hockney had been sent an entry card, where a 'gestapo-like' waiter told Hervé to put on his jacket when he got up to dance. 'He was the smartest person in the place . . . Anyway when we were leaving they told me to put on my jacket in a most unpleasant manner. I said . . . it was everybody's privilege who was leaving to do it how they wished. I tore up the card (it was plastic so it took some time, rather spoiling the effect) and gave it back to them.'[75] He later exclaimed to Ossie Clark, 'Paris would be beautiful if only the English lived there.'[76]

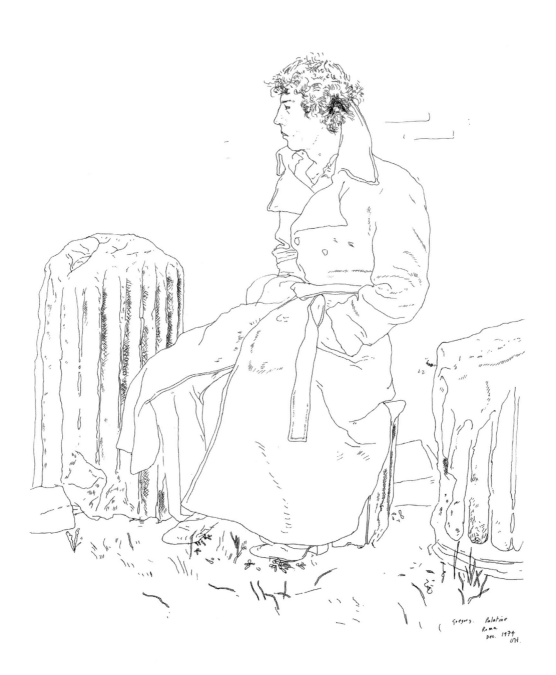

CHAPTER THIRTEEN

THE RAKE'S PROGRESS

In late March 1974, the calm of Hockney's Paris life was shattered. He had a call from Jack Hazan telling him that the film he had been working on for the last three years was completed, and inviting him to come over to London to view it. The trip was a disaster from the moment he arrived. 'I went with Yves-Marie on the train on Sunday,' he recounted to Henry Geldzahler, 'and when we arrived at Powis Terrace, it was as though we weren't expected. Ossie has taken over the whole place, and we were just shoved into the back bedroom. Anyway it was so depressing with all of Ossie's models running around that we immediately went out to dinner with George and Wayne.'[1] Worse still was the fact that Clark had ripped out the beautiful fireplace in the studio, which had been lovingly chosen by Peter Schlesinger, leaving nothing but a large black hole. Nor had the sheets been washed. 'They crackled with the filth,'[2] Hockney told Melissa North. He was beside himself with anger. To compound it all, Clark let the bath run over, in doing so destroying one of Hockney's favourite jackets. 'David confused, uptight, silly, spiteful, ratty,' was Clark's comment in his diary. 'First time no clean sheets on his bed – I've really upset him on top of overflowing the bath, wrecking his trendy jacket and flooding Mo's basement.'[3]

The following morning Hockney set off for a screening room off Curzon Street to watch Jack's film, *A Bigger Splash*, which turned out to be, not the documentary about an artist that he had been expecting, but a semi-fictional account of the break-up of his relationship with Peter Schlesinger. It brought back too many painful memories. 'He sat through the movie,' says Hazan, 'and at the end of it I have never seen a more distraught person. He just said to me, "Jack, it's too heavy. It's too heavy."'[4] Hockney poured out his heart to Henry Geldzahler.

Gregory, Palatine, Roma, December 1974

'It shattered me. I didn't know what to think or how to react. Its main story is about my brake [sic] with Peter, and then painting that picture of him looking into the swimming pool. My first reaction was that it was a schmaltzy [sic] view of an artist and homosexuality. I couldn't understand Peter's reactions to it, and realised he had almost collaborated with Jack on it. I had a conversation with him on the telephone, finally asking him why, when he had been living with me he had hated Jack and hated taking part in the movie . . . and why afterwards he had been such an eager actor and collaborator. He replied he did it for the money, which if it is true (which I doubt) seems too cheap. I hung up on him eventually. . .'[5]

Hockney attempted to cheer himself up by going to watch Wayne Sleep as Puck in *A Midsummer Night's Dream* at Covent Garden, before heading off to the King's Road Theatre to see Clark's latest fashion show, a glamorous event bankrolled by Mick Jagger, and attended by numerous stars including Paul McCartney, Ringo Starr, Rod Stewart, Marianne Faithfull, Bryan Ferry and Britt Ekland. It was an evening that further blackened his mood. 'Our reserved seats had been taken,' he wrote to Geldzahler, 'by some drugged-up hooray layabouts, so we sat at the back. Ossie then says he had asked a "few people back for a drink at Powis Terrace"– which of course turned out to be 200 drugged-up boring hoorays and hangers on,– including Peter, so Yves-Marie and myself just left and went down to Mo's basement. I left the next day after having a small row with Ossie.'[6]

As a result of both the film and the whole weekend, Hockney decided, once and for all, to get rid of Powis Terrace. 'I don't think I ever want to go back and work there,' he told Geldzahler, 'so I'm definitely going to sell it and buy some small house or flat in central London.'[7] Since Henry featured in *A Bigger Splash*, both in a scene at Powis Terrace and another at the Emmerich Gallery in New York, Hockney advised him to see it. 'You are very good in it, but the portrait of Mo is too cruel, and I just think that it gives a wrong picture of me. There's a scene of Peter making love to some boy – again he must have done it for money. I dread its release, yet as my first reaction had been that anyway it was far too long and boring it didn't really matter, but Anthony Page saw it . . . and said he thought it had commercial potential – it's like a real "Sunday Bloody Sunday", he said. This made me worry about it, but luckily I have some Valium.'[8]

Hockney was right in believing that Peter was paid to appear in the film. It had been the only way that Hazan had been able to persuade him to cooperate. 'He kept asking me to take part and be in it,' recalls Schlesinger, 'and I always said no. But after he'd been doing it for about two years, he took me to lunch in Soho – I remember Pearl Bailey was sitting at the next table – and I was movie mad, so I said I'd do it on the condition that it was treated like a job and I got paid for it. "If you hire me, then I'll do it," I told him.'[9] Hazan then paid him £170 as a fee, followed later on by two payments of £25 and £20 for doing the love scene. But whatever reason people had for appearing, Hockney felt betrayed. '. . . deep down I think I've been exploited,' he told Geldzahler, 'not just by Jack – in some ways I sympathise with his position as an artist at taking material in front of him – but almost more by close friends, especially Peter, as I did think he should know better than Mo.'[10] This preyed on his mind and when he returned to Paris, he could think of nothing but the film. His first reaction was to get it stopped at all costs. 'I didn't hear from David for two or three weeks,' Hazan remembers, 'and then I got a message through Kasmin saying that they wanted to stop the movie going out, and they were prepared to pay £20,000 to have it destroyed, which happened to be the cost of the movie. There was stalemate there.'[11]

Hockney therefore decided to seek a second opinion, and sent Shirley Goldfarb, a keen movie buff, to London to see it. 'She sat through the film,' Hazan recalls, 'and when she came out she said to me, "Jack, this is the greatest film on art that has ever been made," and then she returned to Paris to relay her opinion to David.'[12] The next person to see it was Ossie who said it was 'truer than the truth'.[13] Now that it had been validated by two of his closest friends, Hockney decided to take another look himself. 'David came over, and I showed it to him again at the Trident Preview Theatre in St Anne's Court, which had these large glass cylindrical ashtrays and he managed to knock down two and smashed them. He kept going to the toilet all the time because he just couldn't bear it, because although it wasn't authentic, it seemed authentic, and showed his terrible distress at the loss of his love, Peter. He was totally distraught, and I should have felt guilty, but I just didn't. I thought I was producing art.'[14]

A Bigger Splash was selected for the critics' week at the 1974 Cannes Film Festival, and received generally excellent reviews, not least from *The Times* critic David Robinson, who wrote that it quite outclassed the British films showing in the main competition, which included Ken Russell's *Mahler*. It achieved more than a straight documentary about a painter, he wrote, because 'the images become in a mysterious way an extension of Hockney's own vision. The colours and compositions are those of the paintings. Here is the world of the painter, his friends, his models, and the quiet rooms in which time seems arrested . . . the film moves in and out of the pictures.' He finished his review: 'A first film of so much fulfilled ambition and so much originality disarms criticism.'[15] Hockney resigned himself to the film, concluding that it would be wrong of him to try to suppress the work of another artist, after Hazan had made a visit to his Paris studio. '"I'm painting this picture of Gregory and Shirley,"' Hockney recalled saying to Hazan, '"and it's nearly finished." Jack looks at it, quite fascinated, and says, "You see, David, that's what you do all the time; look at what you're doing to them." And I said, "I know, I see your point; if Shirley and Gregory say We don't like that picture, I'm not going to destroy it, if I like it."'[16]

As it happened, *Shirley Goldfarb and Gregory Mazurovsky* was causing Hockney problems, once again because of his fears about finding himself turning into a portrait painter. Rescue came from an unexpected quarter, in the form of a letter from John Cox, an opera director who was about to start work on a new production of Stravinsky's *The Rake's Progress* for Glyndebourne Opera House in Sussex. Glyndebourne had had a considerable success with their previous production, designed by the cartoonist Osbert Lancaster, and it had occurred to Cox that a young contemporary artist such as Hockney, who had the same strong feeling for graphics as Lancaster had, might be just the right person to create a new production, especially since he had already done his own

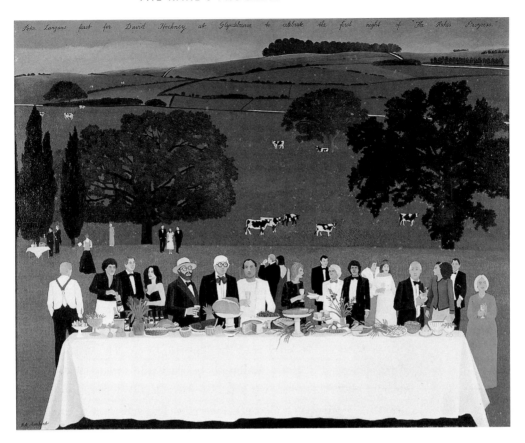

The Glyndebourne
Picnic, 1975

take on Hogarth's paintings. What he did not know was that Hockney
had been an opera lover since he was a boy, when his father had taken
him to see *La Bohème* at the Bradford Alhambra. It also occurred to
Hockney that to work in a new medium was perhaps a way out of the
rut he was in. 'When you're working suddenly in another field,' he
said, 'you are much less afraid of failure. You kind of half expect it, so
therefore you take more risks, which makes it more exciting.'[17]

The weekend of 14 June, Hockney, Yves-Marie Hervé and Gregory
Evans went to Glyndebourne to watch a production of Richard Strauss's
Intermezzo, directed by John Cox and starring the great Swedish
soprano Elisabeth Söderström. It was only Hockney's second visit, his
first having been in the sixties to see Massenet's *Werther*, and he loved
it. 'We stayed in the house,' he recalls, 'and we were having dinner

with the owners, George and Mary Christie, in the dining room and I remember hearing Gregory saying to a woman sitting next to him that he didn't know a thing about the opera. And I thought, "Good for you Gregory admitting that." Later he used to tell me how he used to be quite intimidated by some of the Opera Houses I'd taken him to, but he said, "Backstage it's just show business."'[18]

Despite falling under the Glyndebourne spell, Hockney still had reservations about taking on the job. 'I felt I didn't know enough technically – the only thing I had ever designed for the stage before was *Ubu Roi*.'[19] John Cox immediately put him at his ease. 'I told him we had plenty of people at Glyndebourne who would help him with the working drawings and with colour. I also told him it was a process of development, rather than anyone just saying, yes, that's lovely. Having finally accepted it, he then asked me what I wanted, and I told him that by asking him I was looking for something a little out of the ordinary, which he would initiate and between us we would then develop.'[20]

As soon as Hockney read the libretto, by W. H. Auden and the American poet Chester Kallman, he was transfixed. 'I loved that straight away,' he wrote. 'It was . . . a wonderful, witty, very literate libretto – which not all operas have.'[21] The music he found more difficult, though he was charmed by Baba the Turk's 'Chatterbox' aria in the second act when she sings, 'As I was saying, both brothers wore moustaches' and breathlessly lists all her favourite treasures – among them snuffboxes, statues of the Twelve Apostles, mummies and the Great Auk. The more he listened to the score, however, the more beautiful he began to find it, and his discovery within it of an element of eighteenth-century pastiche made him decide to return to Hogarth's paintings for inspiration.

That the Glyndebourne commission had come about at exactly the right point in Hockney's career is reflected in a review of an exhibition of some of his recent drawings, which opened in July at Garage Art in Earlham Street, Covent Garden. Though the critic Paul Overy admired the skill with which he captured the 'foibles and eccentricities' of subjects such as Kasmin, Warhol and Geldzahler, and was impressed by 'a surprising understanding of the way a woman projects her sexual personality through her clothes and poise' in the coloured drawings of Celia Birtwell, he sensed that the artist had come up against a wall. '. . . as with much of Hockney's recent work, one feels he has become too wrapped up in this world in which he moves . . . Hockney's talent needs themes (literary, usually) which extend it beyond the immediate circle of his personal world.'[22]

Before he could give *The Rake's Progress* his full attention, there were pressing problems to deal with. One was his rapidly deteriorating relationship with Clark, whom he was now desperate to remove from Powis Terrace. Their friendship was compromised because Celia was threatening Clark with divorce owing to his heavy drug-taking, his promiscuity and his violence towards her, and Hockney, now nicknamed 'Mr Magoo' by Clark, had, not surprisingly, taken her side. 'Mr Magoo whining from Bradford,' wrote Clark in his diary on 5 July '– move out by the end of this month etc,'[23] and two days later, 'It's a lovely day but at 11.30 David came in on the warpath and played all his old songs again including two new ones: he's going to store the furniture and cut off the telephone.'[24] Having finally got Clark's agreement to leave by the end of August, Hockney told Mo McDermott, 'Do make sure he doesn't pinch anything,'[25] a sensible precaution as it turned out, as Clark confided to his diary on 29 August: '11 o'clock the big move to Cambridge Gardens. Ordered a telephone to be installed. The beasts won't put in the pink thirties phones. Dare I take them from Big Brother Hockney?'[26]

On 2 September, Clark noted, 'Organise my bed, work-room and laundry and final exit from "Doomsville" Powis Terrace.'[27] For Hockney, however, this was by no means the end of the story, since he was inextricably bound up with the Clarks and their unravelling relationship. There were times when he muddied the waters, rather than poured oil on them. On a visit to London four days later, for example, he took a gang of friends including Celia to Odin's for dinner. 'At one point the conversation came round to what we might all really like,' Birtwell recalls, 'and I said, "A diamond ring," and David, who had had a few drinks, said, "I'll buy you a diamond ring, love. Come round tomorrow morning and we'll go and buy one." So in the morning

I went round to his studio and he'd quite changed his mind. I felt quite embarrassed. Obviously he wasn't lit up any more when he thought about it. Anyway, Maurice Payne happened to be there and he said, "Come on, David, if you don't go now you'll never get there before the shops close" – it was early closing on a Saturday – so we tootled off to Kutchinsky in the Brompton Road. They kept bringing out these modern settings and I said, "Well, I want one that looks like it came out of a Christmas cracker," and David said, "Well, why don't you tell them, lovey?" So I got this lovely three-carat ring. Of course he didn't want me tell Ossie as he felt guilty on his behalf that he'd bought me a diamond ring.'[28] When Clark found out, it did little either for his self-confidence or for his feelings towards Hockney, who, he was now convinced, was pushing Celia to divorce him.

Things eventually came to a head in October, around the time of the opening of *David Hockney: Tableaux et Dessins*, Hockney's first retrospective in Paris. This show, at the Musée des Arts Décoratifs in the Louvre, consisted of thirty paintings and seventy-five drawings, the majority of them from 1970 onwards, and they included the three paintings and most of the drawings he had completed in the Cour de Rohan. Hockney chose the pictures himself, and there was only one that he had to fight for, which was *Mr and Mrs Clark and Percy*. This was because the Tate Gallery claimed it was too fragile to ship. Hockney was furious and demanded a meeting with the chief conservator, a Hungarian called Stefan Slabczynski. 'He was in the cellar,' says Hockney. 'I said, "Where are the cracks?" He said, "They haven't occurred yet." I went up to see Norman Reid, the director, and I said, 'The conservator doesn't think there's anything wrong with it yet. If something happens to it, I'll repaint the whole bloody picture for you. Really, it's not fair – you won't lend a picture for a British artist having a big show in Paris – I'm appalled."'[29] The fuss he made was worth the trouble: Reid finally relented, and the picture went to the Louvre.

Stephen Spender wrote the introduction to the catalogue. The celebrated English poet had been an early collector of Hockney's work, buying etchings from him while he was still at the Royal College, and had been responsible for introducing him to Christopher Isherwood. They had subsequently formed a friendship and had collaborated on the Alecto edition of the Cavafy poems. Spender compared Hockney and his contemporaries to the irreverent and antisocial tradition of art that emerged after the Industrial Revolution, as exemplified by the Pre-Raphaelites, such as Samuel Palmer and, particularly, William Blake, an artist who 'remained outside the main tradition all his life, mocking at the religious and artistic institutions of his time, and producing his own totally original poetry and art'.[30] Also included in the catalogue was an interview with the influential French art critic Pierre Restany, in the course of which Hockney talked about his experience in Paris. 'It's very British,' he said, 'to go abroad to see something unusual and paint it . . . I need constant stimuli of all kinds, visual and others, that is why I travel a lot and enjoy working in lots of different places . . . in the paintings and drawings I've done here there is much more of Paris than there is of London in all I've been able to do in London. The reason is simple: it is easier for me to get the necessary detachment in Paris because I don't understand much of the French character or the language. But on the other hand I know how to use my eyes and I like the sensation of detachment I can experience in Paris and which stimulates my work.'[31]

The show opened to the public on 11 October and the night before, Hockney's friends flew in for the private view. Clark was not among them. 'Celia goes to Paris tomorrow,' he wrote in his diary on 9 October, 'and I thought of going myself – but got very negative vibes from Mo who I spoke to on the phone – David is very off me (I hope he doesn't brainwash Celia too much).'[32] The private view was a glamorous affair, with a dinner for sixty afterwards at Maxim's, which was paid for by an American socialite, Barbara Thurston. 'She had bought a painting of mine,' Hockney recalls, 'and she was one of those rich women with quite a bit of money and not many friends who thought that if they bought a painting they could take you over.'[33] Kasmin remembers her as being 'dotty about David. She wanted to be in the game both as a patron and a friend, and in the end she was pleading on her knees to be allowed to give the big dinner for the opening, and she forked out for a pretty grand dinner ... The thing was that everyone was competing to capture a bit of the Star. It was rather like having Elvis Presley around and people asking, "Who is going to hold the autograph album?" The show was a big deal for David.'[34]

'To stand in a clear space,' wrote *The Times* critic, Michael Ratcliffe, 'with the sleeping nude of *The Room, Tarzana* to one's left, the arrested sensations of *A Bigger Splash* to one's right, with the parquet floor underfoot ending in four high windows and beyond them four stone arches of the Rivoli arcade, the eye finally resting on the scrawled announcements of Bar Mona Lisa and the Tentation du Mandarin boutique, is to feel for a moment the astonishing effect of actually standing inside a painting by David Hockney.'[35] Out of everything on show, Ratcliffe selected the crayon drawings as his favourites. 'The exuberance and economy,' he noted, 'with which he has taken the child's scribbling toy and transformed it – particularly in the portraits of Mark Lancaster, Mo McDermott, Peter Schlesinger, Ossie Clark and, above all, Celia Birtwell, make these in some way the crowning, sophisticated glory of the Paris show.'[36]

When Birtwell returned home, Clark made one last attempt to persuade her to have him back, telling her he was working hard on a new collection and had been four weeks without drugs. But to no avail. 'Celia remains firm,' he wrote, '– she rubbed it in about Paris: wonderful party, photos with St Laurent etc . . . I left Linden Gardens in tears.'[37] Things came to a head the following day when Clark, who had been drinking heavily, went to see his lawyer to discuss the divorce, and discovered during their conversation that Celia had had a secret affair some years previously with the illustrator Adrian George. On hearing this he became, as he wrote in his diary, 'like a bull with a red flag . . . So I split to Linden Gardens and was so furious I beat her and kicked her and her nose was a bloody mess – then I forced her to speak to her lawyer lady, and it was she who sent the police round and told me to leave . . .'[38] A few days later he was in Paris on a working trip and went to a party given by Hockney's French dealer, Claude Bernard. Among the guests, he wrote, was 'big-mouth Shirley Goldfarb, who said to me, at the top of her voice so everyone could hear, "You can

break your wife's nose but you're still very sexy to me.'"[39] Hockney had
made sure that everybody knew what Clark had done.

For Hockney, there was one downside to the success of this show:
the publicity around it alerted people to the fact that he was now living
in Paris. Then, a few days after the opening, Jack Hazan's film opened
in a small art cinema near the Étoile. 'The film became a great success
in Paris,' Hockney wrote. '. . . people kept stopping me in the street:
loved your film. *My* film! . . . They would go to the film, then go to
the exhibition to see the real paintings. People say it was a marvellous
experience to watch the film and then be able to go and see the real
paintings.'[40] But for Hockney, now wanting to throw himself into
working on his designs for *The Rake's Progress*, which he had promised
to deliver by Christmas, life and art were converging uncomfortably.
'A lot of people were coming over and coming to see me,' he says, 'and
I thought, "This won't be very good," so I took Mo and we went to LA
and took a suite in the Chateau Marmont hotel.'[41]

Hockney's research for the Glyndebourne project had led him back to
Hogarth's engravings of *The Rake's Progress* from his original sequence
of paintings: he felt that Hogarth's precise cross-hatching technique,
in which shading is achieved by the drawing of closely spaced parallel
lines set at an angle, perfectly suited the jagged, linear character of
the score. Stravinsky's music, he thought, 'was a pastiche of Mozart's,
and my design was a pastiche of Hogarth's'.[42] He was also convinced
that the setting must remain in the eighteenth century. 'I thought you
couldn't put it in the twentieth century,' he said. 'The story would
seem a bit too ridiculous. Even in the nineteenth century it would seem
ridiculous. Instead of being at first a kind of innocent, you'd have just
thought [the Rake] a fool straightaway, and therefore less interesting.
I told John Cox this before I began. I said . . . "Somehow we have to
look at the eighteenth century and give it a twentieth-century look,"
which of course is easier than one thinks anyway. You can stylize it.'[43]

Apart from wanting to get away from what he would have called the
'natterers', there was another, more emotional reason why Hockney

wanted to do the designs in Hollywood. Stravinsky himself had lived at the Chateau Marmont from March to April 1941, had first seen the Hogarth paintings at an exhibition in Chicago in 1947, and had written the opera in Los Angeles. Hockney left for LA on 25 October, with a penitent Mo McDermott. McDermott was in trouble on two counts, the first being that he had been plundering the Powis Terrace wine cellar. 'I used to go to Burgundy with Kasmin to buy wine,' Hockney recalls, 'not Rothschild-style wine, but good quality. I must have had about two hundred bottles. Then I went away to Paris, and when I came back, it was all gone. Mo had been saying to people, "Have a glass of plonk," and he'd been pouring them my nectar.'[44]

Worse was his heroin addiction. There are references in Ossie Clark's diary to McDermott being 'smacked out', a situation which Hockney had only just discovered. One problem had been that McDermott's whole life had revolved around Hockney, and with Hockney away in Paris, there had been nothing to occupy him. 'I had left Mo in London and he had moved into the basement of Powis Terrace,' Hockney recalls, 'but the moment I wasn't there, there was nothing for Mo to do, and he didn't keep asking me what he should do. Then I found out that he'd got hooked on heroin . . . people were quite prepared to let him have the drugs and pay them later, because they knew he would somehow get the money from me. Of course, I didn't know this was going on. When I was told about it, I came over and threw everybody out – the basement was full of about twenty people. I then got Mo into some clinic, the first of many times I dried him out.'[45] The heroin addiction also explained a number of missing drawings. 'I used to see people with drawings on their walls which would say "For Mo With Love". I gave Mo a lot of drawings if he liked them, to put up on his walls, and then as soon as they got to be worth a hundred quid, he'd start selling them. Then he used to steal drawings and sell them. I just wish he'd asked.'[46]

Along with a newly clean McDermott, Hockney also took with him to Chateau Marmont the original recording of *The Rake's Progress*, directed by Stravinsky himself, and a set of very expensive pens, with red, blue, green and black inks, sourced in Germany. They borrowed a record player to listen to the music, and, working in a small apartment at the hotel, they completed sets for more than half of the eight scenes that made up the opera, making meticulous scale models in cardboard, each one 16 × 21 × 12 inches in size, the cross-hatching done in the colours that would have been standard for printing inks in the eighteenth century – red, blue, green and black. McDermott turned out to be an invaluable asset. Having once worked for the celebrated theatre designer Ralph Koltai, he understood the process by which ideas on paper become reality. 'Mo advised me straight away to make models,' Hockney wrote, 'because, he said, if you only make a drawing, somebody else then translates it into the space. The moment he said that I thought, I don't want anybody else to do that, I want to do that myself. So I thought, I will make scale models. I wanted pictorialism, I wanted to bring my own attitude to sets.'[47]

On 27 November, Hockney flew to Paris to meet his parents and his brother Paul and family, for whom he had arranged a trip to see his show, while McDermott travelled to London with the models to prepare for a meeting with John Cox. Flying from Heathrow, Kenneth had a small problem with security. 'Comical when we checked thro (precaution against carrying bombs),' wrote Laura, 'as Ken made a "Ping" sound – had to go back – same again – thought it was his "hearing aid" – but he said "Don't think I would carry guns. I'm a pacifist." . . . Met by David. Went to Hotel and then on to exhibition at the "Louvre". We all enjoyed it & thought exhibits just wonderful . . . David very tired after travel from California and time change.'[48] The following morning they went to David's flat. 'He, much refreshed, did drawing of me. Shirley called with "Sarah", little dog. We all went to the "Coffee Pot" (lovely restaurant) for meal & dog sat on a stool covered with serviette at table. Other dogs too, but very well behaved. They certainly respect dogs in Paris!!! I hoped to do some shopping while Dad was sitting for portrait – But he kept falling asleep, so David could not go on . . . Later, walking back through Montmartre . . . a pavement artist wanted to draw Lisa – but she said, "Oh no! My Uncle is a famous artist!"'[49]

The following week, John Cox and all the Glyndebourne production team came to London to look at the completed work. 'When I showed what I had done to the people at Glyndebourne,' Hockney recalls, 'they were amazed that I had made models. They had expected me to do just a few drawings. What I didn't know at the time was that some of the people thought what I was doing wouldn't work at all, but they didn't say so. I'm glad of that because I think if they had they would probably have put me off; I would have believed them, thinking they knew more about the theatre than I did.'[50] What the doubters felt, but did not say, was that cross-hatching on such a massive scale was simply too mad an idea and would never work. As it happened, Hockney himself had doubts, and went down to Glyndebourne to test his idea. 'We made lots of samples of cross-hatching in different sizes, and hung them up on the stage. I sat at the back of the theatre with binoculars, deciding what the scale should be. If it was done too small, it would look like a solid colour. If it was too big it would look like a chequerboard – and that would be ridiculous. So I made some calculations and came up with the exact size.'[51]

Having delivered the finished models to Glyndebourne, from where they would be taken to Harkers Studio in Bermondsey to be translated into full-size sets, Hockney took a much needed break. This also had a romantic element to it. For some months he had been feeling a growing affection for Gregory Evans, largely based on their mutual love of art, and Evans's quick, dry wit, which made Hockney laugh, particularly in the way he would take things literally. They were once hiring a car, for example, and the girl at the car-hire desk asked Gregory if he also wanted to drive. 'Oh, you mean it's got two steering wheels?' he said.[52]

It was on their trip to see *Intermezzo* that Hockney realised how his feelings for Evans had deepened. 'Gregory fell asleep on the train returning from Glyndebourne,' he later wrote, 'and I thought he looked very sweet because he was wearing a suit, something he does not normally wear. In most pictures he is very casually dressed, but for Glyndebourne he borrowed a suit from Ossie Clark. I thought he looked very handsome and suddenly saw him in a slightly different way . . .'[53] They went to Rome for a few days, where Hockney drew his new lover sitting among the ruins on the Palatine hill. 'It was the first time I'd ever been to Italy,' Evans remembers, 'so it was very exciting. We didn't do that much, because we weren't there for very long, and most of the time I ended up posing for him. He drew me a lot in those days, and he always seemed to capture something in me that I can relate to. He presented a side of me that I was unaware of, and the drawings gave me a bit of identity that I didn't have before, that I hadn't seen.'[54]

That Hockney was serious about Evans is clear from the fact that he invited him to join him in Bradford to celebrate the eightieth birthday of his mother's oldest sister, Rebecca, known in the family as Aunt Rebe. 'Busy all morning preparing a cold lunch,' wrote Laura in her diary. 'At 2.30pm David, Margaret & Gregory arrived. Had cup of tea and David suggested going to Harry Ramsdens for "Fish & Chips". Left my meal covered and all went to Guisely. Returned to Eastbrook for 4pm. Met old friends and had a happy birthday tea . . . Rebe was delighted – looked lovely in her black gown (1935) but "up to date".'[55]

Evans loved the trip to Yorkshire. 'I felt incredibly at home there,' he recalls, 'as it didn't feel to me that different in spirit to Kansas, which is where my parents were raised. It was dark and full of Gothic gloom, which appealed to me.'[56] The party took place at Eastbrook Hall, and later that night he had his first proper meeting with Kenneth Hockney. 'David's father was magical, and eccentric. I remember we came in late and he was up tinkering. He had this twinkle in his eye as he smiled, and he was excited and wanted to show me all his current projects. The first thing he wanted to show me was this old adding machine which he had converted over from the old system to the decimal system, using dayglo stickers. Then he showed me other things he was working on, like decorated postcards and the posters that he'd made for his anti-war marches. Then – this was what I thought was brilliant – he had a recording of a train which he had taken, and he had the recording machine under his chair in the kitchen near the fire, so he would take naps in his chair and relax listening to it. He was quite right. Nowadays people sell those recordings to help you sleep. He was avant-garde.'[57]

Gregory Evans brought new happiness into Hockney's life at a time when he was under considerable stress, not just from the huge task of designing his first opera, but from the ongoing dramas surrounding Clark and Birtwell, McDermott's heroin addiction, and the continuing fallout from Jack Hazan's film. The last finally came to the attention of Hockney's parents in late March, after a write-up in the *Bradford Telegraph and Argus*. 'It was rather a shock,' Laura confided to her diary. 'At first it did not hit me – I guess I am very naive – tho I'm not quite ignorant. I am very sorry David has allowed himself to be filmed in these private corners of his life, whatever he feels about it. Publicity can be very cruel. He is famous & well liked & well loved – but there are always those ready to see evil rather than good. Sometimes I feel choked. Sometimes I feel who really cares!! I mean in the world! Of course I care – he is my darling boy & he has been lonely & down & distressed – but he has stood alone!!'[58]

It was hard for Laura, who felt embarrassed by the publicity, and when she went to chapel on Sunday, she was convinced that everyone was staring at her, especially since the pastor, the Reverend Thewliss, gave his sermon on 'The Prodigal Son'. 'In my heart,' she wrote, 'I was running to meet David – oh how I love him!'[59] After the service, Mrs Thewliss tried to reassure her by telling her that the film was not showing in any public cinemas, but only at certain 'clubs' and that she should not worry. When Laura did finally see the film two months later, after it had opened in Bradford in a public cinema, she found it on her first viewing 'a revelation – suppose I am a very slow learner & because my upbringing puritanical – but am eager to learn & to broaden my mind according to the times without lowering my standards and principles'. She went a second time with one of her sisters, writing afterwards, 'If I had not known the people taking part, I don't think I should have been interested – but I felt no qualms about David & saw nothing "awful". He I suppose lives a very different life to ours – but I can accept it & only pray that my boy keeps clean & good as he is always to us. I have learned to accept the world & our beliefs in a broader way & realize how much more our children have gained knowledge & understanding more than ever we did.' Kenneth held no such enlightened views when he delivered his verdict. 'It was just "muck",' he told her, adding that David should 'get some different friends'.[60]

Hockney's drawings of Evans in Rome were shown in Paris in April, at the Galerie Claude Bernard, in the Rue des Beaux Arts. Claude Bernard, a wealthy dealer who represented Francis Bacon in Paris, loved stars, and had seen at once that having Hockney in his stable would bring a lot of kudos to his gallery. His first show, *David Hockney: Dessins et Gravures*, consisted of thirty-one drawings and thirteen etchings, including many sketches of Yves-Marie Hervé and Gregory Evans, portraits of Kenneth and Laura Hockney, Man Ray and Douglas Cooper, several studies of Henry Geldzahler, including one of him nude, and a number of drawings of Celia Birtwell, which also included two nude and one semi-nude study. 'I think the nudes were done in Philippe de Rothschild's house outside Paris,' she recalls. 'I posed nude for him there, which is something that my mother said you should never do.'[61]

The show was a triumph, a dazzling demonstration of technique that proved that when it came to draughtsmanship, there were few artists to touch Hockney. Among them all was one nude study of Evans, drawn in coloured crayon, which brings out a touching vulnerability in his character. 'His coloured drawings were very hard to sit for,' Evans says, 'because they could take two or three days. To begin with it is seductive, and you feel flattered. Then reality sets in, when you think about how many times your leg goes numb, or your arm goes, or you're drifting off to sleep. I've never said no, not now, which is probably my own vanity. David can be overwhelming, because in the end it is the David Hockney show, and that's the way things are.'[62]

At Glyndebourne, they were working overtime to turn Hockney's vision into reality. 'Unfortunately, David got all the measurements completely wrong,' George Christie remembers. 'We were using imperial measurements at that time, and he was using metric, so it was a real nightmare to begin with, because nothing fitted properly and we had to translate everything.'[63] When the first set was finally installed, Hockney came down to take a look. 'When he saw the opening scene, he simply couldn't believe that all the cross-hatching, when brought into the theatre in a magnified state compared with his small drawings, came out completely right. He was in absolute awe. He didn't believe they would translate so perfectly and just stared at it absolutely enthralled and bemused that people could do this. It was a skill that he was completely unaware of, and as soon as he saw what was going on, he became fascinated and very involved in the whole process, and started painting some of the props himself.'[64]

Though Hockney took terrific pride in what he was doing, he also welcomed the input and experience of the other departments. 'An example of this,' Christie recalls, 'was when the wig department didn't get a clear picture from him as to what he wanted so far as the wigs were concerned. So they then decided that they would do some multicoloured string wigs, where you take different-coloured strands of wool and knit them together so you get a kind of Neapolitan ice cream of a result. They did this using quite sturdy pieces of string, which, when all put together, formed the wig. David looked at this and he was absolutely in heaven. He adored this inventiveness.'[65] John Cox concurs that the cohesion on this production was tremendous. 'It is impossible to exaggerate the genius of David's work in this, but of course I brought it to life, so it was a perfect convergence of talents and ideas. He was never dismissive of ideas. What David gave us in the model, and what we then adapted so that it would fit this stage, was of a very powerful integrity, but it did give room to move, and that was very important, and he was very keen on that. He was keen on the idea of collaboration, which nobody expected.'[66] All through the month of June, Hockney worked onstage at Glyndebourne helping to put the finishing touches to the production. He was completely engaged in the process, even to the point where he put his camera down. 'I did not take a great number of photographs,' he wrote, 'partly because there was a lot of work in putting on the production, and also because in taking photographs you'd have to somehow isolate yourself from the production work: you can't bother too much with the camera, your loyalty is to the theatre production.'[67]

The opening night of *The Rake's Progress*, 21 June 1975, Midsummer Night, was a never-to-be-forgotten occasion. The master of ceremonies was Peter Langan, who devised an evening of eating and drinking that would meet the demands of any rake. It was agreed with the Christies, though it had never happened before, that Langan would be allowed to take over the whole of Glyndebourne's front lawn, where he would set up long tables and chairs. 'The first thing I remember about the incredible event of the opening night,' John Cox recalls, 'was that we dress-rehearsed the dinner, because Peter didn't want anything to go wrong . . . He arrived with some extraordinary food and a few tables and chairs and some assistants to whom he gave instructions, and they shared ideas and so on. It was very, very carefully planned.'

Langan stage-managed the evening and Hockney cast it, with a glamorous cross section of friends from his past. His parents were not included, having attended the dress rehearsal on 19 June which Laura described as having been 'thrilling and lovely'. On the first night everyone gathered outside Odin's, where a coach was awaiting them. There was champagne on the bus, which got everybody into high spirits, while Tony Rudenko, a friend of Wayne Sleep's, handed out LSD to any takers, including the brewing heiress Henrietta Guinness. It was a perfect balmy June evening, and when the coach arrived and the guests spilled out onto the lawns, they were met with a fairy-tale scene. 'Peter had made a table along the length of the Glyndebourne ha-ha,' George Lawson remembers, 'and put silver candlesticks and cut flowers on it with a white linen tablecloth. It was a wonderful sight.'[68]

Fuelled on champagne, Hockney's guests joined the rest of the audience in the auditorium for curtain-up, and the excitement was palpable. 'The audience was gung-ho for it,' John Cox says, 'and it wasn't just David's friends. We all had people down, who were determined to make the evening history, and that made a marvellous core of response. The whole thing had an incredible buzz and brio to it.'[69] When they filed out of the theatre for the dinner interval, the bacchanalian scene included handsome Cuban waiters handing out more champagne and the tables now groaning with food. The cover of each menu had a Hockney drawing of Langan and his French wine merchant, together with the words 'An Evening of Excess'. 'The picnic was supposed to be for about thirty people,' recalls Hockney, 'but

Peter took 120 bottles of champagne and none went back. I did point out to him, "That's four bottles each, Peter!" The food was fantastic — enormous lobsters, best hams, marvellous smoked salmon — he knew where to get the good stuff. It was spectacular.'[70]

Not everybody managed to make the second half. Henrietta Guinness, for one, high on LSD, was found head down in a flower bed, and Peter Langan was later scooped out of the ha-ha. For those who did, it was a triumph. Spirits were high as the curtain came down at about nine thirty, the applause was long and loud, and Hockney was beside himself with excitement. 'At the end,' George Lawson recalls, 'David came up to me and said, "Well, George, what did you think of *my* opera?" I replied, "Well, David the *music* is so wonderful," and I just shut my eyes. He loved that and I heard him going round saying, "Did you hear what George said?"'[71] At that point the party was by no means over. There was still so much food and drink it was decided to invite the whole company to join the celebrations. Even the few stragglers left from the audience, who were quite bemused coming upon the scene, joined in and as the sun set everyone got stuck into the banquet as if they'd never seen such a spread in all their lives. It made Hockney the hero of the company for weeks after. 'So we watched the sun setting,' he remembers, 'and then the moon came up so bright that it cast shadows on the lawn. We were there till after midnight, when we took it all away, back on the bus, and there was more champagne on the bus, and even buckets for people to throw up in. Peter had just assumed quite rightly that people would be in that state. We got back to Odin's about 3 a.m., where there were waiters with more champagne on trays.'[72]

Only one person missed this great event, and that was Mo McDermott, who was in a drying-out clinic. He wasn't forgotten, however — Hockney made sure that his name was on the drop curtain along with those of the composer, the librettists, the director and himself.

The reviews for *The Rake's Progress* were mixed. William Mann, writing in *The Times*, thought it 'more Hockney than Hogarth', but considered his approach 'even while stealing prime attention . . . well suited to the icy artificiality and mannered wit of the Auden–Kallman libretto and the emotional pendulum of Stravinsky's music; and it makes an ideal background for John Cox's scrupulously characterized and timed production.'[73] The *New Statesman*'s critic, Bayan Northcott, found it 'very good indeed. In his own butterfly way, David Hockney . . . slants the given rather than inventing from scratch. Almost every detail of his sets and costumes can be found somewhere in Hogarth's engravings, a medium further evoked in the printer's ink colours and ubiquitous cross-hatchings – even down to the wigs.' He ended his review with the words 'Stravinsky would surely have approved'.[74]

Rodney Milne, however, writing in the *Spectator*, hated it, and began his review: 'By the end of the evening I was so out of sympathy with the new production of *The Rake's Progress* . . . that I asked my Aunt Jennifer, who came as my guest, to write the notice.'[75] There followed a pastiche review by this imaginary aunt. 'It was a lovely warm evening as we motored down, and we arrived in good time to walk round the gardens, which were looking simply gorgeous. It was Midsummer's Night, of course, and one half expected to see fairies popping out of their little holes and gambolling around the shrubbery. I was terribly excited to see so many people from that picture about David Hockney . . . I recognized that nice-looking Peter Something-or-other, the co-star, wearing a white suit . . . there was Celia Birtwistle looking radiant (I'm told she absolutely *loved* the opera) . . . Then there was that New York art dealer with the beard, Henry Kissinger, I think . . . and Udo Keir, who is the new Warhol superstar . . . Just before we went in, we passed a pretty gel who seemed a bit under the weather. Someone thought she'd tripped over, but I expect she'd taken something that didn't agree with her . . . Rodney says I must mention the opera. He thinks it's a precious pastiche, as pointless as it is puerile, but he will get carried away with alliteration.'[76]

Though the early performances of *The Rake's Progress* were slow to sell out, it wasn't long before it became the hottest ticket of the season. Hockney felt a little wistful when the first night was over. 'I enjoyed it enormously especially the last three weeks,' he wrote to John Cox from Fort William in Scotland, where he had gone for a short holiday

with Henry Geldzahler, 'watching it all grow and take shape. I loved
the performance; – the acting the singing the orchestra, and even my
bit . . . I told you I felt sad last Saturday as for me it had all ended
. . .'[77] He did have something to look forward to, however: before the
first performance was over, John Cox had already asked if he might be
interested in collaborating on a future *Magic Flute*.

For Hockney, *The Rake's Progress* was a dazzling success, opening up
a whole new artistic world in which he could employ his talents. More
importantly, being able to run riot with his imagination had released
him from the rut in which he perceived himself to have got stuck.
'Suddenly I realised I'd found a way to move into another area. In a
sense I'd broken my previous attitudes about space and naturalism,
which had been bogging me down. I'd found areas to step into which
were fascinating: the space of the theatre. It also helped that it was a
success, both critically and with the audiences . . . I then went back to
Paris and started painting.'[78]

Hockney returned to Paris on a positive note, with the applause
for *The Rake's Progress* still ringing in his ears. He felt energized. The
trials and tribulations of the previous few years – his break-up with
Peter Schlesinger, the problems with Ossie Clark, the spectre of Jack
Hazan's *A Bigger Splash*, and his struggles with how to move forward
in his painting – were behind him. He had a new, happy relationship
with Gregory Evans, and his faith in his work had returned: inspired by
John Kirby's eighteenth-century book *The Perspective of Architecture* he
now started a new picture, *Kerby (After Hogarth)*, in which, for the first
time, he played with the idea of reverse perspective. His willingness to
experiment with new ideas was undimmed. Ahead lay a time of great
excitement.

NOTES

CHAPTER ONE
MY PARENTS
(Appearing between pages 1 and 25)

1 *Bright Day*, J. B. Priestley, Heinemann 1946
2 *Yorkshire: West Riding*, Lettice Cooper, Robert Hale, 1950
3 *Brotherhood and Democracy*, William Ward, a pamphlet published by the Brotherhood Publishing House, 1910
4 *Bright Day*, op. cit.
5 Interview with Laura Hockney by John Hockney
6 Ibid.
7 Ibid.
8 Ibid.
9 Ibid.
10 Interview with DH, June 2009.
11 *Postscript*, a radio talk, J. B. Priestley, 29 September 1940
12 Interview with DH, June 2009
13 Interview with Paul Hockney, June 2009
14 Interview with Philip Hockney, August, 2010
15 Ibid.
16 Interview with DH, June 2009
17 Interview with Laura Hockney by John Hockney
18 Interview with Margaret Hockney, June 2009
19 *Postscript*, op. cit.
20 Interview with DH, June 2009
21 *David Hockney: My Early Years*, David Hockney, Thames & Hudson, 1976, p. 28
22 Interview with DH, June 2009
23 Interview with John Hockney, August 2010
24 Interview with DH, June 2009
25 Ibid.
26 Interview with Margaret Hockney, June 2009
27 Interview with DH, June 2009
28 Ibid.
29 Ibid.
30 Ibid.
31 *That's the Way I See It*, David Hockney, Thames & Hudson, 1993 pp. 11–12
32 Interview with DH, June 2009
33 Ibid.
34 Ibid.
35 Wellington Road School Reports, Hockney Archive, Bridlington
36 Ibid.
37 Ibid.
38 Ibid.
39 *A World to Build: Austerity Britain 1945–48*, David Kynaston, Bloomsbury, 2008, p. 28
40 Diary of Laura Hockney
41 Interview with DH, June 2009
42 Ibid.
43 Information from Mike Powell, a fellow pupil
44 Bradford Grammar school report, 21 December 1948
45 *David Hockney: My Early Years*, op. cit., p. 29
46 Interview with DH, June 2009
47 Letter from R. B. Graham to Kenneth Hockney, 11 March 1950, Hockney Archive, Bridlington

CHAPTER TWO
SELF-PORTRAIT
(Appearing between pages 26 and 54)

1   Letter from R. B. Graham to Kenneth Hockney, 21 March 1950, Hockney Archive, Bridlington

2   Letter from A. Spalding to Kenneth Hockney, 5 April 1950, Hockney Archive, Bridlington

3   Interview with DH, February 2010

4   *David Hockney: My Early Years*, David Hockney, Thames & Hudson, 1976, p. 29

5   Bradford Grammar school report, 21 December 1950

6   Interview with DH, February 2010

7   Bradford Grammar school report, 27 July 1951

8   Interview with Laura Hockney, January 1973

9   Interview with DH, February 2010

10 *Family Britain 1951–1957*, David Kynaston, Bloomsbury, 2009, p. 545

11 Interview with Philip Naylor, October 2009

12 Diary of Laura Hockney

13 Interview with DH, February 2010

14 Information from Mike Powell

15 Diary of Laura Hockney

16 Ibid.

17 *Portrait of David Hockney*, Peter Webb, Chatto & Windus, 1988, p. 8.

18 Bradford Grammar school report, 24 July 1953

19 Interview with DH, February 2010

20 Ibid., June 2009

21 Interview with Laura Hockney by John Hockney

22 Interview with DH, May 2006

23 Ibid., February 2010

24 Interview with Dave Oxtoby, February 2010

25 *David Hockney: My Early Years*, op. cit., p. 34

26 Interview with DH, February 2010

27 Ibid.

28 Ibid.

29 Ibid.

30 Ibid.

31 Anecdote told in 'Special Effects', Anthony Bailey, *New Yorker*, 30 July 1979

32 Memoir by John Hockney, February 2010

33 *David Hockney: My Early Years*, op. cit., p. 34

34 Interview with Derek Stafford, February 2010

35 *The Forgotten Fifties*, Exhibition Catalogue, Graves Art Gallery, Sheffield, 1984, p. 46

36 *Encounter*, December 1954

37 Interview with Derek Stafford, February 2010

38 Ibid.

39 Interview with DH, February 2010

40 Interview with Derek Stafford, February 2010

41 Interview with DH, February 2010

42 Interview with John Loker, February 2010

43 Interview with Derek Stafford, February 2010

44 Interview with DH, February 2010

45 Diary of Laura Hockney

46 *David Hockney Portraits*, Exhibition Catalogue, National Portrait Gallery, 2006, p. 26

47 Interview with Dave Oxtoby, February 2010

48 *David Hockney: My Early Years*, op. cit., p. 34

49 Interview with DH, February 2010

50 Interview with Philip Naylor, October 2009

51 Ibid.

52 Interview with Dave Oxtoby, February 2010

53 Interview with Derek Stafford, February 2010

54 Information from Mike Powell

55 Interview with DH, February 2010

56 Ibid.

57 *David Hockney: My Early Years*, op. cit., p. 39

58 Memoir by John Hockney, February 2010

59 Diary of Laura Hockney

60 Interview with Laura Hockney, January 1973

61 *David Hockney: My Early Years*, op. cit., p. 39

62 Interview with DH, October 2009

63 *David Hockney: My Early Years*, op. cit., p. 38

64 Interview with Paul Hockney, October 2009

65 Interview with Derek Stafford, February 2010

66 Interview with Dave Oxtoby, February 2010

67 Interview with Derek Stafford, February 2010

68 Interview with Dave Oxtoby, February 2010

69 Diary of Laura Hockney

70 Letter to DH from RCAB, 4 March 1957, Hockney Archives, Bridlington

71 Interview with DH, February 2010

72 Interview with Derek Boshier, March 2010

73 Interview with DH, February 2010

CHAPTER THREE
DOLL BOY
(Appearing between pages 55 and 84)

1 *Writing Home*, Alan Bennett, Faber & Faber, 1994, p. 227

2 Interview with John Loker, March 2010

3 Ibid.

4 Ibid.

5 Interview with DH, March 2010

6 Interview with John Loker, March 2010

7 Ibid.

8 *The Parting Years: Diaries, 1963–74*, Cecil Beaton, Weidenfeld & Nicolson, 1978, p. 400

9 Quoted in 'Special Effects', Anthony Bailey, *New Yorker*, 30 July 1979

10 Interview with DH, March 2010

11 Quote from a letter written to John Hockney by Audrey Raistrick, 30 August 2002

12 Interview with John Hockney, May 2010

13 Interview with John Loker, March 2010

14 Letter from DH to his parents, Hockney Archives, Bridlington

15 Ibid.

16 Interview with John Loker, March 2010

17 *The Royal College of Art*, Christopher Frayling, Barrie & Jenkins, 1987, p. 137

18 Ibid., p. 132

19 Ibid., p. 133

20 Letter from DH to his parents, 3 October 1959, Hockney Archive, Bridlington

21 Interview with DH, April 2010

22 Interview with Roddy Maude-Roxby, July 2010

23 Interview with Allen Jones, May 2010

24 *The Last of England*, Derek Jarman, Constable, 1987, p. 46

25 Interview with DH, April 2010

26 Ibid.

27 Interview with Allen Jones, May 2010

28 *David Hockney: A Retrospective*, LACMA / Thames and Hudson, 1988, Introduction by R. B. Kitaj

29 Interview with Allen Jones, May 2010

30 *David Hockney: My Early Years*, David Hockney, Thames & Hudson, 1976, p. 41

31 *Jackson Pollock: Meaning and Significance*, Claude Cernuschi, Icon Editions, 1992, p. 129

32 'The Quest for Fulfilment', Ken Martin, *Observer* magazine, 16 March 1969

33 Interview with DH, April 2010

34 *David Hockney: My Early Years*, op. cit., p. 41

35 'The Quest for Fulfilment', op. cit.

36 Interview with DH, May 2010

37 *David Hockney: My Early Years*, op. cit., p. 41

38 Interview with Adrian Berg, May 2010

39 Interview with DH, May 2010

40 Ibid.

41 *David Hockney: My Early Years*, op. cit., p. 42

42 Interview with Allen Jones, May 2010

43 Ibid.

44 Ibid.

45 *David Hockney: My Early Years*, op. cit., p. 63

46 Ibid.

47 Interview with DH, May 2010
48 Ibid.
49 Interview with Mark Berger, April 2010
50 Ibid.
51 Interview with DH, May 2010
52 *David Hockney: My Early Years*, op. cit., p. 44
53 Ibid., p. 62
54 Ibid., p. 68
55 *Not Drowning, But Waving*, Peter Adam, André Deutsch, 1995, p. 207
56 Interview with Derek Boshier, March 2010.
57 *David Hockney: My Early Years*, op. cit., p. 64

58 Interview with Keith Howes, *Gay News*, August 1976
59 Interview with Mark Berger, April 2010
60 Interview with DH, February 2010
61 Ibid.
62 Interview with Allen Jones, May 2010
63 *Listener*, 16 February 1961
64 *David Hockney: My Early Years*, op. cit., p. 42
65 Interview with DH, April 2010
66 The real title of this painting was *Adhesiveness*.
67 *The Parting Years: Diaries, 1963–74*, op. cit., p. 400

CHAPTER FOUR
'WE TWO BOYS CLINGING TOGETHER'
(Appearing between pages 85 and 112)

1   Interview with John Kasmin, May 2010
2   *London Calling*, Barry Miles, Atlantic Books, 2010, p. 78
3   Interviewed in *Kasmin*, a film by Henry Herbert.
4   Interview with John Kasmin, May 2010
5   Ibid.
6   Ibid.
7   Ibid.
8   Ibid.
9   'The Kasmin Gallery', Lisa Tickner, *Oxford Art Journal*, Vol. 30, No. 2, see note 20
10 Interview with John Kasmin, May 2010
11 Interview with Jane Kasmin, July 2010
12 Interview with John Kasmin, May 2010
13 Interview with Derek Boshier, March 2010
14 *David Hockney: My Early Years*, David Hockney, Thames & Hudson, 1976, p. 43
15 Interview with Mark Berger, April 2010
16 *Portrait of David Hockney*, Peter Webb, Chatto & Windus, 1988, p. 35
17 Interview with DH, May 2010
18 Interview with Mary Fedden, November 2008
19 Letter from DH to MB, 28 May 1961. Quoted in *Portrait of David Hockney*, Peter Webb, Chatto & Windus, p. 40

20 See *Canberra's First Trip*, www.britishpathe.com
21 Letter from DH to Hockney family, 4 May 1961, the Hockney Archive, Bridlington
22 Letter from DH to Laura Hockney, June 1961, the Hockney Archive, Bridlington
23 Interview with DH, May 2010
24 Interview with Mark Berger, April 2010
25 Letter from DH to Hockney family, 19 July 1961, the Hockney Archive, Bridlington
26 Interview with Mark Berger, April 2010
27 Interview with DH, May 2010
28 Letter from DH to RBK, August 1961, R. B. Kitaj Papers, UCLA Research Library, 1741/Box 59/F.17
29 Letter from the RCA registrar to Fred Colecough, 3 November 1961, RCA Archives, RCA, London
30 Interview with Grey Gowrie, October 2010
31 *David Hockney: My Early Years*, op. cit., p. 66
32 Interview with John Kasmin, June 2010
33 Ibid.
34 Interview with DH, May 2010
35 Ibid.
36 Letter from the RCA registrar to Fred Colecough, 3 November 1961, RCA Archives, RCA, London

37 Interview with Derek Boshier, March 2010

38 Interview with DH, May 2010

39 *David Hockney: My Early Years*, op. cit., p. 87

40 *Patrick Proctor: Art and Life*, Ian Massey, Unicorn Press, 2010, p. 41

41 'Beautiful or Interesting', *Art & Literature*, No. 5, Summer 1964

42 *David Hockney: My Early Years*, op. cit., p. 67

43 *The Times*, 13 February 1962

44 'David Hockney, 1960–1965', Mark Glazebrook, Mark Glazebrook Papers

45 Interview with DH, May 2010

46 *David Hockney: My Early Years*, op. cit., p. 88

47 'Words in Pictures', Charles Ingham, University of Essex, 1986, p. A85

48 *New Statesman*, 16 March 1962

49 Story told to author by Roddy Maude-Roxby, July 2010

50 Interview with DH, May, 2010

51 Letter from J. Moon to F. Coleclough, RCA Archives, RCA, London

52 Interview with DH, May 2010

53 Diary of Laura Hockney

54 Ibid.

55 Ibid.

56 *Sex and Violence, Death and Silence*, Gordon Burn, Faber & Faber, 2009, p. 16

57 *The Royal College of Art*, Christopher Frayling, Barrie & Jenkins, 1987, p. 164

58 *Town* magazine, September 1962

59 Diary of Laura Hockney

60 Interview with Roddy Maude-Roxby, July 2010

61 Diary of Laura Hockney

62 Ibid.

CHAPTER FIVE
MAN IN A MUSEUM
(Appearing between pages 113 and 139)

1 Interview with DH, August 2010

2 Interview with Mark Berger, April 2010

3 Interview with DH, August 2010

4 'Beautiful or Interesting', *Art & Literature*, No. 5, Summer 1964

5 Interview with Grey Gowrie, October 2010

6 Interview with John Kasmin, August 2010

7 DH to Paul Hockney, April 1961

8 *Image in Progress*, Exhibition Catalogue, Grabowski Gallery, London, August 1962

9 'David Hockney: A Note in Progress', Guy Brett, *London Magazine*, April 1963

10 *David Hockney: My Early Years*, David Hockney, Thames & Hudson, 1976, p. 89

11 Interview with DH, July 2010

12 Interview with John Kasmin, July 2010

13 Interview with Anne Graves, September 2010

14 Ibid.

15 Interview with DH, July 2010

16 Ibid.

17 *David Hockney: My Early Years*, op. cit., p. 89

18 Interview with Mark Berger, October 2009

19 *David Hockney: My Early Years*, op. cit., p. 90

20 'Hockney Abroad: A Slide Show', Henry Geldzahler, *Art in America*, February 1981

21 *David Hockney: My Early Years*, op. cit., p. 90

22 Diary of Laura Hockney

23 Interview with DH, August 2010

24 Interview with John Kasmin, August 2010

25 *David Hockney: My Early Years*, op. cit., p. 92

26 Ibid., p. 93

27 Interview with DH, August 2010

28 Diary of Laura Hockney

29 Quoted in *The Pearl of Days: An Intimate Memoir of the Sunday Times*, Harold Hobson, Phillip Knightley and Leonard Russell, Hamish Hamilton, 1972, p. 350

30 Quoted by Mark Amory on the British Cartoon Archive, www.cartoons.ac.uk/artists/markboxer

31 *Editor-in-chief*, Sir Denis Hamilton, Hamish Hamilton, 1989, p. 108

32 Ibid., p. 110

33 'Roy's Coloured Baby', Francis Williams, *New Statesman*, 29 February 1962

34 'British Painting Now', David Sylvester, *Sunday Times* magazine, 2 June 1963

35 'The Point is in Actual Fact', *Ark*, No. 10, 1967

36 Diary of Laura Hockney

37 Ibid.

38 Interview with DH, September 2010

39 *The Life and Death of Andy Warhol*, Victor Bockris, Fourth Estate, 1998, p. 139

40 Interview with DH, September 2010

41 Interview with Paul Cornwall-Jones, October 2010

42 *David Hockney: My Early Years*, op. cit., p. 92

43 Ibid., p. 94

44 *Groovy Bob*, Harriet Vyner, Faber & Faber, 1999, p. 70

45 'The Kasmin Gallery', Lisa Tickner, *Oxford Art Journal*, 2007, Vol. 30. No. 2

46 Ibid., note 41, Kasmin to John Russell, 9 July 1962

47 Ibid., Kasmin to Clement Greenberg, 29 May 1963

48 *Private Eye*, 2 May 1963

49 Diary of Laura Hockney

50 *David Hockney: My Early Years*, op. cit., p. 94

51 Interview with DH, August 2010

52 Diary of Laura Hockney

53 *Editor-in-chief*, op. cit., p. 387

54 Diary of Laura Hockney

55 Interview with John Kasmin, November 2010

56 Ibid., August 2010

57 Letter from Peter Bird to John Kasmin, 9 December 1963, Kasmin Gallery Papers. Getty Centre, Los Angeles, CA

58 *Sunday Telegraph*, 1 December 1963

59 *Sunday Times*, 15 December 1963

60 *Listener*, 19 December 1963

61 *Spectator*, 20 December 1963

62 Diary of Laura Hockney

63 Ibid.

64 Interview with DH, August 2010

65 *Self Portrait with Friends: The Selected Diaries of Cecil Beaton, 1926–74*, Richard Buckle (ed.), Weidenfeld & Nicolson, 1979

66 Diary of Laura Hockney

67 Ibid.

68 Interview with John Kasmin, August 2010

CHAPTER SIX
A HOLLYWOOD COLLECTION
(Appearing between pages 140 and 168)

1   *The Ossie Clark Diaries*, Lady Henrietta Rous (ed.), Bloomsbury, 1998, p. xviii

2   Interview with DH, August 2010

3   *City of Night*, John Rechy, Grove Press, 1963, p. 100

4   Interview with DH, September 2010

5   *Los Angeles Art Community: Group Portrait*, Oliver Andrews Oral History Transcript, 1977, p. 102, UCLA Library Centre for Oral History Research

6   *David Hockney: My Early Years*, David Hockney, Thames & Hudson, 1976, p. 94

7   *Big Table: 3*, Periodical Publications, Chicago, 1959–60

8   *David Hockney: My Early Years*, op. cit., p. 97

9   Interview with DH, September 2010

10 Ibid.

11 *David Hockney: My Early Years*, op. cit., p. 97

12 'Hockney Abroad: A Slide Show', Henry Geldzahler, *Art in America*, February 1981, p. 132

13 *Listener*, 22 May 1975

14 Interview with DH, August 2010

15 *David Hockney: My Early Years*, op. cit., p. 125

16 'Monday Night on La Cienega', *Time* magazine, 26 July 1963
17 Interview with DH, September 2010
18 Interview with Jack Larson, September 2010
19 Interview with Don Bachardy, September 2010
20 Ibid.
21 *David Hockney: My Early Years*, op. cit., p. 98
22 Interview with John Kasmin, September 2010
23 Ibid.
24 Ibid.
25 Interview with DH, September 2010
26 *David Hockney: My Early Years*, op. cit., p. 99
27 Interview with DH, September 2010
28 *David Hockney: My Early Years*, op. cit., p. 68
29 Interview with John Kasmin, August 2010
30 Ibid.
31 Interview with DH, September 2010
32 Ibid.
33 *Beaton in the Sixties*, Hugo Vickers (ed.), Weidenfeld & Nicolson, 2003, p. 26
34 Interview with DH, September 2010
35 *The Ossie Clark Diaries*, op. cit., p. lviii
36 Interview with DH, September 2010
37 *The Ossie Clark Diaries*, op. cit.. p. lviii
38 Interview with DH, September 2010
39 Interview with Derek Boshier, September 2010
40 Interview with Celia Birtwell, November 2010
41 Diary of Laura Hockney
42 *David Hockney: My Early Years*, op. cit., p. 100
43 Ibid.
44 Ibid.
45 Interview with DH, September 2010
46 *Self Portrait*, Patrick Procktor, Weidenfeld & Nicolson, 1991, p. 85
47 Interview with DH, September 2010
48 *Self Portrait*, op. cit., p. 85
49 *David Hockney: My Early Years*, op. cit., p. 101
50 Interview with DH, September 2010
51 *Self Portrait*, op. cit., p. 89
52 Interview with DH, September 2010
53 *Self Portrait*, op. cit., p. 90
54 Interview with DH, September 2010
55 Ibid.
56 *Portrait of David Hockney*, Peter Webb, Chatto & Windus, 1988, p. 72
57 Ibid.
58 *David Hockney: My Early Years*, op. cit., p. 102
59 Interview with John Kasmin, November 2010
60 *The Times*, 9 December 1965
61 *London Magazine*, 5 January 1966
62 *Studio International*, January 1966
63 *New Statesman*, 10 December 1965
64 Diary of Laura Hockney
65 Ibid.

CHAPTER SEVEN
IN THE DULL VILLAGE
(Appearing between pages 169 and 184)

1 *Sunday Times*, Atticus, 9 January 1966
2 Diary of Laura Hockney
3 *David Hockney: My Early Years*, David Hockney, Thames & Hudson, 1976, p. 159
4 *The Times*, 7 March 1958
5 *White Heat: A History of Britain in the Swinging Sixties*, Dominic Sandbrook, Little, Brown, 2006, p. 320
6 *The Roy Strong Diaries: 1967–1987*, Roy Strong, Weidenfeld & Nicolson, 1997, p. 35
7 *Dictionary of National Biography*
8 *The Essential Cavafy*, K. P. Kavaphēs, Ecco Press, 1995
9 Interview with DH, September 2010
10 Diary of Laura Hockney
11 Interview with DH, September 2010
12 *Dancing Ledge*, Derek Jarman, Quartet, 1984, p. 62
13 *A History of the World in 100 Objects*, Neil MacGregor, Radio 4, 2010

14 *David Hockney: My Early Years*, op. cit., p. 157

15 *The Times*, 3 May 1966

16 Interview with Maurice Payne, February 2011

17 *Fourteen Poems of C. P. Cavafy*, Director James Scott

18 *David Hockney: My Early Years*, op. cit., p. 103

19 *The Fool on the Hill*, Max Wall, Quartet, 1975, p. 226

20 *A Sense of Direction*, William Gaskill, Faber & Faber, 1988, p. 75

21 Diary of Laura Hockney

22 *David Hockney: My Early Years*, op. cit., p. 103

23 Interview with Jack Larson, September 2010

24 'The Fast Life and Artful Times of Nicholas Wilder', William Wilson, *LA Times*, 27 November 1988

25 Interview with DH, September 2010

26 Ibid.

27 Ibid.

28 *A Chequered Past*, Peter Schlesinger, Thames & Hudson, 2004, p. 11

29 Interview with DH, September 2010

30 Interview with Peter Schlesinger, April 2010

31 Interview with Jack Larson, September 2010

32 Interview with Don Bachardy, September 2010

33 *David Hockney*, Marco Livingstone, Thames & Hudson, 1981, p. 103

34 Diary of Laura Hockney, 23 July 1966

35 *The Times*, 22 July 1966

36 Ibid.

37 Ibid.

38 *Listener*, 4 August 1966

39 Ibid.

CHAPTER EIGHT
A BIGGER SPLASH
(Appearing between pages 185 and 210)

1 Interview with DH, December 2010

2 *David Hockney: My Early Years*, David Hockney, Thames & Hudson, 1976, p. 151

3 Ibid., Introduction by Henry Geldzahler, p. 18

4 Interview with DH, December 2010

5 *Portrait of David Hockney*, Peter Webb, Chatto & Windus, 1988, p. 80

6 Interview with DH, December 2010

7 Interview with Peter Schlesinger, April 2010

8 *David Hockney: My Early Years*, op. cit., p. 104

9 Interview with DH, December 2010

10 *David Hockney: My Early Years*, op. cit., p. 124

11 Interview with Peter Schlesinger, April 2010

12 Ibid.

13 *A Chequered Past*, Peter Schlesinger, Thames & Hudson, 2003, p. 15

14 *David Hockney: My Early Years*, op. cit., p. 151

15 Interview with DH, December 2010

16 *David Hockney: My Early Years*, op. cit., p. 124

17 Interview with Peter Schlesinger, April 2010

18 Interview with DH, December 2010

19 *David Hockney: My Early Years*, op. cit., p. 124

20 Interview with DH, December 2010

21 Interview with Peter Schlesinger, April 2010

22 Diary of Laura Hockney

23 Interview with Peter Schlesinger, April 2010

24 Ibid.

25 *The Times*, 22 July 1967

26 *Beaton in the Sixties*, Hugo Vickers (ed.), Weidenfeld & Nicolson, 2003, p. 185

27 Interview with Peter Schlesinger, April 2010

28 Interview with DH, December 2010

29 Interview with Peter Schlesinger, April 2010

30 Interview with DH, September 2010

31 Interview with Peter Schlesinger, April 2010

32 Interview with DH, September 2010

33 *Patrick Procktor: Art and Life*, Ian Massey, Unicorn Press, 2010, p. 125

34 *David Hockney: My Early Years*, op. cit., p. 149

35 Diary of Laura Hockney

36 *The Times*, 26 January 1968

37 *David Hockney: My Early Years*, op. cit., p. 152

38 Ibid.

39 'Special Effects', Anthony Bailey, *New Yorker*, 30 July 1979

40 Ibid.

41 Interview with Don Bachardy, September 2010

42 *The Sixties: Diaries, Volume Two, 1960–1969*, Christopher Isherwood, ed. Katherine Bucknell, Chatto & Windus, 2010

43 *David Hockney: My Early Years*, op. cit., p. 157

44 Interview with Don Bachardy, September 2010

45 *David Hockney: My Early Years*, op. cit., p. 158

46 Ibid.

47 Diary of Laura Hockney

48 Ibid.

49 Interview with Peter Schlesinger, April 2010

50 Ibid.

51 *Precious Little Sleep*, Wayne Sleep, Boxtree, 1996, p. 63

52 *David Hockney: My Early Years*, op. cit., p. 194

53 *David Hockney and His Friends*, Peter Adam, Absolute Press, 1997, p. 81

54 Quoted by Alan Bennett in his review of *Auden in Love*, *London Review of Books*, 23 May 1985

55 *The Long-Distance Runner*, Tony Richardson, Faber & Faber, 1993, p. 203

56 *The Sixties: Diaries, Volume Two, 1960–69*, op. cit., p. 110

57 Ibid., p. 121

58 *Not Drowning, But Waving*, op. cit., p. 294

59 *A Chequered Past*, op. cit., p. 31

60 Interview with Peter Schlesinger, April 2010

61 Interview with Arthur Lambert, February 2011

62 Interview with DH, December 2010

63 'Hockney Abroad: A Slide Show', Henry Geldzahler, *Art in America*, February 1981

64 'Hockney Paints a Portrait', David Shapiro, *Art News*, May 1969

CHAPTER NINE
PETER 1969
(Appearing between pages 211 and 234)

1 Interview with DH, December 2010

2 Ibid.

3 Ibid.

4 *David Hockney: My Early Years*, David Hockney, Thames & Hudson, 1976, p. 193

5 Interview with Benedict Birnberg, February 2011

6 *The Guardian*, 13 December 1968

7 'Special Effects', Anthony Bailey, *New Yorker*, 30 July 1979

8 Interview with DH, December 2010

9 Interview with Benedict Birnberg, February 2011

10 'Hockney Paints a Portrait', David Shapiro, *Art News*, May 1969

11 *David Hockney and His Friends*, Peter Adam, Absolute Press, 1997, p. 83

12 *Portrait of David Hockney*, Peter Webb, Chatto & Windus, 1988, p. 103

13 Interview with Mark Glazebrook in catalogue to 1970 Whitechapel retrospective, p. 15

14 *David Hockney: My Early Years*, op. cit., p. 194

15 Interview with DH, March 2011

16 *David Hockney: My Early Years*, op. cit., p. 158

17 *The Sixties: Diaries, Volume Two, 1960–1969*, Christopher Isherwood, ed. Katherine Bucknell, Chatto & Windus, 2010, p. 503

18 Diary of Laura Hockney

19 Interview with Peter Schlesinger, April 2010

20 Ibid.

21 Interview with DH, December 2010

22 Interview with Peter Schlesinger, April 2010

23 Interview with Celia Birtwell, November 2010

24 *Ossie Clark, 1965–1974*, Judith Wyatt, V&A Publications, 2003, p. 24

25 *The Ossie Clark Diaries*, Lady Henrietta Rous (ed.), Bloomsbury, 1998, p. liii

26 Interview with Celia Birtwell, November 2010

27 Ibid.

28 Ibid.

29 *The Ossie Clark Diaries*, op. cit., p. lxxiii

30 Interview with Melissa North, May 2011

31 *Sex and Violence, Death and Silence*, Gordon Burn, Faber & Faber, 2009, p. 17

32 Interview with DH, December 2010

33 Ibid.

34 Interview with Peter Schlesinger, April 2010

35 Diary of Laura Hockney

36 Interview with John Kasmin, February 2011

37 Interview with Paul Cornwall-Jones, October 2010

38 Interview with Mark Glazebrook in catalogue to 1970 Whitechapel Gallery retrospective

39 Ibid.

40 Interview with Paul Cornwall-Jones, October 2010

41 *David Hockney: My Early Years*, op. cit., p. 202

42 *The Parting Years: Diaries, 1963–74*, Cecil Beaton, Weidenfeld & Nicolson, 1978, p. 399

43 *The Roy Strong Diaries: 1967–1987*, Roy Strong, Weidenfeld & Nicolson, 1997, p. 39

44 *The Parting Years: Diaries, 1963–74*, op. cit., p. 399

45 'The Big Picture', Peter Conrad, *Observer*, 23 May 2010

46 *Self Portrait with Friends: The Selected Diaries of Cecil Beaton, 1926–74*, Richard Buckle (ed.), Weidenfeld & Nicolson, 1979, p. 88

47 Interview with Melissa North, May 2011

48 Interview with Celia Birtwell, November 2010

49 Ibid.

50 Ibid.

51 *The Ossie Clark Diaries*, op. cit., p. lxvii

52 Interview with DH, December 2010

53 *Portrait of David Hockney*, op. cit., p. 110

54 *Journals, 1939–1977*, Keith Vaughan, John Murray, 1989, p. 165

55 *Precious Little Sleep*, Wayne Sleep, Boxtree, 1996, p. 88

56 *David Hockney: My Early Years*, op. cit., p. 202

57 Interview with John Kasmin, February 2011

58 Ibid.

59 Quoted by Nicholas Shakespeare in a review of *City Boy* by Edmund White, *Daily Telegraph*, 9 January 2010

60 *David Hockney*, Marco Livingstone, Thames & Hudson, 1996, p. 119

61 *David Hockney: My Early Years*, op. cit., p. 202

62 Ibid., p. 203

63 Diary of Laura Hockney

64 *The Times*, 2 April 1970

65 *Spectator*, 11 April 1979

66 *Apollo*, April 1970

CHAPTER TEN

MR AND MRS CLARK AND PERCY

(Appearing between pages 235 and 258)

1 *The Ossie Clark Diaries*, op. cit., p. lxvii

2 Interview with DH, March 2011

3 'Celia's Art Works', Chrissy Iley, Daily Mail, 18 November 2006

4 Interview with DH, March 2011

5 *David Hockney: My Early Years*, David Hockney, Thames & Hudson, 1976, p. 203

6 Interview with Peter Schlesinger, April 2010

7 Letter from DH to HG, 7 August 1970, Henry Geldzahler Papers, Beinecke Library, Yale University, New Haven, CT

8 Diary of Laura Hockney

9 Ibid.

10 *David Hockney: Photographs*, David Hockney, Petersburg Press, 1982, p. 12

11 Letter from DH to HG, 17 September 1970, Henry Geldzahler Papers, op. cit.

12 Diary of Laura Hockney

13 Ibid.

14 Ibid.

15 Letter from DH to RBK, 2 January 1970, R. B. Kitaj Papers, UCLA Research Library, Los Angeles, CA

16 Diary of Laura Hockney

17 *Patrick Procktor: Art and Life*, Ian Massey, Unicorn Press, 2010, p. 145

18 *A Life with Food*, Peter Langan, Bloomsbury, 1990, p. 87

19 *Self Portrait with Friends: The Selected Diaries of Cecil Beaton, 1926–74*, Richard Buckle (ed.), Weidenfeld & Nicolson, 1979, p. 166

20 Interview with George Lawson, April 2011

21 Ibid.

22 Ibid.

23 Diary of Laura Hockney

24 Interview with DH, March 2011

25 *David Hockney: My Early Years*, op. cit., p. 204

26 Diary of Laura Hockney

27 Interview with DH, March 2011

28 Letter from DH to HG, 8 March 1971, Henry Geldzahler Papers, op. cit.

29 Interview with Celia Birtwell, November 2010

30 *David Hockney: My Early Years*, op. cit., p. 239

31 Interview with DH, March 2011

32 *The Times*, 24 March 1971

33 *David Hockney*, Marco Livingstone, Thames & Hudson, 1996, op. cit., p. 137

34 'Hockney Abroad: A Slide Show', Henry Geldzhaler, *Art in America*, February 1981, p. 135

35 *David Hockney: My Early Years*, op. cit., p. 241

36 Interview with Jack Hazan, March 2011

37 Ibid.

38 Interview with DH, March 2011

39 Interview with Jack Hazan, March 2011

40 Interview with DH, March 2011

41 Interview with Peter Schlesinger and Eric Boman, February 2011

42 Ibid.

43 *David Hockney: My Early Years*, op. cit., p. 204

44 Interview with DH, March 2011

45 Interview with Arthur Lambert, February 2011

46 Ibid.

47 Interview with Peter Schlesinger, February 2011

48 *Sex and Violence, Death and Silence*, Gordon Burn, Faber & Faber, 2009, p. 18

49 *David Hockney: My Early Years*, op. cit., p. 204

50 Letter from DH to HG, 16 June 1971, Henry Geldzahler Papers, op. cit.

51 Interview with Jack Hazan, March 2011

52 Ibid.

53 *Dancing Ledge*, Derek Jarman, Quartet, 1984, p. 93

54 Letter from DH to HG, 16 June 1971, Henry Geldzahler Papers, op. cit.

55 Diary of Laura Hockney

56 *David Hockney: My Early Years*, op. cit., p. 239

57 Interview with George Lawson, April 2011

58 Interview with Peter Schlesinger and Eric Boman, February 2011

59 Ibid.

60 Ibid.

61 Interview with George Lawson, April 2011

62 Interview with Jack Hazan, March 2011

63 *David Hockney: My Early Years*, op. cit., p. 240

64 Interview with Maurice Payne, February 2011

65 *David Hockney: My Early Years*, op. cit., p. 240

66 Interview with Peter Schlesinger and Eric Boman, February 2011

CHAPTER ELEVEN
PORTRAIT OF AN ARTIST
(Appearing between pages 259 and 284)

1 *David Hockney: My Early Years*, David Hockney, Thames & Hudson, 1976, p. 240
2 Interview with Peter Schlesinger, February 2011
3 *David Hockney*, Marco Livingstone, Thames & Hudson, 1996, p. 147
4 *David Hockney: My Early Years*, op. cit., p. 241
5 'Hockney Abroad: A Slideshow', Henry Geldzhaler, *Art in America*, February 1981
6 *David Hockney: My Early Years*, op. cit., p. 247
7 Ibid.
8 Diary of Laura Hockney
9 Ibid.
10 Letter from DH to HG, 29 October 1971, Henry Geldzhaler Papers, Beinecke Library, Yale University, New Haven, CT
11 Interview with Don Bachardy, September 2010
12 Interview with Jack Larson, September 2010
13 *David Hockney: My Early Years*, op. cit., p. 242
14 Letter from DH to HG, 20 November 1971, Henry Geldzhaler Papers, op. cit.
15 Ibid.
16 Ibid.
17 Letter from DH to RBK, 20 November 1971, R. B. Kitaj Papers, UCLA Research Library, Los Angeles, CA
18 Letter from DH to HG, 20 November 1971, Henry Geldzhaler Papers, op. cit.
19 Ibid.
20 Letter from DH to HG, 23 November 1971, Henry Geldzhaler Papers, op. cit.
21 Ibid., 28 November 1971
22 Ibid.
23 Ibid., 10 December 1971
24 Ibid.
25 Ibid.
26 Ibid.
27 Interview with Peter Schlesinger, February 2011

28 Letter from DH to HG, 15 December 1971, Henry Geldzhaler Papers, op. cit.
29 Ibid.
30 Letter from DH to RBK, 20 November 1971, R. B. Kitaj Papers, op. cit.
31 'Hockney Abroad: A Slide Show', op. cit., p. 137
32 Quoted in 'Special Effects', Anthony Bailey, *New Yorker*, 30 July 1979
33 Ibid.
34 Diary of Laura Hockney
35 *David Hockney: My Early Years*, op. cit., p. 247
36 Ibid.
37 Ibid., p. 248
38 Ibid.
39 *David Hockney: Photographs*, David Hockney, Petersburg Press, 1982, p. 13
40 *David Hockney*, Livingstone, op. cit., pp. 145, 146
41 *David Hockney: My Early Years*, op. cit., p. 248
42 'Hockney Abroad: A Slide Show', op. cit., p. 138
43 Ibid., p. 136
44 *David Hockney: My Early Years*, op. cit., p. 241
45 Ibid., p. 249
46 Ibid.
47 Interview with George Lawson, April 2011
48 *David Hockney: My Early Years*, op. cit., p. 249
49 *David Hockney: Photographs*, op. cit., p. 15
50 'Hockney Abroad: A Slide Show', op. cit., p. 140
51 Diary of Laura Hockney
52 Ibid.
53 Ibid.
54 *David Hockney: My Early Years*, op. cit., p. 249
55 Interview with John Kasmin, March 2011
56 *David Hockney: My Early Years*, op. cit., p. 250
57 Interview with George Lawson, April 2011
58 *David Hockney: My Early Years*, op. cit., p. 250
59 *The Times*, 12 December 1972

60 Interview with John Kasmin, May 2011
61 Letter from DH to RBK, 31 January 1973, R. B. Kitaj Papers, op. cit.
62 Ibid., 24 February 1973
63 Interview with Celia Birtwell, November 2010
64 Ibid.
65 Letter from DH to RBK, 24 February 1973, R. B. Kitaj Papers, op. cit.
66 Interview with DH, March 2011
67 Interview with Celia Birtwell, November 2010
68 Interview with DH, March 2011
69 Letter from DH to RBK, 1 April 1973, R. B. Kitaj Papers, op. cit.
70 'The Fast Life and Artful Times of Nicholas Wilder', William Wilson, *LA Times*, 27 November 1988
71 Interview with Gregory Evans, September 2010
72 Ibid.
73 Ibid.
74 *David Hockney: Photographs*, op. cit., p. 15
75 Letter from DH to RBK, 1 April 1973, R. B. Kitaj Papers, op. cit.
76 *That's the Way I See It*, David Hockney, Thames & Hudson, 1993, p. 16
77 *David Hockney: My Early Years*, op. cit., p. 288
78 *David Hockney: A Retrospective*, LACMA/ Thames & Hudson, 1988, p. 14

CHAPTER TWELVE
CONTRE-JOUR IN THE FRENCH STYLE
(Appearing between pages 285 and 308)

1   Diary of Laura Hockney
2   Letter from DH to HG, 23 April 1973, Henry Geldzahler Papers, Beinecke Library, Yale University, New Haven, CT
3   Ibid.
4   Letter from DH to HG, 4 June 1973, Henry Geldzahler Papers, op. cit.
5   Interview with DH, March 2011
6   Letter from DH to HG, 4 June 1973, Henry Geldzahler Papers, op. cit.
7   Ibid.
8   Interview with DH, March 2011
9   *David Hockney: My Early Years*, David Hockney, Thames & Hudson, 1976, p. 288
10 Ibid., p. 294
11 Interview with DH, March 2011
12 *David Hockney: My Early Years*, op. cit., p. 293
13 Ibid., p. 288
14 Letter from DH to HG, 22 June 1973, Henry Geldzahler Papers, op. cit.
15 *David Hockney: A Retrospective*, LACMA/ Thames & Hudson, 1988, p. 16
16 Letter from DH to HG, 4 June 1973, Henry Geldzahler Papers, op. cit.
17 Ibid., 22 June 1973.
18 Ibid.
19 Letter from DH to his parents, 3 May 1973, Hockney Archive, Bridlington
20 *David Hockney: Photographs*, David Hockney, Petersburg Press, 1982, p. 16
21 Letter from DH to RBK, 15 August 1973, R. B. Kitaj Papers, UCLA Research Library, Los Angeles, CA
22 Letter from DH to his parents, August 1973, Hockney Archive, Bridlington
23 Interview with George Lawson, May 2011
24 *Portrait of David Hockney*, Peter Webb, Chatto & Windus, 1988, p. 131
25 Letter from DH to RBK, 27 August 1973, R. B. Kitaj Papers, op. cit.
26 Ibid.
27 Interview with Celia Birtwell, May 2011
28 Letter from DH to HG, 4 June 1973, Henry Geldzahler Papers, op. cit.

29   Diary of Laura Hockney

30   *The Times*, 5 September 1973

31   *Portrait of David Hockney*, op. cit., p. 132

32   Letter from DH to HG, 27 September 1973, Henry Geldzahler Papers, op. cit.

33   Interview with Celia Birtwell, May 2011

34   Interview with DH, July 2010

35   Ibid.

36   Ibid.

37   Ibid.

38   Letter from DH to HG, 27 September 1973, Henry Geldzahler Papers, op. cit.

39   Ibid., 2 October 1973

40   Ibid.

41   Ibid.

42   *David Hockney and His* Friends, Peter Adam, Absolute Press, 1997, p. 95

43   Letter from DH to HG, 23 October 1973, Henry Geldzahler Papers, op. cit.

44   Interview with DH, May 2011

45   Letter from DH to HG, 23 October 1973, Henry Geldzahler Papers, op. cit.

46   *That's the Way I See It*, David Hockney, Thames & Hudson, 1993, p. 17

47   Interview with Celia Birtwell, May 2011.

48   'Essays in Naturalism', Paul Melia, in *David Hockney: A Drawing Retrospective*, Exhibition Catalogue, Royal Academy of Arts/Thames & Hudson, 1995, p. 144

49   Interview with DH, May 2011

50   Interview with Gregory Evans, September 2010

51   Ibid.

52   Ibid.

53   Interview with Jack Hazan, March 2011

54   Interview with Celia Birtwell, May 2011

55   Interview with DH, March 2011

56   *David Hockney: My Early Years*, op. cit., p. 286

57   *Not Drowning, But Waving*, Peter Adam, André Deutsch, p. 184

58   *Precious Little Sleep*, Wayne Sleep, Boxtree, 1996, p. 65

59   Interview with Celia Birtwell, May 2011

60   *Not Drowning, But Waving*, op. cit., p. 219

61   Interview with Celia Birtwell, May 2011

62   Interview with DH, May 2011

63   Letter from DH to HG, 17 January 1974, Henry Geldzahler Papers, op. cit.

64   Interview with John Kasmin, May 2011

65   Interview with Celia Birtwell, May 2011

66   *That's the Way I See It*, op. cit., p. 19

67   Interview with DH, March 2011

68   'Remembering Douglas Cooper', John Richardson, *New York Review of Books*, 25 April 1985

69   Interview with DH, March 2011

70   Letter from DH to HG, 17 January 1974, Henry Geldzahler Papers, op. cit.

71   Ibid., 15 December 1973

72   Ibid., 17 January 1977

73   *David Hockney. My Early Years*, op. cit., p. 285

74   Letter from DH to HG, 22 February 1974, Henry Geldzahler Papers, op. cit.

75   Ibid.

76   *The Ossie Clark Diaries*, Lady Henrietta Rous (ed.), Bloomsbury, 1998, p. 6

CHAPTER THIRTEEN
THE RAKE'S PROGRESS
(Appearing between pages 309 and 330)

1   Letter from DH to HG, 7 April 1974, Henry Geldzahler Papers, Beinecke Library, Yale University, New Haven, CT

2   Interview with Melissa North, May 2011

3   *The Ossie Clark Diaries*, Lady Henrietta Rous (ed.), Bloomsbury, 1998, p. 9

4   Interview with Jack Hazan, March 2011

5   Letter from DH to HG, 7 April 1974, Henry Geldzahler Papers, op. cit.

6   Ibid.

7 Ibid.

8 Ibid.

9 Interview with Peter Schlesinger, October 2010

10 Letter from DH to HG, 7 April 1974, Henry Geldzahler Papers, op. cit.

11 Interview with Jack Hazan, March 2011

12 Ibid.

13 Ibid.

14 Ibid.

15 *The Times*, 22 May 1974

16 *David Hockney: My Early Years*, David Hockney, Thames & Hudson, 1976, p. 286

17 *David Hockney*, Marco Livingstone, Thames & Hudson, 1996, pp. 172–3

18 Interview with David Hockney, May 2011

19 *That's the Way I See It*, David Hockney, Thames & Hudson, 1993, p. 21

20 Interview with John Cox, March 2011

21 *That's the Way I See It*, op. cit., p. 21

22 *The Times*, 9 July 1974

23 *The Ossie Clark Diaries*, op. cit., p. 26

24 Ibid.

25 Ibid., p. 31

26 Ibid.

27 Ibid., p. 32

28 Interview with Celia Birtwell, May 2011

29 'Special Effects', Anthony Bailey, *New Yorker*, 30 July 1979, p. 68

30 *David Hockney: Tableaux et Dessins*, Exhibition Catalogue, Musée des Arts Decoratifs, Hillingdon Press, 1974, p. 9

31 Ibid., pp. 21–2

32 *The Ossie Clark Diaries*, op. cit., p. 38

33 Interview with DH, May 2011.

34 Interview with John Kasmin, May 2011

35 *The Times*, 17 October 1974

36 Ibid.

37 *The Ossie Clark Diaries*, op. cit., p. 38

38 Ibid., p. 39

39 Ibid.

40 *David Hockney: My Early Years*, op. cit., p. 287

41 Interview with DH, March 2011

42 *Hockney Paints the Stage*, Martin Friedman,

Stephen Spender, John Cox and John Dexter, Thames & Hudson, 1983, p. 100

43 *David Hockney*, Livingstone, op. cit., p. 175

44 Interview with DH, September 2010

45 Ibid., May 2011

46 Ibid., September 2010

47 *That's the Way I See It*, David Hockney, Thames & Hudson, 1993, p. 22

48 Diary of Laura Hockney

49 Ibid.

50 Interview with DH, May 2010

51 *Hockney Paints the Stage*, op. cit., p. 102

52 Interview with DH, September 2010

53 *David Hockney: Photographs*, David Hockney, Petersburg Press, 1982, p. 16

54 Interview with Gregory Evans, September 2010

55 Diary of Laura Hockney

56 Interview with Gregory Evans, September 2010

57 Ibid.

58 Diary of Laura Hockney

59 Ibid.

60 Ibid.

61 Interview with Celia Birtwell, May 2010

62 Interview with Gregory Evans, September 2010

63 Interview with George Christie, May 2011

64 Ibid.

65 Ibid.

66 Interview with John Cox, March 2011

67 *David Hockney: Photographs*, op. cit., p. 18

68 Interview with George Lawson, May 2011

69 Interview with John Cox, March 2011

70 Interview with DH, May 2011

71 Interview with George Lawson, May 2011

72 Interview with DH, May 2011

73 *The Times*, 23 June 1975

74 *New Statesman*, 27 June 1975

75 *Spectator*, 28 June 1975

76 Ibid.

77 Letter from DH to John Cox, June 1975

78 *That's the Way I See It*, op. cit., p. 29

BIBLIOGRAPHY

BOOKS ON DAVID HOCKNEY

Adam, Peter, *David Hockney and His Friends*, Absolute Press, 1997

Evans, Gregory, *Hockney's Pictures*, Thames & Hudson, 2004

Friedman, Martin, Stephen Spender, John Cox and John Dexter, *Hockney Paints the Stage*, Thames & Hudson, 1983

Hockney, David, *David Hockney: My Early Years*, Thames & Hudson, 1976

——, *David Hockney: Photographs*, Petersburg Press, 1982

——, *that's the Way I See It*, Thames & Hudson, 1993

Livingstone, Marco, *David Hockney*, Thames & Hudson, 1996

—— and Kay Heymer, *Hockney's Portraits and People*, Thames & Hudson, 2003

Melia, Paul (ed.), *David Hockney*, Manchester University Press, 1995

Melia, Paul and Ulrich Luckhardt, *David Hockney*, Prestel, 2007

Webb, Peter, *Portrait of David Hockney*, Chatto & Windus, 1988

CATALOGUES

David Hockney: A Drawing Retrospective, Royal Academy of Arts/Thames & Hudson, 1995

David Hockney: Egyptian Journeys, Islamic Art Society, 2002

David Hockney: Paintings, Prints and Drawings, 1960–1970, Foreward by Mark Glazebrook, Whitechapel Gallery, 1970

David Hockney: A Retrospective, LACMA/Thames & Hudson, 1988

David Hockney: Tableaux et Dessins, Musée des Arts Decoratifs, Hillingdon Press, 1974

David Hockney, 1960–1968: A Marriage of Styles, Nottingham Contemporary, 2009

David Hockney Portraits, National Portrait Gallery, 2006

Image in Progress, Exhibition Catalogue, Grabowski Gallery, 1970

GENERAL BACKGROUND

Adam, Peter, *Not Drowning, But Waving*, André Deutsch, 1995

Beaton, Cecil, *The Parting Years: Diaries, 1963–74*, Weidenfeld & Nicolson, 1978

Bennett, Alan, *Writing Home*, Faber & Faber, 1994

Bockris, Victor, *The Life and Death of Andy Warhol*, Fourth Estate, 1998

Buckle, Richard (ed.), *Self Portrait with Friends: The Selected Diaries of Cecil Beaton, 1926–74*, Weidenfeld & Nicolson, 1979

Burn, Gordon, *Sex and Violence, Death and Silence*, Faber & Faber, 2009

Cernuschi, Claude, *Jackson Pollock: Meaning and Significance*, Icon Editions, 1992

Cooper, Lettice, *Yorkshire: West Riding*, Robert Hale, 1950

Dictionary of National Biography

The Forgotten Fifties, Exhibition Catalogue, Graves Art Gallery, Sheffield, 1984

Frayling, Christopher, *The Royal College of Art*, Barrie & Jenkins, 1987

Gaskill, William, *A Sense of Direction*, Faber & Faber, 1988

Hamilton, Sir Denis, *Editor-in-chief*, Hamish Hamilton, 1989

Hobson, Harold, Phillip Knightley and Leonard Russell, *The Pearl of Days: An Intimate Memoir of the Sunday Times*, Hamish Hamilton, 1972

Isherwood, Christopher, *The Sixties: Diaries, Volume Two, 1960–1969*, ed. Katherine Bucknell, Chatto & Windus, 2010

Jarman, Derek, *Dancing Ledge*, Quartet, 1984

——, *The Last of England*, Constable, 1987

Kavaphēs, K. P., *The Essential Cavafy*, Ecco Press, 1995

Kynaston, David, *Family Britain: 1951–57*, Bloomsbury, 2009

——, *A World to Build: Austerity Britain 1945–48*, Bloomsbury, 2008

Langan, Peter, *A Life with Food*, Bloomsbury, 1990

Lister, Derek, *Bradford Born and Bred*, Bank House Books, 2008

Massey, Ian, *Patrick Procktor: Art and Life*, Unicorn Press, 2010

Miles, Barry, *London Calling*, Atlantic Books, 2010

Priestley, J. B., *Bright Day*, Heinemann, 1946

Procktor, Patrick, *Self Portrait*, Weidenfeld & Nicolson, 1991

Rechy, John, *City of Night*, Grove Press, 1963

Richardson, John, *The Sorcerer's Apprentice*, Jonathan Cape, 1999

Richardson, Tony, *The Long-Distance Runner*, Faber & Faber, 1993

Rous, Lady Henrietta (ed.), *The Ossie Clark Diaries*, Bloomsbury, 1998

Sandbrook, Dominic, *White Heat: A History of Britain in the Swinging Sixties*, Little, Brown, 2006

Schlesinger, Peter, *A Chequered Past*, Thames & Hudson, 2003

Sleep, Wayne, *Precious Little Sleep*, Boxtree, 1996

Strong, Roy, *The Roy Strong Diaries: 1967–1987*, Weidenfeld & Nicolson, 1997

Vaughan, Keith, *Journals, 1939–1977*, John Murray, 1989

Vickers, Hugo (ed.), *Beaton in the Sixties*, Weidenfeld & Nicolson, 2003

Vyner, Harriet, *Groovy Bob*, Faber & Faber, 1999

Wall, Max, *The Fool on the Hill*, Quartet, 1975

Ward, William, *Brotherhood and Democracy*, a pamphlet published by the Brotherhood Publishing House, 1910

Wyatt, Judith, *Ossie Clark, 1965–1974*, V&A Publications, 2003

ARCHIVES

Hockney Archive, Bridlington

Hockney Archive, Los Angeles, CA

Henry Geldzahler Papers, Beinecke Library, Yale University, New Haven, CT

Mark Glazebrook Papers, London

Kasmin Gallery Papers, the Getty Centre, Los Angeles, CA

R. B. Kitaj Papers, UCLA Research Library, Los Angeles, CA

RCA Archives, RCA, London

INDEX

Figures in italics indicate captions. 'DH' indicates David Hockney.

100 Club, Oxford Street, London
  193
ABK 131
Abse, Leo 171
abstract expressionism 68, 82, 128,
  152, 233
Academy Cinema, Oxford Street,
  London 248
Acropolis of Pergamon, Asia Minor
  114
acrylic paint, properties of 145
Acton, Harold 290
Adam, Peter 77, 204, 300
Adam, Theo 268
Adams, Linda 289
Aire Valley, West Yorkshire 16
Airedale Combing Co. 33
Akademie der Kunst, Berlin: *Young
  Generation: Great Britain* (1968)
  220
Alan, Charles 141–44, 230
Alan Gallery, Madison Avenue,
  New York 141, 154, 156, 230
Albany, the, off Piccadilly, London
  292
Albers, Josef 165
Aldermaston atomic weapons
  establishment, Berkshire 60
Aldermaston marches 60, 125, 127
Alecto Editions 129, 136, 165, 174,
  221, 223, 233, 315
Alexandria, Egypt 135, 171–72
Alhambra Theatre, Morley Street,
  Bradford 18, 20, 311
Allen, Woody 264
Alloway, Lawrence 81, 82
Allsop, Kenneth 136
Amacker, Ferrill 97–98, 102–3, 113,
  114, 156, 195
Amaya, Mario 288
American painting
  DH first exposed to 65–66
  and Abstract Expressionists 82
  DH influenced by 99
American Physique magazine 106
Amherst College, Massachusetts 179
Anderson, Sir Colin 94

Anderson, Donald 94
Andrews, Oliver 142, 143, 144
Animals, the 156
Année dernière à Marienbad, L' (film)
  81
anti-hanging bill (passed 1956) 59
Antonioni 193
Apollo magazine 234
Apperley Bridge, Bradford 51
Aram furniture store, King's Road,
  London 216
Arcadian cinema, Bradford 30
Archer, David 85
Architectural Association 237
Ardizzone, Edward 94
Argyll Road, Kensington, London
  294
Arizona 153
Ark (college magazine) 64
Armitage, Kenneth 87
Arp, Jean 146
  Self Absorbed 201
Arran, Earl of 170, 171, 194
Art and Literature magazine 104
Art Deco 229, 245, 252
Art Institute of Chicago 163, 285
Art News 213
Art Nouveau 166, 229
Art Review 71
Arts Council 105, 175
  Collection 102
Asher, Betty 152
Ashley, Mo 93
Ashton, Sir Frederick 203–4, 293,
  300
Ashton, Mr (form master) 27, 61
Ashville College, Harrogate, North
  Yorkshire 205
'Assemblage' 88
Athens 257
Athletic Model Guild (AMG) 124,
  149–51
Atlan, Jean 87
Atlantic Records 279
Attlee, Lord 170
Auden, W.H. 204, 221, 312, 326
Auerbach, Frank 81, 126

Autry, Gene 149
Ayers, Eric 130, 221

Baby Doll (film) 93
Bachardy, Don 147, 148, 162, 181,
  190, 200–201, 213, 215, 262–63
Bacon, Francis 66, 87, 90, 99, 104,
  126, 131, 137, 138, 146, 265, 323
Bailey, Anthony 200, 246
Bailey, David 194
Bailey, Pearl 309
Baker, Carroll 93
Baker, Margaret 24
Bakes, Irvine R. 22
Baldry, 'Long' John 106
Balliol College, Oxford 99, 115
Balthus 296
Bangkok, Thailand 265
Barbirolli, Sir John 45–46
Barcelona
  Museum of Modern Art 254
  Picasso Museum 254
Bardot, Brigitte 80
Barney's Beanery, Los Angeles
  146, 164
Barstow, California 144
Bart, Lionel 76
Bastian, Heiner 221
Bates, Barrie 95
Bathurst, David 99
Battle of Britain (1940) 16
Bawden, Edward 39
BBC 165, 247, 251
  "BBC Tonight" programme 136
  Home Service: "The Critics" 136
  Radio 4: *Desert Island Discs* 267–68
  World Service 290
Beach Boys 155
Beatles, the 154, 155, 165, 193, 194,
  294
Beaton, Cecil 82–83, 138–39, 154,
  194, 203, 224–26
Beaumarchais, Jacques de Bascher
  de 301
Beethoven, Ludwig van 46
  5th Symphony (Liszt piano
  transcription) 268

Beirut, Lebanon 172
Bela Vista Hotel, Macau 265
Belgrade: DH's exhibition at the
    National Gallery 238–39
Bell, Graham 38
Bell, Larry 146
Belsen concentration camp,
    Germany 39
Bengston, Billy Al 146
Bennett, Alan 80
    Writing Home 55
Bennett, John 64, 73
Benson, James 241, 242
Benson, Kirsten 242
Bentine, Michael 28
Berg, Adrian 70–71, 73
Berger, Benjamin 96, 97
Berger, Helen 96, 97
Berger, Mark 79, 124
    an American mature student 764
    meets DH 74–75
    profound influence on DH 74, 91
    openly gay 75
    Royal College Christmas Revue
      79–80
    DH stays with him in New York
      95, 141, 159
    hepatitis 96
    lives in Florence 102, 103, 113–14
    models for DH 121
    appearance 141
    macrobiotic diet 159
    Gretchen and the Snurl 91
Berkeley, California 190, 191
Berlin 114, 116
    "Homage to Picasso" 287
Berlin Wall 114
Bernard, Claude 316, 323
Berne, Switzerland 103
Bertram Rota Booksellers, Long
    Acre, London 242
Best of Cinerama, The (film) 127
Beveridge plan 65
Beverly Hills, California 150, 162,
    163
Beverly Hills Hotel 245
Beyond the Fringe show 80
Bigger Splash, A (film) 247–48, 251–
    52, 255, 269, 270, 275, 307–10,
    317, 322–23, 328
Biggles series (W E Johns) 18
Bird, Peter 137
Birds, The (film) 245
Birmingham, Bishop of 170
Birmingham College of Art 65
Birnberg, Benedict 212, 213
Birtwell, Celia 216–17, 227, 252,
    269, 270, 276, 283, 293, 295, 304
    family background 217

meets Clark 217
a talented fashion student 106
relationship with Ossie Clark
    140, 157, 219, 253, 278, 291, 296,
    313, 316–17
works at the Hades coffee bar
    140, 217
first sees, then meets DH 217–18
on Schlesinger's transformation
    of Powis Terrace 216–17
friendship with Schlesinger 217,
    218
personality 218, 278, 279
friendship with DH 219
marriage to Clark 228, 235
on *Mr and Mrs Clark and Percy*
    235–36
DH's parents visit her shop 243
in Marrakesh 245–46
advises DH 266
visits DH in Malibu 277, 278, 279
DH draws her 296–97, 323
visits de Nobili 300
on Yves-Marie Hervé 301
DH buys her a diamond ring
    313–14
Birtwistle, Harrison 186
Blackpool, Lancashire 21
Blahnik, Manolo 249, 252
Blake, Peter 81, 167
Blake, William 39, 137, 315
    Elohim Creating Adam 90
    'The Flames of Furious Desire'
    79
Blenheim Crescent, London 218
Blow-Up (film) 193
Blum, Irving 146, 147
Bolton Abbey, Yorkshire Dales 6
Boman, Eric 249, 250, 251, 252,
    254, 267
Bomberg, David 82
Bosch, Hieronymous: *The Virgin
    and Child and the Three Magi* 222
Boshier, Derek 52–53, 65, 68, 71,
    77, 79, 80, 81, 82, 90, 102, 116,
    119, 155, 156
Boty, Pauline 80, 217–18
Boucher, François: *Reclining Girl*
    192
Boulder, Colorado 159, 160–61
Boulez, Pierre 186
Bowery, New York 98, 101, 159
Boxer, Mark 125, 134, 135
Boys Town, Santa Monica 280
Bradford, Lord Mayor of 102
Bradford, West Yorkshire viii,
    122, 134
    described (as 'Bruddersford')
    2–3, 6

Charles Thompson sets up as a
    coal merchant 6
DH's grandparents move to 4
Methodist halls and chapels 5
pubs and clubs 5
German bombing raid (31 August
    1940) 1–2, 15–16
cinemas 20
near beautiful countryside 21
Kenneth's placards in Town Hall
    Square 46–47
DH becomes a familiar sight in 50
Bradford Beck 2
Bradford City Art Gallery 137, 292
Bradford Corporation Buses 18
Bradforddale 2
Bradford Education Committee 33
Bradford Grammar School 21
    DH studies at viii, 22–25, 26–29,
    32–33, 36, 42
Bradford Mechanics Institute,
    Bridge Street, Bradford 12–13
Bradford Regional College of Art
    (later Bradford College) 73
    DH's failed application to study
    at the junior school 25, 26, 28
    staff impressed by DH's drawings
    32
    DH awarded a grant 33, 35
    DH's nickname 35
    DH transfers from graphics to
    painting 36–37
    and the Yorkshire Artists
    Exhibition 48
    National Diploma in Design 38, 52
    DH's passion for his work 44, 47
    extracurricular activities 44–45
    easel smuggled out of college 56
    DH's knowledge of lithography
    79
Bradford Telegraph and Argus 15, 322
Bradford Town Hall 3, 26
Bradfordian (school magazine) 24
Bragg, (Lord) Melvyn 145
Brancusi, Constantin 302
Braque, Georges 285, 302
Bratby, John 39–40, 77, 81, 119
Brausen, Erica 87
Brett, Guy 117, 199, 234, 246, 276
Brice, Bill 144
Bridges, Jim 147, 190, 263
Bridlington, East Yorkshire viii, 21
British Camouflage Committee 63
British Council 304
British Museum, London 41, 173
Brontë family 18
Brooke, Celia 227
Brown, Ford Maddox: *The Last of
    England* 90

Buckle, Richard 'Dickie' 226, 244
Buhler, Robert 64
Buñuel, Luis 81
Burford, Byron 153
Burlington House, Piccadilly,
    London 42
Burma 266
Burn, Gordon 219, 250
Burn, Rodney 53
Burnley, Lancashire 170
Burr, James 234
Burroughs, Edgar Rice: Tarzan
    books 191
Burton, John 57
Burton, Margaret 57
Burton, Richard (architect) 131
Butler Act (1944) 22

Cadaqués, Catalonia 254, 256, 260,
    262
Café de Flore, Paris 296, 298, 299
Cage, John 186
Cairo 135, 172
Cairo Hilton 134
Cairo Museum 135
California 227
    DH decides to make a long trip
        to 136
    DH's series of paintings 186, 187,
        234
    Schlesinger visits his parents in
        238
    DH visits 'for some adventure'
        249–50
    DH recuperates in (1973) 277–82
Callaghan, James (Baron Callaghan
    of Cardiff) 212
Callas, Maria 300
Cambridge Gardens, London 292
Camden, north London 247
Camelot (musical) 162
cameras
    box Brownie 5
    Cameflex movie camera 248
    Kodak Instamatic 186
    Pentax 197, 199, 258
    Pentax Spotmatic II 269–70
    Polaroid Land 186
    quarter-plate 5
Campaign for Nuclear
    Disarmament (CND) 59, 60, 127
Canberra, S.S.: Pop Inn room 94–95
Cannes Film Festival (1974) 310
Capote, Truman: Breakfast at
    Tiffany's 231
Carennac, France 196, 227, 230, 253,
    255, 289
Carl Rosa Opera Company 18
Carlos 301

Caro, Anthony 81, 131, 158, 231
Carter, Floyd: Route 69 268
Cartwright Hall, Lister Park,
    Bradford 18
    "First Biennale of Prints" 202
Casa Santini, near Lucca 288
Casablanca Conference 245
Casino Cinerama cinema, Soho,
    London 127
Caskey, Bill 147
Casson, Hugh 94
Cat on a Hot Tin Roof (film) 231
Cavafy, Constantine 70, 73, 77, 97,
    171–75, 183, 224, 250
    'In the Boring Village' 173–74
    'Waiting for the Barbarians' 99
Cave de France, London 85
Cecil Gee stores 110
Ceeje Gallery, Los Angeles 147
Central City, Colorado 161
Cézanne, Paul 89, 158
Chadwick, Lynn 87
Champion magazine 211
Chaplin, Charlie 8, 20, 290
Charles II, King 22
Chassay, Tchaik 237, 243
Château de Castile, Uzès 195
Chateau Marmont hotel, Los
    Angeles 207, 277, 317, 318
Chelsea School of Art, London 70
Chemosphere, Torreyson, Los
    Angeles 145
Chicago 153, 155, 318
China News 59
Chinnery, George: The Balcony,
    Macao 245
Chisman, Dale 161–62, 167, 173
Christ Church, Oxford 100
Christie, George 312, 323, 324
Christie, Mary 312
Churchill, Sir Winston 245
Ciccolini, Aldo 268
Cipriani Hotel, Venice 231
City Lights Bookstore, San
    Francisco 221
Clandeboye House, Northern
    Ireland 223
Clark, Albert 277, 279
Clark, George 277, 279
Clark, Kay 228
Clark, Sir Kenneth 39, 212, 263
    Penguin Modern Painters series 251
    The Nude 212
Clark, Ossie 140–41, 193, 203, 216,
    218, 227, 232, 240, 255, 267, 269,
    304, 313, 316, 320, 328
    a friend of Mo McDermott 123,
        140
    a talented fashion student 106

models for DH 124
relationship with Celia Birtwell
    140, 157, 219, 253, 278, 291, 296
affair with DH 140–41
personality 140
wins a competition for shoe
    design 154, 157
in New York 154–55, 156
appearance 154–55, 156
downturn in relationship with
    DH 157
returns to London 157
on Earles 165
fame and the money go to his
    head 219, 277–78
drug-taking 219, 278, 279, 316
ill-treatment of Celia 219, 316–17
marriage to Birtwell 228, 235
in Vichy 229, 230
Lawson on 242
fashion show at the Royal Court
    252
and Mick Jagger 256
treatment of Powis Terrace 307,
    308
on A Bigger Splash 309
moves out of Powis Terrace 313
and Celia's diamond ring from
    DH 314
hopes DH doesn't brainwash
    Celia 315
Classic cinema, Notting Hill,
    London 81
Cliff Sings (album) 76
Clifford Street Gallery, London
    275, 289
Coats, Peter 294
Cocteau, Jean 173, 303
Cohen, Bernard 131
    Alonging 158
    Fable 158
Cohen, Harold 126
Cohn, Harry 162
Cohn, Joan 162, 163, 164
Coldstream, Sir William 38, 126
Colecough, Fred 36, 40, 51–52, 102
Coliseum cinema, Bradford 30
Colony Room, London 85
Colorado 161, 199
Colquhoun, Robert 39
Columbia Pictures 162
Colville Square, London 120
Colville Terrace, London 259
Commonwealth Institute,
    Kensington, London 157
communism 47, 114
Communist Party 13
Compagnie Generale
    Transatlantique 164

Constable, John 55
Cook, Peter 80, 133
Cookham, Berkshire 50
Cooper, Douglas 195, 302–3, 323
Cooper, Lettice 3–4
Corberó, Xavier 255
Corbett, Bobby viii
Corman, Roger 121
Cornell, Joseph 272
Cornwall 55, 56
Cornwall-Jones, Paul 129, 130, 163, 171, 196, 221, 223
Corona del Mar, California 202
Corsica 274
Coupole, Paris 296, 299
Cour de Rohan, Paris 300, 314
Courcel, Mme de 240
Coward, Sir Noël 122
Cox, John 310, 311, 312, 317, 319–20, 324, 325, 327, 328
Cozens, Alexander 34
Craxton, John 39
Crib, Don 288
Crispo, Andrew 232
Crommelynck, Aldo 283, 285
Crommelynck, Piero 285
Crutch, Peter 92–93, 92, 97
Cubism 69, 287, 302
Cunard 128
Cuthbert, Ken 57
Cuthbertson, Iain 175, 176, 182

Daily Express 17, 60, 170
Daily Mail 60
Daily Mirror 169
Daily Sketch 76
Daily Worker 47, 60
  Bazaar 59
Dali, Salvador 254
Damascus 172
Dandy (comic) 40
Daniell, William 275
Danton, Georges 296
Danube River 239
Danvers-Walker, Bob 95
Darwin, Robin 62–63, 72–73, 101, 108, 109–10
David Murray Landscape Scholarship 55, 56, 58
Davie, Alan 68, 239
Davis, Bette 155
Davis, Ron 179
de Botton, Gilbert 232
de Botton, Jacqueline 232
de Grey, Roger 53, 63–64, 91, 119
de Nobili, Lila 299–300, 301
de Rose, Gerard 117–18
Deakin, Michael 129
Dean, James 128

Deane, Earl 150
Death in Venice (film) 248
Degas, Edgar 49
Delaunay, Robert 64
Denny, Robin 53, 81, 131
Dent, Harold 22
Deuters, Jane 66, 80, 102
Deutsche Grammophon 45
Devine, George 177
Devis, Arthur: *Mr and Mrs Atherton* 235
Dewsbury, West Yorkshire 2
Dewsbury Gazette 15
Dickens, Charles 18
  Bleak House 3
Dietrich, Marlene 245
Dilhorne, Lord 171
Dimbleby, David 194
Disneyland 155
Dobson, Miss (neighbour in Bradford) 1
Domenichino: *Apollo Killing Cyclops* 121
Doyle, Peter 76
Driberg, Tom, MP 194
Drummond, Hon. Sarah 99
Drury Lane Theatre, London 162
Dubuffet, Jean 71, 110, 115, 131, 158
Duccio di Buoninsegna: *Crucifixion* 103
Duchamp, 'Teeny' 254
Dufferin, Lindy viii, 193, 203, 204, 218, 223
Dufferin and Ava, Maureen, Marchioness of 165
Dufferin and Ava, Sheridan Blackwood, Marquess of vii, 132, 165, 193, 218, 223, 232, 275, 277
  at Oxford 99–100
  partnership with Kasmin 100, 130
Dufy, Raoul 264
Dulac, Edmund 221
Duchamp, Marcel 254
Durassier, Marcel 163
Durbin, Deanna 15
Dürer, Albrecht 222
Durrell, Lawrence 77
  The Alexandria Quartet 172
Dylan, Bob 156, 162
Dyson, Sir Frank 12

Ealing Art School, London 174
Earles, Bobby 164, 165, 181
Earls Court, London 122, 297
Earls Court Underground station, London 75
East Riding 34
East Yorkshire Wolds vii, viii, 34

Eastbrook Hall Methodist Chapel, Bradford 12, 32, 321
Eastbrook Methodist Mission, Bradford 10
Eccleshill, Bradford 52
Eccleshill Library, Waltham 18
Eccleshill Methodist Chapel, Bradford 26
École du Louvre, Paris 301
Edinburgh Festival 80
Egerton Crescent, South Kensington, London 227
Egypt
  tomb paintings 99
  DH in 134–35, 171
Eisenstein, Sergei 81
Ekland, Britt 308
Elgin pub, Ladbroke Grove, London 106
Eliot, T.S. 67
Elizabeth II, Queen 165
Elysian cinema, Bradford 30
Embarcadero YMCA, San Francisco 162, 191
Emmanuel College, Cambridge 129
Emmerich, André 230–31
Emmerich Gallery, New York 308
  David Hockney: Paintings and Drawings exhibition (1971) 267, 269, 271–74
Empire State Building, New York 98
Empress cinema, Bradford 30
Encino, Los Angeles 180, 191
Encounter (journal) 39
English Stage Company 205
Ennals, Martin 212
Epstein, Brian 154, 155
Epstein, Jacob 216
Ernst, Max 260
Erskine, Hon. Robert 93–94, 95
Ertegun, Ahmet 279, 291
Esther Robles Gallery, Los Angeles 146
etching process 175
  coloured etching 286–87
Euston Road School 38, 44
Evans, Gregory 280–81, *281*, 282, 286, 297–98, 311, 320–22, 323, 328
Evans, Mrs (grocer in Notting Hill) 119, 294
Evening Standard 137
Exchange Station, Bradford 3, 6
Exeter, Bishop of 170
Exile on Main Street (album) 256
Expresso Bongo (film) 76

Factory, the, New York 157

Faithfull, Marianne 308
Fauvism 107
Fawcett, David 37, 62
Fedden, Mary 64, 94
Feingarten Gallery, Los Angeles
    146
Felix Landau Gallery, Los Angeles
    146
Felixstowe Amateur Arts Show
    57–58
Felsen, Sid 277
Fénelon, François: *Télémaque* 196
Ferry, Bryan 308
Ferus Gallery, Los Angeles 146
Fini, Leonore 87
Finney, Albert 205
Fischer, Harry 87, 88, 89
Flash Gordon (film serial) 20
Flatirons, Colorado 161
Flaubert, Gustave 286
Fleming, John 36
Florence, Italy 102, 103, 113–14, 195
Forbidden Planet, The (film) 90
Fort William, Scotland 327
Forum cinema, Fulham Road,
    London 95
Foster, Sir John 231, 232
Foster Square, Bradford 46
Fountains Abbey, North Yorkshire
    240
Fourth Bradford East Scouts,
    Eccleshill Church, Bradford 30
Foxcovert Farm, Huggate,
    Yorkshire Wolds 34
France, DH visits during European
    tour 194–96
France, SS 164–65
Frankenthaler, Helen 179, 231, 260
Fraser, Robert 130–31
Freeman, Betty 152, 185–86, 202
French House pub, London 85
Freud, Sigmund 288
Fruit Street area, Brooklyn
    Heights, New York 97
Fuller, Ron 79

Gainsborough, Thomas: *Mr and Mrs
    Andrews* 235
Gaitskell, Hugh 170
Galerie Claude Bernard, Paris:
    David Hockney: Dessins et Gravures
    323
Galerie Mikro, Berlin: DH's one-
    man show (1968) 220
Gallard, André 198
Gallery One, D'Arblay Street,
    London 85, 86
    Yves le Monochrome exhibition
    (1957) 86

Gandhi, Mahatma M.K. 77, 79, 287
Garage Art, Earlham Street,
    Covent Garden, London:
    exhibition of DH's recent
    drawings 312–13
Garcia House, Mulholland Drive,
    Los Angeles 145
Gaskill, Bill 175, 176, 177
Gatwick airport 298
Gay News 80
gay rights 77, 170
Geldzahler, Henry 113, 213, 226,
    227, 270, 290, 291, 303, 312, 323,
    327
    family background 129
    works at Metropolitan Museum
    of Art 128, 129, 207, 267
    personality 129, 207–8
    relationship with DH 129, 207,
    282, 289
    tells DH of his adventures 157
    and *Beverly Hills Housewife* 185
    gives DH critical feedback 207
    and Schlesinger 207–8
    on the Webster portrait 246–47
    advice to DH on his break-up
    with Schlesinger 259
    and DH's attitude to modernism
    261
    and *Portrait of an Artist* 271
    DH's drawing 271
    in Corsica 274
    and *Artist and Model* 287–88
    in Italy 288–91
    in *A Bigger Splash* 308
Gemini Ltd, Melrose Avenue, Los
    Angeles 163, 164, 277, 278
Gene Autry's Hotel Continental,
    Los Angeles 149
Geneva, Switzerland 108
George, Adrian 316
George Trippon School of Fashion
    Design, Los Angeles 298
Getty family 246
GI Bill 67
Giacometti, Alberto 285
Giant (film) 128
Gielgud, Sir John 122, 203, 227
Giggleswick, North Yorkshire 12
Gillinson, Bernard 49
Gimpel, Charles 87
Gimpel, Peter 87
Gimpel Fils 87
Giordano, Umberto: *Fedora* 268
Giza, Egypt 136
Glazebrook, Mark 44, 105, 130, 214,
    222, 223, 233
Glyndebourne Opera House,
    Sussex 310, 311–12, 320, 323–28

Goering, Hermann 16
Golden Boys magazine 211
Golden Gate Park, San Francisco:
    Gathering of the Tribes (1967)
    190
Goldfarb, Shirley 298–99, 305, 309,
    310, 316–17
    Carnets Montparnasse, 1971-1980
    299
González, Julio 302
Goodman, Jeff 113, 113, 114, 117, 128
Goon Show, The (radio programme)
    28
Gorge de Tarn, France 253
Gottlieb, Adolph 272
Gould, Glenn 268
Gowrie, Grey Ruthven, 2nd Earl
    of 99, 115
Goya, Francisco de 138, 246
Grabowski, Mieczyslaw 116
Grabowski Gallery, Sloane Avenue,
    London 116
Graham, Mr (headmaster) 23–26,
    28, 32, 33
Graham, Robert 179
Grand Canyon, Arizona 155
Grand Hotel, Perpignan, France
    255
Grand Hotel, Vittel, Italy 288
Grant, Alistair 93
Grant, Keith 247
Greaves, Derek 115
Greaves, Derrick 39–40, 115
Greek Embassy, London 171
Green Mountain, Colorado 161
Greenberg, Clement 132
Greengates Cinema, New Line,
    Bradford 20
Greenwich Village, New York
    95, 98
Gregory Fellowship in Painting,
    Leeds University 68
Grimm's Fairy Tales (DH project,
    1969) 204, 220–24
Grinke, Paul 234
Gris, Juan 302
Grose, Kenneth 24, 27
Guardian 212
Guinness, Henrietta 325, 326
Guinness, Jonathan 254
Guinness, Sue 254
Guinness family 99
Guiseley, Leeds 321
Gypsy (musical) 80

Hades coffee bar, Exhibition Road,
    London 81, 140, 217
Haight-Ashbury district, San
    Francisco 280

Hair (musical) 280

Halifax, West Yorkshire 2

Hallé Orchestra 45–46

Hamilton, Denis 125, 135

Hamilton, Richard 90–91, 151, 213,
    254, 285
    *Just What Is It That Makes Today's
    Homes So Different, So Appealing?*
    90

Hamilton-Fraser, Donald 98

Hanover, Germany 239

Hanover Gallery, London 87

Hanson Junior School, Bradford
    12, 14–15

Hardy, Mr (at Foxcovert Farm)
    34, 35

Harkers Studio, Bermondsey 320

Harland and Wolff shipyard,
    Belfast 94

Harlem, New York 98, 129

Harrington, Curtis 129

Harrods department store, London
    197, 216

Harrogate, North Yorkshire 238,
    261

Harry Ramsden's fish restaurant
    321

Harvard University 171

Harvey, Laurence 162, 163, 164

Hastings, East Sussex 61

Hastings College of Art 61

Haworth, Jan 134, 167

Hayes, Colin 53, 64

Hayward, Brooke 128

Hazan, Jack 247–48, 251–52, 255,
    269, 270, 275, 298, 307–10, 317,
    322, 328

Heath, Edward 304

Hedges Place, Los Angeles 250

Hedrick, Cecil 147

Heilman, Mary 190

Helena Rubinstein 297

Henneky's pub, Portobello Road,
    London 217

Hepworth, Barbara 55, 56

Herbert, George: 'The Elixir' 221

Herbert, Henry viii, 165

Hervé, Yves-Marie 301, 302, *303*,
    305, 307, 308, 311, 323

Heyworth, Peter 204

Hilton, Roger 68

hippy movement 180

Hitchcock, Alfred 245

Hitler, Adolf 13, 16

HM Customs and Excise 211, 212,
    213

"Hockeylok Apples Inc" 61

Hockney, Alwyn (DH's sister-in-
    law) 240, 241

Hockney, Audrey (DH's aunt) 8

Hockney, David
    birth (Bradford, West Yorkshire,
        9 July 1937) 2
    evacuated to Nelson 14
    school education 12, 14–15, 18,
        21–25, 26–29, 32–33
    start of ambition to become an
        artist 16–17
    early drawing 17–18, *18*
    early influences 18, 24, 49
    love of the cinema 20–21, 29–30,
        74, 81, 119, 121
    in the Cubs and Scouts 30–32, *31*
    awarded grant to study at
        Bradford Regional College of
        Art 33, 35
    summer holiday job in Yorkshire
        Wolds 34–35
    at Bradford art college 35–42
    appearance vii, *31*, 35, *43*, 44, 47,
        52, *55*, 67, *70*, 74, 89, 97, 98, 108,
        110, 134, 138, 148, 152, 153, 177,
        180, 217, 248, 287, *291*, *294*, 298
    first trip to London (1954) 41
    series of self-portraits 42–44, *43*
    love of classical music 45–46, 76
    first serious portrait in oils 47–49
    first sale of work (1955) 49
    experiments with colour 51
    applies and is accepted at the
        Royal College of Art 51–53
    Yorkshire accent vii, 52, 64, 89,
        138, 148, 152, 180, 304
    conscientious objector 55
    wins David Murray Landscape
        Scholarship 55, 56, 212
    summer with Loker in Cornwall
        and Suffolk 55–58
    works in hospitals instead of
        national service 58–59, 61, 62
    Aldermaston marches 60, *60*
    starts Royal College course 62
    first exposed to American
        painting 65–66
    early experiments in abstraction
        68
    looks upon Kitaj as his mentor 68
    use of words on paintings 69,
        75, 79
    in Painting School 70, 79
    graffiti 71, 75, 93, 94, 95
    Berger's influence 74, 91
    numbers codes 76–77, 92, 93, 94
    brief encounter with pop art
        77, 79
    first printing 79
    first significant moment in his
        student career 82

    meets Kasmin 88–89
    etching skills 91, 102
    prize for *Three Kings and a Queen*
        93–94
    visits America 95–98, 128–29
    dyes hair blond 97, 108
    contract with Kasmin 100, 108
    first trip to Europe 103, 161
    Young Contemporaries show of
        1962 sets him on the road to
        fame 105
    awarded RCA gold medal 109–12,
        114, 127
    teaches at Maidstone School of
        Art 117–18
    finds a studio in Notting Hill
        118–20
    health 122, 208
    starts to paint domestic scenes
        123
    photographed for *Sunday Times
        Magazine* 125, 126–27
    Geldzahler and Cornwall-Jones
        as key figures in his life 129
    first Kasmin Gallery show 134,
        136–39, 141
    in Egypt 134–35, 171
    first one-man show 136–39
    affair with Ossie Clark 140–41
    embarks on US trip (1963) 141
    learns to drive in LA 143–44
    first successful use of acrylic
        paint 145
    start of key friendship with
        Isherwood 148–49
    visits AMG 149, 150
    first swimming pool painting
        152
    teaches in Iowa 153–54, 159
    sees the Beatles at Hollywood
        Bowl 155
    first American show 156
    Dubuffet's and Bernard Cohen's
        influences 158
    flirts with abstraction 158–59
    teaches at Boulder 159, 161
    and Bobby Earles 164, 165
    second Kasmin Gallery show
        165–67
    decides to leave Britain 169
    solidarity with his working-class
        roots 170
    designs sets and costumes for *Ubu
        Roi* 175–77
    teaches at UCLA 177
    meets Peter Schlesinger 180
    relationship with Schlesinger
        181–82, 214–15, 227, 238,
        244–46, 248–57, 259–66, 271,

276, 278, 282, 283, 302, 307–8, 310, 328
early use of camera as a composition tool 186
teaches graduates 190
becomes interested in light 192
smoking 193, 212
European tour (1967) 194–97
prolific photographer 197, 199, 245
John Moores Prize for Contemporary Painting 198
first double portrait 200–201
fights HM Customs and Excise 211–13
develops the portrait as drama 214
tea parties at Powis Terrace 218–19
picture prices 220
growing international reputation 220
cross-hatching technique 224, 317, 319, 320, 323–24
stain technique 260
as a Yorkshireman viii, 265
composite photographs 271
studies with Crommelynck 285–87
lives in Paris 296–305, 307, 315
buys Celia a diamond ring 313–14
relationship with Evans 320–22, 328
success of The Rake's Progress opens up new artistic world for him 328
use of reverse perspective 328
personality
anarchic attitude 44, 47, 72
charisma 119
confidence 37, 229, 265
energy 77, 98
enthusiasm viii, 224, 225
generosity 198, 202, 220, 240, 244, 261
gregariousness 119
humour 28–29, 30, 40–41, 64, 89, 119, 152, 234, 245
modesty 77, 229
openness 37, 89, 130, 152
self-assurance 77, 108
subversiveness 23
unpretentiousness 224
vegetarianism 69, 96, 98, 100, 123
wit 23, 108, 151, 163, 279
work ethic 118, 120
works
According to the Prescriptions of Ancient Magicians 173

The Actor 154
Adhesiveness 76–77, 83
American Collection 202, 231
Arizona 154, 156
Artist and Model 285, 287
The Artist's Father 262
The Artist's Mother 262
Bedlam 102
Beverly Hills Housewife 185–86, 192
A Bigger Splash 188, 190, 191, 192, 198, 316
Blue Interior and Two Still Lifes 158
Bob, France 1965 165
Boy About to Take a Shower 150
Boys in Bed, Beirut 173
California 158
California Art Collector 152, 186
California Seascape 202
Canberra mural 94–95
Carennac 184, 196
Celia in a Black Dress with Red Stockings 297
Celia in a Black Dress with White Flowers 297
Celia in a Black Slip, Reclining 297
Celia Wearing Checked Sleeves 297
Cha-Cha-Cha that was Danced in the Early Hours of 24th March, 1961 93, 115
Chair and Shirt 263, 272
Christopher Isherwood and Don Bachardy 200–201, 202, 204, 207, 213, 231, 234
Contre-jour in the French Style - Against the Day dans le Style Français 304–5
The Cruel Elephant 96
Cubist Boy with Colourful Tree 154, 156
Different Kinds of Water Pouring into a Swimming Pool, Santa Monica 158
The Diploma 108, 109
Doll Boy 76, 82, 88, 92, 233
Domestic Scene, Broadchalke, Wilts. 226
Domestic Scene, Los Angeles 124, 247
Domestic Scene, Notting Hill 123–24, 137
The Door Opening for a Blonde 102
Edward Lear 141
Erection 68
The Fires of Furious Desire 79
The First Marriage 120
Flight into Italy - Swiss Landscape 1962 103–4
Four Different Kinds of Water 190

French Shop 272
'Fuck' drawings 71
A Glass Table with Glass Objects 260
A Grand Procession of Dignitaries in the Semi-Egyptian Manner 99, 104, 115
Great Pyramid at Giza with Broken Head viii, 136, 137
Gregory Evans + Nicholas Wilder Appian Way Hollywood 281–82, 281
Gregory, Palatine, Roma 306, 320–21
Growing Discontent 68
Henry and Christopher 207
Henry Geldzahler and Christopher Scott 207, 208–9, 213, 214, 226, 231
A Hollywood Collection 163–64, 278
    Picture of a Landscape in an Elaborate Gold Frame 163
    Picture of a Pointless Abstraction Framed under Glass 164
    Picture of a Portrait in a Silver Frame 163
    Picture of a Simply Framed Traditional Nude Drawing 163–64
    Picture of a Still Life that has an Elaborate Silver Frame 163
    Picture of Melrose Avenue in an Ornate Gold Frame 163
The Hypnotist 121, 137
Illustrations for Fourteen Poems from C.P. Cavafy 173, 183, 224, 250
In the Dull Village 167, 169, 173
Iowa 154, 156
The Island 247, 248, 272
Jane in a Straw Hat 196
Japanese Rain on Canvas 276
Jungle Boy 141
Kaisarion with all his Beauty 96–97, 171
Kasmin in Bed in his Chateau in Carennac 196
Kerby (After Hogarth) 328
A Lawn Sprinkler 190
A Less Realistic Still Life 159
Life Painting for a Diploma 106, 133
Lila de Nobili 300
The Little Splash 188
'Love' paintings 75–76
Man vii-viii, *vii*
Man in a Museum (or You're in the Wrong Movie) 117, 120

Man in Shower in Beverly Hills
150, 153, 154
Man Taking Shower 150
*Mark, Strand Hotel, Rangoon
1971* 266
Marriage paintings 117
The Master Printer of Los Angeles
279
Mirror, Mirror on the Wall 97, 171
A More Realistic Still Life 159
*The Most Beautiful Boy in the
World* 93, 115
Mother in a Wicker Chair 262
Mount Fuji and Flowers 267, 276
*Mr + Mrs Ossie Clark, Linden
Gardens London* 236
Mr and Mrs Clark and Percy
228—29, 235—38, 238, 243, 244,
246, 314
My Bonnie Lies Over the Ocean 97
Myself and My Heroes 79, 287
A Neat Lawn 198
Nude 52
Olympic Games poster
(Munich, 1972) 239—40
Ossie and Derek in Grand Canyon
155
Panama Hat 272
Le Parc des Sources, Vichy 232—33,
233
Paris, December 1967 215
Peter 211
Peter C 92, 93
Peter Getting Out of Nick's Pool
187, 190, 198
Peter in Carennac 185
Picture Emphasizing Stillness
116—17
*Picture of a Hollywood Swimming
Pool* 158
Plastic Trees Plus City Hall 145
Play Within a Play 121—22, 124,
137, 230, 233
Pool and Steps, Le Nid de Duc 260,
261, 267, 272
Portrait of an Artist 227, 261, 271,
272—73
Portrait of Jean Léger 297
Portrait of my Father 47—49, 93,
187
Portrait of Nick Wilder 187, 192
*Portrait Surrounded by Artistic
Devices* 158
Pretty Tulips 233
Priestley pen-and-ink drawings
292—93
A Rake's Progress 122, 127—28, 130,
136, 138, 147, 148, 311
   Cast Aside 128

Disintegration 128
*The Gospel Singing, with the
Good People wearing ties with
God is Love on them* 101—2
Receiving the Inheritance 102
The Seven Stone Weakling 101
The Wallet Begins to Empty 101
The Rake's Progress (stage
designs) 310—13, 317—20,
323—28
A Realistic Still Life 159
Road Menders 61
Rocky Mountains and Tired Indians
161, 166
The Room viii
The Room, Manchester Street
197—98
The Room Tarzana viii, 191—92,
198, 316
*Rubber Ring Floating in a
Swimming Pool* 260—61
Rue de Seine 297, 305
Rumpelstiltskin 221
The Second Marriage 120—21
Self Portrait 43
*Shirley Goldfarb and Gregory
Masurovsky* 299, 304, 310
Showing Maurice the Sugar Lift
286
Simplified Faces 286
Sir David Webster 243—46, 249
*Six Fairy Tales from the Brothers
Grimm* 204, 220—24
   'The Boy Who Left Home to
   Learn Fear' 222—23
   'The Enchantress with the
   Baby Rapunzel' 242
   'The Little Sea Hare' 222
   'Old Rinkrank' 221—22
   'Rapunzel' 222
Skeleton 63, 66—67, 73
Some Neat Cushions 198
The Splash 188
Still Life on a Glass Table 260, 272
The Student - Homage to Picasso
287
Sunday lunch Hutton Terrace 27
Sur la Terrasse 245, 250, 259,
260, 272
Swiss Landscape in a Scenic Style
104, 115, 116
A Table 198
*Tea Painting in an Illusionistic
Style* 104
'Tea' paintings 77, 79, 82, 83
Teeth Cleaning 115
Third Love Painting 75—76, 82
Three Kings and a Queen 79, 94
Two Boys Aged 23 or 24 172—73

Two Figures by Bed with Cushions
151
Two Men in a Pool, LA 166
Two Men in a Shower viii, 137
Two Stains on a Room on a Canvas
198
Two Vases in the Louvre 305
Typhoo Tea No.4 115
Ubu Roi sets and costumes
175—77, 177, 183, 312
"Untitled" [drawing] 17—18, *18*,
28, *29*
Vichy 233
Vichy Water and 'Howards End'
196
View from the Nile Hilton 134
Waiting for the Barbarians 171
We Two Boys Together Clinging
91—92, 93
Weather series 277, 278—79
   Lightning 277
   Mist 277
   Rain 277, 278—79
   Snow 277, 278
   Sun 277
   Wind 277, 279
Yves Marie, New York 303
Hockney, Harriet (DH's aunt) 8
Hockney, Harriet (DH's paternal
great-grandmother) 4
Hockney, James William (DH's
paternal grandfather) 4, 8
Hockney, John (DH's brother) 76
birth 14
on DH's drawing as a child 17
relationship with DH 37—38
on his father's teaching 59—60
and DH's homosexuality 133
lives in Australia 240
Hockney, Kenneth (DH's father)
111
birth (9 May 1904) 4
and education 4, 12—13, 18, 25,
26, 28
first job as a telegram boy 4
works at Stephenson Brothers
4—5, 11
serious interest in photography
5, 6
takes evening classes in art 5
meets Laura Thompson 5
involvement in Methodism 5,
7, 12
appearance 8, 9, 262
Laura's letter to him 9—10
marries Laura *1*, 10
conscientious objector 13—14, 55
pram business 15, 16—17
at the cinema 20—21, 127

deafness 20
and DH's use of his Hutton
    Terrace home as studio 43
anti-war and anti-nuclear views
    46–47
at the Yorkshire Artists
    Exhibition 49
political campaigning 59
encourages his children to
    question everything 59–60
his posters confront people with
    his ideas 69
and DH's RCA gold medal 110,
    111
Aldermaston baggage and
    banners stolen 127
visits Paris 133, 304, 319
and DH's first one-man show 138
greets Margaret at Tilbury Docks
    157
visits DH for his second Kasmin
    Gallery show 166
diabetes 177–78, 202–3, 274
sees Ubu Roi 182
visit to son Philip in Australia
    198, 203, 220
visits DH's fourth Kasmin
    Gallery show 198–99
visits DH's Whitechapel
    retrospective (1970) 234
colour television 239
at Odin's restaurant 240–41
at Birtwell's shop 243
visits Lake District 253
DH buys clothes for him 261
sittings for a portrait 274–75
Evans enthuses on his projects
    321
and Hazan's film 322–23
Hockney, Laura (née Thompson;
    DH's mother) 111, 323
birth (10 December 1900) 6
and education 7, 12, 22, 23, 25,
    26, 28
pattern-maker 7
nervous breakdown due to
    bullying at work 7
works in a draper's shop 7
importance of Methodism to
    her 7
meets Kenneth Hockney 5, 7
obstacles to marrying Kenneth
    7–8
letter to Kenneth 9–10
marries Kenneth 1, 10
domestic duties 11, 12
in Second World War 2, 13–14,
    15
on DH's scouting 30–32

shows DH's drawings to Bradford
    Regional College of Art 32
complains about DH's use of his
    home as a studio 42–44, 48–49
on DH's first serious portrait in
    oils 47
at the Yorkshire Artists
    Exhibition 49
DH buys her a sewing machine
    108
unimpressed by DH's blond hair
    108
and DH's RCA gold medal 111,
    112
on DH's Christmas visits 122, 139
first sees Powis Terrace 127
visits Paris 133, 304, 319
on Kasmin 133
and DH's homosexuality 133–34
on Kennedy's assassination 135
pride in DH 136
and DH's first one-man show 138
visits DH for his second Kasmin
    Gallery show 166–67
sees Ubu Roi 182
visit to son Philip in Australia
    198, 220
visits DH's fourth Kasmin
    Gallery show 198–99
worries about Ken 202–3
visits DH's Whitechapel
    retrospective (1970) 234
health 238, 239
seventieth birthday 240
at Odin's restaurant 240–41
at Birtwell's shop 243
visits Lake District 253
DH buys clothes for her 261
sittings for a portrait 274–75
pride in son Paul 292
and Hazan's film 322
at the Glyndebourne dress
    rehearsal 325
Hockney, Lillian (DH's aunt) 8
Hockney, Lisa (DH's niece) 234
Hockney, Louisa Kate (née Jesney;
    DH's paternal grandmother)
    4, 8, 10
Hockney, Margaret (DH's sister)
    239
birth (1935) 10
childhood 12, 14
education 12, 14–15, 18, 33
on DH as a child 18
greeted by parents on her return
    from Australia 157
Hockney, Great-Aunt Nell 21
Hockney, Nicky (DH's nephew)
    234

Hockney, Paul (DH's brother)
birth (1931) 10
childhood 12, 14
education 12, 14–15, 18, 22, 33
fails to find a job in commercial
    art 33
clerk in a firm of accountants 33
engagement 47
national service 50
visits Stanley Spencer 49–50
and DH's homosexuality 133–34
visits DH's Whitechapel
    retrospective (1970) 234
Liberal councillor in Bradford
    292
and Priestley 292
sees DH's Paris show (1974) 319
Hockney, Philip (DH's brother)
birth (1933) 10
childhood 2, 13, 14
education 12, 14–15, 18, 33
lives in Australia 157, 198, 240
Hockney, Robert (DH's paternal
    great-grandfather) 4
Hockney, Willie (DH's uncle) 4,
    10, 13
Hodgkin, Howard 196
Hodgkin, Julia 196
Hogarth, William 137
    The Rake's Progress 101, 136, 311,
        312, 317, 318
Hokusai 267
Holland, Tom 179
Holly, Buddy 16
Hollywood 20, 318
Hollywood Bowl, Los Angeles 154,
    155, 162
Homage to Picasso portfolio 283, 287
Honolulu 263
Hoop and Toy pub, Thurloe Place,
    London 80
Hopalong Cassidy (film serial) 20
Hopper, Dennis 128–29, 164
Hopper, Mrs Dennis 155
Hornsey School of Art 64, 81
Hôtel Nice et Beaux Arts, Rue des
    Beaux Arts, Paris 287
House, Gordon 136, 221
House & Garden 294
House of Commons 59, 171
House of Lords 170
Houses of Parliament 127
Huddersfield, West Yorkshire 2
Huggate, Yorkshire Wolds 34
Huggate Arms 34
Hughes, Fred 248, 249
Hughes, Robert 166
Hull, East Yorkshire 4, 21
Hunt, Randy 301

Hunt Wesson Foods empire 201
Hutton Terrace, Eccleshill,
    Bradford (No.18) 16, *27*, 42–45,
    48–49, 60
Hyde Park, London 127, 270

Idle cinema, Bradford 30
Ifield Road, Fulham, London 88,
    130
Ilkley, West Yorkshire 6, 21, 240
Illinois 153
I'm All Right Jack (film) 47
'I'm Through with Love' (song)
    268
Independent Group 90
Independent Order of Rechabites 13
Indiana, Robert 156
Industrial Revolution 2, 34, 315
Inland Revenue 115
Institute of Contemporary Arts
    (ICA) 81, 90, 115
    *The Wonder and Horror of the
    Human Head* exhibition (1953) 90
    DH lectures on gay imagery in
    America 151
International Film Theatre,
    Westbourne Grove, London 81
Iowa 153, 156, 160, 199
Iowa City, Iowa 153–54, 159, 160
iPad, DH's experiments with viii
iPhone, DH's experiments with viii
Ironside, Professor Janey 123, 140
Isherwood, Christopher *148*, 162,
    194, 204, 221, 233
    emigration to US 147
    relationship with Don Bachardy
    147, 200, 214
    DH meets 147, 315
    loves DH's accent 148
    nostalgia for his childhood 148
    friendship with DH 148–49
    DH and Schlesinger visit 190
    and DH's double portrait 200,
    201, 214, 231, 232
    on Tony Richardson as host 205,
    206
    and DH's break-up with
    Schlesinger 262–63
    Berlin Stories 114, 147
Issigonis, Alex 112
Istanbul 266
Italy 192–93
    DH visits 104, 113–14, 161, 195,
    288–91
It's a Date (film) 15

Jackson, Mahalia 102
Jackson, Tommy 34
Jagger, Bianca 291

Jagger, Mick 227, 256, 291, 308
James, Henry 67
Japan
    DH's interest in 247
    DH's visit with Mark Lancaster
    262, 263–64
Jarman, Derek 65, 173, 252
Jarry, Alfred: *Ubu Roi* 176–77,
    182–83, 204, 312
Jerome, Jerry 147
Jesus College, Cambridge 129
Joan (dry cleaners) 294
John Herron School of Art, Indiana
    163
John Moores Prize for
    Contemporary Painting 198
Johns, Jasper 163
    Map 201
Johnson, David 31
Jones, Allen 64–65, 67, 72–73,
    81–82, 101, 116, 239
Juda, Annely 87

Kalinowski, Egon 131
Kallman, Chester 312, 326
Kansas 153
Kaplan Gallery, Duke Street, St
    James's, London 87
Karlsbad, Czech Republic 239
Karr, Ida 86
Kasmin, Jane (née Nicholson) 87,
    89, 218, 289
Kasmin, John vii, 83, *85*, 193, 218,
    219, 221, 227, 247, 252, 312, 318
    family background 85
    education 85
    in New Zealand 85
    unpaid assistant to Victor
    Musgrave 86
    on the sex life at Gallery One
    86–87
    at the Kaplan Gallery 87
    marriage 87
    at the Marlborough Gallery 88, 89
    on DH's work 88
    meets DH 88–89
    in partnership with Dufferin
    99, 130
    contract with DH 100, 108, 130
    DH on 100
    Tuesday-night gatherings 100–
    101, 115
    relentless propaganda for DH
    114–15, 152
    sale of DH's work 115–16
    on the Powis Terrace area 118
    as portrayed by DH 121–22, 124
    end of DH's vegetarianism 123
    and *A Rake's Progress* 128

and Noland 132, 158
    Laura Hockney on 133
    and DH's one-man show at the
    gallery 136
    on DH's move to New York 139
    visits AMG 149, 150
    taken to LA gay bars 151–52
    rents properties in France 195, 196
    US road trip with DH and
    Schlesinger 199
    and DH's battle with Customs
    and Excise 211
    and prices of DH's pictures 220
    and Emmerich 230–31
    and the Whitechapel
    retrospective of 1970 233
    and George Lawson 242, 243
    DH visits in Carennac 253, 255
    and speculators 272
    on Sheridan Dufferin 275
    Kasmin Gallery closure 277
    and royalties 188
    flees from his incandescent wife
    189
    on Yves-Marie Hervé 301
    and *A Bigger Splash* 309
    on Barbara Thurston 315–16
Kasmin, Paul 87
Kasmin Gallery, New Bond Street,
    London vii, 131–34, *132*, 252
    DH's first one-man exhibition
    (*Paintings with People in*) 134,
    136–39, 141
    DH's second show (*Pictures with
    Frames and Still-Life Pictures*)
    165–67
    show of *Ubu Roi* sets and
    costumes with Cavafy etchings
    183
    DH's fourth one-man show (*A
    splash, a lawn, two rooms, two
    stains, some neat cushions and a
    table...painted*) 198–99
    last show before closure 275–77
Kasmin Ltd, start of 100
Katz, Alex 272
Kaye, Peter 61, 62, 73
Kazan, Elia 93
Keats, John 117
Keighley Road, Frizinghall,
    Bradford 23
Kelly, Ellsworth 101, 207
Kempsford Gardens, Earls Court,
    London (No.47) 64, 66, 73–74,
    77, 93, 118
Kennedy, John F., assassination
    of 135
Kensington Registry Office,
    London 228

Kent, Katharine, Duchess of 213
Kerouac, Jack: *On the Road* 85
Kienholz, Ed 146
    The Beanery 146
kinetic art 146
King's Road Theatre, London 308
Kirby, John: *The Perspective of Architecture* 328
Kirkgate Chapel, Bradford 15
Kirkman, James 89
Kirton, Suffolk 56
Kitaj, R.B. (Ronald Brooks) viii, 65, 67–71, 77, 82, 90, 99, 138, 203, 204, 239, 240, 242
kitchen sink movement 39–40
Klee, Paul 101
Klein, Yves 86
Kleist Kasino gay nightclub, Berlin 114
Kline, Franz 147
Kloss, John 156
Kobe, Japan 264
Kodachrome 178
Kodak 179
Koltai, Ralph 319
Kramer, Jacob 45
Kullman, Michael 103, 107–8, 110, 161
Kutchinsky jewellers, Brompton Road, London 314
Kyoto, Japan 264

La Cienega Boulevard, Los Angeles 146–47, 178, 179, 250, 280
La Dell, Edwin 79
La Mamounia, Marrakesh 245
La Pietra, near Florence 290
LA Times 146
Labour Party 170
Lacourière, Roger 285
Lady Clairol hair dye 97, 102
Lagerfeld, Karl 301
Laguna Beach, California 165
Lake District 253
Lalique, René 216, 217, 252, 259
Lambe, Eugene 289–90
Lambert, Arthur 249–50
Lancaster, Mark 187, 218, 254, 256, 262, 316
    trip to Japan with DH 262, 263, 264, 266
Lancaster, Osbert 310
Lancaster Road, Notting Hill Gate, London 110
Landau, Felix 146
Langan, Peter 241, 242, 325, 326
Lanyon Gallery, Palo Alto, California 179
Larabee Drive, Los Angeles 178

Larson, Jack 147–48, 152, 162, 164, 178, 181, 186, 190, 263
Lartigue, Jacques Henri 225
Las Vegas 144
Latham, John 88
Laurel and Hardy 21
Lautner, John 145
Lawson, George 242–43, 253, 254, 255, 268, 273, 276, 281, 282, 289–90, 296, 307, 325, 326
Le Corbusier 186, 285
Le Nid de Duc, near La Garde-Freinet, France 205, 227, 233, 253, 256, 269, 303
Lear, Amanda 252
Leary, Timothy 190
Leave My Ball Alone (soft-porn movie) 151
Lebanon 172
Lebrun, Rico 146
Leeds, West Yorkshire 4, 21
Leeds City Art Gallery 45, 261
    biannual Yorkshire Artists Exhibition 48–49, 62
Leeds Road, Bradford 10, 11, 12
Leeds School of Art 45
Leeds Town Hall 45
Leeds University: Gregory Fellowship in Painting 68
Left Bank, Paris 296
Léger, Fernand 101, 285, 302
Léger, Jean 297, 305
Leonardo da Vinci 188, 222
    Leonardo Cartoon 105
Les Deux Magots, Paris 296
Leverson, Ada 208
Lewes bonfire, East Sussex 62
Lewis, Wyndham 45
Lichtenstein, Roy 152
Lieberman, William S. 96–97
Lincolnshire 4
    Wolds 34
Linden Gardens, London 218, 236, 292, 316
Lindner, Richard 131
Lindos 257
Lingards department store, Bradford 15
Lion and Unicorn Press 101, 122
Lippscombe, Mark 301
Listener 82, 137, 145, 183
Listerhills, Bradford 11
Liszt, Franz 268
Littlewoods department store 198
Littlewoods football pools company 198
Littman, Marguerite 231–32
'Living Doll' (song) 76
Livingstone, Marco 182, 246, 260, 271

Lloyd, Frank 87, 88
Loker, John 55
    starts studies at Bradford College 41
    London art trips 41
    skiffle group 45
    summer with DH in Cornwall and Suffolk 55–58
    Aldermaston marches 60, 60
    leaves Bradford College 61
    conscientious objector 61
    agricultural work 61, 62
    starts studies at Royal College 73
London
    Kenneth and Laura visit the zoo 10
    DH's first trip (1954) 41
    Earles unimpressed with 165
    swinging London 193
    difficult for DH to get peace and quiet in 282, 287
London Magazine 117, 166
London Midland railway 3
London University Union: DH wins first prize in student art competition 102
Long Beach, Nassau County 96, 97
Lord Mayor's Show, London 157
Lorre, Peter 121
Los Angeles 263
    DH's limited knowledge of 141, 142
    glamorous appeal to DH 141, 142, 144–45
    DH explores Pershing Square area 142–43
    DH's first picture in LA 145
    Monday Night Art Walk 146–47
    DH meets Isherwood 147
    Kasmin shares a room with DH 149
    gay scene 151
    DH's depiction of 166
    DH visits Wilder 280
    The Rake's Progress written in 318
Louis, Morris 104, 131, 152, 231, 260
Louvre, Paris 286, 296, 298, 304–5, 319
Luard, Nicholas 133
Lucca, Italy 195, 288, 290, 296
Lucie-Smith, Edward 166, 174
Lund family 14
Luxor, Egypt 135
Lyle, Fred 38, 49
Lyons Corner Houses
    off Trafalgar Square, London 41
    South Kensington, London 77

Macau 265

MacBride, Terri 47
MacBryde, Robert 39
McCartney, Paul 308
McCracken, John 179
McDermott, Mo 140, 165, 196, 216, 218, 252, 255, 256, 267, 276, *294*, 304, 307, 309, 316
  textiles student from Salford 105
  family background 105
  introduces Birtwell to Ossie Clark 217
  meets DH 106
  models for DH 106, 123, 124, 133, 173, 222, 269
  sexy evenings at Powis Terrace 141
  Lawson on 242–43
  low spirits 293
  a valuable studio assistant 293
  self-confident about his sexuality 293–94
  in *A Bigger Splash* 308
  heroin addiction 318
  and work on *The Rake's Progress* 317, 318–19, 326
MacDonald, Jeanette 268
MacDonald, Joe 270
McEwen, Rory viii
McGrath, Camilla 290
McGrath, Earl 290
McGregor, Neil: *A History of the World in a Hundred Objects* (radio series) 173
MacInnes, Colin 86
  Absolute Beginners 86
  City of Spades 86
McKechnie, Anne 119–20, 159
Mackintosh, Charles Rennie 216
McLeod, Mike 110
Macmillan, Harold, 1st Earl of Stockton 133, 170
Macy's department store 191
Maddox, Reggie 24
Madison Square Gardens, New York 98, 102
Madrid 246
Mafia 149
Magdalen College School, Oxford 85
Magic Flute, The (Mozart) 328
Magritte, René: 'stone age' paintings 222
Mahler (film) 310
Maidstone School of Art 117–18
Malibu 277, 279, 280
Man Ray 323
Man Who Knew Too Much, The (film) 245
Manchester 140

Manchester City Art Gallery 51
Manchester College of Art 217
Manchester Guardian 60
Manchester Street, London (no.25) 197–98
Mann, William 326–27
Mao Tse-tung 59
Marchant, Bob: *The Glyndebourne Picnic 311*
Margaret, Princess 125, 193, 194
Marienbad, Czech Republic 239
Marlborough Gallery, London 87, 88, 89, 99, 100, 136
Marrakesh, Morocco 227, 245
Martin, Ann 107
Marvin, Lee 277
Mason, Don 118
Massenet, Jules: *Werther* 311
Masurovsky, Gregory 299, 305, 310, 312
Maude, Judge John 166
Maude-Roxby, Roddy 64, 80, 111
Mavrogordato, John 73, 171
Maxim's, Paris 305, 315
Maya, Mario 195
Melia, Paul 297
Melly, George 194
Melville, Robert 166
Methodism
  Kenneth Hockney's conversion by 'Gipsy' Smith 5, 7
  the Brotherhood 5, 6, 12
  Kenneth becomes a lay preacher and Sunday school teacher 5, 7
Methodist Central Hall, Westminster, London 127
Metropolitan Museum of Art, New York 128, 129, 199, 207, 267, 304
  New York Painting and Sculpture: 1940-1970 exhibition 207
Michelangelo 17, 26
Middleditch, Edward 40, 81
Midsummer Night's Dream, A (Shakespeare) 308
Miers, France 272
Miller, Jonathan 80, 194
Miller, Mrs (DH's "help") 215, 216
Milligan, Spike 28
Milne, Rodney 327
Milo, Mr (in Cairo) 135
Mingay, David 251–52
Ministry of Education 49
Ministry of Labour and National Service 58
Minton, John 39
Miranda, Paul 250
Miró, Joan 101, 163, 254, 285
Miró Foundation 227
Missouri 153

Mizer, Bob 124, 149, 150
modernism 261
Mojave Desert 144
Monet, Claude 247
Monroe, Marilyn 90, 113, 128, 268
Montague Burton stores 8, 48
Monte Carlo Opera Orchestra 268
Montmartre, Paris 319
Montparnasse, Paris 285
Moon, John 102
Moore, Henry 66, 146, 202
Moores, John 198
Morecambe, Lancashire 21
Morocco (film) 245
Mortimer, John 227
Mougins, France 285
Mount Fuji, Japan 267
Mountain, Dick 161
Moynihan, Rodrigo 294
Mozart, Wolfgang Amadeus 45, 317
Mr Chow restaurant, Knightsbridge, London 248, 249, 252
Mullins, Edwin 137
Munich 114
Municipal Gallery, Kyoto: *Modern Painters in the Japanese Style* exhibition 264
Munnings, Sir Alfred 42
Murray, David 55
Musée d'Art Moderne, Paris 115, 302
Musée des Arts Décoratifs, Paris: *David Hockney: Tableaux et Dessins* exhibition (1974) 304, 314–17
Musée du Petit Palais, Avignon 302
Musée Galleria, Paris 300
Museum of Modern Art, Barcelona 254
Museum of Modern Art, New York 95, 96, 102, 160
  DH's one-man show (1968) 220
Musgrave, Victor 86–87

Naked City (detective series) 129
Nasser, Gamal Abdel 59, 135
National Council for Civil Liberties 212, 297
National Gallery, London 41–42, 121
National Museum of Art, Tokyo 115
National Portrait Gallery, London 232
  Beaton exhibition 224–25, 226
  Snap exhibition 246
National Theatre 175
naturalism 274, 278, 281, 296, 328
Nauman, Bruce 179

Naylor, Philip 30, 45, 46
Nebraska 199
Ned Kelly (film) 227
Neiman Marcus store, Houston,
    Texas 156
Nelson, Lancashire 14
Nelson, Rolf 164
neo-Impressionists 305
neo-Romantics 39
Nevada 155
New London Gallery 87–88, 89, 99
New Mexico 153
New Orleans 95, 154, 155, 156
New Statesman 107, 126, 166, 327
New Victoria cinema, Bradford 30
New York 199, 263
    DH visits 95–98, 128–29
    DH moves to 139, 141
    Ossie Clark in 154–55
    DH's first American show 156
    Procktor's attitude to 159
    Earles dislikes 164
Newlyn Art Society 56
Newman, Barnett 179, 201
Newman, Paul 156
Nicholas Wilder Gallery, Los
    Angeles 179
Nicholson, Ben 55, 87, 101
Nicholson, E.Q. 196
Nicholson, Sir William 87
Night Tide (film) 129
Noland, Kenneth 104, 131, 132, 158,
    159, 179, 231
North, Mary 257
North, Melissa 218–19, 227, 237, 307
Northcott, Bayan 327
Northern Ireland 212
Notting Hill, London 118, 140, 215
Nureyev, Rudolf 203, 271

Observer 204
Odeon Cinema, Manchester Road,
    Bradford 15–16, 30
Odin's restaurant, Devonshire
    Place, London 240–42, 243, 313,
    325, 326
O'Hara, Frank 147
Ohio 199
Oklahoma (musical) 102
Olitski, Jules 131, 158, 179
Olympic Games (Munich, 1972)
    239–40
O'Murphy, Marie-Louise 192
op art 146
Ormsby-Gore, Alice 252
Orwell, George: *The Road to Wigan
    Pier* 67
Osborne, John 205
    The Hotel in Amsterdam 206

Ottringham, East Yorkshire 4
Overy, Paul 183, 312–13
Oxford cinema, Bradford 30
Oxford University Press 223
Oxtoby, Dave
    painting student at Bradford
        College of Art 35
    friendship with DH 35
    a Teddy boy 37
    on DH's passion for his work 44
    skiffle group 45
    on Derek Stafford 46
    on DH's innovative painting
        50–51
    in Hastings 61
    at Royal Academy Schools 62, 73
    works at Maidstone School of
        Art 117

P&O shipping line 94
Page, Anthony 309
Palazzo Vecchio, Florence 3
Palmer, Samuel 39, 315
Panton Street, London 85
Paolozzi, Eduardo 131
Parc des Sources, Les, Vichy 230
Paris 227
    Jacob Kramer as a link with
        bohemian Paris 45
    Allen Jones influenced by
        Delaunay 64
    Ken and Laura visit 133, 304, 319
    premiere of *Ubu Roi* in 176
    art materials bought in 194–95
    DH on 240
    DH escapes to 282, 283, 285–87
    Crommelynck brothers open a
        studio in 285
    DH lives in 296–305, 307, 315, 328
Paris Biennale: Graphic section 102
Paris Opéra 299
Paris Pullman, Drayton Gardens,
    London 81
Paris Salon 185
Partch, Harry 186
Pasadena Museum 202
Pasmore, Victor 38
Pathé Pictorial 94
Pavillon Sévigné hotel, Vichy 229
Payne, Maurice 218, 223, 253
    studies at Ealing Art School 174
    Alecto Editions 174
    takes to DH and his coterie
        174–75
    DH's assistant 175
    and DH's break-up with
        Schlesinger 256
    and sugar lift 286
    and Celia's ring 314

Peace News 59, 60
Pearson, John 119
Pecci-Blunt family 290
Pelham Place, London 83
Penguin Books 251
Pennines 10
Pennsylvania 199
Penrose, Roland 90
Percy Lund Humphries & Co. 33
Pergamon Altar 114
Pergamon Museum, East Berlin
    114, 117
Perlman, Joel 190
Perpignan, France 255
Pershing Square, Los Angeles
    142–43
Peter Stuyvesant Foundation 166
Peters, Mrs (head of Commercial
    Art department, Bradford
    Regional College of Art) 32
Petersburg Press 221, 297
Phaidon 288
Philadelphia Museum 272
Philip, HRH The Duke of
    Edinburgh 23, 111
Phillips, Ewan 87–88
Phillips, Peter 65, 68, 71, 73, 77, 81,
    82, 116, 119, 239
Phoenix House Project 272
Physique Pictorial magazine 75, 95,
    124, 141, 149, 151
Picasso, Claude 302
Picasso, Pablo 66, 163, 195, 248, 249
    DH first sees his work 42
    philistinism about 42
    exhibition at Tate Gallery (1960)
        105
    Crommelynck as his etching
        printer 283, 285
    makes own prints in traditional
        way 285
    Cooper's attack on his late work
        302–3
    death 282
    Guernica 233
    Massacre in Korea 42
    'Series 347' intaglio plates 285
Picasso, Paloma 248, 249, 302
Picasso Museum, Barcelona 254
Pico Boulevard studio/apartment,
    Los Angeles 185, 189–90, 192
Pidgeon, Walter 15
Piper, John 39, 129
Piranesi, Giovanni Battista 145
Pirelli 132
PJ Clarke's, New York 154
Plomley, Roy 267, 268
Pointillism 305
Polanski, Roman 80

Pollock, Adam 105
Pollock, Alice 219
Pollock, Jackson 66, 68, 99, 147, 233
Pompidou, Paris 296
Pontings department store,
    Kensington, London 127
pop art 77, 79, 81, 82, 90, 126, 128,
    146, 264
Pope-Hennessy, John 290
Porteous, Hugh Gordon 137–38
Portobello Road, London 127, 157,
    216, 217, 218
Poulenc, Francis: Les Biches 268
Pound, Ezra 67
Powell, Mike 31, 46–47
Powis Gardens, London 289
Powis Terrace, Notting Hill,
    London (No.17) 118–20, 122,
    123, 124, 127, 130, 141, 157, 158,
    165, 175, 193, 203, 209, 213, 215,
    216, 218, 223, 228, 236, 237, 238,
    240, 242, 243, 246, 248, 249, 250,
    252, 259, 264, 281, 283, 293, 296,
    307, 308, 313, 318
Prado, Madrid 246
Pratt Institute, Brooklyn, New
    York 97, 101, 128, 141
Pre-Raphaelites 90, 247, 315
Presley, Elvis 65, 76, 316
Price, Vincent 121, 152
Priestley, J.B. 11–12, 16, 134, 170,
    292–93
    Bright Day 2–3, 6
    The Good Companions 2
Print Centre, Holland Street,
    Kensington, London: A Rake's
    Progress exhibited 136, 138
Private Eye magazine 133
Prizeman, John 289, 290
Procktor, Patrick 154, 167, 193, 197,
    215, 218, 241, 270
    studies at the Slade 80, 159
    and DH's appearance at the drag
        ball 80
    and 'Young Contemporaries'
        exhibition 81, 104
    works at Maidstone School of
        Art 117
    teaches at Iowa 154, 159, 161
    Russian interpreter with British
        Council 159
    appearance 159, 160, 195
    attitude to New York 159
    and Laurence Harvey 162, 163
    first lithograph 164
    travels in Europe with DH and
        Schlesinger 194, 195
    love of watercolour 195
    DH's portrait of him 197–98

on Odin's 241–42, 243
    Seated Crowd on the Grass 164
Propyläen Verlag 283
Proust, Marcel 253
    À la recherche du temps perdu 59
Prunier's restaurant, St James
    Street, London 88
Puccini, Giacomo: La Bohème 18,
    311
Pyramids, Egypt 135, 136

Queen magazine 125
Queen Elizabeth, RMS 128, 192
Queen Mary, RMS 192, 199
Quorum boutique, King's Road,
    London 219

Race Relations Act 212
Rachman, Peter 118
Rackham, Arthur 221
Radio Times 28
Raistrick, Audrey 59
Rake's Progress, The (Stravinsky)
    310–13, 317–20, 323–28
Rand, Mike 174, 223
Raphael 285
Ratcliffe, Michael 316
Rauschenberg, Robert 128, 152,
    163, 233
Raven, The (film) 121
Ravilious, Eric 39
Rawson Market, Bradford 15
Read, Sir Herbert 112
Rebel Without a Cause (film) 128
Rechy, John: City of Night 141,
    142–43
'Recording Britain' project 39
Red Raven gay bar, Los Angeles
    164
Reddish, near Salisbury, Wiltshire
    224–26
Redfern Gallery, Cork Street,
    London 159, 162, 193
Redgrave, Vanessa 206
Regent's Park, London 203
Régine's nightclub, Paris 305
Reich, Steve 186
Reid, Sir Norman 212, 314
Rembrandt van Rijn 26, 285
Renoir, Jean 81, 282
Repton School, Derbyshire 148
Repulsion (film) 80
Restany, Pierre 315
Rhine River 204, 223
Rhodes, Mr (Principal, Bradford
    Regional College of Art) 32, 33
Richard, Cliff 76, 91, 92, 93
Richards, Ceri 53, 64
Richardson, Joely 206

Richardson, John 302
Richardson, Natasha 206
Richardson, Sir Ralph 227
Richardson, Tony 218, 237
    friendship with DH 204
    DH visits in the south of France
        204
    Yorkshire background 204–5
    distinguished career in theatre
        and films 205
    Le Nid de Duc 205, 227, 256
    as host 205–6
    DH rents his apartment in Paris
        296
    and Lila de Nobili 300
Richmond, Surrey 271
Ripon Street, Bradford 6
Rivers, Larry 104, 114–15, 138
Robert Fraser Gallery, Duke
    Street, London 131
Robert's Pie Shop, Godwin Street,
    Bradford 11–12, 16
Roberts, William 45
Robertson, Bryan 66, 131, 233
Robinson, David 310
Robinson, Derek 30
Rocky Mountains 161
Rolf Nelson Gallery, Santa Monica
    Boulevard, Los Angeles 146, 164
Rolling Stones, the 193, 213, 219,
    256
Rome 195, 227, 266, 320–21, 323
Roosevelt, Franklin D. 245
Rosenquist, Jim 272
Rothko, Mark 233
Rothmans cigarettes 115
Rothschild, Philippe de 323
Rotterdam 239
Roundhay Park, Leeds 12
Rowan Gallery, Lowndes Street,
    Belgravia, London 122
Rowntree, Kenneth 39
Royal Academy, London 42
    Summer Exhibition 61–62
    Leonardo Appeal 105
    exhibition of new work (January
        2011) ix
Royal Academy Schools 62, 73,
    119, 120
Royal Army Medical Corps 38
Royal Ballet 203, 300
Royal College of Art, South
    Kensington, London 217, 296
    Derek Stafford's studies 38, 39
    DH's application 49, 51–53
    DH accepted on postgraduate
        course in painting 53
    national service delays DH's
        arrival 55

DH starts his course (September 1959) 62
described 62–63
hostility of some staff 71–72, 107
Christmas Revue 79–80, 102–3
film club 81
visitors to the painting studios 82–83
DH's achievements while at RCA 90–91, 102
general studies course 107–8, 110
DH awarded gold medal 109–12, 114, 127
Fashion Design School 123
etching studio 174
turns Schlesinger down 196–97
print department 223
Royal College of Music, London 111
Royal Court Theatre, London 175, 176, 182, 183, 204
Ossie Clark's fashion show 252
Royal Hawaiian Hotel, Waikiki Beach, Honolulu (Pink Palace) 263
Royal Opera House, Covent Garden, London 129, 243, 308
Royal Society of British Artists, Suffolk Street, London: 'Young Contemporaries' exhibitions 81–82, 88, 90, 104–5, 159
Rudenko, Tony 325
Ruscha, Ed 147, 152, 164, 201
Ruskin College, Oxford 67
Russell, Bertrand 170
Russell, John 131, 137, 166
Russell, Ken 310
Russia, Kenneth Hockney's view of 47
Rye, East Sussex 61

St Andrew's Villas, Princeville, Bradford 5, 8
St Austell, Cornwall 56
St Clair, John 269
St Francis Hotel, Union Square, San Francisco 263
St George's Gallery, Cork Street, London: *The Graven Image* exhibition 93–94
St George's Hall, Bradford 3, 45–46
St Helen's Hospital, Hastings 61, 62
St Ives, Cornwall 55, 56
St John's Market, Bradford 11
St Laurent, Yves 316
St Luke's Hospital, Bradford 58, 61, 274
St Margaret's Road, Bradford 4

St Martin's School of Art (later merged with Central School of Art and Design), London 105
St Petersburg Place, London 223
St Saba, Church of, Alexandria 172
St Thomas's Hospital, London 213
Salford Art School 217
Salt, Sir Titus 21
Saltaire, West Yorkshire 21, 205
Salvation Army 6, 127
San Fernando Valley, California 180, 181
San Francisco 141, 161–62
'Summer of Love' 190, 280
San Francisco Chronicle 191
'San Francisco' (song) 268
Santa Cruz, California 180, 182, 189
Santa Monica, California 144, 149, 153, 162, 199–200, 207, 280
Santa Monica Mountains 152, 180
Satie, Erik: 'La Belle Excentrique' 268
Savoy Hotel, London 277
Scarning, Norfolk 6
Schlesinger, Peter 232, 233, 242, 316
family background 180
studies at University of California, Santa Cruz 180, 189
meets DH at UCLA 180
appearance 181
personality 181, 218
relationship with DH 181–82, 214–15, 227, 238, 244–46, 248–57, 259–66, 271, 276, 278, 282, 283, 302, 307–8, 310, 328
DH's first paintings featuring him 187
transfers to UCLA 189
parents send him to a psychiatrist 189
trip to Europe 192–97
rejected by RCA but accepted by the Slade 196–97
photographer 197, 225–26
at the Slade 202, 203
DH's interest in his painting 203
and DH's sitters 203–4
and Richardson's house parties 206
lack of a double portrait with DH 214–15
meets DH's parents 215–16
friendship with Birtwell 217, 218
Christmas on his own 220
DH's drawings 226–27
in Vichy 229, 230
longs for his own identity 237
love of Paris 240
at Odin's 242, 243

in Marrakesh 245–46
affair with Boman 249, 250, 251
poses for photographs for DH 270–71
friendship with Gregory Evans 280
in *A Bigger Splash* 307–10
Schwab's Coffee House, Los Angeles 149
Scotch of St James's nightclub, London 165
Scott, Christopher 207, 213, 226
Scott, James 175
Scott's Club, London 193
Secombe, Harry 28
Second World War
declaration of war on Germany 13
Kenneth's conscientious objection 13–14
Hockney family evacuated 14
Bradford bombed (31 August 1940) 1–2, 15
Battle of Britain 16
Hockney family moves 16
war ends 18
Jarman on 65
Secunda, Chelita 228
Self, Colin 161, 162
Sellers, Peter 28, 29
Sévigné, Marquise de 229
Sewell, Brian 241
Sexual Offences Act (1967) 170–71, 194
Shapiro, David 213
Shell 104, 135
Shepherd, Jack 176
Shipley, West Yorkshire 2, 175
Shipley Glen, West Yorkshire 12, 21
Sibelius, Jean 46
Sibylla's Club, London 193
Sickert, Walter 38, 48, 49
Silverman, Sidney 59
Simon, Meyer 201
Slabczynski, Stefan 314
Slade School of Fine Art, Gower Street, Bloomsbury, London 52, 53, 80, 82, 90, 197, 199, 202, 203
Sleep, Wayne 203–4, 230, 242, 243, 253, 255, 273, 276, 281, 282, 289, 296, 307, 308, 325
Smith, Dick 53, 202
Smith, Jack 40
Smith, Richard 81, 131
Smith, Rodney 'Gipsy' 5, 7
Snowdon, Lord (Anthony Armstrong-Jones) 125, 126, 127, 194
social realism 40, 115, 205

Söderström, Elisabeth 311
Soho, London 85, 86, 309
Some Like It Hot (film) 268
Southampton 94, 164
Soviet Weekly 59
Spalding, Mr (Director of
  Education, Bradford) 26
Spanish Civil War 13, 233
Spear, Ruskin 53, 64, 72, 94, 107
Spectator 137, 234, 327
Spence, Sir Basil 112
Spencer, Sir Stanley 39, 49–50
  Christ Preaching at Cookham Regatta
  50
Spender, Humphrey 94
Spender, Stephen 147, 170, 171,
  314–15
Spoleto international festival, Italy
  300
Spring Bridge, Bradford 51
Stable Gallery, East 74th Street,
  New York 128
Stafford, Derek
  education 38, 39
  war service 38–39
  tutor at Bradford Regional
    College of Art 38, 40
  falls out with the Principal 40
  on DH's behaviour in classes
    40–41
  encourages his students to go on
    London trips 41–42
  and importance of evolution at
    work 42, 44
  parties at his new studio 46, 47
  encourages DH 49
  on DH's paintings 50, 51
  teaches students to be committed
    to their work 58
Stalin, Joseph 59
Stanford University 179
Stangos, Nikos 171, 250–51
Stanhope Hotel, Fifth Avenue,
  New York 199
Stanton, Larry 249–50
Starr, Ringo 165, 308
Steadman Terrace, Bradford
  (No.61) 1–2, 10–11, 12, 16
Steele, Tommy 76
Stella, Frank 131, 158, 207
Stephenson Brothers 4–5, 11
Sternberg, Josef von 245
Stevens, Norman 35, 65
  friendship with DH 37
  his disability 37
  in the Tate Gallery 41
  skiffle group 45
  Royal College of Art application
    52, 53

visits Hastings while at Royal
  College 62
DH lodges with him in Earls
  Court 64
Yorkshire accent 64
warns Berg about DH 70
graduates 73
works at Maidstone School of
  Art 117
visits DH in US 161, 162
Stevenson, Harold 131
Stewart, Rod 106, 308
Still, Clyfford 99, 201
Stott Hill, Bradford 23
Strachey, Lytton 289
Strand Hotel, Rangoon 266
Strand Palace Hotel, London 240
Strauss, Richard: *Intermezzo* 311,
  320
Stravinsky, Igor: *The Rake's Progress*
  310–13, 317–20, 323–28
Strong, Dr Roy 170, 224–25
Studio magazine 136
Studio International 166
Suffolk 55, 56–58
sugar lift 285–86
Sunday Mirror 133
Sunday Telegraph 137
Sunday Times 131, 134, 136, 226
  Atticus column 169
Sunday Times Magazine 125–27, 135
Superman (film serial) 20
Sutton, Keith 82
Sutton, Philip 134
Swan Arcade, Bradford 11
Sykes Wardrobes, Bradford 35
Sylvester, David 39, 107, 126, 134

Taplin, Denis 57
Tate Gallery, London 41, 117, 132,
  212, 314
  Picasso exhibition (1960) 105
Taylor, Elizabeth 231
Taylor, Rod 37, 46, 60
Teenage Nudist magazine 211
Theatre of the Absurd 176
Thewliss, Mrs 322
Thewliss, Reverend 322
Thompson, Charles (DH's
  maternal grandfather) 6, 7, 10
Thompson, John 292
Thompson, Mary (née Sugden;
  DH's maternal grandmother)
  6–7, 32
Thompson, Rebecca (Aunt Rebe;
  DH's aunt) 321
Thompson, Robert (DH's maternal
  great-grandfather) 6
Thomson, Roy 125, 126

Thurston, Barbara 315–16
Tidman, Bruer 241
Tilbury Docks, London 157
Time magazine 146, 156, 193
Times, The 59, 104–5, 166, 170, 174,
  182, 194, 199, 234, 246, 276, 292,
  310, 316, 326
Times Educational Supplement 22
Tinguely, Jean 87
  Meta-Matics 87
Tokyo 263–64
Tolson's of Bradford 7
Torino's, Soho, London 85
Town magazine 110
Trevelyan, Julian 94, 129
Trials of Oscar Wilde, The 73
Trident Preview Theatre, St Anne's
  Court, London 309–10
Trinity College, Dublin 290
Troubador pub, Old Brompton
  Road, London 80–81
Trust Houses Ltd 94
Tulane University, New Orleans 74
Tumble Inn Motel, Santa Monica
  142, 143, 147, 155, 162
Turnbull, William 152, 186, 202
Turner, Alan 190
Turner, J.M.W. viii, 34
Twelfth Night (Shakespeare) 32
Twiggy 252
Twombly, Cy 179
Tyler, Ken 163, 277, 279
Typhoo tea 79, 83

Uccello, Paolo: *The Hunt in the
  Forest* 222
Uffizi, Florence 103
Under Milk Wood (Thomas) 176
United States
  Jarman on post-war America 65
  DH visits (1961) 95–98
  DH's love of America 124
  DH leaves London for New York
    (30 December 1963) 139
  DH's first American show 156
  DH teaches at UCLA 175
  DH's road trip with Kasmin and
    Schlesinger 199
  Supreme Court rulings 211
  recession 275
  DH prefers to work on *The Rake's
    Progress* in 317–18
University of California, Berkeley
  190
University of California, Los
  Angeles (UCLA) 196, 197
  DH teaches 177, 179–80, 181
  DH meets Schlesinger 180
  Schlesinger transfers to 189

University of California, Santa Cruz 180, 189
University of Colorado at Boulder 159, 161
University of Iowa 153, 154, 161
Upton, Anne 218
Upton, Michael 117, 119, 120, 159, 167
Utah 199
Uzès, near Nîmes, France 195, 302

van Gogh, Vincent 51, 89
Vaughan, Keith 39, 77, 229
Vega restaurant, off Leicester Square, London 100, 127
Velázquez, Diego 246
Velvet Underground, the 156
Venice, California 142, 144
Venice Biennale, Italy 39–40, 220
Viareggio, Italy 113, 114, 195
Vichy, France 227, 229–30, 238
Victoria and Albert Museum, London 41, 69, 70, 290
Victoria Road, Bradford 17
Vidal, Alexis 297
Viehmann, Katarina Dorothea 222
Vietnam War 161
   anti-war meetings 191
Villa Nellcôte, Nice 256
Villa Reale, Lucca 290
Visconti, Luchino 300
Vogue 193, 224
   American 156
von Bülow, Claus 132
Vorticism 45
Vreeland, Diana 156

Wagner, Richard
   'Liebestod' from Tristan und Isolde 268
   Lohengrin 10
   Die Meistersinger 268
Waiting for Godot (Beckett) 176
Wakefield, West Yorkshire 2
Wakefield City Art Gallery: Alan Davie retrospective (1958) 68
Walker Art Gallery, Liverpool 115, 198
Walker Galleries, 118 New Bond Street, London 131

Wall, Max 176–77, 182
Wallis, Neville 138
Ward, Eleanor 128
Ward, James 34
Warhol, Andy 113, 128, 129, 152, 156, 157, 187, 201, 207, 208, 248, 312
   first solo exhibition 146
   first exhibition of the Soup Cans 146
   Birtwell on 300–301
   Mao portraits 300
   Mona Lisa paintings 128
Warwick, Mrs Wally 192–93
Warwick, Wally 192
Waterloo Station, London 165
Waugh, Evelyn: Brideshead Revisited 290
Webb, Peter: Portrait of David Hockney 228–29
Webster, Sir David 243–46, 249
Weight, Carel 53, 64, 72, 73, 74, 81, 107, 110
Weimar Republic 114
Weisman, Fred 201–2
Weisman, Marcia 201–2
Welles, Orson 45
Wellington Road Primary School, Bradford 18, 22
West Riding 34
West Side Story (musical) 65
Westbourne Grove, Notting Hill, London 140
Western Electric Sound System 20
Westminster School, London 129
White Star Line 128
Whitechapel Gallery, London 131, 214
   This Is Tomorrow exhibition (1956) 90, 233
   Jackson Pollock exhibition (1958) 65–66
   DH's retrospective (1970) 233–34, 235, 239, 247
Whitehead, Mr (art teacher) 28, 35, 36
Whiteley, Brett 106
Whitman, Walt 70, 73, 76, 77, 79, 287
   'I Hear It Was Charged Against Me' 79

'So Long!' 77
'We Two Boys Together Clinging' 92
'When I Heard at the Close of Day' 76
Whitworth Art Gallery, Manchester: DH's mini retrospective (1969) 220
Wigmore Place, London 273
Wilde, Oscar 194, 208
Wilder, Nick 178–79, 187, 189, 190, 249, 280–82, 281, 297
Williams, Francis 126
Williams, Kyffin 159
Williams, Tennessee 231
Wilson, Harold (Baron Wilson of Rievaulx) 170
Wilton's restaurant, Jermyn Street, London 88, 100
Wishnick, Robert I. 185
Withernsea, East Yorkshire 21
Wolfenden, Sir John 170
Wolfenden Committee 170
Woodcock, Dr Patrick 122
Woodfall Films 206
Woodward, Bernard 37
Wool Exchange, Bradford 3
Woolf, James 162
Woolner, Thomas 90
Woolworths 21, 80
Wordsworth, William 253
Wright, John 94
Wyberslegh Hall, High Lane, Greater Manchester 148
Wyndham, Violet 208
Wyoming Building, Seventh Avenue, New York 207

Yeovil College of Art, Somerset 52, 65
York 21
Yorke, Emma 110
Yorkshire Artists Exhibition 48–49, 62
Yorkshire Dales 2
Young Physique magazine 75

Zajac, Jack 146
Zapata Boutique, London 249

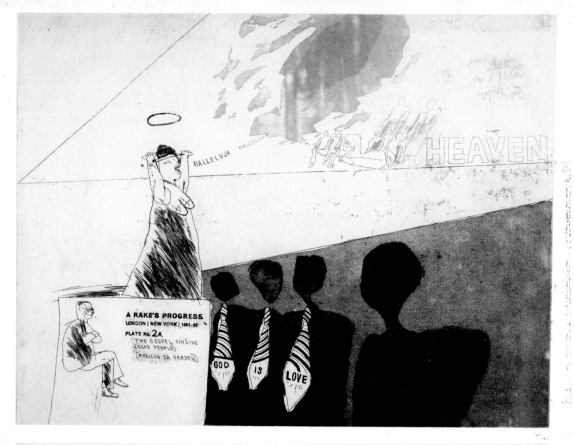

A RAKE'S PROGRESS
LONDON | NEW YORK | 1961-62

PLATE No. 2A
THE GOSPEL SINGING
(GOOD PEOPLE)
(MADISON SQ. GARDEN)

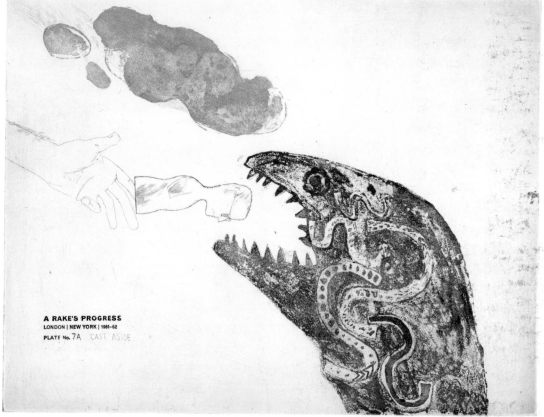

A RAKE'S PROGRESS
LONDON | NEW YORK | 1961-62
PLATE No. 7A CAST ASIDE